FREEDOM TIME

D1521506

FREEDOM TIME

Negritude, Decolonization, and the Future of the World

GARY WILDER

Duke University Press   Durham and London   2015

© 2015 Duke University Press All rights reserved
Printed in the United States of America on acid-free paper ∞
Designed by Courtney Leigh Baker
Typeset in Univers by Westchester Book Group

Library of Congress Cataloging-in-Publication Data
Wilder, Gary.
Freedom time : Negritude, decolonization, and the future of the world / Gary Wilder.
pages cm
Includes bibliographical references and index.
ISBN 978-0-8223-5839-8 (hardcover : alk. paper)
ISBN 978-0-8223-5850-3 (pbk. : alk. paper)
ISBN 978-0-8223-7579-1 (e-book)
1. Césaire, Aimé.   2. Senghor, Léopold Sédar, 1906–2001.
3. France—Colonies—Africa—20th century.
4. France—Colonies—America—20th century.
5. Negritude (Literary movement).   I. Title.
JV1818.W553 2015
325'.3—dc23
2014040365

Cover art: (*top*) Léopold Senghor. Felix Man/Picture Post/Getty Images; (*bottom*) Aimé Césaire. © Mario Dondero.

FOR RACHEL & ISABEL

In memoriam Marilyn Wilder & Fernando Coronil

NON-TIME IMPOSES ON TIME THE TYRANNY OF ITS SPATIALITY. —AIMÉ CÉSAIRE

CONTENTS

PREFACE

This book was born of an intuition while writing a conference paper about Aimé Césaire's nonnational orientation to decolonization. I wondered whether it would make sense to suggest that the Haitian Revolution exemplified Marx's subsequent demand that the new social revolution draw its "poetry" from the future. All I wanted was one quote from Toussaint Louverture to set up a discussion of why Césaire committed himself to departmentalization in 1946. But I fell into a deep rabbit hole.

I reread James's *The Black Jacobins*, Marx's *The Eighteenth Brumaire*, DuBois's *Black Reconstruction*, and, of course, Césaire's writings about abolition and decolonization. The conjuncture of freedom struggles and historical temporality in these texts led me back to Walter Benjamin, Theodor Adorno, and Ernst Bloch. Césaire was helping me grasp their arguments in a new way, and vice versa.

I had regarded this paper as unfinished business, a loose thread dangling from the edge of the book I had recently published on the interwar matrix out of which the Negritude movement emerged. But the more I pulled, the longer it got. I suspected that I should make myself stop but was unable to contain the fascinating mess. My twenty-five-page paper blossomed into a fifty-page essay, which then grew into a two-hundred-page pile. I wondered whether it would be wiser to just write the paper on Léopold Sédar Senghor's nonnationalist thoughts about decolonization. So I read his parliamentary speeches from the forties and fifties and began to puzzle over what he meant by federalism and what relation it might have with departmentalization. I read Proudhon and revisited Marx's "On the Jewish Question." When I then turned back to Césaire's parliamentary interventions I realized, with some misgiving, that I was now facing a book on freedom, time, and decolonization. I conceded that I was not finished writing about Césaire and Senghor. But *this* book, I thought, on figures whom I already knew, would be comparatively quick and easy. Hah!

That was the summer of 2006, a moment when I was personally preoccupied with time and reckoning, opening and foreclosure, potentiality and loss . . . pasts conditional and futures anterior. I began writing that original paper while recovering from major surgery to robotically repair a severely leaking heart valve. This was only a few months after I became a parent and lost a parent— following an unraveled year not knowing whether I would miss my daughter's birth in California because I was saying good-bye to my dying mother in New York or miss the chance to say good-bye to her because I was attending to a newborn.

By then, a few events had already been moving me into the intellectual space from which this book was written. These included a 2001 conference in Guadeloupe about the legacy of slavery, organized by Laurent Dubois; this was where I first wrote about temporal legacies and spoke with Michel Giraud. The 2005 session of the Irvine Summer in Experimental Critical Theory, hosted by David Theo Goldberg, where, nourished by discussions with Dipesh Chakrabarty, Lisa Lowe, and Achille Mbembe, I presented a speculative talk on the "decolonization that might have been." And a 2006 conference on "imperial debris," organized by Ann Stoler at the New School, for which I first wrote about Césaire and Toussaint.

Equally catalyzing were the Critical Theory Group at Pomona College; the seminars I taught at Pomona on the History and Politics of Time, Decolonization, and Postcolonial France; the year I spent on a Mellon New Directions Fellowship as a Visiting Fellow of the Human Rights Program at Harvard Law School, where I audited international law classes with David Kennedy and grappled with questions of global politics and planetary justice with Mindy Roseman and a group of international lawyers and activists then in residence from Brazil, Iran, Kenya, and Palestine; and the opportunity to share and discuss my work on Césaire with Michel Giraud, Justin Daniel, Jean Crusol, and their colleagues in the Department of Law and Economy at the Université des Antilles et de la Guyane.

I then reworked a rough version of this manuscript in my new intellectual home at the CUNY Graduate Center, where I am now a member of the anthropology PhD program and director of the Mellon Committee on Globalization and Social Change. This has been an especially rich intellectual milieu that has provided a space for the kind of transdisciplinary inquiry and collaborative community that I'd only dreamt about. The GC has also allowed me to work closely with inspiring doctoral students from whom I am constantly learning.

The journey to and through this book was also inflected by worldly developments. As the contours of my particular questions, object, and argument became clearer to me, concerns that seemed to emerge from a personal crucible, I realized that academic discussions about temporality, utopianism, and potentialities were unfolding in all directions—and this at a moment of converging "crises." An apocalyptic sense of impending global catastrophe at the intersection of financial, political, and ecological breakdown. On the left a reluctance to name or envision the kind of world or life for which it is worth struggling, even as popular and horizontal antiauthoritarian and anticapitalist movements surged worldwide. Intellectually, a sense that critical theory may have reached certain impasses regarding how to think radical democracy for these times partly by recuperating concepts such as freedom, autonomy, and justice, and above all Marx's human emancipation. It struck me that we do not have a robust critical language with which to speak postnational democracy, translocal solidarity, and cosmopolitan politics in ways that have not already been instrumentalized by human rights, humanitarianism, and liberal internationalism.

In some way *Freedom Time* proceeds from the same basic point as my first book, *The French Imperial Nation-State*. For twentieth-century African and Antillean populations there did not exist a simple "outside" from which to contest empire or pursue different futures, an outside that was not already mediated by relations of colonial domination. In my first book this starting point led to an analysis of the disabling antinomies of colonial racism and the impossible situations that they created. Situations that Senghor, Césaire, and their cohort negotiated and reflected upon. That same starting point has now led me away from a critique of impossibility and toward a reflection on utopian potentiality. It provides the basis for taking seriously Senghor's and Césaire's attention to the transformative possibilities that may have been sedimented within existing arrangements—as well as their hope, through decolonization, to remake the world so that humanity could more fully realize itself on a planetary scale. That starting point has provoked the concern in this book with critical history as a dialogue with past and future and with politics as practices oriented toward pasts present, not yet realized legacies, and supposed impossibilities that may be already at hand.

This book feels overdue; I am past ready to abandon it. At the same time I also feel like I might just now be ready to begin writing it.

ACKNOWLEDGMENTS

Much of this book was written thanks to the Mellon Foundation's shockingly generous New Directions Fellowship. It owes singular debts to Laurent Dubois, who talked me through almost every step of this project and read carefully two versions of this manuscript; Fernando Coronil, thanks to whom I am at the Graduate Center—his belief in my work was sustaining, and his intellectual spirit inspiring; Susan Buck-Morss, a passionate and committed thinker, with whom I have enjoyed the adventure of intellectual collaboration; and Louise Lennihan, whose extraordinary efforts have made me at home at the Graduate Center. Special thanks are due to Souleymane Bachir Diagne, Jean Casimir, Mamadou Diouf, Michel Giraud, and Achille Mbembe, specialists in the areas that I explore, whose encouragement and suggestions made all the difference.

My thinking in this book has been incubated through dialogue with dear friends and colleagues whose insights have been invaluable gifts: Dan Birkholz, Yarimar Bonilla, Mayanthi Fernando, Jennifer Friedlander, Vinay Gidwani, Manu Goswami, Philip Gourevitch, Henry Krips, Jeffrey Melnick, Paul Saint-Amour, Marina Sitrin, Judith Surkis, Massimiliano Tomba, and Matthew Trachman. It has benefited greatly from discussions with CUNY colleagues who humble me with their intelligence and generosity: notably Anthony Alessandrini, Talal Asad, Herman Bennett, Claire Bishop, Kandice Chuh, John Collins, Vincent Crapanzano, Gerald Creed, Duncan Faherty, Sujatha Fernandes, David Harvey, Dagmar Herzog, Mandana Limbert, Michael Menser, Uday Singh Mehta, Julie Skurksi, and Neil Smith. Stellar doctoral students who commented on sections include Neil Agarwal, James Blair, Lydia Brassard, Megan Brown, Ezgi Canpolat, Jill Cole, Jennifer Corby, Sam Daly, Mark Drury, Melis Ece, Mohammed Ezzeldin, Timothy Johnson, Ahilan Kadirgamar, Anjuli Fatima Raza Kolb, Fiona Lee, Shea McManus,

Amiel Melnick, Junaid Mohammed, Andy Newman, Kareem Rabie, Jeremy Rayner, Ahmed Sharif, Samuel Shearer, Chelsea Shields, and Frances Tran.

I had the good fortune to present various pieces to engaged audiences at Columbia University, Cornell, CUNY Graduate Center, Duke, Hanyang University (Korea), Harvard, Northwestern, the New School, NYU, Princeton, the University of Chicago, University College, Cork (Ireland), the University of Missouri (Columbia), Universitat Pompeu Fabra (Barcelona), Université des Antilles et de la Guyane (Martinique), the University of Stirling (Scotland), the University of Texas–Austin, Yale, and Wesleyan. For their invitations and comments I am grateful to Nadia Abu El-Haj, Vanessa Agard-Jones, Mamadou Badiane, Ed Baring, Benjamin Brower, Kamari Clarke, Frederick Cooper, Michaeline Crichlow, Patrick Crowley, Michael Dash, Gregson Davis, Brent Edwards, Charles Forsdick, Duana Fulwilley, Kaiama Glover, Brian Goldstone, Julie Hardwick, Antony Hopkins, Abiola Irele, Stephen Jacobson, Deborah Jenson, Alice Kaplan, Sudipta Kaviraj, Trica Keaton, Ethan Kleinberg, Yun Kyoung Kwon, Laurie Lambert, Brian Larkin, Mary Lewis, Jie-Hyun Lim, Tessie Liu, Claudio Lomnitz, Anne-Maria Makhulu, Gregory Mann, Bill Marshall, Joe Masco, Tracie Matysik, Alfred McCoy, Julia Mickenberg, Sam Moyn, David Murphy, Nick Nesbitt, Patricia Northover, Charlie Piot, François Richard, Kristin Ross, Emmanuelle Saada, David Scott, Jerrold Segal, Charad Shari, Carroll Smith-Rosenberg, Ann Laura Stoler, Tyler Stovall, Stephen Tyre, Aarthi Vaade, Frederic Viguier, Patricia Wald, and Jini Kim Watson.

Much needed last-minute research assistance was offered by Jessie Fredlund, and heroic editorial work by Clare Fentress and Andrew Billingsley. Thanks are due to Willa Armstrong, Elizabeth Ault, Amy Ruth Buchanan, Christopher Robinson, Jessica Ryan, and Ken Wissoker at Duke University Press.

My deepest gratitude is reserved for Paula Gorlitz, for showing me the difference between a setback and a catastrophe; Arthur Wilder, my beacon for how to be human; Rachel Lindheim, whose sharp insights, unflagging belief, loving patience, and inspiring midcareer bravery nourished my writing; and Isabel Wilder, whose boundless heart, vitality, and imagination compel me to live in the present and believe in the future.

ONE Unthinking France, Rethinking Decolonization

An emancipated society . . . would not be a unitary state, but the realization of universality in the reconciliation of differences. —THEODOR ADORNO

This book is about "the problem of freedom" after the end of empire.[1] The title refers not only to the postwar moment as a time *for* colonial freedom but to the distinct types *of* time and peculiar political tenses required or enabled by decolonization. Decolonization raised fundamental questions for subject peoples about the frameworks within which self-determination could be meaningfully pursued in relation to a given set of historical conditions. These were entwined with overarching temporal questions about the relationship between existing arrangements, possible futures, and historical legacies. The year 1945 was a world-historical opening; the contours of the postwar order were not yet fixed, and a range of solutions to the problem of colonial emancipation were imagined and pursued.[2] At the same time, the converging pressures of anticolonial nationalism, European neocolonialism, American globalism, and UN internationalism made it appear to be a foregone conclusion that the postwar world would be organized around territorial national states.

Freedom Time tells this story of opening and foreclosure through unrealized attempts by French African and Antillean legislators and intellectuals during the Fourth and Fifth Republics to invent forms of decolonization that would secure self-determination without the need for state sovereignty. Central to this account are Aimé Césaire from Martinique and Léopold Sédar Senghor from Senegal who, between 1945 and 1960, served as public intellectuals, party leaders, and deputies in the French National Assembly.[3] Their projects proceeded from a belief that late imperialism had created conditions for new types of transcontinental political association. They hoped to overcome colonialism without falling into the trap of national autarchy. Their constitutional initiatives were based on immanent critiques of colonialism *and* republicanism, identifying elements within each that pointed beyond their existing forms. They not only criticized colonialism from the standpoint of constitutional democracy and self-government; they also criticized unitary republicanism from the standpoint of decentralized, interdependent, plural, and transnational features of imperialism itself.

In different ways Césaire and Senghor hoped to fashion a legal and political framework that would recognize the history of interdependence between metropolitan and overseas peoples and protect the latter's economic and political claims on a metropolitan society their resources and labor had helped to create. Rather than allow France and its former colonies to be reified as independent entities in an external relationship to each other, the task was to institutionalize a long-standing internal relationship that would persist even after a legal separation. They were not simply demanding that overseas peoples be fully integrated within the existing national state but proposing a type of integration that would reconstitute France itself, by quietly exploding the existing national state from within. Legal pluralism, disaggregated sovereignty, and territorial disjuncture would be constitutionally grounded. The presumptive unity of culture, nationality, and citizenship would be ruptured.

Given these colonies' entwined relationship with metropolitan society, decolonization would have to transform all of France, continental and overseas, into a different kind of political formation—specifically, a decentralized democratic federation that would include former colonies as freely associated member states. This would guarantee colonial emancipation and model an alternative global order that would promote civilizational reconciliation and human self-realization. At stake, for them, was the very future of the world.[4]

Refusing to accept the *doxa* that self-determination required state sovereignty, their interventions proceeded from the belief that colonial peoples cannot presume to know a priori which political arrangements would best allow them to pursue substantive freedom. Yet this pragmatic orientation was inseparable from a utopian commitment to political imagination and anticipatory politics through which they hoped to transcend the very idea of France, remake the world, and inaugurate a new epoch of human history.[5] Their projects were at once strategic and principled, gradualist and revolutionary, realist and visionary, timely and untimely. They pursued the seemingly impossible through small deliberate acts. As if alternative futures were already at hand, they explored the fine line between actual and imagined, seeking to invent sociopolitical forms that did not yet exist for a world that had not yet arrived, although many of the necessary conditions and institutions were already present. This proleptic orientation to political futurity was joined to a parallel concern with historicity. They proclaimed themselves heirs to the legacies of unrealized and seemingly outmoded emancipatory projects.

This book may be read in at least two ways. On one level, it is an intellectual history of Aimé Césaire and Léopold Senghor between 1945 and 1960. As such, it extends the account provided in my last book of the genesis of the Negritude project in the 1930s in relation to a new form of colonial governance in French West Africa, the political rationality of postliberal republicanism, and the development of a transnational black public sphere in imperial Paris.[6] *Freedom Time* follows that story into the postwar period, when these student-poets became poet-politicians participating directly in reshaping the contours of Fourth and Fifth Republic France and pursuing innovative projects for self-determination. On another level, it attempts to think *through* their work about the processes and problems that defined their world and continue to haunt ours. Their writings on African and Antillean decolonization may also be read as reflections on the very prospect of democratic self-management, social justice, and human emancipation; on the relationship between freedom and time; and on the links between politics and aesthetics. They attempted to transcend conventional oppositions between realism and utopianism, materialism and idealism, objectivity and subjectivity, positivism and rationalism, singularity and universality, culture and humanity. The resulting conceptions of poetic knowledge, concrete humanism, rooted universalism, and situated cosmopolitanism now appear remarkably contemporary.[7] Their insights, long treated as outmoded, do not only speak to people interested in black critical thought, anticolonialism, decolonization, and French Africa and the Antilles. They also warrant the attention of those on the left now attempting to rethink democracy, solidarity, and pluralism beyond the limitations of methodological nationalism and the impasses of certain currents of postcolonial and poststructural theory.

Decolonization beyond Methodological Nationalism

Historians have long treated decolonization as a series of dyadic encounters between imperial states and colonized peoples: the former are figured as powerful nations possessing colonial territories, and the latter as not yet independent nations ruled by foreign colonizers. Such stories are often tethered to parallel accounts of nation formation. Whether focused on European powers or Third World peoples, policymakers or social movements, international strategy or political economy, a certain methodological nationalism has persisted in this scholarship. But to presuppose that national independence is the necessary form of colonial emancipation is to mistake a product of decolonization for an optic through which to study it.

Rather than evaluate decolonization from the standpoint of supposedly normal national states, this book seeks to historicize the postwar logic that reduced colonial emancipation to national liberation and self-determination to state sovereignty. It does so in part by recognizing that decolonization was an epochal process of global restructuring that unfolded on a vast political terrain inhabited by diverse actors and agencies. The outcome of this process was the system of formally equivalent nation-states around which the postwar order was organized.

Historical accounts typically focus on stories of confrontations between national states losing overseas possessions and oppressed nations winning independence. Debates often focus on decolonization's causes, mechanisms, or outcomes as well as the so-called transfer of power. However important, these discussions tend to treat the meaning of decolonization as self-evident by reducing colonial emancipation to national liberation.[8] Underlying such dyadic accounts is the assumption that European states *had* empires but were not *themselves* empires.

Alternatively, an approach that begins with empire as an optic emphasizes the real, if problematic, ways that colonized peoples were members of imperial political formations. It proceeds from the fact that European states did not simply surrender colonies but abandoned their overseas populations. Decolonization was among other things a deliberate rending whereby populations were separated, polities divided, and communities disenfranchised.[9] Rather than focus on the mechanisms, pace, or implementation of national independence for colonized peoples, histories of decolonization should inquire into the range of political forms that were imagined and fashioned during what was a process of economic restructuring and political realignment on a global scale. Historians have recently demonstrated that however important liberation struggles and metropolitan transformations were in the process of decolonization, colonized peoples and European policymakers were not always the primary actors in this drama. Other agents—the United States, the Soviet Union, China, the United Nations, international public opinion—were no less important in dismantling Europe's empires and creating the neocolonial system that would succeed them.[10]

Histories that do not start with methodological nationalism can also focus less on who may have helped or hindered programs for state sovereignty than on the various ways that colonial actors confronted freedom as a problem with no intrinsic solution. Public struggles over the shape of the postwar world questioned the meanings of terms long treated as synonyms: freedom, liberty, emancipation, independence, sovereignty, self-determination, and autonomy. This study attends to the historical processes through which these terms came to refer to one another. It does so by engaging seriously Césaire's and Senghor's attempts to fashion political forms that were democratic, socialist, and intercontinental. This method fosters an appreciation of the novelty of their attempts to envision new forms of cosmopolitanism, humanism, universalism, and planetary reconciliation, forms that were concrete, rooted, situated, and embodied in lived experiences and refracted through particular but porous lifeworlds.

Unthinking France, Working through Empire

The French Imperial Nation-State was less concerned with the familiar fact that the republican nation-state exercised autocratic rule over colonized peoples than with how imperial history had transformed the republican nation into a plural polity composed of multiple cultural formations, administrative regimes, and legal systems.[11] Such multiplicity also enabled novel types of political association, identification, and intervention. The crucial question was not how France behaved overseas or how its populations experienced colonial rule. Rather, it was how the fact of empire, including how colonial subjects reflected upon it, invites us to radically rethink "France" itself. I suggested we follow the lead of the expatriate student poets associated with the Negritude project who since the mid-1930s grappled with the imperial form of the interwar republic. In contrast, *Freedom Time* explores how French imperialism created conditions for an alternative federal democracy that might have been. Underlying both works is a challenge to the methodological nationalism that often conditions the study of French colonial empire. They proceed from the conviction that historians should not simply turn their research attention to colonial topics; we need to do so in ways that turn inside out the very category "France."[12]

Freedom Time again engages the contradiction between France as an actually existing imperial nation-state and the territorial national categories that formed both French self-understanding through the colonial period and historiographic common sense in the postcolonial period. Any attempt to understand the French empire through those same national categories unwittingly reenacts that initial contradiction. But engaging French history from the standpoint of empire invites and compels us to unthink a series of assumptions about the territorial national paradigm concerning the isomorphism among territory, people, and state; the symmetry between nationality and citizenship; the national state as a unitary juridical and administrative space; or the scale and composition of political terrains, public spheres, discursive communities, and intellectual fields.

Treating empire as an irreducible unit of analysis and refiguring France as an imperial nation-state confounds conventional distinctions among national, transnational, and international phenomena and recognizes that the challenge of cultural multiplicity for a democratic republic was an imperial problem that did not begin with decolonization and postwar immigration. In many ways the imperial republic was a profoundly cosmopolitan space in which legal pluralism and disaggregated sovereignty were institutionalized in ways that might illuminate current debates over plural democracy in the French postcolony.[13] In order to "work through" empire, to treat France as an imperial formation and consider French history from an imperial perspective, we must unthink France as object and unit.[14]

Here I am borrowing from Immanuel Wallerstein, who calls on scholars to unthink nineteenth-century social scientific categories and paradigms that once enabled but now obstruct understanding of time, space, and development. He distinguishes the act of *rethinking* an interpretation based on new evidence from the more radical gesture of *unthinking* the very categories by which we apprehend such evidence.[15] The concept of working through has multiple associations. On a common-sense level it suggests careful analysis, coming to terms with a topic by unpacking it. But it also indicates how a perceived topic may also serve as an optic through which to rethink and to unthink. Working through thus signals an operation akin to Marxian immanent critique: identifying elements *within* an existing formation that point beyond it. *Working through* is also a psychoanalytic term that suggests a different kind of overcoming, another type of emancipation through critical self-reflexivity: mastering an impasse by confronting and untangling it; moving inside and through it in order to get beyond it. Dominick LaCapra has written about the relationship between historiography and the Freudian concepts of acting out and working through. He warns of the danger of "historical transference," the tendency among historians to act out in their work the processes about which they are writing. Working through thus also implies a self-reflexive distance from the object rather than an unthinking identification with it.[16]

Aimé Césaire and Léopold Senghor spent their public lives "working through" empire and "unthinking" France in just these ways. Proceeding from the insight that Africans and Antilleans were integral parts of the (imperial) nation, they refused to accept that "France" referred to a metropolitan entity or a European ethnicity. They rejected the idea that they existed outside radical traditions of "French" politics and thought. Even as student-poets in the 1930s, they did not simply call for political inclusion but made a deeper demand that "France" accommodate itself legally and politically to the interpenetrated and interdependent realities its own imperial practices had produced. Treating imperial conditions as the starting point for emancipatory projects, they claimed France as theirs and thus challenged the unitary and territorialist assumptions upon which the national state had long depended.

Though their decolonization projects differed, Césaire and Senghor were more interested in reclaiming and refunctioning than rejecting the categories and forms that mediated their subjection. This recalls Adorno's insight about the revolutionary efficacy of a "literalness" that "explodes [an object] by taking it more exactly at its word than it does itself,"[17] an approach we might call the politics of *radical literalism*. Césaire and Senghor repeatedly insisted that while *they* did not feel alienated from French and France, those who assumed that they should—whether on the left or right—needed to revise their own understanding of these categories. Their politics of radical literalism thus linked immanent critique to poetic imagination, aiming less to negate the empire or the republic than to sublate and supersede them. Rather than counterpose autarchic notions of Africa, the Caribbean, or blackness to a one-dimensional figure of France, they claimed within "France" those transformative legacies to which they were rightful heirs and attempted to awaken the self-surpassing potentialities that they saw sedimented within it. Rather than found separate national states, they hoped to elevate the imperial republic into a democratic federation.

Without understanding this distinctive orientation to anticolonialism, it is difficult to appreciate the political specificity of Césaire's and Senghor's pragmatic-utopian visions of self-determination without state sovereignty. Their radically literalist approach to decolonization cannot be fully grasped without understanding their aesthetic orientation to images as self-surpassing objects. For example, when they invoke "France" in their postwar legislation, criticism, or poetry they are often referring not to the existing national state but to the future federation they hoped to create.

Deterritorializing Social Thought

Césaire and Senghor were canny readers of their historical conjuncture in relation to the macrohistorical trends of imperial history. Like many of their contemporaries—Third World nationalists, regionalists, panethnicists, and socialist internationalists—they were acutely aware that decolonization would entail the reconfiguration rather than the elimination of imperial domination. But rather than offer a territorial response to this threat, they formulated epochal projections and projects. Their ambition exceeded a commitment to protecting the liberty and improving the lives of the populations they represented. They also felt themselves to be implicated in and responsible for remaking the world and redeeming humanity. Their interventions thus remind us that during the postwar opening, the world-making ambition to reconceptualize and reorganize the global order was not the exclusive preserve of imperial policymakers, American strategists, international lawyers, or Third International Communists. But to even recognize this dimension of anticolonialism requires us to move beyond the dubious but entrenched assumption that during decolonization many in the West thought globally while colonized peoples thought nationally, locally, concretely, or ethnically—and those that didn't were somehow inauthentic.

Scholarship long promoted one-sided understandings of Césaire and Senghor as either essentialist nativists or naive humanists.[18] Tied to the territorialism that dominated histories of decolonization, Negritude, whether embraced or criticized, was treated as an affirmative theory of Africanity rather than a critical theory of modernity. Scholars have typically viewed their writings as expressions of black subjectivity or anticolonialism and read their political proposals reductively, seeking information or messages, or in relation to Césaire's or Senghor's public records *after* decolonization.

Like *The French Imperial Nation-State*, this book endorses more recent attempts to understand these figures' writings as multifaceted engagements with modern politics, philosophy, and critical theory.[19] I extend the effort of my earlier book to treat Césaire and Senghor as situated thinkers whose reflections illuminate not only the black French or colonial condition but their own historical epoch and the larger sweep of political modernity by engaging the elemental categories around which political life at various scales was organized. Regarding them as epochal thinkers and would-be world makers who grappled with global problems at a historical turning point raises questions about territorial assumptions underlying strong currents in both European historiography and postcolonial criticism, assumptions that often lead scholars to relate texts to the ethnicity, territory, or formal political unit to which their authors appear to belong or refer.

Critics often treat Césaire or Senghor as representatives of black thought or African philosophy whose thinking may have been *influenced* by French or European ideas but whose writings refer to local lifeworlds that are somehow separate from "the West."[20] But their reflections should be read in relation to contemporaneous attempts, between the 1920s and 1960s, to overcome conventional oppositions between speculative rationalism and positivist empiricism by developing concrete, embodied, lived, intuitive, or aesthetic ways of knowing through which to reconcile subject and object, thought and being, transcendence and worldliness. Their work thus exists within a broad intellectual constellation including not only surrealist modernism or Bergsonian vitalism but ethnological culturalism, Christian personalism, and Marxist humanism (as well as Jewish messianism and philosophical pragmatism).[21] They also contributed to the critical engagement with instrumental reason, state capitalism, the reification of everyday life, the domestication of western European socialism, and the limitations of Soviet Communism.[22] Yet these thinkers are rarely included in general considerations of interwar philosophy or postwar social theory. This despite their novel attempts to link the search for a concrete metaphysics, poetic knowledge, and lived truth to a postnational political project for colonial and human emancipation that built upon traditions of mutualist socialism, cooperative federalism, and cosmopolitan internationalism. Or their attempts to reformulate humanism and universalism on the basis of concrete historical conditions and embodied experience.

The point is not to reduce their thinking to continental or hexagonal parameters nor speciously to elevate or legitimate it by placing it alongside canonical works. It is, rather, to use their work and acts to rethink, or unthink, the supposedly European parameters of modern thought. Just as Césaire and Senghor refused to concede that "France" was an ethnic category or continental entity, they resisted the idea that they should approach modern philosophy as foreigners. So rather than debate whether their writings were African-rooted or European-influenced, we should read them as *postwar* thinkers of the *postwar* period, one of whose primary aims was precisely to question the very categories "Africa," "France," and "Europe" through an immanent critique of late-imperial politics. They attempted in ways at once rooted and global to grapple with human and planetary problems at a moment of world-historical transition.

Understandable fears of totalizing explanation and Eurocentric evaluation have led a generation of scholars to insist on the singularity of black, African, and non-Western forms of thought. But we now need to be less concerned with unmasking universalisms as covert European particularisms than with challenging the assumption that the universal is European property. My aim is not to provincialize Europe but to deprovincialize Africa and the Antilles. Dipesh Chakrabarty's landmark critique demonstrated that supposedly universal categories were in fact produced within culturally particular European societies.[23] Césaire's and Senghor's multiplex reflections on Negritude resonate in many ways with Chakrabarty's argument about the existence of incommensurable forms of being and thinking that are often ungraspable by the rationalist protocols of modern historiography.[24]

But their thinking also provides a perspective from which to question Chakrabarty's critique of general, abstract, and universal thought from the standpoint of local, concrete, and particular lifeworlds.[25] It reveals how the "provincializing Europe" argument depends partly on a set of territorial assumptions about lifeworlds; how it tends to collapse people, place, and consciousness and to ethnicize forms of life; how it equates the abstract and universal with "Europe" and the concrete and lived with India or Bengal. Chakrabarty argues persuasively that there is an intrinsic connection between forms of life and forms of thought but does not then inquire directly into the scales of lifeworlds in relation to which thinking is often forged. He seems reluctant to recognize that large social formations and political fields, such as empires, are also concrete places.

Yet if there exists a determinate relationship between dwelling and thinking and if in certain cases we identify an empire to be the relevant social formation within which lives are lived and consciousness shaped, then that imperial form and scale, rather than a culture or ethnicity, must be relevant for understanding a form of thought. If we *begin* with empire as our unit of analysis, the case for insisting on cultural singularity or epistemological incommensurability weakens.

An imperial optic, for example, may help us to appreciate how postwar Martinique or Senegal really *were* "European" places and integral parts of "France." Or that putatively French or European forms of thought were elaborated through the dialogic exchanges, antagonistic confrontations, and transcontinental circulation that characterized life and thought in mid-twentieth-century European empires. It then follows that the supposedly European categories of political modernity belong as much to the African and Antillean actors who coproduced them as to their continental counterparts. These black thinkers also produced important abstract and general propositions about life, humanity, history, and the world.

My argument pushes against a recent tendency in comparative history and colonial studies to insist upon multiple, alternative, or countermodernities, thus granting to Europe possession of a modernity which was always already translocal. What is the analytic and political cost of assigning to Europe such categories or experiences as self-determination, emancipation, equality, justice, and freedom, let alone abstraction, humanity, or universality? Why confirm the story that Europe has long told about itself? Modern, concrete universalizing processes (like capitalism) were not confined to Europe. Nor were concepts of universality (or concepts that became universal) simply imposed by Europeans or imitated by non-Europeans. They were elaborated relationally and assumed a range of meanings that crystallized concretely through use. Moreover, African traditions of being and thinking entailed abstract ways of conceptualizing humanity. All humanisms, after all, are rooted in concrete ways of being, thinking, and worlding.

Chakrabarty recognizes that the intellectual heritage of Enlightenment thought is now global and that he writes from within this inheritance. He concludes with an eloquent reminder that "provincializing Europe cannot ever be a project of shunning European thought. For at the end of European imperialism, European thought is a gift to us all. We can talk of provincializing it only in an anticolonial spirit of gratitude."[26] So clearly he is not himself a provincial or nativist thinker. Yet this conception of gratitude concedes too much at the outset—to Europe as wealthy benefactor and to a liberal conception of private property. For if modernity was a global process its concepts are a common legacy that already belong to all humanity; they are not Europe's to give. They are the product of what Susan Buck-Morss has recently called "universal history," the "gift of the past," and "communism of the idea."[27]

In short, Césaire's and Senghor's postwar work invites us to deterritorialize social thought and to decolonize intellectual history. This is not matter of valorizing non-European forms of knowledge but of questioning the presumptive boundaries of "France" or "Europe" themselves—by recognizing the larger scales on which modern social thought was forged and appreciating that colonial societies produced self-reflexive thinkers concerned with large-scale processes and future prospects. The point is not simply that Césaire and Senghor were also interested in humanism, cosmopolitanism, and universalism. More significantly, they attempted to reclaim, rethink, and refunction these categories by overcoming the abstract registers in which they were conventionally formulated and attempted to realize them through intercontinental political formations.

Not satisfied with securing a favorable place for their peoples within the existing international order, they sought to transcend it; rather than simply pursue sovereignty, they envisioned unprecedented arrangements for dwelling and thinking through which humanity could realize itself more fully. From the evanescent opening of the postwar moment they anticipated a new era of world history in which human relations would be reorganized on the basis of complementarity, mutuality, and reciprocity. Through these novel political arrangements, humanity might overcome the alienating antinomies that had impoverished the quality of life in overseas colonies *and* European metropoles.

Thinking With: Intellectual History as Critical Theory

Freedom Time proceeds from the conviction not only that a global or imperial optic is necessary for grasping Césaire's and Senghor's thinking about decolonization but that intellectual history is crucial for grasping decolonization as a process of global restructuring. Historians concerned with colonial politics typically move from published texts to archival documents to peek behind the scenes, where "real" meanings supposedly reside. We also need to move in the other direction, from practical interventions to actors' texts. It is only through a nonreductive engagement with such textual material, for example, that we can understand the underlying relations for Césaire and Senghor among politics, aesthetics, and epistemology.

This book attempts to think *with* Césaire and Senghor, by regarding their world and moment from their perspective, to appreciate their constraints and the possibilities they discerned, in order to understand their political and intellectual goals. But *thinking with* is not just an exercise in contextualization; it also means listening carefully to what their analysis of that world might teach us about ours, treating them not only as native informants symptomatic of their era but as critical thinkers whose formulations about politics, aesthetics, and epistemology might help us fashion frameworks with which to reflect upon related phenomena.

In short, this book contains a normative dimension which makes it a work not only of intellectual history but of critical theory. Thinking *with* Césaire and Senghor means reading their work to inform our contemporary understanding about their moment, and ours, and the covert links between them. We should also search their writings for potentialities within them that might exceed them. While a first step would require a faithful reading, a second would attend to what a particular intervention might open or signal beyond what they might have intended. Thinking *with* them thus entails a deliberate strategy of generous reading that gives these writers the benefit of the doubt. To read generously is not to suspend critical evaluation but sometimes to extend the logic of their propositions far beyond where they may have stopped.

Thinking with Césaire and Senghor is to practice what Dominick LaCapra has referred to as "dialogical history"—whereby the historian enters a critical dialogue with texts that are allowed, in some sense, to speak back. Such histories stage a dialogue between past and present in which historians are compelled to attend to how they too are implicated in their objects of study.[28] *Freedom Time* proceeds from this belief that critical history must always seek to relate pasts and present dynamically. It contends that we who want to imagine alternative futures have much to gain by thinking with these figures about the world they envisioned, the realization of which was foreclosed by the postwar order whose ruins we currently inhabit. Insofar as political imagination pivots around historical reflection, it requires us not only to examine the paths that led to our present but to remember futures that might have been.

Historical Constellations

In thinking with Césaire and Senghor about modern categories as universal property, I have found especially useful the concept of "constellations" developed by Walter Benjamin and later taken up by Theodor Adorno.[29] For them, thinking entailed arranging concrete objects of inquiry into particular constellations through which the elements, the whole, and the hidden relations among them may be illuminated. They sought to grasp the dialectical character of historically specific truths that are constructed yet revealed, present within objects yet mediated by subjective reason, nonintentional yet disclosed by critical reflection. Especially important was their idea that constellations are actually existing arrangements that must, nevertheless, be arranged. For these peculiar entities to illuminate problems, they must be simultaneously objective and subjective. It is only *after* they have been created by a critical imagination that the creator can discover and recognize as real the relations he or she crafted by thinking together seemingly disparate ideas, places, peoples.

Freedom Time attempts to discover and construct constellations through which to explore non-self-evident connections across conventional geographical boundaries and historical epochs. These include those linking Césaire, Senghor, Benjamin, Bloch, Adorno, Hannah Arendt, Albert Camus, and John Dewey; Marx's human emancipation, Proudhon's mutualism, and Senghor's and Césaire's federalism; Césaire's postwar program for abolition through integration, Victor Schoelcher's utopian vision of slave abolition in 1848, and Toussaint Louverture's 1801 attempt to create a constitutional federation with imperial France; Senghor's redemptive solidarity, Emmanuel Levinas's and Jacques Derrida's commitment to hospitality, and contemporary efforts to institute cosmopolitan law and global democracy.

Césaire and Senghor were especially attentive to the complex relationship between politics and time. They explored separately how inherited legacies may animate current initiatives and how present acts may liberate the not yet realized potential sedimented within reified objects. Alternatively they were each concerned with the proleptic character of politics, which sought to call forth nonexistent worlds by acting as if an unimaginable future were at hand. Their sensitivity to the politics of time and the temporality of politics calls attention to the marvelous but real relations that often implicate disparate times, places, peoples, and ideas in one another, relations that historians should attend to directly.

Although *Freedom Time* focuses primarily on the postwar opening, it also attempts to trace a constellation between that period and earlier moments of epochal transition when self-determination and colonial emancipation became public problems (i.e., the 1790s and 1840s) and likewise between the postwar opening and our contemporary conjuncture. My examination of Senghor's and Césaire's programs for decolonization thus moves backward and forward from the postwar fulcrum, analyzing their self-conscious relationship to predecessors who also believed nonnational colonial emancipation might create conditions for real self-determination. These included Schoelcher and Louverture, as well as Marx and Proudhon. But this study also looks forward from the postwar period to a future that Césaire and Senghor anticipated, one we now inhabit and are still seeking to construct from within what Jürgen Habermas has called the "postnational constellation."[30]

Structural transformations have unmade the postwar order that decolonization created and against which Césaire and Senghor sought alternative arrangements. These shifts make their works newly legible and politically resonant insofar as they anticipated and addressed many of the conceptual and empirical predicaments that democracy in an age of globality must now confront. Our political present is characterized by issues and proposals that circulated in the immediate postwar period—autonomy, self-management, legal pluralism, cultural multiplicity, disaggregated sovereignty, and federalism. Césaire's and Senghor's political initiatives thus speak to current movements among Francophone Africans and Antilleans to reimagine and renegotiate their relationship to France, the European Union, and the international community. They also resonate with efforts today by scholars, activists, and international lawyers to fashion new frameworks for postnational democracy, cosmopolitan law, and planetary politics.

This study, which, despite its length, I regard as an essay, is also meant to be an inquiry into the politics of time, paying special attention to how a given historical epoch may not be identical with itself and historical tenses may blur and interpenetrate.[31] And it examines the untimely ways that people act as if they exist or can address a historical epoch that is not their own, whether strategically or unconsciously. Such connections can be grasped only abstractly; they cannot be indicated or documented in traditional empirical fashion. To tack between past and present thus requires a certain movement between empirical and abstract levels of analysis. Identifying and fashioning "historical constellations" is one way of writing a "history of the present" that is related to but distinct from the more familiar strategy of producing genealogies. *Freedom Time* thus works simultaneously to elaborate contexts, trace lines of descent, and construct constellations.

A crucial precedent and reference point for this study is anthropologist David Scott's important book *Conscripts of Modernity*, which powerfully challenges the nationalist orthodoxies of anticolonial thinking and demands that scholars attend directly to historical temporality as an analytic and political problem. Scott contends that "morally and politically what ought to be at stake in historical inquiry is a critical appraisal of the present itself, not the mere reconstruction of the past."[32] Regarding the unexamined persistence of certain anticolonial research questions that were once formulated by C. L. R. James for a now unavailable future, he offers a warning for scholars today: "the task before us is not one of merely finding better answers . . . to existing questions—as though [they] were timeless ones" but of reflecting on "whether the questions we have been asking the past to answer continue to be questions worth having answers to."[33] *Freedom Time* accepts this urgent invitation to rethink history—including our stories about colonialism and our methods for approaching the past—in relation to the demands of our political present.

In the following chapters I develop a different understanding of the provocative notion of "futures past" that Scott adapts from the historian Reinhart Koselleck.[34] For Scott, revolutionary anticolonialism's dream of national sovereignty became a historically superseded and politically obsolete future past after failing to secure political freedom for colonized peoples and can no longer meaningfully animate emancipatory projects in our radically transformed conditions. I am not primarily concerned with futures whose promise faded after imperfect implementation nor with those that corresponded to a world, or to hopes, that no longer exist but instead with futures that were once imagined but never came to be, alternatives that might have been and whose unrealized emancipatory potential may now be recognized and reawakened as durable and vital legacies.

TWO Situating Césaire: *Antillean Awakening and Global Redemption*

I believe what one has to do as a black American is to take white history, or history as written by whites, and claim it all—including Shakespeare —JAMES BALDWIN

The Problem of Freedom

The populations of Martinique and Guadeloupe contemplated decolonization in relation to the fraught history of openings and foreclosures that had characterized successive acts of emancipation in the French Antilles. In 1794 and 1848, abolition had freed a black population not only *from* slavery but *for* new regimes of colonial domination from which they would then struggle to be emancipated.

Marx identified this double-sided character of modern freedom—*from* feudal constraints and *for* economic exploitation—in his account of the development of capitalism in early modern Europe. Liberation from direct political domination (wherein position in a social hierarchy determined legal status) enabled indirect social domination (wherein legal equivalence grounded social stratification, operating through the production of value by formally free labor).[1] For Marx, capitalism was a system of socially embedded compulsions presupposing and producing a certain individual liberty; in bourgeois society, alienating processes operated in and through the putatively "free" domain of civil society, while real forms of liberty, equality, and universality were abstracted from everyday social life and restricted to a reified state alienated from the people in whose name it existed. Marx therefore warned against confusing *political emancipation*, which allowed society to become a

Hobbesian realm of animalistic competition among atomized individuals, with *human emancipation,* which would require abolishing the very distinction between state and civil society. Then abstract forms of equality and universality could be reclaimed from the liberal state and realized concretely in people's everyday social relations.[2]

Marx underscored the historically specific character of capitalist arrangements by describing the difficulty of establishing a system of free wage labor in the American colonies, given low population density and large supplies of available public land. Without slavery, independent cultivators could easily resist incorporation into modern labor markets. States would then have to induce autonomous producers to act like "free" laborers.[3] Thomas Holt illustrates this "problem of freedom" in his landmark study of colonial Jamaica.[4] He shows how after Britain abolished slavery in 1833, the colonial state compelled "free" populations to accept the unnatural conditions of plantation wage labor, thus indicating how emancipation marked the commencement of a modern form of colonial racism and expropriation from which freed slaves would have to free themselves.

A similar dynamic linking abolition and domination emerged decades later in struggles over the most Caribbean region of the United States *after* the Emancipation Proclamation of 1863. In *Black Reconstruction* (1935), W. E. B. DuBois demonstrates how a contingent alliance of northern industrialists, abolitionists, and freed blacks against a defeated plantation oligarchy created conditions for the "southern experiment" that "could have led the way to an American social revolution."[5] By confiscating land and redistributing wealth, the government's Freedman's Bureau challenged the legal basis of property. But poor southern whites could not recognize their common interest with free black workers and aligned with their planter adversaries, resulting in a "counter-revolution of property" that disenfranchised white workers and let the weakened planter oligarchy reassert its violent rule over freed southern blacks. DuBois writes that "the world wept" as the progressive "dictatorship of labor" was replaced by an oppressive "dictatorship of capital" in the service of a corporate plutocracy that "murdered democracy in the United States."[6]

Three years after *Black Reconstruction,* C. L. R James published *The Black Jacobins,* which also explored how emancipation could raise rather than resolve the problem of freedom.[7] After leading a successful slave revolt in Saint-Domingue, Toussaint Louverture needed to balance the individual liberties of freed slaves against the strict labor discipline necessary for an economy still dependent on plantation production. Believing that only economic autonomy could protect the population's fragile freedom from foreign interference, Toussaint calculated that peace and liberty demanded the repressive supervision of a military dictatorship in cooperation with sympathetic white planters. This difficulty of reconciling territorial sovereignty (against foreign states and capital) with popular sovereignty (against an autocratic postemancipation elite) challenged successive regimes after the creation of an independent Haitian state on January 1, 1804.[8] Laurent Dubois traces this persistent struggle in Haiti between a repressive state, preoccupied with protecting its territorial sovereignty, international standing, and economic viability, and peasant masses who engaged in regular uprisings against any interference with their local autonomy and agricultural self-sufficiency.[9]

Between the 1790s and the 1840s Haiti also served as a projective screen for the fears and hopes of planters, colonial states, imperial powers, and enslaved masses in Europe, the USA, and across the Caribbean.[10] The specter of Haiti reminded whites that revolutionary uprising in the Antilles was an ever-present possibility. It confirmed the abolitionist argument that immediate and total emancipation would not lead to social anarchy. But it also underscored the fact that national independence and state sovereignty would not necessarily protect a "free" people from economic impoverishment, political instability, territorial insecurity, and international isolation, let alone financial and military interference by foreign powers.

This drama of dashed expectations unfolded across the French Antilles through cycles of popular insurrection, constitutional reform, and state reaction seeking to circumscribe the meaning and substance of various emancipations. The National Assembly's 1794 decision to abolish slavery was not a republican initiative; it was compelled by the revolutionary insurrection in Saint-Domingue.[11] In Guadeloupe, abolition preceded a system of gradual emancipation and restricted liberty that compelled freedmen to continue working on their former plantations.[12] In May 1802, after a failed invasion meant to restore French authority in Saint-Domingue, Napoleon reestablished slavery in the other Antillean colonies. It was not fully abolished until the 1848 revolution when, against the backdrop of unfolding insurrection in Martinique, Victor Schoelcher compelled the Provisional Government in Paris to decree the immediate and unconditional end of slavery—*against* the wishes of most metropolitan republicans.[13] But as in Jamaica, this emancipation inaugurated an era of colonial domination based on exploitation of a racialized population's "free" labor. Between 1850 and 1940, Guadeloupe and Martinique experienced periodic insurrections against the economic oppression of the old white plantocracy (*békés*) and the new capitalist employers. Power struggles also persisted between elected municipal leaders and unelected representatives of the metropolitan government who ruled nominal citizens like a colonial state.[14]

Given this long-term history of emancipation and foreclosure, Antillean actors after World War II approached the prospect of decolonization mindful that freedom was a problem with no ready-made solution. Consequently, it would be a mistake for us to treat demands for national independence as an index of an Antillean commitment to self-determination. Rather, we should ask how Antilleans at that moment understood the meaning of self-determination.

Situating Césaire

Aimé Césaire's distinctive approach to the problem of freedom between 1946 and 1960 was anticipated in his wartime writings in the journal *Tropiques*. But to understand his initiatives we need first to unthink inherited narratives of this iconic figure, often themselves artifacts of the historical period and processes they purport to explain. A paradigmatic example is provided by the Martinican novelist Raphaël Confiant, who condemns Césaire for having "betrayed" his heirs by committing the "original sin . . . of assimilation" when he sponsored the 1946 law that transformed the Antillean colonies into departments of the French state.[15] Confiant ascribes Césaire's support for departmentalization to his cultural alienation and self-hatred as a member of the *petite bourgeoisie noire*, which he dismisses as descendants of "house slaves."[16] He concludes that Césaire's "visceral refusal of any idea of independence" makes him "doubt that Césaire loves the country of Martinique (and the Antilles) with a carnal love."[17]

Not all critics of Césaire have condemned his support for departmentalization so absolutely.[18] But Confiant's underlying logic, identifying integration with alienation and nationalism with emancipation, has long guided critical and political evaluations of Césaire. Many scholars have shared Confiant's inability to reconcile "the yawning gap that exists between the radicality of the *Discourse on Colonialism* and the extreme moderation of [Césaire's postwar] demands and political practices."[19] Commentators often try to overcome this supposed tension by splitting off what are regarded as his radical writings and militant poetry from his seemingly cooperative politics.[20] But this tendency to split stems from the erroneous assumption that anticolonialism must be oriented toward national independence.

A different starting point would recognize that emancipation posed a genuine problem with no obvious solution. There were tensions within and among the different aspects of Césaire's postwar initiatives. But once we challenge the political logic that opposes departmentalization to decolonization, it becomes easier to recognize the underlying relations between Césaire's anticolonial writing and his legislative initiatives, his aesthetics and politics, and his desires and acts. And what is often treated as a problem—that Césaire was not a nationalist—becomes an opportunity—to reconsider entrenched assumptions regarding Césaire's legacy, anticolonialism more generally, the postwar moment, and the very meaning of self-determination.

Revisiting Césaire requires us to recognize that he developed a *pragmatic* relationship to colonial emancipation and political freedom.[21] I am not referring to the political moderate's willingness to compromise principles so as to achieve something rather than nothing. Nor do I use pragmatism as synonym for opportunism and realism or antonym for utopianism and idealism. Rather, I use it philosophically to signal an antifoundational, nondogmatic, and experimental approach to truth and politics that refuses ready-made a priori certainties about the best means to desirable ends.[22] To say that the pragmatist focuses on what works is not to say that the pragmatist settles for what can be got or is willing to compromise on ends, but that he or she does not presuppose the necessary route to reach any given end. Césaire's pragmatism, which refused to fetishize means but never lost sight of ends, was not only consistent with ethical principles and utopian ideals but was dialectically related to them.[23] It resonated with John Dewey's observation that politics is "a matter of finding out the particular thing which needs to be done and the best way, under the circumstances of doing it."[24] For him "all proposals for social action" should be regarded as "working hypotheses, not as programs to be rigidly adhered to and executed . . . experimental . . . subject to ready and flexible revision in light of observed consequences."[25]

In light of the political orthodoxies produced by the Cold War order, Césaire's postwar politics may now appear complacently prosaic (practical, moderate, reformist) compared to his insurgent poetics. But his aesthetics suggest that we read in his multivalent poetry a warning against presumptively treating his political acts as self-evident or one dimensional. Rather than ask why this incendiary anticolonial poet "failed" to demand independence, perhaps we should ask why he regarded departmentalization as a creative anticolonial act.

Tropical Occupation

Césaire's epistemological orientation was also pragmatic; he distrusted a priori approaches to knowledge and truth, whether idealist or materialist. During the late 1930s while studying in Paris, Césaire participated in overlapping social circles drawn from expatriate colonial students, a transnational black public sphere, and the literary avant-garde. These were the spaces from and in relation to which he helped to fashion the cultural and political project that would become known as Negritude. The latter aimed to refigure imperial France as a plural society within which cultural particularity and political universality could be reconciled.[26] Césaire engaged deeply with writings about African, African American, and black diasporic culture and history, with varieties of anticolonial criticism, and with diverse currents of modernist aesthetics, vitalist philosophy, and cultural theory.

Beginning in 1936, Césaire distilled these interwar experiences and orientations into an early masterwork, *Notebook of a Return to My Native Land*,[27] simultaneously the aesthetic high point of interwar negritude and a radically self-reflexive questioning of its fundamental assumptions and objectives. Contrary to its typical reading, this exorbitant poem was neither a straightforward transcription of black subjectivity nor an allegory of coming to racial consciousness. Rather, it staged a set of impossible dilemmas concerning colonial racism, alienation, and emancipation.[28] The *Notebook*, whose form is as complex and self-interrupting as its content, underscores the dangers of treating Césaire's texts as containing direct propositions and prescriptions, as if his clear-sighted critique of the actual is separable from his darkly lyrical conjuring of the possible. It is a powerful example of what Césaire would later characterize as "poetic knowledge," a process of aesthetic understanding that points beyond easy oppositions between form and content, thought and action, art and politics, universalism and particularism, freedom and necessity, subjective will and objective constraints.

Césaire composed the *Notebook* while studying English literature at the École Normale Supérieure. He failed the *agrégation* exam but wrote a master's thesis titled "The Theme of the South in the Negro-American Poetry of the United States." In December 1939 he returned to Martinique with his wife, Suzanne, and young son Jacques to teach at the Lycée Schoelcher in Fort-de-France, his alma mater. He was only twenty-six years old, but his courses in Greek, Latin, and modern French literature catalyzed a younger generation of Antillean intellectuals, including Frantz Fanon, Édouard Glissant, the novelist Georges Desportes, and Marcel Manville, a longtime advocate of Martinican independence.[29] Glissant recalls that Césaire introduced students to the works of Lautréamont, Rimbaud, and Malraux.[30] Césaire relates that his crucial reference points also included Mallarmé, Baudelaire, Claudel, Nietzsche, and the German ethnologist Leo Frobenius as well as Langston Hughes, Countee Cullen, and Claude McKay.[31] Fanon recounts that Césaire's call for students to recognize their African heritage was so antithetical to Antillean norms that his teaching "created a scandal" and his colleagues believed him to suffer from some "delirium."[32]

Césaire spent the war in Martinique, which was closed off from the rest of the Caribbean by a de facto U.S. naval blockade. The colony was governed by the authoritarian Admiral Georges Robert, a Vichy loyalist, who sought to introduce Marhsal Pétain's National Revolution in the Antilles by replacing black elected officials to the Conseil Général with his own white appointees.[33] Furthermore, thousands of white French sailors were confined to Fort-de-France, fueling racial hostility throughout the city.

In these conditions, Aimé, along with his wife and their friend René Ménil, both also teaching at the lycée, founded *Tropiques*, the legendary journal of avant-garde philosophy, criticism, poetry, and ethnology, history, and politics whose eleven issues appeared between 1941 and 1945.[34] Like Césaire's courses, *Tropiques* conjugated Antillean specificity with European modernism. Like his *Notebook*, this journal was less interested in criticizing modern universality from the standpoint of black particularity than in refiguring the relationship between universality and particularity by fashioning an original Antillean modernism that was simultaneously rooted and cosmopolitan. Articles on Martinican flora, fauna, and folktales and Antillean literature and culture were published alongside pieces on Péguy, Alain, Breton, Mallarmé, and Lautréamont, as well as poetry and aesthetic manifestos by Césaire and his colleagues.

René Ménil later recollected that the audience for *Tropiques* was composed almost entirely of local students. Government repression prevented them from mentioning Marxism or criticizing the Vichy state directly.[35] Nevertheless, Césaire later explained, "the situation becoming more unbearable with each passing day, we had to take more and more political positions."[36] In May 1943, after six issues had appeared, Suzanne was notified by the authorities that further publication would be prohibited. The director of the Information Services called it a "revolutionary, racial, and sectarian review" written by ungrateful and antipatriotic functionaries of the French state who were "poisoning minds, seeding hatred, and destroying morality."[37] He admitted that he had originally assumed a journal concerned with Antillean identity would promote a "vigorous [and] desirable regionalism" based on the Pétainist conviction that "excessive centralization, a malady from which all French provinces have suffered, threatened to smother [true] personality, and substitute for it a conventional and uniform being, to kill art and dry up the source of truth."[38]

In a letter of reply, the editors of *Tropiques* denounced this culturalist assumption that regional identity and racial identification were synonymous with reactionary antirepublicanism. Declaring that "we do not speak the same language [as you]," they invoked the revolutionary spirit of Racine, Zola, Hugo, Rimbaud, Lautréamont, Toussaint Louverture, Claude McKay, and Langston Hughes.[39] This ambition to challenge racism and redeem Europe by recuperating submerged critical traditions *within* a multifaceted French history in which the Antilles had played an integral role characterized the novelty of *Tropiques*. After the end of the Robert administration in June 1943, the journal resumed publication. Subsequent issues more directly criticized Vichy ideology, denounced the Catholic Church's complicity with the Occupation, and called for a new Fourth Republic.

Prophetic Vision: Antillean Awakening, Global Redemption

Tropiques is often remembered either as a journal focused on the Martinican recovery of authentic black identity or as an overseas outpost of international surrealism. Each characterization contains a grain of truth, but these were precisely the alternatives that the editors of the journal hoped to overcome. Césaire's inaugural editorial called for a cultural awakening in Martinique which, as in the *Notebook*, he characterized as a "sterile and mute land" marked by absence and silence: "No city. No art. No poetry. No true civilization."[40] This situation was "a death more dreadful than death, where the living wander [*dérivent*]" and cultural seeds are sown in vain. Against this gathering darkness, "we are those who say *no* to the shadows." The objective of *Tropiques* was to create "true civilization" through the "projection of man on the world; a modeling of the world by man."[41] Not merely aiming to spark a regional renaissance by affirming Antillean particularity but to project a model of humanity onto the world stage from an Antillean perspective, Césaire declared, "the time has passed for parasitizing the world. Now, rather, it is a matter of saving it"; "the earth needs . . . the most humble . . . [to] create a new light in the world."[42]

Césaire's "Fragments of a Poem," appearing in the first issue of *Tropiques*, enacts this vision of Antillean humanism in the service of global redemption.[43] It is filled with figures of delirious plenitude, ecstatic self-obliteration, and transcendent reconciliation.

> As everything was dying,
> I did. I did grow—as big as the world—and my conscience wider than
> the sea!
> Last sun.
> I explode. I am the fire, I am the sea.

The world is dissolving but I am the world.
[...]
and here we are caught in the sacred
whirling primordial streaming
at the second beginning of everything.
[...]
The whole possible at hand.
Nothing excluded.[44]

These images could be interpreted to signify some primordial reconciliation, for the poet and through poetry, of word and world, language and being, self and cosmos, whether figured as a return to a primitive state of preverbal or prerational plenitude or as anticipating a future state of utopian reconciliation. But this process should not be understood as an expression of "the African's original reality" that "affirms the inviolability of the self."[45] Rather than a description of cultural return or projection of subjective sovereignty, we can read these verses as signaling the self-surpassing potentialities that inhere in the given world of appearances. They manifest as "poetic knowledge" whereby through surreal images rather than logical concepts the speaker seeks to transcend conventional oppositions between subject and object, self and universe, humanity and nature, microcosm and macrocosm, waking and dreaming, existent and transcendent, past and future. By writing "All one has lived sputters on and off," he offers vital pasts persisting within a multiplicitous present. The "setting sun" and "new dawn" indicate the world-making possibilities potentially enabled by a historical opening when a "second beginning of everything" may be fashioned out of the "sacred whirling primordial streaming" because the "whole possible [is] at hand."

This prophetic concern with future vision is underscored by Césaire's use of an epigraph (omitted in the later published version) from Rimbaud: "I say that it is necessary to be a visionary [voyant], to make oneself clairvoyant [voyant]."[46] This identification of the poet as seer who conjures a new world is echoed in the poem's concluding verses:

The end!
[...]
and I speak
and my word is peace
and I speak and my word is earth
and I speak
and

Joy
bursts in the new sun
... time glides
[...]
and the earth breathed under the gauze of mists
[...]
Its sleep peeled off like an August guava tree
on virgin islands thirsty for light

These images of reconciliation imply a return to the youth of the world, a harmonious premodern equilibrium. But they may also refer to the coming (cultural) revolution that Césaire prefigures and *Tropiques* envisions. Such images of awakening and illumination are simultaneously ancient and contemporary, earthly and transcendent. That this poem is a cosmopolitan charter for future possibilities and not simply a retreat into primordial being or culture is evident in its closing line: "my ear to the ground, I heard Tomorrow pass." This is the prophetic voice of poetic clairvoyance. Rather than mourn a lost past, it anticipates an alternative future that this Antillean awakening might help call forth, signaling not only the end of colonial domination but the inauguration of a new humanity that has recovered its poetic relationship to knowledge and life, one that has reconjugated the relation between painful histories and possible worlds, one that has reconciled human, natural, and supernatural dimensions of life.

Tropiques was animated by precisely this concern with (Antillean) aesthetics, humanity, and futurity. Suzanne Césaire, for example, reclaimed the concept of *païdeuma*, developed by Leo Frobenius to describe the impersonal vital force that acts on humans through culture to create civilizations. While the German ethnologist employed it to distinguish reductively between "Ethiopian" and "Hamitic" civilizations,[47] Suzanne argues that the modernity of capitalism, imperialism, and catastrophic wars also enabled "the eruption [*éclatement*] of a new [type of] life-feeling [*sentiment de la vie*] ... a new gushing of the Païdeuma ... of which we cannot yet be fully conscious, whose real significance still remains hidden from us."[48] Echoing Aimé's call for poets to become seers, she declares that "man's role ... is to prepare ... to live this other future." The task for Martinicans is not only to "dare to know themselves" but to "dare to ask who they want to be."[49]

Suzanne thus attempted to conjoin Antillean awakening with a revolutionary humanism mediated by poetic imagination. "We feel that our unsettling epoch will cause a ripe fruit to burst forth ... on this peaceful sunny land, the formidable, inescapable pressure of destiny [*destin*] ... has covered the whole world with blood, in order to give it, tomorrow, its new face."[50] Surrealist poetry, she believed, had a uniquely creative power to liberate individuals, emancipate peoples, and ground human emancipation.[51] It represented "freedom to make and unmake." In it "space is abolished ... past, present, and future are merged [*confondus*] ... [and] we live in this undivided state that allows us to recover the plenitude and meaning of the moment."[52] In this way, "the poet becomes a prophet" by tracing "yesterday's routes and tomorrow's routes ... where man freed from the fetters of duration [*la durée*] and extension [*l'étendue*] by the omnipotence [*toute-puissance*] of poetry, *sees* clearly ... into his past which is at the same time his future."[53] Poetry thereby allows for "total knowledge" through which "clairvoyant minds" are able to recognize the simultaneity of past, present, and future.[54]

For Suzanne, this clairvoyant poetics could overcome the impoverished range of false alternatives that had long imprisoned modern thought and being. Surrealism, for example, would allow man "to finally act to transcend the sordid existing antinomies: blacks-whites, Europeans-Africans, civilized-savages. ... Purified of colonial stupidities."[55] Poetry as medium for collective emancipation would work not simply to oppose black to white or separate colonies from Europe but to create a world wherein these distinctions no longer made sense. She envisioned peoples of African descent as vanguards in this struggle: "Millions of black hands, across the furious skies of world war, will be raised against their horror. Freed from a long drowsy torpor [*engouridisse-ment*], the most disenfranchised of all peoples will rise up from the fields of ashes."[56]

Similarly, in the first issue of *Tropiques*, René Ménil invoked Nietzsche to distinguish between a sterile "sphere of erudition," mere form without living content, and "the sphere of real art," creation rooted in actual experience, flowing from living collectivities, and expressing cultural singularity.[57] He too called on Antilleans to overcome alienation through rooted and vital art that would express "the original life that we lead and that leads us ... [our] fears and hopes, desires and passions, acts and dreams, sadness and joy, unique in the world."[58] But rather than fetishize Antillean singularity, Ménil called for situated art that "expresses the universal through the expression of the individual man, rooted in his provincial [*villageoise*] existence. And universality is attained, not by the suppression of the most particular aspects that the artist language."[59] The task of Antillean poets "who want to reclassify [themselves] within humanity" is to "bring to our life a content worthy of being universally taken into consideration."[60] Ménil sought not to critique (European) universality from the standpoint of (Antillean) particularity but to overcome this antinomy through art expressing *concrete universality*. As he wrote, "in the imperial concert of a common culture we have a special sound to contribute which until now we have not been able to utter."[61]

Like Suzanne, Ménil was interested in poetic anticipation: "works of the imagination . . . announce our best future [*avenir*]. The marvelous . . . projects, onto the furthest edge of the future [*devenir*], a light that pierces the darkness . . . The story [*conte*] is a prophecy."[62] Ménil is not suggesting that art can predict the future or know what forms might be appropriate to it, but that it is a performative act that conjures futures, a call that calls into being. In jazz, "[t]he 'musician' does not know, must not know, his next phrase, his next utterance, the next adventure, however, it advances, like the acrobat, on the tight-rope of circumstances."[63] Politics might be similarly imagined as a clairvoyant high-wire act and improvisational art whose form cannot be known in advance but must project forward even while adjusting dynamically to ever changing circumstances. For Ménil, "our task is to prepare for the arrival of the Poet . . . who will create that which we conceive."[64] He explains that "every renaissance" depends on "the renewal of a content rooted in human realities" as well as "a new form" appropriate for it.[65] However, creative rebirth is often misrecognized "precisely because it denies, by its novelty, the old formulas."[66] Such terms might have described subsequent responses to Césaire's political projects.

Ménil's prophetic poetics were as concerned with historicity as futurity. Reminding readers that every epoch contains "all the previous instances of this future," he writes,

> The present existence [*actualité*] of a being is its present [*présent*] but this present is this very being marked by the extreme temporal sign of his duration [*durée*]. There does not, therefore exist, for a living being, an irreconcilable contradiction between his present [*présent*] and his past . . . similarly, in a social milieu, no antinomy between modernity and old works.[67]

Challenging the simplistic dichotomy between tradition and modernity, he concludes: "The poet, therefore, is not modern by abandoning or ignoring the past, but by surpassing dialectically the stages of this past, which is to say by a simultaneous negation and living conservation of all previous cultural forms."[68] These forms crystallize a multiplicity of enduring pasts that they also supersede. Like the Césaires, Ménil regarded creative acts as entwined with untimely artifacts and untimely acts with creative artifacts. In this view criticism identifies potentialities within inherited forms and enacts future possibilities by inventing novel forms. "Such is the necessity of poetry: all of the past in the self. Such is the freedom of poetry: before oneself, the future without a face."[69] This ambition—for prophetic poets to conjure a future society by reclaiming legacies that persist within a disjunctive present and by anticipating forms that would be adequate to it—animated these thinkers' orientation to aesthetics, epistemology, and politics.

Poetic Knowledge

In 1941 Césaire met André Breton, who had arrived in Martinique on a ship full of émigré intellectuals and artists seeking the United States, including Claude Lévi-Strauss and Cuban painter Wilfredo Lam. Breton discovered the first issue of *Tropiques* in the window of a bookshop owned by René Ménil's sister; he proclaimed Césaire's writing "a shaft of light."[70] Césaire recollected that meeting Breton was a "very important" turning point for him as a poet, marking "the end of hesitation."[71] Césaire characterized his relation to surrealism in terms of dialogue and convergence rather than imitation or derivation. During this period, Césaire wrote the poems eventually collected in *Les Armes Miraculeuses* (many originally published in *Tropiques*) and the poem he would later rework as his first play, a neoclassical tragedy titled *And the Dogs Were Silent*, whose central character, The Rebel, embodied a spirit of absolutist revolt.

Equally formative was a trip to Haiti from May to December 1944. Invited to serve as a French cultural ambassador by Breton's friend and fellow surrealist Pierre Mabille, then conseiller culturel of the French Embassy,[72] Césaire taught at the University of Haiti and gave a series of public talks.[73] He later recalled feeling overwhelmed by the cautionary example of "this terribly complex society. . . . Most of all in Haiti I saw what should not be done! A country that had conquered its liberty, that had conquered its independence, and which I saw was more miserable than Martinique, a French colony! . . . It was tragic, and that could very well happen to us Martinicans as well."[74] If his trip provoked a long engagement with the world-making history of the revolution in Saint-Domingue, it also further demystified the idea of state sovereignty as a self-evident good.

Césaire's trip coincided with the Congrès International de Philosophie, from September 24–30 in Port-au-Prince. Organized around the theme "Problems of Knowledge," the conference was presided over by the Catholic philosopher Jacques Maritain. Ethnologist Roger Bastide presented "The Sociological

Theory of Knowledge," and W. E. B. DuBois wrote a supporting letter recalling his past studies with pragmatist philosophers William James, George Santayana, and Josiah Royce.[75] Césaire, there as an official delegate of the French government, presented his anti-Kantian essay "Poetry and Knowledge."[76] Unlike the other conventionally academic papers, Césaire's was written in a poetic form. It was published first in the *Cahiers de Haiti* in October 1944 and reprinted the following year in *Tropiques*.

In the essay, Césaire criticizes instrumental reason, not to celebrate madness or unreason, but in service of a more elevated form of reason that he called "poetic knowledge" and "poetic truth."[77] He suggests that "in the first days of humanity" man was a "primitive scientist" who "discovered in fear and rapture the throbbing newness of the world. Attraction and terror. Trembling and wonderment. Strangeness and intimacy. . . . It is in this state of fear and love, in this climate of emotion and imagination that mankind made its first, most fundamental, and most decisive discoveries."[78] This "fulfilling knowledge" was gradually superseded by an "impoverished" scientific knowledge, "poor and half starved," that "enumerates, measures, classifies, and kills."[79] But the ancient form of knowing did not disappear; it persisted in "the nocturnal forces of poetry."[80]

Césaire identifies "the ground of poetic knowledge" as "an astonishing mobilization of all human and cosmic forces." He writes,

> it is with his entire being that the poet approaches the poem . . . all lived experience. All the possibility. . . . And the most extraordinary contacts: all the pasts, all the futures. . . . Everything is summoned. Everything awaits. . . . Within us, all the ages of mankind. Within us, all humankind. It is *universe*. . . . Surrender to the vital movement, to the creative *élan*. Joyous surrender . . . one man is the salvation of humanity, one man puts humanity back in the universal concert, one man united the human flowering with the universal flowering; that man is the poet.[81]

This is a vitalist vision of recovery, reconciliation, and salvation through poetry. But if Césaire evoked this primordial unity to reject modern forms of instrumental rationality, this was not a romantic rejection of modernity. Rather, "poetic knowledge" represented a modern modality of knowing through which modern antinomies are not denied but transcended: "There we see resolved—and by the poetic state—two of the most anguishing antinomies that exist: the antinomy of one and the other, the antinomy of Self and World."[82] He thus identified nineteenth-century modernism as a revolutionary "leap into the poetic void" through which figures like Baudelaire, Rimbaud, Mallarmé,

Apollinaire, Breton, Lautréamont, and Freud recovered the ancient insights of Lucretius (who "divines the indestructibility of matter, the plurality of worlds, the existence of the infinitely small") and Seneca (who "sends forth ships on the trail of new worlds").[83] Césaire's "poetic knowledge" is a dialectical form of knowing that overcomes "the barriers . . . the law of identity, the law of noncontradiction, the logical principle of the excluded middle."[84] Its privileged epistemological instrument is the poetic *image*, which contrasts with (Kantian) rational judgment.[85] He explains, "because the image extends inordinately the field of transcendence and the right of transcendence, poetry is always on the road to truth . . . the image is forever surpassing [*dépasse*] that which is perceived because the dialectic of the image transcends antinomies. . . . When the sun of image reaches its zenith, everything becomes possible again. . . . Accursed complexes dissolve, it's the instant of emergence."[86]

Césaire extends to time itself this capacity of poetic images to transcend the impoverished antinomies of philosophical rationalists and scientific empiricists.

> Here we are . . . at the very heart of mankind, in the babbling hollow of destiny. My past is there to show and to hide its face from me. My future is there to hold out its hand to me. Rockets flare. It is my childhood in flames. It is my childhood talking and looking for me. And within the person I am now, the person I will be stands on tiptoe. And what emerges [are] . . . hereditary images that only the poetic atmosphere can bring to light again for ultimate decoding. The buried knowledge of the ages.[87]

Poetic knowledge thus reveals how past and future, heritage and destiny, may be contemporaneous with one another . . . even as it also produces such contemporaneity.

Césaire's poetic images enable a revolutionary form of knowing that unsettles the existing order. Referring to Rimbaud, he declares, "the result is known to you . . . worlds twisted, crushed, torn apart, the cosmos given back to chaos, order given back to disorder, being given over to becoming, everywhere the absurd, everywhere the incoherent, the demential."[88] He explains,

> it is appropriate to speak of poetic violence, of poetic aggressivity, of poetic instability. In this climate of flame and fury that is the climate of poetry, money has no currency, courts pass no judgment, judges do not convict, juries do not acquit. Only the firing squads still know how to ply their trade. . . . Police functions are strangulated. Conventions wear out.[89]

Césaire thus conjures a poetically mediated revolutionary situation in which the conventional coordinates of capitalist exchange, constitutional legality, and parliamentary democracy are overturned. Yet this is not simply an apocalyptic vision of catastrophe. "And at the end of all that! What is there? Failure! No, the flashing vision of his own destiny. And the most authentic vision of the world."[90] Poetic knowledge moves through, or moves humans through, a state of violent upheaval into a prophetic vision of destiny, an elevated truth, an illuminated world. Similarly, rather than negate exchange, law, and democracy as such, poetic knowledge may elevate them. This is precisely the argument that Césaire began to develop about political form in *Tropiques*.

The Politics of Inflection

Consider "Panorama" in the February 1944 issue of *Tropiques*. Declaring that "this country suffers from a repressed revolution [*revolution refoulée*]," Césaire contends that "Martinican capitalism" has created an "Antillean malaise" among a people whose creativity has been stifled and humanity impoverished—a malaise that intensified *after* the abolition of slavery.[91] He asserts that "under the regime of slavery the *nègre* was magnificent," resisting with humor when they "treated him like a beast . . . broke his body . . . [and] tortured his soul." Césaire attributes this resilience to slaves' connections to African societies; they were "swollen with life, with strength. And rich. Rich with sensuality, with spirituality."[92] In contrast, "one shudders at the thought of the quality of souls created here for almost a century. A century of insidious slavery, of resignation, of individual and collective cowardice. A ferocious egoism. A repugnant conformism."[93] Worse, for Césaire, this soul-destroying system was maintained by a cowardly and conformist black bourgeoisie.

Because "the logical end point of three centuries of Antillean history" was "the triumph of total *servitude*," Césaire insisted that colonial emancipation would require a renaissance in moral and intellectual life.[94] He explained that "the Martinican Revolution will of course be made in the name of bread, but also in the name of air and of poetry (which is the same thing). I am saying that we are suffocating. Principle of a healthy Antillean politics: open the windows. Air. Air."[95] If overcoming colonial capitalism was necessary so was creative self-expression through which Martinicans could fully realize themselves as free human beings. And he emphasized that the revolutionary awakening must be initiated by the people of Martinique themselves, through direct action. Change would have to be seized not requested, invented not inherited. "We want to live passionately. And it is the blood of this country that will de-

cide [*statuer*] in the last instance. . . . This blood does not vote."[96] Césaire is
not so much calling for revolt as recalling the long history of popular uprisings that regularly compelled the French state to institute substantive reforms

Although "Panorama" calls for a renaissance, it does not advocate state sovereignty. Césaire actually writes, "I condemn any idea of *Antillean independence*. . . .
But . . . Martinican *dependence*, desired, calculated, as reasoned as sentimental,
will neither be de-graded nor under-graded [*ni dé-chéance ni sous-chéance*]."[97]
He thereby envisions the Antillean revolution as an integral element of a
broader revolution aiming to transform—and redeem—France itself. Thus
his declaration: "The Fourth Republic must be."[98] Following Ménil's insights
about future forms, we should not assume that Césaire was referring to the
anemic, imperial republic that was actually instituted in 1946. A clue may be
found in his crucial qualification: "I only know one single France. That of
the Revolution. That of Toussaint Louverture. Too bad for the Gothic cathedral."[99] With this poetically layered phrase, Césaire reminds readers that by
definition a republican polity must be singular and indivisible. If, after the Liberation, France was to create a new state including overseas territories, then
the Antilles must enter on terms of unconditional equality. Simultaneously,
his formulation invites Antilleans to identify not with the integral French nation or cultural *patrie* ("too bad for the Gothic cathedral") but with France's
revolutionary republican tradition, which they should recognize as their own.
Césaire subversively identifies this tradition with the anticolonial *and* truly republican acts of Toussaint Louverture but keeps the reference ambiguous by
leaving "revolution" unqualified, suggesting both that Toussaint most fully
embodied the spirit and values of the French Revolution and that Toussaint's
revolution in Saint-Domingue most fully embodied the revolutionary ideals
of a single, indivisible French republic.

Thus Césaire's seemingly moderate call for a Fourth Republic works a kind
of transgressive magic. An ostensibly straightforward formulation is followed
promptly by a call to rethink received understandings of categories like emancipation, revolution, republic, and even France. He identifies *within* traditions
linked to each of these inherited concepts transformative political possibilities that point beyond their apparent meanings. The faint distinction between
de Gaulle's France and Césaire's "France" marks a potentially revolutionary difference. This is an example of radical literalism. Like Arendt's historical "treasure hunter," Césaire seeks to reclaim traditional concepts "in order to distill
from them anew their original spirit."[100]

In a telling interview, the literary critic Jacqueline Leiner practically badgers
Césaire into conceding that he could never fully express his authentic Creole

self and sensibility in French as an imposed foreign language. Césaire calmly responds:

> I am not a prisoner of the French language! Only, I try, I always wanted to *inflect* French. Thus, if I loved Mallarmé so much, it is because he showed me . . . that language is, ultimately, arbitrary. It is not a natural phenomenon . . . my aim was to inflect French, to *transform* it to express, let's say, 'this me, this black-me, this creole-me, this Martinican-me, this Antillean-me.' This is why I am much more interested in poetry than in prose, and this *insofar as the poet creates his language*, while, in general, the prose writer uses language. . . . I am re-creating a language that is not French. Whether or not French people recognize themselves in it is their problem.[101]

Like Mallarmé, Césaire turns French inside out; he finds within the linguistic legacy resources through which to create a language that is simultaneously known and new, familiar and foreign, French and not.

When Leiner pushes Césaire to admit to an alienated relationship to French language and culture, he patiently reiterates that as a Martinican, he speaks French or Creole depending on the context but, like everybody educated in the Antilles, was instructed in French and had learned to write in French. He also stresses that languages, like selves, are neither fixed nor determining. The boundary between French and Creole is porous. Writers don't just use languages instrumentally; they inhabit them creatively. They inflect and invent. Leiner's questions reveal the monocultural, territorialist, and identitarian assumptions that even sympathetic critics have brought to Césaire's work and acts. Ultimately she has difficulty recognizing him as really French. He graciously reminds her "my self is *vague*, it is *blurry* [*flou*], it is *uncertain* . . . The self, it is a sort of *stupor* [*torpeur*]."[102] While *he* did not feel alienated by French, perhaps those who assume that he did should revise *their* understanding of "France."

Césaire's critical strategy regarding language, culture, *and* politics is condensed in his will to "inflect" rather than reject; to bend, refigure, and refunction French was inseparable from his ambition to expand, explode, and elevate France.[103] He, like Senghor, developed a political poetics and poetic politics that turned France into an uncanny object, simultaneously familiar and fearful.[104] It is precisely because their political and aesthetic interventions sometimes appeared to comport with dominant norms that they produced an uncanny experience among metropolitans who felt estranged and disoriented precisely where or when they expected to feel "at home."

Césaire's subversive commitment to immanent critique reappears at the interview's closing. When he asserts that poets are seers and "poetry is prophetic," Leiner says, "I recognize in you, precisely, a primitive belief, an African belief, in poetry?" Césaire responds,

> That's it, but just *primitive*, not necessarily *African!* The prophet! [*Le vatès!*] What interests me is primitive Greek poetry, primitive Greek tragedy. Moreover, whether Latin [*latinité*] or Greek [*grécité*], I only appreciate them in their primitivity. . . . At bottom, we can glimpse that Roman civilization or Greek civilization, at their start, were not very far from African civilization.[105]

Césaire thus refigures a stereotypical distinction between rational Europeans and primitive non-Europeans as one between prosaic modernity and a poetic primitivity that once animated *both* European and African civilizations but had been lost by the former. Confessing to prefer the richness of self-surpassing poetic images to the poverty of logical concepts, Césaire explains, "all that was gained through reasoning was lost for poetry. It seems to me that the surrealist conception of the image is the meeting point! Through this conception, Europe admits its guilt and returns, finally, to *primitive* traditions."[106] Césaire is less interested in challenging French colonialism by retreating into primordial Africanity than in identifying within European and Antillean history those unrealized revolutionary possibilities through which colonialism could be overcome and a lost primitive-poetic relationship to knowing and being recuperated.

By conceiving the "image" as both embodied and self-surpassing, able to condense within itself more than it appears to be, Césaire offered a way to think beyond conventional oppositions between sensibility and intelligibility, empiricism and rationalism, subjectivity and objectivity, concrete and abstract, particular and universal, immanent and transcendent, actual and possible, being and becoming, cause and effect, past and future. As he said to Leiner, "I suppose that the Image, it is a *dépassement*."[107] Through such "poetic knowledge," Césaire attempted to overcome antinomies, to liberate sedimented histories, and unlock future potentialities in existing arrangements. Radical literalism became the medium for a politics of *dépassement*.

Tropical Legacies

In later recollections, Césaire relegated *Tropiques* to a specifically cultural phase of his anticolonial engagement, explaining, "if, suddenly, with the Liberation, [it] stopped appearing, it was precisely because the cultural struggle gave way to the political struggle."[108] Césaire, like Senghor, stepped abruptly onto the postwar political stage. But we should not accept at face value his claim that the last issue of *Tropiques* marked a straightforward shift from cultural to political engagement.

Tropiques, after all, challenged the distinction between art and politics. Through it Césaire developed a critical aesthetics and aesthetics of critique that disclosed the poetic dimensions of political acts and the political efficacy of poetic acts. Rhetoric was the medium of his poetry *and* his politics; each pursued transformation through inflection, refraction, and radical literalism. Understanding his peculiar orientation to postwar emancipation requires attention to his rhetorical practices and strategies whereby multilayered and polysemic images disclosed themselves to be more or other than they appeared. Whether on the stage of the National Assembly, at metropolitan commemorations, before municipal microphones in Martinique, in campaign speeches and party programs, or in his historical plays, Césaire was acutely sensitive to the theatrical—aesthetic, poetic, performative, prefigurative—dimensions of politics. In the spirit of *Tropiques* he sought to invent political forms adequate to late imperial historical conditions and to employ new aesthetic forms to call forth novel political realities.

Rather than critique abstract universality from the standpoint of concrete particularity—or empty form from that of living content, or alienated modernity from that of rooted tradition, or a faceless future from that of a lived past, or a generic humanity from that of a local culture—René Ménil, Suzanne Césaire, and Aimé envisioned an elevated form of concrete universality. *Tropiques* wagered that cultural revolution in the Antilles would precipitate revolutionary change in metropolitan France even as socialist revolution in France would fuel for cultural renewal in the Antilles. The resulting renovated "France" would include Antillean colonies on terms of equality, mutuality, and solidarity. This formation would become a model and instrument for global renewal and human redemption.

Their criticism targeted not only white planters but bourgeois black functionaries, not only French racists but black cultural essentialists, not only hypocritical republicans but vulgar socialists. They challenged anyone, regardless of cultural or political identity, who regarded human action as motivated only by material well-being and did not attend to the creative spirit and poetic imagination. Rather than challenge French colonialism from the perspective of a static Antillean cultural tradition, or capitalism from the perspective of an idealized Antillean peasantry, they criticized the reactionary dimensions of each tradition from the standpoint of critical currents *internal* to that tradition. They looked to history neither for confirmation of past suffering nor escapist compensation for present stasis but for living legacies through which to revive traditions of struggle and revitalize a demoralized population.

In this version of modernist Antillean humanism and humanist Antillean modernism, the writers for *Tropiques* did not limit their inheritance to traditions of knowing, making, and acting associated with Caribbean folktales, black American writers and jazz musicians, African dancers, sculptors, and sages, and Haitian revolutionaries. They also identified themselves as the rightful heirs of European vitalists, symbolists, psychoanalysts, surrealists, socialists, communists, and revolutionaries. Their transcultural embrace of these critical currents served a cosmopolitan project of human emancipation through prophetic poetic illumination. Their anticolonial modernism could only be understood as a sign of cultural alienation from a perspective that deems immutable the invidious distinctions that they themselves sought to transcend. *Tropiques* promoted a poetics of clairvoyant futurism that invited Antilleans to act as if these distinctions had already been overcome.

Excursus: Untimeliness

Aimé and Suzanne Césaire and René Ménil attempted to grasp the aesthetic and political possibilities of the *untimely* quality of social life in a disjointed historical present. Their retrospective and prospective meditations on historical rupture, blurred tenses, and possible futures provides a useful starting point for a history of postwar France that attends explicitly to the relation between the problem of freedom and the politics of time.

I use "untimely" to refer to ways that the historical present is not—or no longer appears to be—identical with itself.[109] Untimeliness may entail processes of temporal confusion or illumination when conventional distinctions between past, present, and future no longer obtain, when tenses blur and times (seem to) interpenetrate.[110] Untimely processes also lead social actors either to misrecognize or deliberately conflate one historical period for another, to act *as if* they inhabited an epoch that had already passed or had not yet arrived. These untimely practices, whether unconscious or intentional, can serve either transformative or conservative ends.[111]

Reinhart Kosellek's metahistory of historical temporality and its corresponding forms of knowledge directs our attention to the qualitative dimensions of time and suggests that historians must attend to the historically specific character of tenses and their relations.[112] Thus his overriding interest in "former futures" or "futures past"—not only specific visions of concrete futures that may have existed in the past but the qualitatively distinct ways that peoples once conceptualized the relation between present and future.[113] He also examines the underlying connections among the sociopolitical organization of time, the lived experience of time, time consciousness, temporal ideologies, and forms of historical knowledge.

In his own research on the "the temporalization of history," Kosellek traces how, sometime in the seventeenth and eighteenth centuries, time assumed a different quality and history was ascribed a temporal character. This "new time" (*Neuzeit*) was characterized by historical acceleration, a growing disjuncture between "the space of experience" and "the horizon of expectation" on the one hand and a new orientation to the future as ever unfolding.[114] Simultaneously, the German concept *Historie*, as a collection of discrete events requiring narration, was displaced by the concept *Geschichte*, as a collective and singular worldwide process.[115] Kosellek identifies a contradiction within "new time." European moderns refigured history as a contingent human process whose outcome would always be unknown, but also viewed history as progressive. Christian eschatology thus joined to Enlightenment humanism to form a new conception of history as global, total, and progressive but whose ever-receding horizon could never be reached.[116]

Kosellek's work demonstrates that modern time is distinctive not simply because it is singular and progressive but because it is untimely. He contends that when future expectations could no longer be derived from past experiences, what was once regarded as the uniformity of time was shattered; past, present, and future came to be regarded as qualitatively different.[117] Yet in modern times fixed boundaries among tenses become porous, and any one time became less identical with itself. Kosellek describes an internally divided *now* in which experience and expectation, memory and hope, do not align. He writes, "the one process of time became a dynamic of a coexisting plurality of times."[118]

For Kosellek this dynamic of differentiation and interpenetration led to a coexisting plurality of nonidentical times, which he calls "the contemporaneity of the noncontemporaneous."[119] In some places he uses this formulation to designate the moment when imperial contact with other civilizations led Europeans to figure the world as composed of different peoples living in distinct historical eras and developing at disparate paces.[120] In others he uses it to signal the fact that modernization unfolded unevenly, such that some places and people appear to exist in dissimilar historical eras, live their lives according to different temporal rhythms, and develop at their own specific pace.[121]

Kosellek also invokes "the contemporaneity of the noncontemporaneous" to signal how the modern *now*, which he calls a "temporal refraction" contains "a diversity of temporal strata which are of varying duration."[122] All manner of untimely phenomena flow from this condition. Kosellek invokes "the prognostic structure of historical time" whereby "each prognosis anticipates events which are certainly rooted in the present and in this respect are already existent, although they have not actually occurred."[123] He contends that in modern times, history no longer refers simply to the past but to the "covert connection of the bygone with the future."[124] And given the accelerating tempo of modernity, he remarks, all past history must continually be revisited and reinterpreted from the standpoint of this ever-shifting present such that the past regularly reveals itself as other than what it earlier appeared to be.[125] With "new time" the past can never fully pass; it remains vital, plastic, and incomplete. To convey this he invokes a Bergsonian image: "it is like the glass front of a washing machine, behind which various bits of the wash appear now and then, but are all contained within the drum."[126]

Similarly, many articles in *Tropiques* attended to the temporal heterogeneity of the political present. A world-historical transition had heightened these intellectuals' sensitivity to the qualities of historical temporality. And such an interruption called forth and rendered newly legible the histories of preceding transitions. Colonial and metropolitan thinkers who wrote from within the historical fissure that opened with the war attended repeatedly to the relationship between the problem of freedom and the politics of time. Moreover, the Occupation set the stage for much of postwar French history, which was often characterized by temporal confusion, conflation, and refraction: uncanny returns, repetitions, and reenactments; belated responses and nostalgic projections; and proleptic practices of conjuring, anticipation, and envisioning. This was a period of anachrony, when politics, whether founded on flashback or animated by anticipation, were often conducted in the subjunctive mode: "as if." Many actors experienced time in an unsteady and disjointed manner. The present was densely layered; incomplete histories were pressed up against imagined futures. There was a great deal of temporal misrecognition and historical acting out, much discussion of unrealized pasts that could now be reactivated and unfolding futures that were already at hand.

From the perspective of the "contemporaneity of the noncontemporaneous," postwar French history can be read as a chain of intersecting and untimely events that created the conditions through which subsequent experiences were refracted. Thus the ongoing instances of conflation involving the occupation, collaboration, and purge; the Resistance myth, the exclusion of communists from government, and the disavowal of Holocaust victims; the violent wars of colonial secession in Indochina and Algeria, including public debates about systematic torture, OAS terrorism, the playing out of the Algerian conflict in metropolitan France, and the descent into quasi-dictatorship in 1958; the extreme violence of the state against students and workers during May 1968; the resurgence of neofascism, anti-Semitism, and anti-immigrant racism in the 1970s and 1980s; the corresponding panic about republican values, national unity, and citizenship laws that criminalized immigration by a xenophobic security state; the spectacular trials of Vichy collaborators and Nazi officials in French courts; debates among scholars over the relationship between history and memory as well as about law and historical truth; the publication of Pierre Nora's *Lieux de memoire* (1984–1992); bitter conflicts over multiculturalism and French Islam; celebrations and debates marking the 150th anniversary of the abolition of slavery; the decision to designate May 10 as a national holiday commemorating this abolition; so-called public revelations about the torture during the Algerian war, which was already well documented and widely known; the debate over the law instructing public schools to teach about the history of slavery followed by the debate over the law instructing them to teach about the "positive" aspects of overseas colonialism; the 2005 uprising in the *banlieues* and the creation of a Museum of National Immigration. The list could be easily extended. Again and again groups of postwar actors may be read as symptomatically acting out a haunting past event through which their present experiences are refracted *and* as providing a new source of untimely refraction for future actors. At every instance we see the "contemporaneity of the noncontemporaneous" at work. Yet historians drawn to these peculiar dynamics have more often regarded them through the optic of memory rather than that of time itself.[127]

The play of remembering and forgetting, memorializing and disavowing traversed postwar French history and deserves critical attention. It is not an accident that much of the innovative historiography on historical memory was developed not only by historians of the postwar years but by those who came of age during this period.[128] Their attention has rightly been attracted to the ubiquitous call for "the duty to remember" that has resounded throughout the postwar period. *Le devoir de mémoire* has been evoked across the political spectrum with respect to a range of historical events and political projects. Whether regarding the legacy of the Occupation and collaboration or, more recently, legacies of slavery and colonialism, the issue of historical memory has fueled countless public debates and provided much raw material for scholarly production. The so-called duty of memory combines intersecting calls for historical truth, legal reparations, state apologies, and public commemoration in order to honor suffering, remember crimes, and assume responsibility. This multilayered injunction has implicated historians in state institutions and state actors in the production of historical knowledge, whether through laws, trials, holidays, protests, textbooks, museum exhibits, media spectacles, symposia, or scholarship. These scholars' attention to the highly mediated and refractive character of postwar politics, as well as to the charged political stakes of historical knowledge, has demonstrated that any history of these events must also be a history of historical memory. And their work makes clear that such an object cannot be grasped through conventional archival empiricism.

The various phenomena grouped under the rubric "historical memory" are clearly bound up with untimely processes. Scholarship on historical memory has indeed troubled many orthodox historiographic assumptions about stable distinctions between past and present and between the scholar and the object of knowledge. But memory studies do not necessarily engage historical temporality directly and critically. In fact, they often accept disciplinary history's understanding of time as a neutral medium within which history takes place rather than treat it as a productive historical force of its own.[129] The untimely character of historical memory is then relegated to the mentalities or ideologies of particular historical actors.

Generally, memory studies have inherited the sociological functionalism of their putative founder Maurice Halbwachs. Like Freud and Bergson, Halbwachs sought to remove memory from the reductive purview of cognitive science. But in Durkheimian fashion, he argued that representations of the past are produced through "social frameworks" in order to serve present needs and interests.[130] Groups construct collective memories in order to maintain social solidarity and temporal continuity.[131] Unlike Freud, Bergson, or Proust, Halbwachs was not interested in exploring the involuntary processes of temporal indistinction or interpenetration that are bound up with memory; he was concerned with maintaining proper boundaries between tenses. Thus his claim that whereas dreams mistakenly lead people to "become fused with the past" and provide them with "the illusion of reliving it," collective memory functions to "differentiate the past from the present."[132]

Studies of historical memory tend to reproduce this functionalist concern with memory construction rather than situate memory within a broader field of untimely processes and practices.[133] Accounts of collective representation often focus on how actors become invested in remembering, memorializing, narrating, or inventing certain accounts of the past. Such approaches do not usually attend to the fact that these memories and sites are also typically endowed with an untimely power to revisit, invest, and possess present social action and perception. To grasp this power, it is not enough to treat past artifacts as repositories of meaning or sources of affective attachment through which actors recall or construct memories of the past. Attention to untimeliness requires us to treat historical remnants more along the lines of fragments of dreams that remain upon waking.

For psychoanalysis, dream fragments do not function as factual evidence to be collected and ordered to reconstruct what actually happened. Nor are they simply symbols that allow us to recall memories of the past. They are charged images that invest and haunt the waking present. In psychoanalysis, the dream fragment is both the product of forgetting and the opening for a certain type of remembering. Through careful attention that is simultaneously focused and distracted, such fragments can suddenly reveal the fuller dream of which they are the traces. And just as they condense within themselves the "lost" and "forgotten" dream, the dream itself condenses structures, revelations, and truths within and about the dreamer.

If dream fragments are charged remnants of persistent pasts, the past can impose itself and make demands upon the present. Yet their meaning and power emerge only after we have tracked and pursued them. Lost and forgotten dreams reveal themselves through a peculiar process of active seeking and patient waiting. Their meanings are both discovered and constructed; their significance is simultaneously immanent to the images and fashioned retrospectively through analysis. Because it is impossible to distinguish clearly between what they present to us and what we bring to them, such dream fragments blur boundaries between then and now, reality and fantasy, experience and imagination, cognition and the unconscious, subject and object. They are fragments of objectified subjectivity and subjectified objectivity that throw us back into the past and disclose truths about the present. They embody pasts present and futures past.

Walter Benjamin attempted to conjugate psychoanalytic, surrealist, and Marxian insights about dreams, poetics, and politics. "Dream images" were the template for his concept of "dialectical images," which he called "the primal phenomenon of history."[134] For Benjamin they serve as relay points among disparate historical epochs by "actualizing" in themselves their own origin (past) and decline (future).[135] He speaks of the crucial moment when "humanity, rubbing its eyes, recognizes [a] particular dream image" from a different epoch; "it is at this moment that the historian takes up, with regard to that image, task of dream interpretation." This is simultaneously an intellectual and political act whose aim is "the realization of dream elements in the course of waking up."[136]

Benjamin's thinking about politics, truth, and time built upon the insights of Marx and Freud. Both figures developed sophisticated frameworks for recognizing untimely phenomena as social facts. In different ways, Marx and Freud each demonstrated the quasi-autonomous power of persistent pasts to dominate present structures and subjects in determinate but not immediately apparent ways. Marx did so through his conception of alienation as the domination of living labor in the present by congealed (past and dead) labor in the form of fixed capital, which is itself nothing but crystallized labor time (i.e., the past).[137] Freud's general theory of neurosis also identified processes of temporal conflation and confusion whereby present perceptions are refracted through and overdetermined by past experiences. This mechanism is especially intense for victims of trauma who misrecognize the present as the past and thus act as if the past were perpetually present; they continually re-experience the earlier trauma as if it were always unfolding.[138]

Marx and Freud also explored how the uneven and layered character of an untimely present may harbor or enable seemingly impossible futures. Marx demonstrates that within existing social formations, ever-present pasts operate below the level of immediate appearances to produce already emergent futures. Revolutionary transformation for Marx is less a matter of leaping out of the present into a phantasmic future than in recognizing within the present a future that is already in formation but is still difficult to imagine or discern. Present praxis seeks deliberately to create a new future by realizing the not yet conscious dreams of the past.[139]

Freud's analysis of condensation, displacement, and representation in "dream work" illuminates a frightening but free domain of life where human being is liberated from the material constraints of space, time, and causality. Within the unconscious, which Freud described as "the general basis of psychical life" and "the true psychical reality," there are no distinctions between past and present, actual and possible, real and imagined.[140] Through treatment, the analyst helps the patient travel back in time to the scene of unfulfilled desires or traumatic injuries in order to act as if the past were present or the future not yet fixed, so he or she can remake an already lived life into something different. Patients are invited not simply to interpret the past but to intervene into the temporal processes that seem to have already fixed their present.

Marx and Freud pointed implicitly to the liberatory dimensions of untimely processes. But neither thematized them directly. They both formulated visions of emancipation that sought to disentangle temporal knots in order to overcome the ongoing power of the past in and over the present. For each, disalienation was above all a matter of restoring proper temporal coordinates so that present subjects could reclaim rightful and rational control over a past seemingly endowed with a quasi-autonomous agency.

In contrast, Benjamin, along with Adorno and Bloch, extended and inflected Marxian and Freudian insights to address how untimely processes, practices, and artifacts could be sources of transformative possibility. By constructing constellations, they believed, philosophy could pursue concrete truths condensed within reified phenomena by recognizing and awakening their self-surpassing potentialities.[141] Adorno, for example, argued that "our thinking heeds a potential that waits in the object." It "sees more in a phenomenon than what it is—and solely because of what it is." He writes, "cognition of the object in its constellation is cognition of the process stored in the object" such that "the history locked in the object . . . is delivered."[142] This may be read as an elegant description of both untimeliness and immanent critique.

Benjamin too was preoccupied with such deliverance. He sought to awaken the "revolutionary energies" crystallized within actually existing but functionally "outmoded" objects.[143] This operation, which substitutes "a political for a historical view of the past" is one method for achieving a "profane illumination."[144] Benjamin directs attention to moments when "what has been comes together in a flash with the now to form a constellation."[145] Such *historical* constellations produce and are revealed by evanescent "dialectical images" through which past objects and epochs "attain to legibility" but "only at a particular time."[146] "Each 'now'," Benjamin argued, "is the now of a particular recognizability."[147] Through such recognition remembrance becomes and enables political action. The critical thinker "grasps the constellation into which his own era has entered, along with a very specific earlier one. Thus he establishes a conception of the present as now-time."[148] For him "every historical moment" carried with it a "peculiar revolutionary chance" grounded simultaneously in the given "historical situation" and in "the right of entry which the historical moment enjoys vis-à-vis a quite distinct chamber of the past, one which up to that point has been closed and locked." He defines this transtemporal "entry" as "political action."[149]

Benjamin's interest in constellating "what has been" with "the now" is bound up with his understanding of revolution as interruption. He proposes that critical "thinking involves not only the movement of thoughts, but their arrest as well. Where thinking suddenly comes to a stop in a constellation saturated with tensions."[150] Rejecting the conventional historicist idea of the present as "a transition," Benjamin's aim is "to blast a specific era out of the homogeneous course of history" in order to "blast open the continuum of history" itself.[151] He famously described revolutions as "an attempt by the passengers on the train [of world history] to activate the emergency break."[152] Radical remembrance thus seeks to explode any conception of linear progress. "Time," Benjamin wrote, "must be brought to a standstill."[153]

But Benjamin's affirmation of the Jewish prohibition against "inquiring into the future" does not mean he abandoned a *political* conception of what is to come.[154] He wrote that "every second was the small gateway in time through which the Messiah might enter" and revolution was a "dialectical leap" into the "open air of history."[155] The movement from a disjunctive present to an unknowable future must be mediated by a "tiger's leap into the past."[156] The critic "articulates the past historically" not to recognize it, like a positivist historian, as "the way it really was"[157] but to grasp the revolutionary possibilities of the present "political situation."[158] Benjamin understands Friedrich Schlegel's claim that "the historian is a prophet facing backward" to mean that "the historian turns his back on his own time, and his seer's gaze is kindled by the peaks of earlier generations as they sink further and further into the past." Indeed, the historian's own time is far more distinctly present to this visionary gaze than it is to the contemporaries who "keep step with it."[159] Paradoxically, the task of the critical historian is to maintain "a prophetic relation to the future" by turning to the past: "he perceives the contours of the future in the fading light of the past as it sinks before him into the night of times."[160] From this perspective Benjamin affirms Turgot's maxim that "politics is obliged to foresee the present."[161]

This recognition that the path to an open future is mediated by what has been is also at play in Bloch's conception of "nonsynchronous contradictions" whereby past forms of life persist in a disjunctive present.[162] Bloch developed a "concrete utopian" approach to politics founded on "the principle of hope" that was also oriented toward the latent power congealed in emancipatory projects that are either "not-yet conscious" or "not yet realized."[163] Adorno, Benjamin, and Bloch all believed, in different ways, that politics often entailed stolen glimpses across epochal divides. But whereas they concentrated on interruption, leaps, and breaks, with punctual moments of awakening, illumination, and recognition, Hannah Arendt, was concerned with worldly politics in the moment *after* the historical continuum has been interrupted.

Arendt's understanding of revolutionary possibility was also informed by a heterodox conception of historical temporality. Discussing Kafka's 1920 parable "He," she contends that "at each single moment" we are "inserted and caught in . . . an extended Now . . . and what [we call] the present is a life-long fight against the dead weight of the past, driving [us] forward with hope, and the fear of a future . . . driving [us] backward."[164] Humans do not merely float along on the surface of a flowing present nor stand still as time rushes past us. Rather we dwell in the charged gap between past and future at the dynamic meeting point of "a no-longer that pushes . . . forward and a not-yet that drives . . . back."[165] This "time construct," according to Arendt, "is totally different from the time sequence of ordinary life, where the three tenses smoothly follow each other and time itself can be understood in analogy to numerical sequences, fixed by the calendar, according to which the present is today, the past begins with yesterday, and the future begins tomorrow."[166]

Arendt explored the "political relevance" of this "extended now" within which a tense-blurring battle between past and future is perpetually staged.[167] Stating that the challenge for modern life was "how to move in this gap," she figured politics as undetermined action in an extended present that is buffeted by the persistent power of pasts present and the prescient power of futures present.[168] She relates, "I . . . believe with Faulkner, 'The past is never dead, it's not even past,' and this for the simple reason that the world we live in at any moment *is* the world of the past . . . it is quite true that the past *haunts* us."[169] But she also recognized that such vital pasts may serve as rich testaments or legacies that can nourish present politics. For her, like Césaire, the "chief aim" of "the critical interpretation of the past" is

> to discover the real origins of traditional concepts in order to distill from them anew their original spirit which has so sadly evaporated from the very key words of political language—such as freedom and justice, authority and reason, responsibility and virtue, power and glory—leaving behind empty shells with which to settle almost all accounts, regardless of their underlying phenomenal reality.[170]

In just this way, she attempted to recuperate the category "freedom," which she believed had been evacuated during the liberal nineteenth century.

Arendt contends that the "treasure" known to French revolutionaries as "public freedom" and to American revolutionaries as "public happiness" was repeatedly created, lost, and recovered in the modern period. She writes, "the history of revolutions . . . could be told in parable form as the tale of an age-old treasure which, under the most varied circumstances, appears abruptly, unexpectedly, and disappears again, under different mysterious conditions."[171] She surmises that "the treasure was lost because . . . no tradition had foreseen its appearance or its reality, because no testament had willed it for the future."[172] In her view, this failure of memory befell not only the heirs but . . . the actors and witnesses [themselves], who for a fleeting moment had held the treasure in the palms of their hands. . . . Thus the first who failed to remember what the treasure was like were precisely those who had possessed it and found it so strange that they did not even know how to name it.[173]

If humans are to be more than mere biological creatures inhabiting a "sempiternal" natural world and if *past* and *future* are to be meaningful terms, she insists, historical actors must create testaments that tell "the heir what will rightfully be his" and indicate "where the treasures are and what their worth is."[174]

Arendt supports her case by citing the French poet and Resistance fighter René Char, who recalled that that during the war "our inheritance was left to us by no testament."[175] She suggests that wartime intellectuals like Char who joined the Resistance had suddenly inherited a legacy that had not been willed to them. They "had been visited for the first time in their lives by an *apparition of freedom* . . . and therefore, without knowing or even noticing it, had begun to create the public space between themselves where freedom could appear."[176] This precious public realm was enabled by the Occupation and was then destroyed not by the Germans or Vichy collaborators, but by the Liberation: "It did not last long. After a few short years they were liberated from what they originally had thought to be a 'burden' and thrown back into what they now knew to be the weightless irrelevance of their personal affairs . . . a private life centered about nothing but itself."[177]

If Char received the untimely gift of an unwilled legacy that was lived and lost, his contemporary Marc Bloch deliberately willed a testament to a future that he feared may never come to exist, but which he nevertheless addressed directly.[178] Bloch, a French Jew who founded the Annales school of history, left his university position to fight with the Resistance. During the struggle, he wrote *Strange Defeat*, in which he attempted to explain the remarkable speed with which the German army occupied France. Bloch indicated the untimely character of this "strange defeat" when he suggested that Germany and France coexisted in the present yet, in some real sense, inhabited different historical epochs; they processed information and adapted to changing conditions at different velocities. Bloch thus projected himself forward to a future standpoint from which to write the structural history of a volatile present whose form had not yet crystallized.

Strange Defeat is an untimely artifact that confounds tenses and leaps across epochs, an attempt by to make historical sense of a story that was still unfolding as it destroyed him. Given the catastrophic threat posed by Nazism, the book was addressed to a possible world in which the French nation and people may have ceased to exist. He did not know if it would ever be discovered or read but, nonetheless, wrote it for his children, offering the text as a gift for and a dialogue with the next generation. In June 1944, shortly before the Liberation, Bloch was captured and killed by the Gestapo. The fact that Bloch's death was a function of the events that he describes combined with a direct address to future readers makes it feel as if the voice of a living ghost speaks to readers across generations. The conditions of the text's production, the perspicacity of its insights, and the untimely fate of its author endow it with a spectral aura of testimony, prophesy, and sacrifice.

Thinkers as different as Aimé and Suzanne Césaire, René Ménil, Ernst Bloch, Walter Benjamin, Theodor Adorno, Hannah Arendt, Marc Bloch, René Char and, as we shall see, Léopold Senghor, Jean-Paul Sartre, and Albert Camus did not only write from within and about the wartime rupture, postwar opening, and premature foreclosure. They also reflected on the deeper temporal implications they entailed. Despite their disparate ideological investments, theoretical orientations, and geographical locations, these figures may all be located in a broad constellation of thinkers concerned with untimeliness; the work of each of them may therefore illuminate the others in unexpected ways. And taken as a group, their writings reveal the dreamlike, poetic, and untimely aspects of the world-historical moment they inhabited. Among them, Césaire and Senghor were remarkably attentive to the triangular diagram that bound politics, poetics, and time together in relation to the problem of colonial emancipation, the promise of a genuinely new beginning, and the perils of historical foreclosure.

THREE Situating Senghor: *African Hospitality and Human Solidarity*

Live with your head in the lion's mouth. I want you to overcome 'em with yeses, undermine 'em with grins, agree 'em to death and destruction, let 'em swoller you till they vomit or bust wide open. —RALPH ELLISON

Être Noir: *From Black Being to Being Black*

In February 1976, President Léopold Sédar Senghor of Senegal became the first African head of state to visit Martinique. Aimé Césaire, then mayor of Fort-de-France, welcomed the "essential Senghor" as a "master of language" and self-proclaimed "diviner [*sourcier*] of the kingdom of childhood."[1] Césaire rejected criticism of Senghor's poetry as mere idyll or elegy and identified Senghor's commitment to "the marvelous dimension of life" as a political act comparable to that of "utopians . . . and maniacs of hope" who become "pioneers of . . . great upheavals and . . . movements to improve the world."[2] Césaire addressed his old friend as if revealing a secret that Senghor had kept not only from the public but perhaps himself as well:

> By creating a contradiction between the present, on the one hand, and the kingdom of childhood, on the other, you condemn yourself to seek a solution that can only be, despite your sense of moderation [*sens de la mesure*], revolutionary, for, there is no other way of transcending [*dépassement*] the contradiction that you feel between lived existence and the marvelous dimension of life, a glimpsed instant [*un instant entr'aperçu*].[3]

Césaire thus regarded Senghor as a retrospective seer whose poetry of the glimpsed instant constellated memory and vision in a revolutionary way. This, he observed, "is why yours is not, as many believed, a poetry of elegiac past-ism, but also of virility, a call to action and presentiment of the future."[4]

Then, in an exemplary poetic gesture, Césaire adds "I have always been struck to see that, for you, the hazel switch [*baton de coudrier*] that makes the waters of childhood well up is the same that makes the great waters of the future burst forth, for such is indeed, by definition, the mission of the poet."[5] The term *baton de coudrier* at once conjures a divining rod, magic wand, con-ductor's baton, royal scepter, and doctor's staff; it invokes the traditional Euro-pean association of the hazel tree with prophetic dreams, magical divination, and the healer's art. This image figures in Rimbaud's 1872 poem "Tear." When the poem's speaker slakes his existential thirst with magical golden liquor that flows beneath a stand of hazel trees, he is seized by a feverish hallucination of transcendent beauty and melancholy barrenness.[6] Césaire's single image, *baton de coudrier*, thus calls forth a flood of associations that relate African to Euro-pean traditions, remembered pasts to conjured futures, and poetic imagination to political possibilities.

Césaire closed by invoking his decades-long friendship with Senghor, dur-ing which they "lived . . . in parallel, parting often, thus is life, but without, for all that, ever separating. And how could we? Our adolescences were merged. We read the same books, and often the same copies; shared the same dreams; loved the same poets. We were seized by the same anxieties and grappled with the same problems."[7] Césaire likened their youthful attempts to revalorize black African traditions to making a "claim on an inheritance without desig-nated heirs."[8] Thus their concern with recuperating "lost kingdoms" and "cities . . . of memory . . . forgotten fraternities and the vast solidarity of those who were violated by history."[9] Césaire thereby welcomed his "very dear friend" to Fort-de-France "in the name of [their shared] past where there still burns the brand that we ignited forty years ago, in the name of the present in which we continue our quest through trial and error and sometimes despair-ingly, [and] in the name of the future of which it is the mission of the poet to have a presentiment, and which can only be the awakening of peoples."[10]

Césaire thus reminded the Antillean public that Senghor's seemingly ele-giac poetry about the marvelous in life indexed a profound political project. He also affirmed continuities between his and Senghor's respective aesthetic and political orientations and links between their interwar reflections and post-war interventions. The following day, President Senghor, responded with a public address titled "Negritude as the Culture of Black Peoples Cannot Be Surpassed." He began by rehearsing his long-standing understanding of negri-tude as referring not only to "the ensemble of values of the civilization of the black world" but, more concretely and above all, to "a black manner of living" or "a way of living as blacks" [la manière de vivre en nègre]. He emphasized the existential rather than merely ideological valence of the term "être Nègre"— not just a "black being" with a distinct way of thinking but a lived and embodied manner of "being black" and "living black." Conjuring Heidegger's sense of *being* as a verb rather than an entity, he explained that "black being [être Nègre] is not only a state [état], an ensemble of objective situations, but also a concrete action, of the black individual and the black collectivity: of black peoples. It is not a simple condition [état], a being-there, a *Da-Sein*, an acted-upon-being [être-agi]; it is above all an acting [agir]."[11]

Reiterating a formulation he had advocated since the 1930s, Senghor characterized this manner of "being black" as a mutual adjustment between a particular form of subjectivity and a specific milieu. Since the birth of Greek civilization, he explained, European "discursive reason" or "eye reason" had enabled human subjects to analyze passive natural objects, aiming to "master nature by making it an instrument of their will to power." In contrast, "Negro-African" civilizations "privileged intuitive reason" which "makes contact with the Universe through their senses [sens], through their *touch-reason*, not to oppose itself to nature, but, in a reciprocal embrace, to unite itself with it. It is the acuity of their touch-reason that explains, along with the taste for life, the . . . *communal* spirit, of Negro-Africans."[12] Senghor credited "this sense and this spirit" for the harmonious forms of political association and socio-economic cooperation he ascribed to precolonial Africa.

Senghor addressed the accusation that the Negritude movement had become outdated (dépassé) insofar as it privileged cultural celebration over political liberation. He asserted that the reflections he, Césaire, and Damas had initiated in the 1930s were motivated by the conviction that "politics must be in the service of culture and not culture in the service of politics."[13] He insisted that cultural creativity must never be subordinated to instrumental interests, explaining that according to Marx "the animal only produces under the constraint of immediate physical need whereas man produces even when he is liberated [libéré] from all physical need . . . man also knows how to work according to the laws of beauty."[14]

Senghor thus figured "being black" and "living black" as forms of being human that could transcend the conventional opposition between abstract universalism and concrete particularism.

I believe that in the Civilization of the Universal into which we entered in the last quarter of century, Negritude will constitute, or already constitutes ... an ensemble of essential contributions ... it will again play its essential role in the edification of a new humanism, more human because it will have reunited in their totality the contributions of all continents, of all races, of all nations.[15]

At once mosaic and mixture, this Civilization of the Universal was a "revolution" which is "nothing other than, on a planetary scale ... the most modern enterprise of civilization that reunites the most contrary and, consequently, the most fecund values: flesh and spirit, intuition and reason [*discursion*], emotion and idea, symbol and logic, discourse and rhythmic song."[16]

Senghor recounts that his experience during World War II propelled an important shift of emphasis in his thinking.

I acknowledge that in the first years of the movement, in the Latin Quarter, Negritude was voluntarily a type of moral ghetto ... tainted by racism ... in the enthusiasm of the return to [our] sources and the discovery of the black Grail ... we found White-European values to be insipid: discursive reason, with its rigid logic and its mathematical coldness ... its symmetrical and monotone parallelisms.[17]

Their confrontation with Nazism challenged this tendency. "Two years in a camp, as a prisoner of war, freed me from it: cured me. ... During two years, therefore, I had time [*le loisir*] to meditate on the 'Greek miracle' whose civilization was founded upon *métissage*."[18] After the war Senghor continued exploring the specificity of black forms of life but increasingly strove to imagine new frameworks for integrating African and European ways of being and knowing. Central was a capacity for memory without hatred and a commitment to African hospitality in service of human solidarity. "I don't have to teach you, Antilleans, about the long suffering of Nègres ... in spite of everything, we remained without hate ... we have transformed suffering into joy and the long lament [*plainte*] into song: into a work of beauty. That is *Négritude*."[19]

The Poetics of Captivity: Suffering and Solidarity

Senghor would identify the decade between 1935 and 1945 as "important because I moved from ghetto-negritude to open-negritude, and from the professoriat to politics, while remaining faithful to [*dans la fidélité*] to poetry: to art."[20] Senghor had arrived in Paris from Senegal in 1928 on a government scholarship to continue his postsecondary education. Despite his preparatory classes at Lycée Louis-le-Grand, he twice failed the entrance exam to the École Normale Supérieure. Instead he studied French, Latin, and Greek at the Sorbonne, obtaining a *license en lettres* in 1931. The following year, after writing a thesis titled "Exoticism in Baudelaire," he received a *diplôme d'études supérieures*. Senghor then devoted himself to preparing for the *agrégation* exam in grammar; though failing in 1933,[21] two years later he became the first student from sub-Saharan Africa to pass this test. He now reached a crossroads where he had to decide whether to return to Senegal as a secondary school teacher or remain in France to continue his studies.

Senghor's dream was to become a poet with a post at the Collège de France, where he had attended seminars on linguistics. He therefore accepted a position in 1935 as a professor of Latin and Greek at the Lycée Desartes in Tours. The proximity to Paris allowed him to pursue a course of studies at the Institut d'Ethnologie, where he took classes with Marcel Mauss, Paul Rivet, and Marcel Cohen. He also studied African linguistics with Lilian Homburger at the École Pratique des Hautes Études. During this time Senghor began his doctoral research on African languages and poetry, planning to write a principal *doctorat d'état* thesis with the title "Verbal Forms in the Senegalese-Guinean Group: Wolof, Sérère, Poular, et Diola." He also returned to his natal village of Joal to conduct research for a secondary thesis, "Sérère Oral Poetry." This immersion in African expressive forms eventually inspired him to burn all the poetry he had written before 1935, rejecting it for imitating European models.[22]

Senghor's decision to remain in metropolitan France obliged him to perform military service (1934/35); he served first in an infantry regiment in Verdun, the only black soldier in his company, then in a regiment in Paris where he was in charge of the officers' library.[23] This felicitous location allowed him to study for the *agrégation*. In September 1939, after he transferred to a new position at the Lycée Marcelin-Bertholot in a Paris *banlieue*, Senghor was again called up for military service and assigned this time to a regiment in Rochefort with other soldiers from overseas colonies. After the German invasion began in May, his company spent four days defending a bridge at La Charité-sur-Loire before surrendering on June 20, 1940. According to Senghor's story, their German captors immediately separated black soldiers from the rest of the prisoners and lined them up against a wall; the moment before they were to be shot, he and his fellow black soldiers cried out "Long live France! Long live Africa!" A French lieutenant was so impressed by this act of courage that he persuaded the Germans to spare their lives.[24]

Senghor created a rich mythology of his two years as a prisoner of war, when he was interned in seven different camps in France. He recalls that while "very difficult" the "experience of captivity was not un-useful for me."[25] Like many contemporaries (such as Jean-Paul Sartre and Emmanuel Levinas), Senghor treated internment as an opportunity for intensive study. He returned to the classics and reflected on the "miracle of Greek civilization," which he now attributed to the fruitful encounter between "Hellenic" and "pre-Hellenic" (including Egyptian and black or "Ethiopian") peoples. "This discovery, remade when confronted with Nazism, helped me to transform my life, to orient myself, little by little, towards the theory of cultural *métissage* as the ideal of civilization."[26] This reaffirmed the very lesson that he had learned from his professors at the Sorbonne and the Institut d'Ethnologie and the German anthropologist Leo Frobenius, whom he and Césaire read eagerly.

Captivity also enabled Senghor to teach himself German and to revisit the German literary and philosophical tradition he had been introduced to as a student. After a year of internment he was able to read the poetry of Goethe in the original, describing the encounter as "a revelation which led me to re-read, in a more attentive spirit, the great works of the master. In my minuscule library I now placed *Faust* and *Iphigenia* next to the *Aeneid*, Pascal's *Pensées*, and Plato's *Dialogues*, which had become my bedside books. It was a veritable conversion."[27] He explains how before the war his circle of black expatriate students was "plunged in the drunkenness of the Kingdom of Childhood, of re-discovered negritude."[28] They abandoned themselves to nostalgia, curious only about griots and sorcerers. Frobenius, teaching them to embrace "Ethiopian" emotion over Western rationalism, inspired them to read Goethe as an anti-imperial and anticapitalist rebel whose protagonists nourished their own desire to "demand, for black peoples, even more than political independence, the autonomy of negritude."[29]

But their tendency to reject Occidental rationalism in the racial language of "blood" immediately changed after "the defeat of France and the West, in 1940." Senghor relates that "stung by catastrophe, naked and sobered, we woke up. That therefore was where, in the odor of the gas chambers and the sound of firing squads, the hatred of reason and the cult of *Blood* had led us. . . . We undertook . . . to re-read our classics with the lucidity of an awakening."[30] In these changed circumstances Goethe became newly legible. He now "taught us about the dangers of cultural solitude, of retreat into the self, of the wish to only build on the foundation of one's own race, nation, and native virtues."[31] *This* Goethe was a cosmopolitan polyglot with an insatiable cultural appetite whose most important lesson was that "everyone must be Greek in his own fashion, but he must be Greek in some fashion."[32]

Such civilizational mixture, Senghor explained, would allow black peoples to *better* "express their negritude" by enabling a "perfect balance between two complementary values, the heart and the head, instinct and imagination, the real and the fact, the perfect balance of Zeus hurling his lightning."[33] In an epiphany beneath "the barbed wire of the camp," he recognized "that our most embodied voice, that our most black [nègre] work will, at the same time, be the most human."[34] Just as Goethe had traveled from the north "in search of the sun . . . we came from the south . . . and lo and behold we met on the shore of the middle sea, navel of the world. And we conversed fraternally in the balmy and luminous air. And we tasted the sweetness of the hybrid sea [mer métisse], of the Mediterranean."[35]

If captivity led Senghor to meditate on the miracle of civilizational métissage, it also connected him with African recruits from a variety of humble backgrounds and ethnic groups. He memorialized these compatriots in Hosties Noires (1948), a volume of poetry appearing three years after his groundbreaking collection Chants d'Ombre (1945).[36]

The volume's title "black hosts" likens France's overseas Africans who served during the war to sacrificial victims. It also signals the "host" of the Christian Eucharist, the wafer that is, through the miracle of transubstantiation, the body of Christ, the man-god who was sacrificed and sacrificed himself for humanity's redemption.[37] This image of a hostie thus joins the profane and divine, matter and spirit, essence and appearance, suffering and joy, abjection and transcendence, victim and benefactor. Through the drama of sacrifice and redemption, "host" conjures images of deliverance or emancipation, tracing a movement from servitude to freedom, sin to absolution, guilt to forgiveness, and division to reconciliation. The book's closing poem addresses Christ directly and refers to Hosties Noires as a "ciborium of suffering," reminding readers that each individual African victim, however humble and anonymous, is a Christlike body who may serve as a vehicle for future-saving redemption, just as each poem is like a wafer through which the miracle of transubstantiation may occur.

By adding the term black to "hosts," Senghor mobilizes a series of associations. Europe sacrifices African soldiers for its future while Africans sacrifice themselves for humanity's future. This new round of suffering and sacrifice will save France, now reduced to an occupied colony, its soldiers forced into camps and fearing for their lives, in payment for its colonial sins. France will seek redemption after the war by according freedom and equality to those Africans who have assumed the moral and human responsibility of standing by their metropolitan countrymen in a moment of mortal crisis.

The opening piece, "Liminary Poem," written in April 1940, before Senghor was imprisoned, sets the tone for the volume. With the famously ambiguous line "Ah! Don't say that I don't love France—I am not France, I know" the speaker identifies with the France that historically had "distributed not only a hunger for liberty but a hunger of the spirit / To all the peoples of the earth solemnly assembled at the catholic feast."[38] This image of a global assembly of peoples at a unified but diverse human banquet commits the speaker to a triple solidarity: with his fellow Africans, metropolitan France, and humanity. That this commitment is difficult—"Ah! Am I not divided enough?"—is expressed throughout the collection.[39]

Many of the poems in *Hosties Noires* meditate on France's exploitation of African soldiers, voice uncertainty about whether colonial Africa's relationship with France will change after the war, and stage the poet's attempt to overcome his own anger and hatred toward an imperial power that has caused centuries of suffering in Africa. "Prayer for the Senegalese Soldiers" laments the sacrifice—likely in vain—of the Africans "who offer their godly bodies, glory of stadiums, for the catholic honor of humanity."[40] It exhorts these soldiers to "savor the ephemeral sweetness of living" for "we do not know if we will breathe the harvest for which just cause we will have fought / If we were only going to be used by them!"[41]

Here Africans do not offer their lives merely to improve their own material position. France's soldiers, "so dissimilar yet so alike on this furthest outpost of peoples assembled for the same battle," fight for a fraternal vision of cross-racial and transcontinental solidarity.[42] "Let the white child and the black child . . . of Confederated France go hand in hand / Like the Poet foresees . . . / Let not the husk of hatred hinder their de-petrified steps."[43] This shift from Africans as sacrificial victims to self-sacrificing martyrs is evident in a poem celebrating Félix Éboué, the Guadeloupean governor of French Central Africa who rejected collaboration with the Vichy government. It concludes with a surging image: "A thousand peoples and a thousand languages have claimed their voices through your red faith / . . . / Look, Africa rises up . . . / Africa is made a *hostie noire*/ So that human hope can live."[44] Through Éboué, the hospitable Antillean intermediary, Africa redeems humanity through a solidarity beyond hatred and self-interest.

This figure of redemptive hospitality assumes a more concrete and intimate form in the poem "Camp," which Senghor wrote while a prisoner in Front-Stalag 230. It opens in "a vast village . . . crucified by two virulent ditches" where "hatred and hunger ferment in the torpor of a lethal summer . . . surrounded by the immobile spite of barbed wire . . . under the tyranny of four twitchy machine guns." Only the Africans "have kept the candor of their laughter, and . . . the freedom of their fiery soul." As "evening falls . . . They watch over the big pink children, their big blond children / Who toss and turn in their sleep, haunted by the fleas of worry and the lice of captivity." Africans' "evening stories cradle them, with deep voices that trace the pathways of silence."[45] Black soldiers willingly provide parental comfort to their white counterparts. "Dirt roads invite them to freedom. But they will not leave. They will desert neither their forced labor [corvées] nor their duty to be cheerful. For who will do the shameful work if not them?"[46] Although possessing every reason to allow these Europeans to slaughter each other, Senghor's soldiers cannot *not* behave like full humans, necessarily concerned with the suffering and fate of others. The speaker is inspired by these selfless African comrades to overcome his own hatred towards a metropolitan France that has so failed them. "No hatred in your soul without hatred, no cunning in your soul without cunning. / Oh black Martyrs of an immortal race, let me say the words that forgive."[47]

Wonder at Africans' willingness to sacrifice "the first fruits of its harvest . . . the most beautiful bodies" to the distant war and to forgive while resisting hatred permeates this collection.[48] Black American troops, messengers "of Peace and hope at the end of the wait," liberate "those who have forgotten how to laugh" (the French people).[49] But a question remains regarding what *kind* of liberation they might have enabled. If Africans and their American descendants gave France-Europe-humanity a second chance to make a different world, the outcome is far from certain. The final poems in *Hosties Noires*, written after Senghor's release from the camp in 1942, suggest melancholy, disillusionment, and bitterness about the possibility that Africans' sacrifices will have been meaningless.

In "Letter to a Prisoner" a freed soldier contrasts the solidarity he had experienced in the camp with his alienation upon returning to the white world of bourgeois Paris. Confined within "the solitude of the closely monitored and dear residence of my black skin," he finds civilian society privatized, class-divided, and racialized,[50] an insipid life filled with "too bright apartments that sterilize . . . even the memories of love" and "substantial dishes that do not nourish . . . sleepwalkers who have renounced their human identity."[51] Ironically, camp conditions had created the equality, fraternity, solidarity, mutuality, and sociability missing from ordinary "free" life in metropolitan Europe.

This frightening presentiment that liberation could institute new forms of oppression emerges in Senghor's protest poem over the demobilized Africans massacred at Camp Thiaroye for demanding the discharge benefits rightfully due them as French soldiers.[52] "Black prisoners, indeed French prisoners, is it true that France is no longer France? / Is it true that the enemy has stripped it of its face?" Addressing the dead, the speaker declares, "You are the witnesses of immortal Africa / You are the witnesses of the new world of tomorrow. / Sleep oh Dead! and let my voice cradle you, my voice of wrath that cradles hope."[53] Here is the tension structuring the asymmetry of African wartime solidarity. On one hand, suffering without recognition and sacrifice for a fore-closed future. On the other, witness to a coming world and the triumph of hope over rage. Note that Senghor wrote this foreboding poem *after* the August 1944 liberation of Paris.

This tension is again staged in the volume's final "Prayer for Peace":

> Lord Jesus, at the end of this book, which I offer you
> like a ciborium of sufferings
>
> . . .
>
> At the feet of my Africa crucified for four hundred years
> and still breathing
> Let me tell you Lord, her prayer of peace and pardon.
> Lord God, forgive white Europe!
>
> . . .
>
> And I want to pray especially for France.[54]

The poem offers an inventory of colonial crimes perpetrated against Africa under the signs of Enlightenment and Christianity.[55] It recognizes that France "too, has brought death and cannons into my blue villages."[56] It presents an image of France "who speaks of the right way and then follows a crooked path/ Who invites me to her table and tells me to bring my own bread . . . who hates the occupiers yet imposes such a severe occupation on me."[57] Moreover, the speaker laments that these African hosts, who have been treated like "merce-naries . . . black mastiffs of the Empire," will be used to recolonize Indochi-nese territories, which had effectively liberated themselves during the war, and then be forced to return to a condition of colonial subjection. But because "crucified Africa" has assumed this Christlike position of host and victim, it can pardon France-Europe.[58]

The speaker struggles to forgive these destroyers of African civilizations, confessing, "Lord . . . the serpent of hatred lifts its head in my heart, this ser-pent that I had believed was dead / Kill it Lord, because I must continue along my path."[59] Like the Senegalese soldiers, who could not refuse to stand in solidarity with their metropolitan counterparts, these overseas peoples must overcome resentment in order to build an alternative future that will require African and European cooperation. These African victims (hosts) sacrifice themselves (as hosts) in order to become hosts that lead and redeem France and Europe, partly through forgiveness and hospitality. Remembering that "there always must be traitors and imbeciles" and that French people too suffered during the war, the speaker pleads, "Oh, Lord, banish from my memory France that is not France, this mask of pettiness and hatred on the face of France."[60] Forcing himself to remember France's emancipatory legacy,[61] he prays, "Bless this bound people who freed its hands twice and dared to proclaim to royalty the advent of the poor / Who made the slaves of the day into free equal fraternal men / Bless this people who brought me Your Good News."[62] A peaceful human future requires that France be forgiven and that Africans, joining all the world's peoples, "encircle the earth with a ring of brotherly hands/ UNDER THE RAINBOW OF YOUR PEACE."[63] As a new world order dawned, Africans whose worlds were devastated in the name of civilizational improvement now volunteer as "hosts" to humanity, partly by taking a missionary responsibility for Europe's big pink children, benighted peoples who must be shown how to be human.

Critics might interpret Senghor's poetics of forgiveness as overidentification with French society by an assimilated comprador elite. But given that Senghor, like Césaire, treated language and objects poetically, as "*pregnant* images," it would be wrong to read his "France" as a self-evident reference.[64] Each poem attempts to look beyond immediate appearances to identify the immanent political potentiality possibly inhering within existing arrangements. Senghor's concern was always with what France might come to be. And Senghor's readiness to forgive historical crimes should recall his commitment to decolonization as a process of global restructuring wherein the fate humanity and the future of the world were at stake. His belief in forgiveness was entwined with his view that despite the boundaries created by sovereign states and recognized by international law, former imperial powers and former colonized peoples had no choice but to create a new set of arrangements *together* since they would remain entangled on this shared earth. Subtending this poetry and his subsequent politics was the conviction that Africans and Europeans were jointly responsible for the common future they were fated to share.[65]

The Coming Community

Through a French doctor's intervention, Senghor was released from his prison camp on medical grounds in February 1942, returning to his post at the Lycée Marcellin-Berthelot.[66] For the remainder of the war, he mentored younger black students in Paris (including Alioune Diop, Mark Sankalé, Guy Tirolien, A. F. Amorin, and Louis Behanzin), hosting gatherings and participating in African student association activities.[67] On May 8, 1943, Vichy officials inaugurated a colonial student center with a party where 200 "blacks of the world" heard performances by Antillean singers and African drummers.[68] In November of the previous year, colonial students led by Alioune Diop had created a study group that published a modest journal, *L'Étudiant de la France d'Outre Mer: Chronique des foyers*.[69] Senghor contributed reviews and poems that would later be included in *Chants d'Ombre*. In the inaugural issue (July 1, 1943), an editorial written by Diop under the psyeudonym Kothj Barma announced that the *Chronique* hoped to promote solidarity among colonial students, to educate metropolitans about overseas cultures, and "to make contact with real France outside of university and intellectual circles."[70]

This group organized a series of discussions about culture and empire, "Problems of Contact," and "Humanity for Us." Senghor attended several of these events and gave lectures titled "The Problem of Education in French West Africa" and "Black African Soul and Civilization," likely reprising two similarly titled public interventions of the thirties.[71]

In the first of these, "The Cultural Problem in French West Africa," delivered to the Dakar Chamber of Commerce in 1937, Senghor called for a reinvention of colonial education to better nourish African students as complex cultural beings. He criticized the government's tendency to offer colonial students practical educations that neglected the humanities. His demand that colonial schools teach African languages, geography, history, folklore, civilizations, and art as well as traditional European humanities was based on three premises. First, education must address the human spirit and not only technical training. Second, since civilizations must be thought of in the plural, courses for Africans should explore African conceptions of the human. Third, given that the colonial milieu compelled Africans to become "bicephalous" beings, education must be bilingual and multicultural. Underlying this educational orientation was Senghor's conviction that culture was a process of "creative dynamism" generated by a "perpetual effort towards a perfect balance" between "man and [a] milieu" that is "never unchanging."[72]

Characteristically, Senghor sought to strike a "bicephalous" balance between, on the one hand, teaching students a West African concept of the "ideal human" based on a "sense of honor, refined manners, and a mind that is more nimble than knowledgeable [*plus délié que savant*]" and, on the other hand, showing them that this African humanism must adapt to the evolving milieu young people actually inhabited.[73] Reminding his audience that Africans and metropolitans were "implicated in a common destiny [*destin*],"[74] he noted that "our milieu is no longer West African, it is also French, it is international; in sum, it is *afro-français*."[75] Rather than submitting to colonial assimilation or preserving a reified tradition, he hoped to explore African cultural singularity *and* rethink African culture in relation to contemporary imperial conditions.

Senghor continued this balancing act in his landmark essay "What the Black Man Contributes," published in a 1939 collection of writings, *L'homme de couleur*, on colonial subjects in the French Empire. Here he discussed the singularity of the "black soul . . . [and] its conception of the world . . . in a humanist spirit."[76] Proceeding from his infamous proposition that "emotion is *nègre* as reason is Hellenic," Senghor presented an idealized portrait of African forms of religion, society, economy, politics, and art in which the West's own humanist ideals were more fully realized than in the alienated societies of modern Europe,[77] characterized by oppositions between subject and object, spirit and matter, mind and body, knowledge and emotion, individual and community, labor and product, owner and worker, humanity and nature, living and dead. In contrast, his Africa resembled the harmoniously integrated ancient Greek societies idealized by European humanism.

Senghor concluded by invoking the myth of Antaeus, the Libyan giant whose formidable strength derived from his contact with the earth. Heracles defeated him in a wrestling match by lifting him off the ground—separating him from the source of his power—and strangling him.[78] Senghor wrote,

> It is not strange, this meeting of the Black and the Greek. I fear that many today who reclaim the Greeks in fact betray Greece. Treason of the modern world that has mutilated man by making him a "reasonable animal." . . . The black gift [*le service nègre*] will have been to contribute, along with other peoples, to remake the unity of man and the World: to link flesh to spirit, man to his fellow man, the pebble to God. In other words, the real to the spiritual surreal—through man, not as the center, but the hinge, the navel of the World.[79]

Senghor's postwar writing would continue to demonstrate how a lost humanism could be recovered through this gift of African civilization and how African forms of life could contribute to the unity of universal civilization, characterized variously as a network of interlinked singularities, a mosaic assembled from many distinct pieces, or a global mélange to which each civilization contributed its most distinctive and fully realized attributes.

After the war, Senghor began to envision new political forms to accommodate the cultural hybridity and social interdependence created by imperialism. He published "Views on Black Africa or Assimilate, Don't Be Assimilated" (1945) in a volume, *The French Imperial Community*, edited by Robert Delavignette, to whom Senghor dedicated his contribution.[80] It warned African elites against either passively acquiescing to assimilation into European civilization or creating a separate system of local institutions to protect their cultural particularity. In contrast, Senghor advocated a framework wherein metropolitan and overseas peoples could become equal "associates" within a common community with a shared future. Although his 1945 position inhabited an imperial paradigm, it anticipated the critical strategy that would inform his more transformative thinking about decolonization in the coming years; it foregrounded how colonial history had created conditions for new types of nonnational political association.

The essay's epigraph is from Maréchal Lyautey, an iconic architect of the French empire: "What I dream is that . . . [colonial] Morocco offers the spectacle of a human assemblage [*groupement d'humanité*] where men of such diverse origins, habits, professions, and races, pursuing, without abdicating any of their individual conceptions, the search for a shared ideal, a common *reason for living*."[81] We might wonder how Senghor can quote Lyautey's ideological rhetoric without qualification. But we also see here Senghor's radically literalist interest in taking Lyautey exactly at his word by envisioning a new form of plural community. Senghor's insight was that imperialism had both created and prohibited the possibility for such an assemblage.

Recognizing the opening created by the Liberation, Senghor presented these reflections in the future anterior tense. "Our reversals of 1940 will have had the result, fecund for us, that they will have led metropolitans and natives from the colonies, not to re-pose the problem of colonialism, but to rethink it. For everyone feels that its solution is the very basis of French *renaissance*."[82] He believed that all considerations of France's postwar form must begin by engaging "the colonial fact."[83] But rather than criticize the French state for past actions, Senghor challenged it to confront the colonial reality it had already created. For better or for worse, he was willing to bracket the question of the legitimacy of French imperialism. "France does not have to justify its colonial conquests any more than it does the annexation of Brittany or the Basque country. It must only reconcile its interests with those of its native inhabitants [*autochtones*]. At base, the colonial problem is nothing other than a provincial problem, a human problem."[84] For Senghor, the only question was whether France *now* will realize its own claims about overseas populations being integral parts of this transcontinental assemblage.

Figuring colonial history as the "contact of *two civilizations*," Senghor's goal became maintaining diversity within unity.[85] Challenging both a "false assimilation which is only identification" and a paternalist "antiassimilationism" designed to keep Africans separate and inferior, Senghor advocated a form of "association" founded on political equality *and* cultural diversity.[86] Each partner in this union would have to *"work in a community of views and interests, to reciprocally assimilate their ideas, each at the same time having to adapt itself to the nature and habits of its co-associate."*[87] Referring back to the Lyautey quote, he argued that only through mutual and reciprocal association could there develop "a shared ideal" and a "common reason to live."[88]

Senghor criticized as incoherent Henri Labouret's proposal, published in the *L'homme de couleur* volume, to create a distinct legal status of "imperial citizenship" that would grant educated and loyal colonial elites citizenship rights that would be valid only in their own countries. Senghor remarked, "I do not see why the rights of imperial citizens would cease to apply in other parts of the Empire. Do they not still remain *humans*?"[89] Outlining a plan for reforming France as a community of equally associated peoples, he proposed that African village chiefs would select regional representatives who would designate representatives for each colony. The latter would choose members to serve in a Federal Assembly composed of "colonial nations," including North Africa, French West Africa, French Central Africa, the Antilles, Indochina, and Madagascar. The metropole would house an Imperial Parliament "concerned with problems of general interest, imperial affairs, foreign affairs, etc."[90]

In a move resembling Césaire's non-self-evident call for a Fourth Republic, Senghor promoted far-reaching reform *and* assuaged metropolitan fears of imperial decline in the postwar period. He explained,

> far from weakening the authority of the Metropole, this system would only reinforce it since it would be founded on the consent and love of liberated men, free men; far from weakening the unity of the Empire, it would secure it since the conductor of the orchestra will have as a mission not to stifle the voices of the different instruments by covering them over by its voice, but to direct them in a unity that will allow the smallest African flute to play its role.[91]

In contrast to his bolder postwar proposals, this sought to improve relations *within* a refigured empire rather than abolish the empire altogether. Yet he was already attempting to identify institutional forms corresponding to the novel solidarities imperial conditions had enabled.

For Senghor, such reciprocal associations must hinge on the recognition that *"every civilization is the singularly marked expression of certain traits of Humanity."*[92] If colonialism created "intellectual ferment" and "spiritual grafts," he argued, this process must be bidirectional. After the war, "along with its factories, fleets, and ports, [the Metropole] will have to reconstruct its spiritual patrimony which has been undermined and bit by bit ruined by a current of materialism that has claimed the intellect."[93] To this end, he argued, "black Africa, can help it to discover . . . [a] sense of community, sense of hierarchy, sense of the divine—in any case of the spiritual—sense of an art that plunges its roots into life."[94] "It is not a question of placing France in the school of Africa" but of "helping [France] to rediscover its ancient and authentic face beneath the deformations to which its modern evolution has subjected it."[95]

In short, Senghor figured Africans as "hosts" whose civilization would redeem a degraded Europe dehumanized by instrumental reason, competitive materialism, and utilitarianism. Educated Africans would not only lead cultural renaissances at home but would revive genuine humanism as the vanguard of a new universal civilization. Senghor cared less about what France had been or done than about what it could become. And insofar as he tended to immanent institutional possibilities, his political thinking was deeply poetic.

Senghor viewed human self-realization through civilizational flourishing as the ultimate aim of sociopolitical arrangements. He regarded aesthetic creation as both means and end of a more fully human form of life. Politics served aesthetics, broadly construed as creative action through which humans could realize their humanity. Conversely, poetics could also infuse and inform politics understood as performative acts and a creative art of seeing realities beneath surface appearances, conjuring something out of nothing, recognizing or condensing myriad possibilities within a single word, concept, image, or object, and overcoming reified distinctions between past, present, and future.

Politics and Poetics

Given his criticism of materialism, instrumentalism, and utilitarianism, Senghor was reluctant to commit to a political career. Despite mentoring student groups, most of his time after the liberation was spent writing poetry and studying linguistics. He recalled, "at the beginning of 1945 I felt ready to accomplish my task: to be a professor and a poet."[96] "Horrified" by the idea of entering politics, he had avoided Senegal because he feared being drawn into local struggles and becoming a professional politician.[97] He eventually "fell into politics . . . by accident" when in 1944 he became professor at the École Nationale de la France d'Outre-Mer, teaching languages to aspiring colonial administrators.[98] This post led de Gaulle to appoint him to the Monnerville Commission, charged with studying how best to organize colonial representation in the Constituent Assembly for the new Fourth Republic.

In 1944, Senghor also received a CNRS grant to research Serer oral poetry in Senegal for his supplementary thesis. While there he was struck by how the war had devastated Senegalese living conditions.[99] That year, Lamine Guèye asked Senghor to join him on the Socialist Federation ticket to run for deputy representing Senegalese noncitizens in the November 1945 elections for the Constituent Assembly. Senghor recalls agonizing over the decision.

> I hesitated for a month. I felt, in effect, that that would be the end of my university career, and perhaps my poetic career. I went to consult with the members of my family who, naturally, pushed me to be a candidate insofar as victory in the election was assured: I was an academic. Finally, I accepted because the war years had been terrible for Senegal. On top of forced labor and requisitions were years of drought. The peasants were suffering from severe poverty.[100]

Despite his hesitations and misgivings he agreed to enter politics "without knowing where I was heading."[101]

Although he would neither complete his thesis nor be appointed to the Collège de France, his intellectual and artistic life continued. Senghor himself drew an epistemological distinction between his prose and poetry. He regarded prose as a rational means to an end inevitably inadequate to address the questions it posed and poetry as an imagistic end in itself whose very existence as creative expression testifies to its success: "the poem attains its objective by the very fact of being put on the page, there, unique, growing richer through the diverse participation [*adhesion*] of readers."[102] Senghor noted, "It is not an accident that the ancient Greeks reserved the word *poesis*, poetry, that is to say 'creation,' only for the production of poems among works of art in the general sense of the term."[103] Although Senghor emphasized this difference between instrumental prose and creative poetry, *poesis* informed his art *and* his politics. In both spheres he was concerned with human self-realization through creative acts.

After the war Senghor continued to refine an aesthetic theory he had begun to formulate in the 1930s. He maintained that in African civilizations the European dichotomy between knowing subject and passive object did not exist. Through intuitive and aesthetic forms of knowing, African subjects surrendered to animated objects that already pulsed to the rhythm of the world:

> For the European, *Homo faber*, it is a matter of knowing nature in order to make it an instrument of his will to power: to *utilize* it. He fixes it through analysis, making it a *dead* thing to dissect. But how can you make

Life from a dead thing? It is, on the contrary, in his subjectivity that the Nègre, "porous to the breath of the world," discovers the object in its reality: its *rhythm*. And it is he who abandons himself, obedient to this living movement, going from subject to object, "playing the game of the world." What does this mean if not that, for the Nègre, to know is to live—life and the Other—by identifying with the object? To know [*con-naître*] is to be born [*naître*] in the Other by dying oneself: it is to make love to the Other, it is to dance the Other. "I feel, therefore I am."[104]

For Senghor, this sympathetic relation of dialogue and merger between subject and object is echoed and preconditioned by the very structure and syntax of "Negro-African" languages, in which sign and meaning are indistinguishable and in which images supersede concepts. These imagistic languages are not neutral media. They are inherently poetic rather than referential. "The sensuous virtues of the word—timbre, tone, and rhythm—reinforce their meaning."[105] The word "is analogical image without even having the aid of a metaphor or comparison. It suffices to name the thing for the *meaning* to appear beneath the *sign* . . . for Black-Africans everything is sign and sense at the same time; every being, every thing, but also matter, form, color, odor, and gesture is rhythm, tone, and timbre."[106] According to Senghor, this essentially poetic system of signification enabled a more creative way of relating to the world and a more vital poetry.

In contrast European poetry collapsed as an embodied creative practice through "the disaggregation of the modern world." Poetry therefore "must be returned to its origins, to the time when it was sung—and danced. Like in Greece, in Israel, and above all in the Egypt of the Pharaohs. Like today in black Africa . . . Poetry must not perish. For if it does, where will be the hope of the World?"[107] Elsewhere, Senghor characterized his own poetry as a type of rhythmic incantation that allowed "access to the essential truth of things: the Strength (forces) of the Cosmos,"[108] explaining that "the power of the analogic image only liberates itself through the effect of rhythm. Only rhythm provokes the poetic short-circuit and transmutes copper into gold, the word into verb."[109] Poetry does not attempt to fix reality; it sets the world in motion or joins itself to the motion and multiplicity of the world. Senghor invoked the example of Césaire's poetry, in which "images are more than ambivalent, they are *multivalent* and doubly so. The same feeling-idea expresses itself through a whole series of images, and each image lives its own life, radiating from all of its facets of meaning like a diamond."[110] In this view, genuine poetry discovers *and* creates truths; it reveals the world as it truly is *and* posits the world as it should be.

Despite attending to the specificity of black African poetics, Senghor did not promote aesthetic nativism. Many of his explicit reflections on black art emerged in response to those who criticized his decision to express African ways of being, knowing, and creating in the French language. He acknowledged the challenges of this approach: "Paradox of Poetry, magic of Poetry. This negritude and its abyssal riches, this thing that is so particular, how to communicate it to others through [poetry]? And how to express it in the bland language of engineers and diplomats?"[111] Senghor thereby underscores not only that it is difficult to express in French the subjective experience of black being but also perhaps impossible for anyone to express one's deepest subjectivity in language. He thus indicates the problem as much deeper than the chosen language of expression; it strikes at the heart of linguistically mediated human creativity, of poetics itself.

Senghor provides several answers to the question of why African poets might choose to write in French. First, he recalls the resources within European aesthetic traditions that resonate directly with his understanding of African approaches to art and knowledge: "only the Surrealist revolution will have allowed our poets to express negritude in French."[112] Second, he notes that language choice is pragmatic and contextual: "We write first of all, but not only, for African French speakers, and, if the French of France find it picturesque, we will accept the consequences."[113] Senghor thereby uses French to decenter, rather than reaffirm, metropolitan culture and readers. He simultaneously acknowledges that "our message is *also* addressed to the French of France and to other men."[114]

French African poetry accords with Senghor's larger ambition to reconcile particular African forms of life with the cosmopolitan cultures created by imperialism: "[we write in French] because we are cultural hybrids [*métis*]."[115] And he suggests that specific qualities of French complement those of African poetry:

> Who said that it is a gray and atonal language of engineers and diplomats? Of course, I too once said this for the purposes of my thesis. Forgive me. Because I know its resources after having tasted, chewed, and taught it and it is the language of gods. Listen therefore to Corneille, Lautréamont, Rimbaud, Péguy, and Claudel. Listen to the great Hugo. . . . For us, words are naturally shrouded by a halo of sap and blood; French words radiate a thousand lights like diamonds. Rockets that illuminate our night.[116]

Senghor thus indicates that if French provides rich semantic resources to African poets, there is nothing essential about the kind of the subjectivity that it can or must express. Echoing Césaire, he recalls that French can be borrowed, bent, reoriented, and repurposed, productively aligned or mixed with other linguistic and aesthetic traditions to invent forms and content that might correspond to a multicultural imperial formation.

Senghor sums up this multiplex project of producing new forms of black French or French African poetry very simply: "Our ambition is modest: it is to be precursors, to open the way for an authentic black poetry that does not . . . renounce being French."[117] There is a deep resonance connecting his aesthetic project (expressing black African experience in French language to create new Afro-French poetics), his cultural commitments (reconciling cultural particularity with universal humanity; establishing relations of reciprocity between African and European civilizations; fashioning a Franco-African civilization), and his political hopes (reconciling French citizenship with African cultural autonomy; transforming the empire into a union of distinct but equal peoples; fashioning new political forms through which to pursue plural democracy, human freedom, and planetary reconciliation). But this simple statement also invites us to question what he means by "French."

Senghor's reflections on language and poetics suggest that he treated "French" and "France" as multivalent poetic images with facets pointing in different directions simultaneously. "France" should then be read as nonreferential, mobilizing many possible Frances, including those of past and future. Such an operation also recalls Senghor's seemingly self-evident prayers for forgiveness for "France" in *Hosties Noires*. What if every "France" in Senghor's postwar writings were substituted with "democratic union of peoples" or "multicultural community of associates" or "postcolonial democratic federation"? We should read Senghor's wartime poetry through the optic of his broader project to reconceptualize and reconstitute "France" and similarly engage his political interventions from the perspective of his poetry and aesthetic theory.

My interpretations of Senghor's postwar political projects are informed by his reflections on poetic language being a noninstrumental end in itself, on *poesis* as creation, language as composed of ramifying and reverberating images that contain multiple realities simultaneously, and poetry as the source of human hope. As we engage Senghor's untimely approach to decolonization as a poet-politician, it helps to recall Césaire's quotation of Senghor: "I therefore only had to name things, the elements of my childhood universe to prophesize the *Cité* of tomorrow, which will be born from the ashes of the old one, which is the mission of the Poet."[118]

Excursus: Forgiveness, Hospitality, Democracy

Rather than presumptively criticize Senghor's willingness to forgive imperial France as an (unforgivable) act of self-hatred or bad faith, we might recall Jacques Derrida's insight that "if one had to forgive only what is forgivable, even excusable . . . then one would not forgive. . . . In order to forgive, one must therefore forgive the unforgivable . . . the worst of the worst . . . forgiveness must therefore *do the impossible*."[119] For Derrida, forgiveness "remains heterogeneous to the order of politics or of the juridical as they are ordinarily understood" precisely because it contests the "*conditional* logic of the exchange" and challenges "calculated transactions" whereby "forgiveness is granted only after it is asked for."[120] He concludes that "sometimes forgiveness . . . must be a gracious gift, without exchange and without condition."[121] He also suggests that forgiving the unforgivable means recognizing the possibility that the roles of perpetrator and victim could be reversed under different circumstances.[122]

Treating the relation of forgiveness as a template for ethical behavior, Derrida follows Emmanuel Levinas, Senghor's contemporary, in arguing that all human subjects should act as if, by their very existence, they have committed an unforgivable wrong for which they are infinitely responsible and require another's forgiveness. Subjects are both constituted and bound by a "rapport of infinite and originary duty and indebtedness . . . incommensurable, irredeemable, and therefore delivered over to the 'asking of forgiveness.'" For Derrida and Levinas, this ethic of forgiveness derives from an even more fundamental relation of "absolute and unconditional" hospitality.[123] Derrida states, "hospitality is . . . not simply one ethic amongst others . . . *ethics is hospitality*."[124] In his view, any sort of norm, rule, expectation, prescription, or hope of reciprocity, even including an invitation, would transgress the ethos of hospitality. Like forgiveness, hospitality "gives without return or else is nothing." Through this welcome without conditions, "the guest [*hôte*] becomes the host [*hôte*] of the host [*hôte*]."[125] Derrida even suggests, following Levinas, that the host becomes a "hostage" of the guest-visitor-other.[126]

Because forgiveness and hospitality, like justice, are absolute and unconditional for Derrida, they cannot be transposed onto the domain of empirical politics founded on laws, prescriptions, or principles of equivalent exchange. Yet Derrida recognizes that "rights and duties . . . are the condition of hospitality" and observes therefore that unconditional hospitality is both heterogeneous to and indissociable from the "determined . . . delimitable . . . [and] calculable" domains of law and right.[127] Derrida wants, after all, to effect positive transformations in the world of conditional politics. For example, he suggests that the ethic of hospitality should serve as the basis for a new internationalism grounded in cosmopolitan law that would exceed the logic and scale of either national states or the existing system of international law based on the principle of state sovereignty.[128] But here too Derrida insists that cosmopolitanism must by definition be absolute and unconditional, based on a "universal hospitality without limit" that is "offered *a priori* to every other, to all newcomers, *whoever they may be*."[129]

Derrida faces a dilemma: he calls for a new politics (founded upon an unconditional ethics of cosmopolitan hospitality) that is supposedly irreconcilable with politics (figured as calculation, institutionalization, specification, rights, duties, reciprocity). One way he confronts this dilemma is through the provocative but allusive concept of "democracy to come."[130] Sometimes Derrida identifies this desirable democracy with the prospect of a novel internationalism or cosmopolitanism. But more often he employs this concept to signify the permanent gap between desirable forms of democracy and any actually existing democratic state. "Democracy to come" figures the series of untranscendable aporias that exist *within* democracy, such as conditional law versus unconditional justice or equality based on measurement versus diversity based on singularity. Democracy becomes an impossible object, a form of politics for which no actual institutional form could be adequate. And yet this impossibility generates a practice of perpetual critique, a refusal of institutional closure, and a permanent openness to uncertain outcomes—which are precisely what, for Derrida, make politics democratic. In his view, any state that claimed to realize democracy would negate the constitutive openness that makes democracy democratic. It is a form of politics that can exist only in the future conditional tense of something "to come."

Derrida seems to want to reintegrate Levinas's ethics into a democratic political project. But his persistent focus on aporias, undecidability, and impossibility leads him to treat politics in either/or terms. His constant warnings about law contaminating justice, politics contaminating ethics, equivalence contaminating incommensurability, and calculation contaminating the unconditional suggest that he privileges the first over the second term in each opposition. By positing a clear distinction, despite his disclaimers, between empirical acts and infinite demands, Derrida, like Levinas, ultimately retreats from the messy and ever-contaminated world of politics into the comforting refuge of an absolutist ethics.[131] He seems ever ready to reduce any political activity associated with empirical laws, existing states, or real places to vulgar calculation and instrumental action which follow the logic of legal contracts or market equivalence among self-interested actors. He implicitly offers us a choice between liberal capitalism or unconditional ethics. In his scheme, there is no middle ground for democracy between instrumental calculation and infinite justice.

This covert absolutism lends Derrida's "democracy to come" a troubling political valence. Of course democratic thinking should attend to his emphasis on the gap between justice and law or to political forms that accommodate rather than erase heterogeneity. A self-identical or monocultural social formation would indeed violate the openness, uncertainty, and dynamism that democracies require. In Rancière's terms, such a democracy would be a regime of police rather than politics.[132] But the Levinasian ethic of "infinite responsibility" for the other, upon which Derrida bases his politics, is fundamentally undemocratic and antipolitical.[133] For it posits an original and unsurpassable *inequality* between the subject and the other whose well-being becomes his inexhaustible concern. Ironically, this ethical relation privileges the responsible subject and reduces the suffering other to a passive object of concern and intervention. The structure of this relationship is hierarchical and paternalistic. The ethical actor assumes the role of a benevolent sovereign (father, king, Christ, God) who reduces "others" to the status of children or wards who have no voice about the care they will receive; they are not accorded a role as autonomous subjects in the ethical transaction. This framework is incompatible with the horizontal forms of equality, based on the dialogue and dissensus of equals inhabiting the same field of public action, upon which any form of real democracy must depend.[134]

By conflating calculation, conditionality, equivalence, reciprocity, equality, and solidarity, Derrida's formulations suggest that any attempt to organize self-determination around a relation of free and equal subjects would be contaminated by the unethical logic of commercial capitalism or parliamentary politics. Rather than use ethics to reclaim politics, as he appears to, he conjures democracy to denigrate politics (thereby disguising theology as democracy). Derrida's and Levinas's interest in infinite responsibility may point to a radical ethics but not to a radically democratic politics.[135]

Derrida's ethical turn offers many insights about justice, forgiveness, hospitality, and cosmopolitanism that may be read in relation to Senghor's thinking about similar issues.[136] His work should lead us to pause before dismissing as self-hating or reactionary Senghor's insistence that Africa forgive imperial France in order to build a common future, call forth a different kind of political association, and enact a form of reconciliation among peoples of the world. For Derrida reminds us that seemingly apolitical ethical acts often have radical political implications and that supposedly radical political acts may have dubious ethical implications. Conversely, Senghor's readiness to forgive the unforgivable reminds us how difficult, painful, and even repellent the kind of radical ethical practice that Derrida and Levinas advocate can actually be.

Like Levinas and Derrida, Senghor rejected the dehumanizing character of calculation as a principle of social organization. He too criticized both traditional liberalism and orthodox Marxism for reducing questions of human well-being to material welfare. And he hoped to reconcile cultural singularity with political equality through alternative forms of plural democracy that would exceed the limits of territorial national states. Yet Senghor's thinking contrasts strongly with the opposition that emerges in their work between unconditional ethics and instrumental politics. He, like Césaire, always sought both to make ethics worldly and to introduce a utopian, anticipatory, and performative dimension to concrete politics. Whereas Derrida identified aporias and impossibilities, Senghor attempted to transcend false antinomies by exploring potentialities immanent within existing conditions. Thus his concern with developing forms of aesthetic and intuitive reason beyond instrumental rationality, forms of mutuality and solidarity beyond parliamentary democracy, and forms of cosmopolitan sociality beyond colonial imperialism.

Like Derrida, Senghor was concerned with the nonreciprocal politics of forgiveness, the ethics of hospitality, and the prospect of cosmopolitan democracy. But he did not relegate these to the regulative or futural space of the "to come." He risked contaminating ethics with politics, politics with calculation, and equality with reciprocity by seeking to create a concrete political form in which such ethical principles and political aims could be legally instituted here and now. Rather than reduce reciprocity to market equivalence, as Derrida does, Senghor revisited European traditions of democracy and socialism, as well as African traditions of corporatism and collectivism, to found a new politics of plural association that would accommodate multiple singularities and universal equality. Similarly, Senghor did not reduce gifting to the statist logic of legal contracts or the market logic of commercial exchange. Rather, in the spirit of his teacher Marcel Mauss, he treated gifts as forms of mutuality. For Mauss the gift was a modality of exchange through which humans created concrete, embodied, and qualitatively meaningful bonds of social solidarity.[137]

For Senghor, reciprocity was less an effect of atomized individuals pursuing interests, as Derrida implies, than it was a matter of interdependent actors creating vital communities. For conceptual resources and historical precedents, Senghor turned to the European mutualist traditions in which labor cooperatives, collective property, social production, and direct democracy related more to federated associations of neighbors or coworkers than to elected representatives. He also identified precisely these values and practices in "African" ways of being, knowing, and making. In his postwar writing, Senghor regularly referred to cultural *métissage*, the politics of federation, and the civilization of the universal through the metaphors of a global human banquet, a festive rendezvous, an intellectual symposium, a public colloquium, or a symphony orchestra.

FOUR   Freedom, Time, Territory

The worldwide paradoxically appears on the horizon as possibilities already
partially (sketchily) realized ... but also resisted ... planetary space gives itself to
the human species as theater and scenario, field of the possible, and sudden
appearance of the unforeseen. —HENRI LEFEBVRE

Spectacular Liberation

The liberation of Paris from German occupation in August 1944 was a spectacular performance through which the problem of freedom intersected with
the politics of time. The Forces Françaises de l'Intérieur (FFI) opened the
spectacle, rising up against the army of occupation. The danger and the deaths
were real enough (Germany had destroyed Warsaw in crushing *its* revolt). But
these were also performances in which French actors sought to make real the
political fiction that the French people, embodied by the Resistance, liberated themselves from German occupation. Although the Americans allowed
a French armored division to lead the final assault into Paris, this was understood as political theater directed at national and international publics.[1] In his
August 25 1944, speech at the Hôtel de Ville, de Gaulle consecrated the event
in a national benediction. "Paris! Outraged Paris! Broken Paris! Martyred
Paris! But liberated Paris! Liberated by itself, liberated by its people with the
assistance of the French army and the support and assistance of the whole of
France, of the France that fights, of the only France, of eternal France."[2]

   In an article published the day before the speech, Jean-Paul Sartre deemed
the uprising "a pompous and bloody ceremony whose ordering was carefully
controlled and which ended fatally in deaths, something like human sacrifice."[3]
Absurdly, Resistance forces struggled to *prevent* German soldiers who were flee-

ing the Allies' advance from evacuating Paris too soon, so that French fighters could symbolically defeat the occupation. He noted sardonically, "these days, if a man isn't willing to say that Paris liberated itself, he is taken for an enemy of the people."[4] Through this act, Resistance fighters "wanted to affirm the sovereignty of the French people; and they understood that the only means they had . . . was to shed their own blood."[5] Although Paris would have been liberated without the uprising, these fighters, by risking and losing lives, enacted an experience of freedom with universal implications. Thus their "sense of fighting not only for France against the Germans but also for man against the blind powers of the machine . . . it makes little difference that the FFI did not, strictly speaking, liberate Paris from the Germans: at each instant, behind each barricade and on each street, they exercised freedom for themselves and for each Frenchman."[6] Moreover, Sartre recognized the untimeliness of this event. "All of them were remembering Paris' great days of wrath . . . The whole history of Paris was there, in that sun, on those naked streets."[7] Mobilizing that legacy of insurrection, these actors "decided that the event would be 'historic'" and were deliberately "writing history" by creating a future memory of self-liberation.[8]

Sartre's account of the Liberation, simultaneously wry and solemn, captures the risks and effects of political performance. It suggests freedom is as much a set of improvisational and self-constituting practices as a legal status or political condition and reminds us that through such popular eruptions, particular battles may articulate with universal struggles, and present acts may awaken past legacies or conjure possible futures.[9] Sartre's dramatic Resistance fighters enjoyed an evanescent moment of what Hannah Arendt called "public happiness" and "public freedom."[10] Referring to the shock many French intellectuals experienced during the Occupation, Arendt described how "they who as a matter of course had never participated in the official business of the Third Republic were sucked into politics as though with the force of a vacuum. Thus without premonition and probably against conscious inclinations, they had come to constitute willy-nilly a public realm," enabling them to experience the "public happiness" that is simultaneously the condition and consequence of political action.[11]

To Arendt, "the Greek *polis* once was precisely that 'form of government' which provided men with a space of appearances where they could act, with a kind of theater where freedom could appear."[12] There freedom was "a worldly tangible reality" that existed only in practice, "through intercourse with others."[13] But this understanding was forgotten both by philosophical idealism, which had banished freedom to a private inner mental state concerned with feeling, willing, and reflection, and by political liberalism, which had conflated freedom with liberation from insecurity and external compulsions. Tracing the Greek and Latin meanings of the verb *to act*, Arendt semantically links action, spontaneity, freedom, and "a beginning by which something new comes into the world."[14] In this sense, public freedom enables and is enabled by political *miracles*: "not supernatural events but only what all *miracles* . . . always must be, namely, *interruptions* of some natural series of events, of some automatic process, in whose context they constitute the wholly unexpected."[15]

Arendt equates the "faculty of freedom" with "the sheer capacity to begin."[16] Political acts are "miracles" that "[break] into the world as an 'infinite improbability,' and yet it is precisely this infinitely improbable which actually constitutes the very texture of everything we call real."[17] Because humanity has received "the twofold gift of freedom and action," because it "can establish a reality of its own," Arendt argues, "it is not the least superstitious, it is even a counsel of realism, to look for the unforeseeable and unpredictable, to be prepared for and to expect "miracles" in the political realm."[18] Politics were creative acts of miraculous interruption performed in service of the infinitely improbable. She describes eighteenth-century revolutionaries confronting the "abyss of freedom," a "nothingness that opens up before any deed that cannot be accounted for by a reliable chain of cause and effect."[19] This "absolute beginning," she explains, "abolishes the sequence of temporality no less than does the thought of an absolute end, rightly referred to as 'thinking the unthinkable.'"[20] Arendt thus refigures the politically improbable and unthinkable as truly real.

Despite her attention to revolutionary interruption, Arendt was especially concerned with the moment *after* a rupture, the "*hiatus* . . . between liberation from the old order and the new freedom . . . between a no-more and a not-yet." She argues that there exists "a decisive distinction between mere liberation and actual freedom,"[21] between "the liberation from oppression" (i.e., external coercion or material constraint) and "the constitution of freedom" as a "political way of life" defined by public speech and action.[22] It was from within this very gap between liberation and freedom, between the no longer and the not yet, that metropolitan and colonial actors sought to fashion a new postwar polity. This historical hiatus allowed and compelled these figures to confront the problem of freedom in relation to actual, possible, and desirable conditions. Arendt, as we saw, also recognized that the historical opportunities presented by such politico-temporal gaps often flash by in an instant. The liberation of Paris in

1944 marked just such an evanescent opening: a new beginning appeared possible, yet the opening's political potentiality could be easily foreclosed.

Henri Lefebvre later recalled, "In the enthusiasm of the Liberation, it was hoped that soon life would be changed and the world transformed. More than that: life had already been changed; peoples were on the move, the masses were in ferment. Their movement was causing new values to 'rise to the surface.'"[23] Many contemporary observers believed that the end of the Occupation provided a historic opportunity and responsibility to radically reconstitute France. Albert Camus wrote in the Resistance journal *Combat*, "It won't be enough to regain the outward appearance of freedom . . . we will have accomplished only an infinitesimal part of our task if the French Republic of tomorrow were to find itself, like the Third Republic, under the strict control of Money."[24] His fellow freedom fighters, "having begun with resistance, [want] to end with Revolution." For Camus this meant instituting "a true people's and workers' democracy."[25]

On March 15, 1944, the alliance of associations known as the Conseil National de la Résistance (CNR) convened a "plenary assembly," elaborating a plan for "installing, after the Liberation on the territory, a more just social order." It pledged to create a "true social and economic democracy" based on the "rational organization of the economy assuring the subordination of particular interests to the general interest" and "the participation of workers in the administration of the economy." Workers would be offered "the possibility of a fully human life." The CNR also called for "an extension of political, social, and economic rights of native and colonial populations."[26]

Echoing Arendt's observation that many French intellectuals were politicized by the Occupation, Simone de Beauvoir wrote, "Through the CNR charter, France was taking the path of socialism. We believed that the country had been shaken deeply enough to permit a radical remodeling of its structure without new convulsions. *Combat* expressed our hopes."[27] She recalled that "the war had effected a decisive conversion" upon Sartre who developed from an anarchistic anticapitalist into a committed socialist. But foreboding tempered Sartre's hopes. He wrote, "it is to be feared that the festival," this "explosion of freedom" and "disruption of the established and effective order . . . will quickly lose its meaning."[28] In similar apprehension, his intellectual comrade, Maurice Merleau-Ponty, warned, "we do not want this year of 1945 to become just another year among many."[29]

To Merleau-Ponty, "unity had been easy during the Resistance" because conditions "offered the rare phenomenon of historical action which remained personal."[30] He argued that this intimate solidarity, a "source of . . . happiness through danger,"[31] transcended divisions between private and public life, social and political spheres, and being and doing. But because "this balance . . . was intimately bound up with the conditions of clandestine actions and could not survive it,"[32] the Resistance "fostered . . . illusions . . . and masked the truth of the incredible power of history which the Occupation taught us in another connection." The truth was that "we have returned to the time of institutions."[33] Public happiness and direct democracy devolved back into the attenuated parliamentary representation of the failed Third Republic. Merleau-Ponty's response was internationalist, beseeching fellow Marxists to make "patriots see . . . that in a weakened country like France which the movement of history has reduced to a second-rate power, a certain political and economic independence is possible only . . . within the framework of a Socialist Confederation of States which has no chance of becoming a reality except through revolution."[34]

Raymond Aron, the center-right anticommunist editor of *La France Libre* and later an editor of *Combat*, did not agree. But even this member of the Gaullist Rassemblement du Peuple Français (RPF), supported worker participation in management and profit sharing ("association") as an alternative to both liberal capitalism and state socialism.[35] Yet Aron also shared Merleau-Ponty's presentiment about institutions, predicting that French politics would quickly return to a parliamentary system defined by the partisan interests of competing parties.[36]

An anguished sense of fragile historic opportunity was expressed with special intensity by Albert Camus, whose movement from hope to despair after the war can be followed clearly in his pieces for *Combat* between 1944 and 1947. Anticipating Arendt's understanding of the gap between no-longer and not-yet, Camus warned that whereas "resistance" had allowed for liberation, only "revolution" could create the conditions for freedom.[37] Several days later, on the eve of victory, Camus remarked that "Paris . . . is aglow with . . . all the splendor not just of liberation but of the liberty to come."[38] Rejecting the reinstatement of any of the failed Third Republic leaders who had betrayed France, he declared that "real democracy—remains to be constructed."[39] He also insisted that *Combat's* conception of revolution was nondogmatic: "We do not believe in ready-made principles or theoretical plans."[40]

Camus viewed the challenge as creating a political system that respected the principles of justice (in contrast to American capitalism) and freedom (in contrast to Soviet communism).[41] Like many contemporaries, he regarded 1945 as an opening for a different kind of world system; his "true people's and worker's democracy" would be integrated into a more ambitious international program.[42] Camus immediately identified the limitations of the proposed United Nations organization, arguing that if the United States, the USSR, Great Britain, China, and France were granted veto power over attempts to regulate or counteract their violations of international justice, the world would "in effect be ruled by a directorate of five powers."[43] He warned that, "either the future League of Nations will be a federal instrument that will strictly enforce the rules of an international democracy, or it will be an organization that will . . . demonstrate the supreme virtue of sanctioning themselves for their own imperialist aims."[44] He lamented,

> millions of people . . . expected that with victory . . . some kind of international law would protect small nations . . . and punish imperial projects . . . They expected the victorious countries to give up a portion of their sovereignty to an international organization. Instead they are confronted with a reinforcement of great-power sovereignty at the expense of the sovereignty of smaller nations.[45]

Camus therefore exhorted France to "say to the world that the only realistic course leads to economic federalism, to the sharing of wealth, and to the submission of all nations to the rule of international democracy."[46]

In a series of articles titled "Neither Victims nor Executioners," Camus attempted to reconcile a revolutionary desire for social justice with a refusal of violence. His radical pledge to reject any program or idea that justified taking a life, directly or indirectly,[47] led him to demand a French constitution transcending national autarchy. He explained,

> today we know that there are no more islands and that borders are meaningless . . . There is no longer any such thing as isolated suffering . . . no economic problem, no matter how minor . . . can be resolved today without international cooperation. Hence we know, beyond a shadow of a doubt that the new order we are seeking cannot be merely national or even continental, much less Western or Eastern. It has to be universal.[48]

This "world unity" and "international revolution" could be achieved in one of two ways.[49] A powerful state like the USA or USSR could unify the world coercively through international dictatorship.[50] Or an "international democracy" could achieve "universal order . . . by mutual agreement of all parties."[51] He warned that despite its claims to the contrary, the UN was in fact establishing an international dictatorship because its actions were dictated by powerful states rather than "being the expression of the will of all."[52] In his view, "the only way out is to place international law above governments, which means that law must be made, that there must be a parliament for making it, and that parliament must be constituted by means of worldwide elections in which all nations will take part."[53] Camus added a crucial caveat; this "World Parliament" must include the "colonized civilizations from the four corners of the earth" who "are making their voices heard."[54]

Camus blamed "anachronistic thinking" for the general reluctance to embrace this plan as a real possibility. "Today's political systems seek to settle the world's future by employing principles shaped in the eighteenth century in the case of capitalist liberalism and in the nineteenth century in the case of so-called scientific socialism." Noting that the "disastrous gap that exists between political thought and historical reality . . . is widening today as the pace of history accelerates," Camus insisted that the future international order will require an entirely new form of political thought.[55] "The choice today is between anachronistic political thinking and utopian thinking. Anachronistic thinking is killing us . . . realism . . . forces us to embrace the *relative utopia* I am proposing. When this utopia has been absorbed into history like so many others before it, people will no longer be able to imagine any other reality."[56] In slightly different terms, he observed that "the battle that will be waged in years to come will not pit the forces of utopia against the forces of reality. Rather it will pit different utopias against each other as they try to gain a purchase on the real, and the only choice remaining will be to decide which form of utopia is least costly."[57]

Camus's attempt to reclaim utopianism as authentic realism addressed traditional revolutionaries who claimed to be more concerned with immediate socioeconomic problems than with "utopian" abstractions such as global peace and international democracy. Camus reminded these provincial leftists that it would not be possible "to revolutionize the mode of property ownership" or to resolve even "the simplest problems" on a national scale. "The fate of people of all nations will not be settled until the problems of peace and world organization have been settled."[58] Camus therefore suggested that traditional revolutionaries themselves had lost touch with reality; their "romantic" conceptions of violently seizing power and changing property relations in particular nations were inherited from 1789 and 1917. "This set of ideas," he argued "makes no sense in the current historical situation."[59] The "repressive apparatus" of states had become too powerful to be toppled and given the world economy, socialist revolution and industrial nationalizations in a single society would be economic suicide.[60]

For Camus, new global interdependencies required that traditional political thinking, focused on territorial national states, be revised. He called on the world peace movement to ally with national labor movements to create "international study groups" and "working communities, organized in a cooperative way" that would "define the values on which the new international order should be based." Their first priority would be to establish "an international code of justice."[61] He explained, "the point" would "not be to elaborate a new ideology" but "to search for a new way of life."[62]

Whether we accept Camus's specific proposals for a social republic and international democracy, we can appreciate the crucial problem that he identified for mid-twentieth-century politics: Given the emerging realities of global economic interdependence and the powerful superstates, what political framework would best allow small or weak peoples to enjoy substantive human freedom and social justice? What political language could be employed to do so? These problems resonated across the colonial periphery. If Europeans could no longer afford the luxury of thinking nationally, how could these new postcolonial societies? Wouldn't they too need to revisit fundamental categories—revolution, independence, liberty, freedom, self-determination, sovereignty, socialism, solidarity, internationalism, humanity—in relation to emerging conditions and constraints? If they were not to seek nineteenth-century solutions to mid-twentieth-century problems, what political traditions, idioms, and frameworks would they invoke or invent?

Equally significant was Camus's refiguring of the relationship between realism and utopia. In his view, international democracy appeared unrealistic only from the anachronistic perspective of a world that ("realists" failed to recognize) no longer existed. In fact, because international democracy corresponded more adequately to new historical conditions, *it* was the more "realistic" option for the postwar world, even if the language for conceiving it did not yet exist. As Camus wrote, "if realism is the art of taking both the present and the future into account at the same time, of obtaining the most while sacrificing the least, then who can fail to see that the most unmistakable reality belongs to" the proponents of international democracy.[63] Camus's "relative utopia," which resonated with Arendt's "political miracle," was a realist utopianism and utopian realism. It attempted to rework the present from the standpoint of an unimaginable future *and* to build that future from the standpoint of an already changed present.

Not Quite Sovereign

De Gaulle, of course, was a traditional realist who intended to renovate French politics through a strong state with an independent executive whose power did not derive from a popularly elected legislature. He instrumentalized the Resistance to domesticate its transformative potential, converting the (image of a) festive uprising and the dream of a people's democracy into a mandate to discipline and unify the nation under a strong central government. In his June 16, 1946, speech at Bayeux de Gaulle offered a narrative of the Resistance as a fight not for popular freedom but for "the future of the *patrie*" on the "soil of the ancestors" in order to protect "the legitimate state" so that it would be "capable of reestablishing national and imperial unity around itself" and "act as an equal among the other great nations of the world"[64]

The overseas empire was integral to his vision. The loyalty of France's colonial populations to the republic during the war was figured in popular discourse by two iconic images. First, the so-called tirailleurs Sénégalais: French troops recruited from African colonies. Second, the dramatic gesture by Félix Éboué, the Guadeloupe-born governor general of French Central Africa, to align with de Gaulle's Resistance and refuse to recognize the Vichy state.[65] In January 1944 de Gaulle convened the landmark Brazzaville Conference, calling on colonial officials to outline a plan of structural reforms to reorganize the relationship between metropolitan France and its colonies. The putative aim was to improve the moral and material condition of colonized peoples. According to de Gaulle France had a "duty" to "elevate them little by little to the level where they will be capable of participating, in their own country, in the management of their own affairs." But despite this allusion to autonomy, he had no intention of allowing them to create sovereign states. On the contrary, he would help them "integrate themselves into the French community with their [own] personality, interests, aspirations, and future." His commitment to restructuring the empire was based on his belief that "concerning the life of the world of tomorrow, autarchy would neither be possible nor desirable for anyone." He thus envisioned "110 million men and women who [would] live under our flag . . . in a federated form."[66] The precise form of such a federation would be the source of chronic struggle in the following years.

In a 1943 article entitled "The Colonial Question and the Destiny of the French People," Simone Weil contended that the challenge of "future reconstruction, cannot be separated from the colonial problem," which must be "rethought."[67] Observing that "Hitlerism consists in the application by Germany to the European continent . . . [of] colonial methods of conquest and domination," Weil argued that France could not claim to deserve liberation from Nazism without recognizing that its subject populations deserved liberation from colonialism. But rather than support political independence for colonized peoples, she hoped to supersede an outmoded system of sovereign states. She predicted that after the war "the nation will be only one possible context for collective life."[68] And if "so-called colored populations . . . must no longer be subject populations . . . to make of them nations on the European model, . . . would be no better."[69] She asserted that "the only hope for Europe, for colonized peoples, and for humanity" would be a "new renaissance" based on postimperial *and* nonnational forms whereby emancipated peoples would remain aligned with larger states. She advocated the same solution for "the weaker populations of Europe."[70]

Weil's paternalist vision may have been as imperial as de Gaulle's "federative form." But it signified a public interest in political alternatives to both colonialism *and* nationalism through new forms of transcontinental partnership. Whereas Weil made an ethical argument, others made a realist case that French reconstruction would require imperial transformation. Aron, for example, argued that France no longer had the financial resources to fund its overseas activities and that imperialism in the new world order would lose its economic and geopolitical utility.[71] He also argued that France's only hope of maintaining its international stature was by joining a new European federal state.[72]

French dependence for its postwar reconstruction on US aid, advisors, and planning experts has been well documented.[73] France's global standing after the war was also largely determined by the United States and Britain. No French representatives were included in the wartime deliberations by the United States, Britain, and the Soviet Union about the shape of the postwar order. France was neither invited to participate in the August 1944 Dumbarton Oaks conference, where the plan for the UN was outlined, nor in the follow-up Yalta Conference (February 1945). It was only through the insistence of Britain, against the wishes of Roosevelt and Stalin, that France was awarded a permanent seat on the UN Security Council in order to counterbalance American power.[74]

When France was invited to the April 1945 San Francisco Conference, the shape of the new system had already been defined. At this conference the signatories of the UN Declaration elaborated the specific rules and structure of the new organization and drafted its charter.[75] The charter established a Trusteeship Council through which responsibility for the old League of Nations mandates would be transferred to metropolitan powers. The council would require regular reports from them, could accept petitions from overseas inhabitants, and conduct local investigations. Signatories also agreed to abide by a declaration on non-self-governing territories. Imperial powers committed themselves to respecting local cultures, promoting economic, social, and political advancement, and developing self-governing political institutions according to a territory's particular circumstances. They also agreed "to transmit regularly to the Secretary-General for information purposes . . . statistical and other information of a technical nature relating to economic, social, and educational conditions in the territories for which they are respectively responsible."[76] These provisions, which were supported especially by the United States, the Soviet Union, and China, challenged the absolute sovereignty of Britain and France over their colonial and mandate territories.

The UN requirement that member states submit regular reports on non-self-governing territories and the ability, generally, of the United Nations to take up colonial questions became a source of contention among imperial powers. During the Mau-Mau rebellion in Kenya and during the war of national liberation in Algeria, Britain and France sought to prevent the UN from discussing colonial disputes by insisting that their overseas territories and populations were internal to their national states, invoking Article 2: "Nothing contained in the present Charter shall authorize the United Nations to intervene in matters which are essentially within the domestic jurisdiction of any state or shall require the Members to submit such matters to settlement."[77]

When France signed the charter in 1945, its sovereignty, authority, and legitimacy as an imperial state were tenuous. By then, its position in Southeast Asia was largely dependent on American support. During the war, the colonies that composed the Federation of French Indochina were formally ruled by a French administration loyal to the Vichy regime. But beginning in August 1940, they were effectively controlled by a Japanese army of occupation, which in March 1945 overthrew the French administration and installed Bo Dai as emperor of a nominally independent state. During the war, Ho Chi Minh, the founder of the Indochinese Communist Party, had been patiently organizing the Vietminh into a national popular revolutionary movement. When Japan surrendered to the Allies in August 1945, the Vietminh seized power through a nationalist uprising and declared independence for the Democratic Republic of Vietnam.[78]

At the conclusion of the war, de Gaulle's provisional government was in a precarious position. France still regarded Indochina as part of its empire, but to exercise colonial authority it would need to reconquer the country. Given the relative poverty and weakness of the French state, an invasion would have to be authorized and financed by the US government. Roosevelt, however, opposed France's plan to recolonize Vietnam. During the war, when the French administration had cooperated with the Japanese army, the US president had already made plans to transform Indochina from a French colony into an international trustee territory under the supervision of China, which he envisioned as one of the "four policemen" of the postwar order.[79] But Roosevelt died before the San Francisco Conference, and Truman's advisors persuaded the new president to recognize French sovereignty over Indochina.[80]

De Gaulle pursued American support for his Indochina policy, insisted that this territory could not be subject to UN jurisdiction, and assured international public opinion that France intended to introduce a form of self-government to the people of Vietnam.[81] But because France's imperial authority depended on American funding and approval, its intervention in Indochina, just like the Paris uprising and liberation, was ultimately a *performance* of state sovereignty.[82] In March 1946 Ho Chi Minh, after concluding an agreement with France whereby Vietnam would be an autonomous state within the framework of a new union, allowed French troops to return to the territory. But in November, France attacked the Vietminh, sought to recolonize the country, and embarked on the military adventure that would last until 1954.[83]

This war against Vietnamese national liberation may also be regarded as an "untimely" event in which French forces restaged the war with Nazi Germany that they had never actually fought in 1940.[84] Many of the French commanders in Indochina had been imprisoned by the Germans, and some of the same paratrooper brigades were transferred directly from the European theater to operations in Southeast Asia. Figures who would play a prominent role as torture advocates and architects of the counterinsurgency during the Algerian War were also veterans of the war with Germany who then served as commanders in Indochina.[85] French journalist Bernard Fall, who covered the war directly as a correspondent, argued that France's spectacular defeat at Dien Bien Phu could be explained partly in terms of a desperate desire to find and fight a large "set-piece battle" against an enemy it could defeat; that is, to perform sovereignty and stage victory as if it were still confronting German divisions on European territory.[86]

France's inability to control Indochina was related to a larger crisis of authority and legitimacy that unfolded across its empire. In Martinique, the months after the Liberation were marked by strikes over salary levels, which Governor Parisot suppressed with troops.[87] In February 1945, Tunisian nationalists demanded political autonomy and Habib Bourguiba, founder of the Neo-Destour party, was forced into exile in Egypt.[88] Beginning on May 8, the day the war ended in Europe, there were uprisings of indigenous Algerians against French settlers in the cities of Sétif and Guelma and in the Kabylia region, followed by the brutal retaliation of the French army.[89] On May 30 France tried to suppress an uprising in Syria by bombing Damascus. Nationalist unrest in Syria and Lebanon led to the evacuation of French troops there in December.[90] In October 1946, the Rassemblement Démocratique Africaine (RDA) convened in Bamako to draft a resolution calling for political independence for French West African colonies. In March 1947, a popular nationalist uprising in Madagascar against French rule erupted; it lasted until November 1948 and was brutally suppressed by colonial authorities.[91] In April the sultan of Morocco denounced the French protectorate there.[92] In October 1947 a mass strike of railway workers across French West Africa thoroughly disrupted everyday life for almost six months.[93] Such unrest developed in the context of growing demands for decolonization worldwide and the granting of national independence to Indonesia (August 1945), India (June 1947), and Israel (May 1948).

France's imperial crisis, beginning while it was itself occupied by its Anglo-American liberators, reminds us that in 1945 it was a not-quite-sovereign state.[94] In September 1944, de Gaulle had established a provisional government of national unity, which the allies recognized the following month. The FFI Resistance forces were incorporated into the regular French army, and a Consultative Assembly was convened. In October, elections were held for a Constituent Assembly, which was dominated by representatives from the Communist Party, the Socialist Party, and the Christian Democratic Mouvement Républicain Populaire (MRP). The following month de Gaulle was elected head of state, during which time he sought to undermine the legitimacy of the communist *Résistants* and replace the institutions of the CNR. But in January 1946, de Gaulle resigned in protest against the assembly's unwillingness to institute his plan for a presidential government dominated by a strong executive.[95]

In May 1946 the first constitution that the assembly drafted for the Fourth Republic was rejected in a public referendum. Elections were then held for a Second Constituent Assembly. Beginning in June 1946 George Bidault, from the center-right MRP, became head of government and supported the second constitution, which was then approved in an October referendum. During the period of Communist-Socialist-Christian Democratic cooperation, major French industries and utilities were nationalized, the principal social security provisions of the new welfare state were passed, and the US Marshall Plan for French reconstruction was approved.[96]

But in April 1947 de Gaulle founded a new right-wing nationalist party, the Rassemblement du Peuple Français, and had success in municipal elections of October 1947. Writing in 1951, the conservative historian Jean-Baptiste Duroselle identified 1947 as a turning point in French politics, after which the tripartite arrangement that began in 1945 collapsed and Communists were effectively expelled from the government. No longer sharing power, Communists supported the waves of militant strikes that erupted across the country in 1947, beginning with Paris newspaper workers and the Renault automobile factory at Boulogne-Billancourt. These intersecting developments—resurgent Gaullism, official anticommunism, and syndicalist social unrest—contributed not only to the end of the wartime dreams of French leftists for a social democratic people's republic but to the commencement of the Cold War fissure that divided the capitalist West from the Soviet East.[97] By this point the postwar opening was already closing.

The Nationalist Logic of Decolonization

The 1960 UN resolutions on ending colonialism and assuring self-government to dependent peoples provides a fruitful starting point for thinking about the nationalist logic of decolonization that became consolidated after World War II. These documents, which attempted to enforce Chapter XI of the original UN Charter, contained an ambivalence about the meaning of self-determination that would haunt anticolonial politics for generations.

Resolution 1513, titled "Declaration on the Granting of Independence to Colonial Countries and Peoples," "solemnly proclaims the necessity of bringing to a speedy and unconditional end colonialism in all its forms and manifestations."[98] It did so on the basis of "the determination proclaimed by the peoples of the world in the Charter of the United Nations to reaffirm faith in fundamental human rights, in the dignity and worth of the human person, in the equal rights of men and women and of nations large and small."[99] Such human and national rights are bound up with the rights of "self-determination of all peoples."[100] But the resolution contains a symptomatic tension between two conceptions of self-determination: one procedural, democratic, and popular and the other territorial, national, and statist. On the one hand, it declared that "All peoples have the right to self-determination; by virtue of that right they freely determine their political status and freely pursue their economic, social, and cultural development."[101] On the other hand, it declared that all "dependent peoples" be allowed "to exercise peacefully and freely their right to complete independence, and the integrity of their national territory shall be respected."[102] This followed from the fact that "all peoples have an inalienable right to complete freedom, the exercise of their sovereignty and the integrity of their national territory."[103] In the first case, "self-determination" did not imply a specific framework; the second formulation presupposed that self-determination should assume a territorial national form. It referred to dependent colonies as "territories which have *not yet* attained independence."[104] The declaration did not mention the possibility that "the peoples of those territories" might decide to exercise their liberty or pursue their freedom in any framework except that of a territorial national state.[105]

The companion resolution passed the following day did recognize other modalities of decolonization. It defined a "non self-governing territory" as one in which the "geographical and ethnical or cultural distinctness of a territory" led it to be placed "arbitrarily" through "administrative, political, juridical, economic, or historical" mechanisms "in a position or status of subordination" with respect to a "metropolitan State."[106] The resolution then elaborated three situations that would allow these territories "a full measure of self-government." These included "(a) Emergence as a sovereign independent State; (b) Free association with an independent State; or (c) Integration with an independent State."[107] It further specified that association or integration should be the result of the free and democratic choice by the population concerned.[108]

Through these specifications, the UN was preempting dubious claims by imperial states to have turned colonies into associated or integrated territories in order to circumvent compliance with Article 73 of the UN Charter. The latter held that all states which administered "non self-governing territories" had to submit annual reports on these colonies to the UN until they reached the "full measure of self-government."[109] When the General Assembly established a Special Committee on Decolonization to monitor compliance with this reporting regulation, it again stressed these peoples' "right to complete independence" and condemned any "acts aimed at the partial or total disruption of national unity and territorial integrity . . . in countries in the process of decolonization."[110] But now there was no mention of freely chosen forms of democratic association or integration. The special committee certainly had strong grounds for supporting the national unity and territorial integrity of colonized peoples who demanded sovereign states. But such resolutions also demonstrate how decolonization was typically narrowed to mean national independence for culturally distinct groups inhabiting a delimited territory. Likewise, a procedural understanding of self-determination as a people's free choice about its future political status, about a specific framework for self-government, was conflated with a limited understanding of self-determination as state sovereignty for a national people. This elision was hardly surprising given that the UN order was organized around an international system of formally equivalent sovereign states. The conflation was symptomatic of longstanding tensions among modern conceptions of sovereignty, self-determination, and internationalism.

Much of the ambivalent internationalist logic of the UN was adapted directly from the League of Nations. Both systems sought to overcome a contradiction between the competing goods of state sovereignty and cosmopolitan internationalism. Each regarded national states as necessary components of *and* as possible impediments to a world order founded upon democratic self-determination. Each questioned the inviolability of state sovereignty even as it established an international order organized around sovereign states.

The 1919 Paris Peace Conference was a watershed moment in the process whereby self-determination became identified with national independence. Its aim was to neutralize interstate antagonisms and to criminalize war through a League of Nations. The league created new national states, redefined boundaries of existing ones, fashioned novel legal instruments for protecting minority and stateless peoples, and established a mandate system to administer the non-European colonies of defeated empires.[111] Supporters of the league included British imperialists, who regarded empire as a template for an international commonwealth, and American nationalists, who saw the Monroe Doctrine as a model for a global hegemony without formal colonies.[112]

Member states agreed to surrender a measure of sovereignty for "international cooperation, peace, and security."[113] They pledged to conduct foreign affairs according to the rules of international law and submit international disputes to league arbitration or settlement by a new Permanent Court of International Justice.[114] This attempt to subordinate interstate conflict to international law challenged state sovereignty as the fundamental principle guiding international relations. Yet the fact that only national states could be members of the league or have standing in its court reaffirmed the nineteenth-century idea that political liberty required national independence. The covenant declared that "Members of the League undertake to respect and preserve against external aggression the territorial integrity and existing political independence of all members."[115] Territorial integrity, political independence, and national sovereignty were the means and ends of the league. Yet how did its proponents understand *self-determination*?

In his Fourteen Points speech to the US Congress on January 18, 1918, Woodrow Wilson announced the need for a postwar settlement that would make the world "safe for every peace-loving nation which, like our own, wishes to live its own life, *determine its own institutions,* be assured of justice and fair dealing by the other peoples of the world."[116] He underscored that "all peoples and nationalities" had a "right to live on equal terms of liberty and safety with one another, whether they be strong or weak."[117] He proposed that "a general association of nations must be formed . . . for the purpose of affording mutual guarantees of political independence and territorial integrity to great and small states alike."[118] But it is not clear here whether its aim was to guarantee the territorial integrity and political independence of existing states, as a means to prevent future wars, or to guarantee peoples and nations the right to determine their own institutions. In his campaign to ratify the covenant, Wilson explained: "the time had come when the people were no longer going to consent to live under masters, but were going to live the lives that they chose themselves, to live under such governments as they chose themselves to erect."[119] Yet Wilson specified neither the people to whom he was referring nor the type of liberation they were being granted.

According to historian Margaret MacMillan, Wilson's own secretary of state, Robert Lansing, was perplexed about whether by self-determination the president meant democratic self-government or the right of any people who identified as a nation to have their own state.[120] Historian Erez Manela notes that Wilson invoked democratic self-government only for the peoples of continental Europe and never directly for colonial subjects of imperial powers.[121] He also contends that it was not until V. I. Lenin began referring to the rights of oppressed peoples to "national self-determination" that Wilson appropriated the specific term, as a synonym for popular consent, to neutralize Bolshevik influence on world opinion.[122]

In 1914 Lenin announced that international socialism sought to balance "the absolutely direct, unequivocal recognition of the full right of all nations to self-determination" with "the equally unambiguous appeal to the workers for *international* unity in their class struggle."[123] He first developed his position on self-determination in relation to specific struggles by oppressed "nationalities" against the despotic czarist state and reactionary Russian nationalism. By "self-determination" he meant "the right of an oppressed nation to secede" from a "dominant nation."[124] But this was only a means for the emancipation of workers within independent states that would enable the "class goal" of an "alliance of all proletarians of all nations."[125] Lenin advocated a "practical" and "historically concrete" approach to the national question, warning that "an abstract presentation of the question of nationalism in general is of no use."[126] For the young Soviet Union Lenin supported a decentralized and federalist system that would "retain the union of Soviet socialist republics only for military and diplomatic affairs, and in all other respects restore full independence to the individual People's Commissariats."[127] He regarded nationality as an instrument to be used against the chauvinism and imperialism of powerful states, not as an end in itself.

The architects of the Paris Peace Conference shared much of Lenin's orientation to national territory and state sovereignty, if for different ends. In addition to creating the league and its court, the Versailles Treaties transformed overseas colonies into mandates, carved new national states out of continental empires, created minority protection laws and reciprocal emigration agreements, and invented "unprecedented international legal forms" in the Saar, Danzig, and Upper Silesia that existed outside the framework of any sovereign state. Legal scholar Nathaniel Berman writes, "in these regions . . . plebiscites, partition, minority protection, internationalization, supranational integration, and international supervision were united in complex and nuanced regimes."[128] Through the league, international law shifted from "the role of supervisor of sovereigns and guardian of nations to that of autonomous creator of institutions that could replace states as the structuring units of the legal order."[129] Such legal experiments undermined the doctrine of state sovereignty, as peoples were often governed directly by international agencies without the intermediation of states.[130]

The league's ambivalent relationship to national self-determination and state sovereignty was also expressed in its mandate system. Article 22 of the covenant stipulated that former colonies of defeated states "inhabited by peoples not yet able to stand by themselves," whose "well-being and development . . . form a sacred trust of civilization," would henceforth become "mandates" placed under the "tutelage" of "advanced nations" acting on behalf of the league. This sanctioned imperialism under a different name by continuing to allow European states to govern non-European peoples. Yet by "entrusting" these territories to members who assumed responsibility for their "tutelage . . . on behalf of the League," this new international confederation superseded the sovereignty of those imperial states. The league thereby challenged the inviolability of state sovereignty in international law. As the legal scholar Frederick Charles Hicks argued in *The New World Order* (1920), the mandate system

> created a curious international situation in which the sovereignty of extensive territory apparently is jointly held, while the inhabitants of these territories . . . are deprived of nationality. . . . Nor are they by virtue of the transfer under the control of a government. But a government there

must be, and until or unless these colonies are made independent that government is provided by the League Covenant.[131]

Certainly this was not emancipation; colonial peoples were turned into wards of the international community, ruled by imperial powers without consultation or consent.[132] But we should note that the mandate system experimented with new kinds of supranational governance. These legal experiments created as many conflicts as they resolved. But in them the very precept of state sovereignty as unitary, centralized, and territorially circumscribed was reworked through the creation of nonsovereign states and nonnational sovereignties.

After World War II, the great powers attempted to resolve the tension between state sovereignty and international cooperation by creating another supranational confederation of independent states willing to surrender a degree of sovereignty in return for global peace and stability. By opening membership to all nations, the UN attempted to correct the failures of the league. But whereas many *interwar* internationalists had attempted to desacralize territorial sovereignty, the architects of the *postwar* system effectively fetishized it.[133]

In the 1941 Atlantic Charter Churchill and Roosevelt had declared that they "respect the right of all peoples to choose the form of government under which they will live; and they wish to see sovereign rights and self government restored to those who have been forcibly deprived of them."[134] But during the war, the US administration had already been drawing up plans for the United Nations as an association of powers that could enforce world peace through force and impose sanctions in the name of the international community. According to this plan, "Four Policemen"—the United States, Britain, the USSR, and China—would be charged with maintaining order and security over the geographical regions within which they were dominant powers.[135] During planning meetings in 1944/45, conflicts and compromises led the United States, Britain, and the USSR to combine aspects of the Four Policemen plan and the discredited League of Nations. All agreed that small nations had to be included directly in the new organization, that the great powers would retain final decisions over certain issues, and that limitations must constrict the UN's ability to interfere in the domestic affairs of sovereign states. All were anxious to retain their zones of autonomous action: the Soviet Union in Eastern Europe, Britain in its empire, and the United States in the Americas.[136]

The first article of the UN Charter, signed in San Francisco on June 25, 1945, announced the organization's primary purpose: "To maintain international peace and security" through "effective collective measures for the prevention and removal of threats to the peace."[137] The following articles made it clear that this would neither be a federation of peoples nor a world parliament, but a confederation of independent national states. Article 2.1: "The Organization is based on the principle of the sovereign equality of all its Members."[138] Article 2.4: "All Members shall refrain in their international relations from the threat or use of force against the territorial integrity or political independence of any state."[139] And, especially, 2.7: "Nothing contained in the present Charter shall authorize the United Nations to intervene in matters which are essentially within the domestic jurisdiction of any state or shall require the Members to submit such matters to settlement under the present Charter."[140] Ultimately, the UN was designed as an association of sovereign equals meant to ensure international peace and security by prohibiting members from interfering with the territorial integrity and political independence of other states. The organization was not permitted to interfere in the domestic affairs of members states unless they violated the Charter. And only independent sovereign states could be members of the UN or bring cases before the International Court of Justice.

This preoccupation with respecting state sovereignty and territorial integrity in the name of national self-determination was partly meant to protect the interests of small and weak states from manipulation by larger powers. The UN indeed became a guardian of the decolonization process.[141] Yet the great powers also had compelling geopolitical and economic reasons to create just such a system of formally equal sovereign states. Geographer Neil Smith argues persuasively that the United States was willing to compromise some of its sovereignty in the Western Hemisphere in exchange for the prospect of dominating the new global economy through free-trade imperialism. American planners believed that an international system of independent states would be amenable to US management, surveillance, and policing. And insofar as interstate conflicts would be neutralized or managed by the UN, the United States would be freer to devote its energy to global economic expansion.[142]

According to historical sociologist Giovanni Arrighi, this system of sovereign states also facilitated American economic domination by globalizing consumer demand. By the end of the war, Fordist capitalism had concentrated world financial power, productive capacity, consumer demand, and purchasing power in the United States. But "unless world liquidity was distributed more evenly, the world could not purchase from the United States the means of production which it needed to supply anything of value to US consumers in whose hands most of the world's *effective* demand was concentrated."[143] American initiatives to organize an international financial system (through GATT, Bretton Woods, IMF, the World Bank) and an international state security system (through the UN) may be regarded as two aspects of this strategy to globalize liquidity.[144]

For its part, Britain believed that an international organization of sovereign states would allow its empire to be protected from outside interference. Historian Mark Mazower demonstrates that the British imperial architects of the League of Nations, who had promoted a federation linking colonial powers and colonized peoples, also supported the UN.[145] As pressure for decolonization mounted in the decade following 1945, European powers attempted to protect their imperial prerogatives by invoking Article 2.7 of the charter, which prohibited UN intervention in states' domestic affairs. In turn, colonized peoples invoked Article 73:

> Members of the United Nations which have or assume responsibilities for the administration of territories whose peoples have not yet attained a full measure of self-government recognize the principle that the interests of the inhabitants of these territories are paramount, and accept as a sacred trust the obligation to promote to the utmost, within the system of international peace and security established by the present Charter, the well-being of the inhabitants of these territories.[146]

This "sacred trust" obligated imperial member states "to develop self-government [for the peoples concerned], to take due account of the political aspirations of the peoples, and to assist them in the progressive development of their free political institutions, according to the particular circumstances of each territory and its peoples and their varying stages of advancement"[147] This charge was paired with provisions to transform the interwar system of colonial mandates into a new "international trusteeship system." Like the League of Nations, the UN granted imperial states the right to administer these trustee territories in exchange for a pledge "to promote the political, economic, social, and educational advancement of [their] inhabitants . . . and their progressive development towards self-government or independence as may be appropriate to the particular circumstances of each territory and its peoples and the freely expressed wishes of the peoples concerned."[148]

The UN Charter envisioned the eventual self-government of colonized peoples even as it also affirmed European colonial rule as legitimate.[149] But this contradiction was only apparent. A national conception of state sovereignty was compatible with the imperial interests of both Britain and the United States. Historians William Roger Louis and Ronald Robinson characterize British decolonization as a process of renegotiating imperial alliances with local intermediaries and establishing informal postcolonial contracts with newly independent states. In many cases, as in Kenya following the Mau-Mau rebellion, British authorities actually rushed political independence to ensure that moderate allies would govern new national states and choose to join the Commonwealth. These British imperialists helped to create a postwar Anglo-American consortium through which former colonial territories could be managed and exploited, albeit under American leadership.[150]

According to Louis and Robinson, the United States after the war undertook a tricky balancing act. By opposing, as outdated, Europe's territorial colonialism, it could dissolve imperial commercial monopolies and open markets to American penetration. Anti-imperial initiatives would disrupt European power and win the ideological loyalty of colonized peoples as the Cold War began to unfold. Yet the United States also regarded European imperialism as an effective bulwark against communist insurgencies in Africa and Asia. Louis and Robinson argue that until the Suez Crisis, American anticommunism trumped its anti-imperialism, but after 1956, the United States assumed an imperial role as leader of a global anticommunist struggle.[151]

After 1955, the center of gravity in the UN began to shift from the West to the newly empowered Third World. But by then the UN-US order had already defined and circumscribed the political field on which decolonization would play out. Struggles developed over the pace of national independence, the political ideologies of postcolonial states, and forms of neocolonialism. But few actors on any side of these conflicts disputed the territorial nationalist logic that reduced colonial emancipation to political independence, and self-determination to state sovereignty.

Citizenship without Territory: A Commonwealth of Nations

UN internationalism may have enumerated conditions under which state sovereignty could be overridden—as when member states violated individuals' human rights through war crimes or crimes against humanity—but it did not meaningfully reconceptualize sovereignty itself. Like the League of Nations, the UN established a system of what Neil Smith called nationalist internationalism.[152] Both organizations nurtured the common-sense belief that self-determination required an independent national state and reproduced the dilemma between state sovereignty and human solidarity they had attempted to resolve.

Arendt addressed precisely this dilemma in a 1940 letter to Eric Cohn-Bendit when she was living as a political refugee in Paris and would soon be interned by the French state at the camp in Gurs for being Jewish.[153] She asserted that "all politics dealing with minorities, and not just with the Jews, have foundered on the existing and abiding fact of state sovereignty."[154] Accordingly, she criticized the League of Nation's minority treaties for proceeding from the illusion that persecuted peoples spread across state borders could be protected on a state-by-state basis.[155] She challenged their assumption that every minority enjoyed a majority status in some established homeland, as if all humans necessarily belonged to a territorial national state.[156]

In her view European Jews after World War I were confronted with equally unacceptable alternatives: to abnegate their community, renounce their status as a people, and surrender their fate to an alien national state or to leave Europe, emigrate to Israel, and embrace political Zionism.[157] Arendt criticized the Zionist option as a misguided territorial solution to the problem of Jewish nationality. She regarded it as an unrealistic fantasy based on "the conundrum of a people without land in search of a land without people," insisting that no such place existed.[158] Moreover, she contended that a Jewish homeland would not serve the mass of Diaspora Jews, who may identify themselves with a distinct Jewish people or nation but who were also at home in Europe, whose cultural identity was inextricably European, and who had neither the possibility nor the desire to constitute themselves as a separate and sovereign national state.

Yet Arendt was equally dubious about Jews who placed their fate in the hands of European states, as the minority treaties instructed them to do. She insisted that the best these treaties could provide was "cultural autonomy" or "culture without politics."[159] In *The Origins of Totalitarianism*, Arendt argued that membership in a polity and the protection of a particular legal regime was the condition of possibility for living like a full human being. If so, then stateless peoples who could not or would not assimilate into host nations would have to find some arrangement by which they could enjoy legal citizenship within a polity that did not require a *patrie*.[160] The challenge for communities such as non-Zionist European Jews was to create a political framework within which a distinct people that neither possessed nor desired state sovereignty could nevertheless enjoy the rights that constitutional states accorded to citizens as humans. Only through such a novel arrangement, according to Arendt, would it be possible to be truly Jewish and fully human.[161]

Arendt recognized that in the modern era human rights presupposed national rights. But this insight did not lead her to promote national sovereignty against abstract humanity. Instead, she spent her life grappling with the challenge of how to reconcile cultural particularity and human solidarity.[162] She developed, not a critique of human rights from the standpoint of national rights, but a critique of the historical conflation of the two from the standpoint of what she called a "political concept of humankind" and the "solidarity of the human race."[163] Rather than reject the politics of humanity, she sought to recuperate them by calling for a political framework that could protect communities without sovereignty through citizenship without territory. She noted that the old order of national states was no longer adequate to this task, and new institutional arrangements had not yet emerged to supersede them. As she later explained:

> humanity, which for the eighteenth century, in Kantian terminology, was no more than a regulative idea, has today become an inescapable fact. This new situation . . . [means] that the right to have rights, or the right of every individual to belong to humanity, *should be guaranteed by humanity itself.* It is by no means certain whether this is possible. For . . . this idea transcends the present sphere of international law which still operates in terms of reciprocal agreements and treaties between sovereign states; and *for the time being a sphere that is above nations does not exist.*[164]

Some kind of postnational political system would have to be fashioned through which "humanity" itself could finally guarantee the right of all humans to have rights.

Arendt relayed to Cohn-Bendit her belief that "the only chance of all small peoples [including Jews]—lies in a new European federal system."[165] In her view it was no longer viable to believe that political rights could be derived from territorial sovereignty. She wrote, "the notion that nations are constituted by settlements within borders and are protected by their territory is undergoing a crucial correction. . . . There may soon come a time when the idea of belonging to a territory is replaced by the idea of belonging to a commonwealth of nations."[166] Surprisingly, Arendt then suggested that existing imperial institutions might provide anti-Zionist Jews with a framework for some future polity. She wrote, "The British Commonwealth reveals—in a distorted form . . . the rudiments of a new arrangement. Someone who is part of the British Empire does not therefore cease to be an Indian or a Canadian . . . this would be our sole salvation. Within such a commonwealth we could be recognized as a nation and be represented in a European parliament."[167] Because such an arrangement had a real, if small, chance of being instituted, she insisted that it was not "utopian to hope for [this] possibility."[168] Arendt thus glimpsed within the already existing (national-imperial) system, though *in a distorted form*, a future political formation that could better serve as a framework for democratic politics on a planetary scale. Mindful of the untimely character of these utopian-realist reflections, she added, "what such a national alliance stretching across all of Europe would look like in juridical terms—that is, what concrete shape it would take—is still fairly enigmatic to my mind, though I pin great hopes on it."[169]

We do not have to accept Arendt's quasi-imperial proposal to appreciate that she was trying to work through the relationship between plurality and democracy, nationality and humanity, political community and universal rights, self-determination and human solidarity. At stake in her reflections on the fate of small peoples being tied to a future commonwealth was the distinction between territorial sovereignty and popular sovereignty.[170] Her proleptic intervention illuminated the distinction between, on the one hand, a state's right to dispose freely of a given territory and population under its jurisdiction without external interference and, on the other hand, a people's inalienable right to constitute a political community; that is, its members' right to elaborate the political norms and legal framework to which they will freely subject themselves. Arendt regarded as politically tragic that, in the modern period, self-government by citizens came to appear to require territorial sovereignty within a national state.

Excursus: Self-Determination without State Sovereignty

Writing from within (and about) the postwar opening, Camus and Arendt, like Césaire and Senghor, were proleptic thinkers, utopian realists who sought to exploit the postwar gap between the no longer and the not yet. However differently, they each hoped to transcend the limitations of the UN's nationalist internationalism by anticipating supranational forms of political association that did not ground citizenship in territory, ethnicity, or community. Lurking within their acts of political imagination was a refusal to conflate popular sovereignty with territorial sovereignty, a recognition that self-determination did not require state sovereignty. Because the democratic dilemma they confronted—between national liberation and human emancipation—had haunted politics since at least the eighteenth century Atlantic revolutions, they may thus be read alongside modern thinkers who also grappled directly with the antinomies of freedom.

In *The Philosophy of Law* (1797), Kant defined "Constitutional FREEDOM, as the Right of every Citizen to have to obey no other Law than that to which he has given his consent or approval."[171] He also identified freedom as "the sole original, inborn, Right belonging to every man in virtue of his humanity."[172] His primary question was how a people can transform itself into a "civil union" or "political state" such that "constitutional freedom" can ground human freedom. He recognized that such freedom implied sovereignty insofar as "a state which is self-governing and free from all external laws will not let itself become dependent on the judgment of other states in seeking to uphold its rights against them."[173] But he was *not* immediately concerned with the right of sovereign peoples to have supreme power over national territories. He used the terms *nation, state,* and *commonwealth* interchangeably to refer to the political form assumed by a sovereign people governing themselves according to principles of political freedom and legal right.

Kant identified a fundamental contradiction at the heart of self-government. On the one hand, constitutional republics expressed a sovereign people's inherent human right to enjoy civil freedom according to the rational principles of public right. On the other hand, the fact that the world was organized into particular territorial units violated the very principle of lawful freedom upon which rational self-government depended: as long as the earth was divided among separate sovereign states free to declare war on others and not subject to a higher legislative authority, humanity was condemned to exist in a state of "lawless freedom."[174] In this sense, the very condition of constitutional freedom was antithetical to real human freedom, which for Kant would require civil freedom on a global scale.

Kant thereby outlines a seemingly intractable dilemma. For humanity to transition from a condition of lawless liberty to one of lawful freedom, it would have to create a legal order and civil union that would encompass all humans. But all free humans as members of sovereign peoples have the right to constitute themselves as self-governing legal states that cannot be legally compelled by an external power to obey any but its own freely elaborated laws.[175] Kant explains that "as states, they already have a lawful internal constitution, and have thus outgrown the coercive right of others to subject them to a wider legal constitution."[176] Globally, this lawless freedom in which people are permanently threatened by war violates the inborn right of all humans to live in a state of perpetual peace, which, for Kant, is the only true ground of human freedom. He explains, "reason, as the highest legislative moral power, absolutely condemns war as a test of rights and sets up peace as an immediate duty."[177] Kant thus stages an antinomy of right; human freedom requires both popular sovereignty and perpetual peace.

In "Perpetual Peace" (1795), Kant concludes that the only rational solution would be for sovereign states to combine into a "federation of peoples" or "federation of free states."[178] He contends that in the absence of a "supreme legislative power" governing relations between states, peace can be guaranteed only through an international "substitute for the union of civil society."[179]

Yet his commitment to constitutional freedom prevents him from endorsing a supranational state whose sovereignty would trump individual humans' inborn right to be self-governing (through a constitutional republic). He therefore turns to the idea of a free union of peoples.

It is unclear whether Kant regards this "free federation" as a desirable solution to the problem of freedom or simply as the best solution that could be expected at that point in human history. He argues that despite the dangers of war posed by sovereign states, a "federal union . . . is still to be preferred to an amalgamation of the separate nations under a single power which has . . . created a universal monarchy" and "soulless despotism."[180] But he also argues that such an "international state," which would "continue to grow until it embraced all the peoples of the earth," is in fact the only rational solution to the problems of perpetual peace and human freedom. He explains that the sole reason this "positive idea of a world republic cannot be realized" is that it "is not in the will of the nations, according to their present conception of international right." So "if all is not to be lost, this [world republic] can at best find a negative substitute in the shape of an enduring and gradually expanding *federation* likely to prevent war."[181] Kant thus vacillates between identifying a federation of free peoples as the preferable solution, one consistent with competing principles of right, or as a practical compromise in the face of existing historical conditions. Similarly, he oscillates between figuring a world republic (or international state) as a dangerous threat *and* an unattainable ideal. According to his logic, public right and human freedom make each alternative both necessary and inadequate. Instead of resolving the contradiction between a people's rights and human rights, Kant ultimately displaces it into one between a federal union and a world republic.

In his related discussion of "cosmopolitan right" or the "universal right of mankind," which he figures as standing above the realms of national and international right, Kant reiterates this dilemma between sovereignty and globality.[182] He grounds the idea of cosmopolitan right on humanity's "communal possession of the earth's surface," which means that "no one originally has any greater right than anyone else to occupy any particular portion of the earth."[183] Yet he also defines cosmopolitan law more restrictively as "the Right of man as a citizen of the world to *attempt* to enter into communion with all others, and for this purpose to *visit* all the regions of the earth, although this does not constitute a right of *settlement* upon the territory of another people."[184] In this second, more limited formulation, what is universal in the cosmopolitan right to intercourse and hospitality is the assumption that all individuals belong to some sovereign people and deserve recognition as such when engaging with another sovereign people. Kant's cosmopolitan right thus presupposes the existence of an interstate system and reinscribes the very territorial division of humanity that it attempted to transcend.[185]

Regardless of what we think of Kant's particular programs, his reflections on the problem of human freedom and the challenge of global democracy remind us that the imperatives of political emancipation worked both to bind self-determination to sovereign national states and to open the prospect that sovereignty might have to be disaggregated and redistributed across diverse territorial scales. Kant's writings on federalism and cosmopolitanism demonstrate that we cannot know a priori the correct political form in which lawful human freedom must be grounded or best pursued. We can only start with an overarching political aim before identifying the form that might best correspond to it in any given historical conjuncture and political field.

Speaking schematically, between 1789 and 1848 territorial national states were normalized as the dominant institutional form for popular sovereignty. The French Revolution, followed by revolutionary wars against ancien régime powers in the name of national-popular liberation, elevated the Jacobin example into a general paradigm for self-government. According to this model, peoples are nations, nations are sovereign, and national-popular sovereignty requires unitary territorial states. With the liberal uprisings of the 1830s, which culminated in the "awakening of peoples" in 1848, popular struggles for self-government against absolutism, aristocracy, and imperial states were expressed primarily as demands for national independence. Such movements emerged within the international system, based on sovereign states, that was defined by the great powers during the 1815 Congress of Vienna, after the Napoleonic Wars.[186] By the twentieth century popular and territorial sovereignty were largely conflated; an enduring equivalence was established between self-determination and national liberation.

But this process of national normalization was also punctuated by political projects that challenged Jacobin assumptions about the necessary relationship between self-determination, unitary states, and undivided sovereignty. In the French "federalist revolt" of 1793, republicans in cities such as Marseille, Lyon, Bordeaux, and Caen challenged Jacobin centralization in the name of regional autonomy for provincial assemblies and municipal councils.[187] Similarly, white planters in colonial Saint-Domingue during the French Revolution responded to Jacobin centralization, abolitionist pressure, and the 1791 slave revolt with reactionary proposals for legislative autonomy within the imperial framework through self-governing colonial assemblies.[188] At a different scale, Napoleon's continental imperialism introduced onto the stage of political modernity an alternative, Roman-inspired framework for linking territory, peoples, and states. Exemplifying the very sort of international superstate that Kant warned against, Napoleon envisioned Europe, led by imperial France, as a confederacy of peoples or autonomous nations united within the framework of a single constitutional state.[189]

There were also progressive anti-Jacobin movements that challenged the assumption that free states were always unitary. During the popular revolution in Saint-Domingue, as we will see, Toussaint Louverture neither accepted metropolitan rule nor established a sovereign state. Instead, he proposed an unprecedented partnership between a self-governing Saint-Domingue and the metropolitan state within a refigured imperial federation. Likewise, we should recall Simón Bolívar's creative attempts to institutionalize colonial emancipation for the peoples ruled by the Spanish empire in Latin America. Called "the Liberator," Bolívar linked self-determination to various plans for regional pan-American federations and confederations through which democracy and plurality might be articulated.[190]

Even in the nationalist nineteenth century unitary state sovereignty was not the only response to the problem of freedom. Instructive here are the political projects of Giuseppe Mazzini from Genoa and Pierre-Joseph Proudhon from Besançon. In relation to the challenges and opportunities of 1848, each, in different ways, addressed the Kantian dilemma between constitutional states and cosmopolitan federations as frameworks for human freedom.

Since the 1830s Mazzini had struggled to unify Italy as a constitutional republic. He regarded 1848 as a battle between the oppressed peoples of Europe, who demanded democratic liberties, human dignity, and self-government, and outmoded absolutist states and associated dynastic empires. He called on Europe's free states to join with peoples fighting for freedom in a "Holy Alliance of Peoples" against the ancien régime.[191] Bound together through the "principle of association," these free states would "enter into a common pact to regulate all matters related to their international life."[192] In this way, "the future Europe of peoples will be united through a new type of federation, which will avoid both the anarchy of absolute independence and the tyrannical centralization that results from conquest."[193] As Mazzini imagined it, this "international democratic association" would be organized around "a series of national Councils" that would "coherently express the special mission of each nation" and "prepare each people for their future membership in the great federation of nations." Each national council would send a representative to a "supreme international Council," which would "promote a Holy Alliance of the oppressed against the oppressors."[194]

Mazzini regarded "country" as the "pivot" of a lever whose task was a "cosmopolitanism" founded on "the destruction of all barriers that separate the Peoples."[195] He believed that nations allowed peoples to realize their full potential as humans through republican self-government.[196] On a larger scale, self-governing nations were means for allowing peoples to join together in associations that could encompass humanity as a whole.[197] According to Mazzini, nationality without cosmopolitanism had no purpose, while a cosmopolitanism that sought to bypass nations had no chance of being realized.[198] His "guiding principle" was *progress of each for the benefit of all.*"[199] And he observed, "the challenge consists in harmonizing things, not in *blending* them together."[200] Mazzini traced a dialectic of nationality and humanity whereby each served as the condition of possibility for the other's realization.[201] In his schema, nations were most fully national when integrated in a cosmopolitan association of countries that knitted together humanity as a whole, and humanity was most fully human when distinct peoples freely pursued and developed their national particularity.

Mazzini's concrete cosmopolitanism was at once pragmatic and utopian, timely and untimely. If, like Kant, he insisted that "our point of reference is the globe's entire surface and our faith lies in unity," he also recognized that existing historical conditions required that global unity be pursued through the medium of nationality.[202] He wrote, "we are practical people above anything else, and so we aim toward the possible. . . . We therefore need to study our epoch and adapt to it: we need to understand what is feasible . . . we cannot choose our battlefield."[203] Yet he tied this practical realism to an expansive vision: "we mean unity in the widest, most comprehensive, and most profound possible sense. Unity in heaven and on earth, unity inside every human being."[204] In this way, he was Arendt's and Camus's utopian realist predecessor.

For Mazzini the issue of feasibility was related to timing. On the one hand, he instructed, "you should not attempt to superimpose a world whose time has not yet come on the world you can presently observe at your feet. . . . We clearly believe in the future unity of the human species. . . . However, we believe that this time of ultimate unity has not yet arrived."[205] On the other, he argued proleptically that rather than accept an inherited definition of "nationality," cosmopolitans "should rather seek [it] in the future, and in all the signs that anticipate what it will look like. . . . When we speak of Nationality, it is of Nationality such as the *Peoples*, free and brotherly associated, will conceive it. Now, this Nationality of the Peoples has never existed so far."[206] Mazzini thereby swung between figuring free peoples and self-governing nations as the *best* form in which to pursue ultimate human aims and as the most *realistic* form, given humanity's current state of historical development.

Mazzini's writings remind us that the art of politics requires situated actors to conjugate means and ends in relation to a given historical epoch. His interventions also underscore that 1848 was a historical opening wherein political freedom reemerged as a public problem that provoked debates about the relationship of self-government, state sovereignty, and human emancipation. Such problems were addressed by Pierre-Joseph Proudhon, who in his 1840 polemic *What Is Property?* argued that collective property, the equalization of wages, and the abolition of profit could best be realized through a process of "free association." In his view, "the government of man by man, under whatever name it is disguised, is oppression. The highest perfection of society is found in the union of order and anarchy."[207] Proudhon spent decades attempting to define the proper political form through which to reconcile this dual imperative to found a political community based on free association and to avoid the government of man by man. He did so through a nondogmatic refusal to begin with a priori certainties about how to achieve the ultimate aim of socialist politics and political revolution, which for him was a new civilization of "universal regeneration" that would "let humanity be free."[208]

Proudhon's thought also developed in the crucible of the 1848 revolution, in which he participated and for which he was imprisoned and then exiled. Alongside his critique of capitalist private property, he formulated a program for mutualist socialism organized around worker, artisanal, and peasant cooperatives, small producers, a democratic credit system, and industrial associations. Believing that labor was social and property collective, he envisioned a society based on direct relations among producers. Proudhon therefore conceptualized self-determination in terms of consensual and decentralized self-management. He was also an advocate of peaceful revolution whereby the autonomous organization of economic forces would make state power unnecessary.[209]

Proceeding from his critique of the unitary and centralized Jacobin state, Proudhon identified federalism as the political orientation that would best correspond to his visions of cooperative socialism and *autogestion*. He believed that democratic republicanism should be based on loosely coordinated and freely associated federations of self-managing communes and municipalities. He opposed unitary sovereignty and believed that federations would best be able to reconcile anarchy and order, individual liberty and collective social force. His vision of international order and world peace simply extended this mutualist and federalist logic on a larger scale: national federations of self-managing municipalities would themselves freely associate to form pacific international federations. This process of ever-expanding association and federation would eventually encompass all of humanity, overcoming distinctions among races and nations while also guarding against conquest and empire.[210]

Like Kant, Proudhon based his cosmopolitan program for a world confederation on the fantasy that transnational commerce would create relations of peaceful global interdependence. But unlike Kant, these international commercial networks would no longer depend on existing forms of capitalist private property and exchange, which Proudhon identified as creating inequality; they would be founded on what Proudhon called a postcapitalist "social economy." In contrast to Mazzini, Proudhon's mutualist and cooperative federalism hoped to reconcile plurality and humanity without the mediation of national states. But whereas Kant's cosmopolitanism began with humanity as a unit, Proudhon's starting point was self-managing communities and producer associations. Kant regarded the existence of distinct political communities as obstacles to the realization of self-government as human freedom; Proudhon treated such multiplicity as the condition of possibility of self-determination and the only guarantee of political liberty.

The writings of Proudhon, Mazzini, and Kant remind us that at epochal turning points in the history of political emancipation, such as 1789 and 1848, the relationships between popular and territorial sovereignty, between self-government and national states, and between constitutional republics and human freedom was not self-evident; it had to be worked out in contingent and contextual, pragmatic and strategic ways. The point was not simply to demand national independence but to determine the best framework through which substantive self-determination could be grounded and human emancipation pursued. Insofar as Mazzini and Proudhon attempted to fashion federal political forms through which to reconcile self-government and human solidarity, they engaged the very problem that Kant had identified in the wake of the French Revolution. These nineteenth-century heirs embraced the German philosopher's cosmopolitan ambitions but challenged his abstract conception of humanity. They were rooted cosmopolitans and concrete humanists who insisted on the possibility of self-determination without state sovereignty. They anticipated twentieth century attempts by political organizations such as the League of Nations and the United Nations, and political thinkers such as Camus and Arendt to reconcile popular sovereignty and human freedom. As we will see, Césaire and Senghor, who refused to reduce colonial emancipation to national liberation, were also their heirs. They too understood self-determination as a people's right to choose the particular form through which to manage its affairs rather than the requirement that it create a sovereign national state.

FIVE   Departmentalization and the Spirit of Schoelcher

The past to which we were subjected, which has not yet emerged as history for us, is however, obsessively present. The duty of the writer is to explore this obsession, to show its relevance in a continuous fashion to the immediate present. This exploration is therefore related neither to a schematic chronology nor to a nostalgic lament. It leads to the identification of a painful notion of time and its full projection forward into the future. . . . That is what I call a prophetic vision of the past. —ÉDOUARD GLISSANT

Revisiting Departmentalization

At the war's conclusion, Aimé Césaire considered the place of the Antilles in the world and concluded that integration into a new French republic on terms of unconditional legal equality would be the best framework for pursuing self-management and substantive freedom. He believed it would be unacceptable to exclude these territories from the society, economy, or polity of which they had always been a part. By exhorting metropolitan France to democratize the plural reality its own imperial history had created, he politicized the defiant challenge in his *Notebook of a Return to My Native Land*: "Accommodate yourself to me. I will not accommodate you!"[1] This accommodation, he believed, would improve the lives of Antilleans *and* fundamentally change France itself.

Rather than criticize Césaire for supporting what became a neocolonial relationship, we should consider why he initially regarded departmentalization as a promising form of decolonization. We might recall his strategy, developed in *Tropiques*, of identifying Antilleans as heirs of French language, thought, and history. Through departmentalization he hoped to "inflect" existing relations to the point of rupture. We should also recall his pragmatic commitment to conjugate given conditions, possible means, and desirable ends. For Césaire departmentalization was an experimental approach to the aims of economic autonomy and effective self-government. As conditions changed and this arrangement became an obstacle to substantive emancipation, Césaire reoriented his decolonization program.

Finally we should recall how, for Césaire, politics and aesthetics were mutually entwined. Fanon recounts that when volunteering for Césaire's 1945 campaign for the French Constituent Assembly, a friend told him that during one of Césaire's speeches an audience member was so overcome by the intensity of his rhetoric and the elegance of his French that she fainted.[2] This anecdote, however apocryphal, reminds us that for Césaire, rhetoric was a "miraculous weapon" through which to overcome distinctions between the intelligible and the sensible, politics and poetics, and instrumental action and dramatic performance. Arendt also related democracy and theater as public acts.[3] This link is condensed in the word *act*, simultaneously signifying concrete activity, performance, and legislation. If Césaire's poetry was saturated by political sensibility, his political rhetoric was shaped by poetic knowledge, challenging the presuppositions of rational critical argument even while practicing immanent critique.

Seizing Historical Opportunity

In July 1943, Martinican officials loyal to de Gaulle's Comité Français de Libération Nationale took control of Admiral Robert's colonial administration. The new governor, Georges Louis Ponton, a protégé of Félix Éboué, countermanded many Vichyist measures, the previously elected conseil général was reinstated, and trade unions were legalized. A period of syndicalist resurgence, fueled by dissatisfaction with prices and wages, followed. According to historian Armand Nicolas, the Martinican Federation of the French Communist Party, founded by Jules Monnerot, assumed a leading role in public life.[4]

The secretary of the Federation was Léopold Bissol, a working-class Martinican who had participated in founding the French Communist Party in 1920 and the Confédération générale du travail in 1936. Thélus Léro, a mathematics professor and member of the earlier *Légitime défense* group, was in charge of propaganda. Other members included Gilbert Gratient, Césaire's former teacher who had contributed articles to *L'Étudiant Noir* (1935) and to *Tropiques*, and Réné Ménil, who called for a union of unions, an anticapitalist alliance of workers, peasants, and the middle class, and for the nationalization of sugar factories, large plantations, local banks, and the electric utility.[5]

The Communist Federation argued that the business *patronat* and white *béké* settler community had profited from the war and should share its illicit wealth with ordinary Antilleans. Militants traveled the county training activists and educating the population about the party's economic and social policies regarding producers' and consumers' cooperatives.[6] The federation endorsed efforts by Governor Ponton to introduce in Martinique progressive social and economic reforms meant to relieve scarcity, increase production, and promote agricultural and industrial development. But in July 1944 he committed suicide.[7] Césaire's public eulogy declared that Ponton had a poet's "human sense," enabling him "simply to look, to see, and to feel." Césaire noted the love and trust that Ponton felt for Martinicans and praised him as a political "artist and artisan" who promoted "cooperative or collective solutions" for a Martinique whose "immense historic [and] human importance" he recognized. Césaire saw Ponton as counterbalancing reactionary attempts to return the colony to the old status quo and "suffocate the Martinican revolution [then] underway."[8]

Although not yet a party member, Césaire supported these communists by organizing events targeting the younger generation, with whom he, as a lycée professor, had direct contact. These included an anticapitalist youth conference and a lecture series by literary scholar René Etiemble criticizing Vichy thought. Césaire helped found the literary review *Caravelle* and an ethnological bulletin called *Franc Jeu* and supported young painters associated with the art gallery Atelier 45. Following his 1944 trip to Haiti, Césaire delivered a public lecture on the black republic to an audience of 1,500. [9]

Minister of Colonies Jacques Soustelle wrote to Governor Ponton about his intention to groom Césaire for a position in the political or educational bureau of the colonial administration.[10] But rather than join the government, Césaire reluctantly entered electoral politics,[11] recruited by Ménil and Gratient to head the Martinican Communist ticket for Fort-de-France in the May 27 municipal elections and to run in the October 21 national election.[12] Césaire later recalled that he and his friend Pierre Aliker were selected because they were widely known intellectuals who could lead the post-Vichy government: "For my part, I was neither communist nor anti-communist, let's say I was a fellow traveler [*sympathisant*], a man of the left who did not belong to any party; I never had the party spirit."[13]

Only thirty-two years old, Césaire was elected mayor and conseiller municipal of Fort-de-France and conseiller général of the canton.[14] Then he and Bissol were elected delegates to the Constituent Assembly in Paris, which would be charged with drafting a new republican constitution. Césaire and Bissol acted with a broad popular mandate *and* as members of the majority party in the metropolitan assembly at a time when, as Governor Parisot reported, the "municipal elections [had] given many [in Martinique] the belief that the [French] government of tomorrow will be communist."[15] In July 1945, Césaire joined the French Communist Party (PCF), later explaining, "in a world not yet cured of racism, where the fierce exploitation of colonial populations still persists, the Communist party embodied the will to work effectively for the coming of the only social and political order we can accept . . . founded on the right of all men to dignity."[16]

According to Nicolas, when Césaire left Martinique for Paris, he carried in his briefcase a draft of the departmentalization law he and Bissol would submit to the assembly.[17] Their January 17, 1946, proposal reiterated a unanimous motion of the local assembly in Martinique and a resolution by the Comité Martiniquais de Libération Nationale to the États-Généraux du Conseil National de la Résistance in July 1945. Whether Césaire and Bissol felt ambivalence or, eventually, regret, no one at home could have been surprised by their support for departmentalization, a long-standing Martinican demand.[18] More remarkable was that the National Assembly passed with minimal debate a law that would have been unthinkable one year earlier and probably impossible one year later.[19]

During the first Constituent Assembly, Césaire served on the Commission des Territoires D'outre-mer, to which he, Bissol, Gaston Monnerville (Guyane), and Raymond Vergès (Réunion) proposed the departmentalization law.[20] It had three simple articles. The first established the colonies of Guadeloupe, Martinique, Réunion, and Guyane as French departments. The second declared that all existing metropolitan French laws and decrees would be applied to these new departments within three months. The third stipulated that all new laws and decrees passed in and for the metropole would automatically be extended to them.[21]

In the report that served as the basis for the legislative debate, Césaire declared departmentalization a simple legal reclassification, "the normal outcome of a historic process and the logical conclusion of a doctrine" that had been evolving since Martinique and Guadeloupe began to participate "in the fate [*destin*] of the metropole" in 1635.[22] He asserted that metropolitan and overseas peoples and territories were historically entwined and that republican principles required their legal and political assimilation on equal grounds. By arguing that this proposed law would liberate these colonial peoples from "an arbitrary regime of decrees," he implicitly compared the outmoded colonial situation both to the authoritarian Vichy state the republicans were charged with replacing and to the ancien régime against which the French Revolution was initially fought.[23]

Comparing overseas living conditions to those of the impoverished French workers that Louis-René Villermé described in his 1840s sociological exposés,

Césaire noted that "almost no effort has been made to assure to workers from the Antilles and Réunion an economic and social status that is in harmony with the political status that they have enjoyed for a century."[24] As a result, "in a country where salaries are abnormally low and the cost of living approaches that in France, the worker is at the mercy of sickness, injury, and age without any guarantees accorded to him."[25] Cultivators too lived in terrible conditions, and local functionaries were paid less than their metropolitan counterparts. Césaire concluded that if France were truly to "assimilate the Antilles," it could only be "by taking the initiative for a policy which . . . will ameliorate [*assainera*] the economy . . . by ending the veritable private monopolies of industries."[26] He thus exhorted the government to equalize wages and prices between metropolitan and Antillean territories by extending to Martinique the nationalizations that had begun in France. For "there should not be two capitalisms: a metropolitan capitalism that is opposed and limited, and an overseas capitalism that is tolerated."[27] Because republicanism required that public good take precedence over private interests, he insisted, all metropolitan social provisions and protections must be extended to these overseas departments. Moreover, he added, the law "has great international importance by satisfying all the conditions that allow it to be said that a constitution is good."[28]

Césaire thus mobilized republican reason and international norms to support departmentalization. He warned that any delays or qualifications would create "diminished departments" or "departments of exception," which would violate the republican doctrine of a singular and indivisible nation.[29] Césaire rejected "federal" proposals that invested local assemblies with the power to decide which metropolitan laws should be applied, contending that in places like Martinique, long dominated by entrenched white elites, such a solution would disenfranchise local populations.[30] He declared, "for us, loyal to a constant republican doctrine, we think that only the National Assembly, repository of the will of the nation, can make the law and determine the geographic field of its application."[31]

Crucially, Césaire believed that legal equality would require corresponding socioeconomic initiatives. In a December 20, 1945, debate on the annual budget, his first intervention in the Constituent Assembly, he passionately demanded economic development and social reforms for the Antilles to challenge the "oligarchy of huge planters still sympathetic to slavery." He called on the state to create an overseas development fund and warned legislators against taking Antilleans' political loyalty for granted, proclaiming, "the workers of Martinique and the Antilles have waited for three centuries, they are at the limit of their suffering and patience."[32]

In presenting this proposal for debate on March 12, 1946, Césaire invoked the great abolitionist Victor Schoelcher, who, according to Césaire, rejected all economic arguments against abolition, declaring emancipation to be a matter of morality not money. Césaire thereby urged the assembly not to "sully its act [geste] through any haggling. Four colonies, having reached maturity, demand a stricter attachment to France. You will appreciate the full value of this thought, I am sure, at this moment when we hear the ominous cracking of the edifices of imperialism."[33] Emphasizing the modest character of departmentalization, he explained that Antilleans wanted only "to know that, in the framework that we are beginning to call the French Union, there will no longer be room . . . for master-servant relations, but that there should be established an active and effective fraternity" as the basis for "a France that is more than ever united and diverse, multiple and harmonious, from which we are allowed to expect the greatest discoveries [revelations]."[34] Regarding Césaire's postwar initiatives, we should remember this image of a multiple, harmonious, and postimperial French nation, simultaneously the simple realization of the republican state and an unprecedented modification of it.[35]

The debates in the Constituent Assembly, for which Césaire served as rapporteur from the Commission of Overseas Territories, revolved around concerns about state form in relation to fiscal responsibility, local autonomy, and republican legitimacy. André Philip, the Socialist Party Minister of Finances, argued that automatic application of metropolitan social and economic legislation would be financially prohibitive.[36] Alternatively, Paul Valentino, the Socialist Party deputy from Guadeloupe, claimed that the centralization of power in Paris would erode the authority of local Antillean assemblies.[37] But legislators were more persuaded by Gaston Monnerville, who denounced the antidemocratic "absurdity" of the existing system, explaining, "as a representative of Guyane to the National Assembly, I vote for laws proposed for the metropole or North Africa. I contribute along with all of you to the administration of the French Community, yet, the laws on which I vote here are not applied in my country which remains subject to a regime of decrees."[38] On March 19, the assembly voted unanimously for the final version of the departmentalization act containing two significant revisions. First, the government would have nine months to apply existing metropolitan laws to these departments. Second, the provision that all future French laws be automatically extended overseas was removed; only those specifically designated as general by the assembly would be valid in the new departments. The radical potential of departmentalization was thus domesticated from the start.

When Césaire and Bissol returned to Fort-de-France after passage of the law, they were acclaimed by a jubilant crowd of 10,000 Martinicans. Departmentalization was supported by all of the island's major political parties (Communist, Socialist, and MRP) and trade unions. Opposition was limited to white businessmen and landowners and a small group of Martinicans associated with the Congrès de l'Union des Évadés Volontaires et Résistants. The latter called for a new economic federation of Martinique, Guadeloupe, and Guyane that would become part of the French Union but maintain local autonomy through a regional parliament.[39] On behalf of the Federation of Communists, Thélus Lero declared that departmentalization would effect "the emancipation of Martinican workers" through metropolitan social laws, public health services, higher taxes on wealthy Antilleans, the nationalization of the sugar industry, modernized agriculture and credit systems, and rational economic development plans.[40]

Césaire too hoped that departmentalization would lead dynamically from formal legal liberty to economic emancipation and then to significant social reorganization within the Antilles. The integration of former colonies into the unitary republic would also reconfigure the French state. This future-oriented vision was nourished by an untimely engagement with past projects for colonial emancipation. It was no accident that in his report to the assembly, Césaire invoked Schoelcher, the socialist architect of abolition following the 1848 revolution.

From Abolitionism to Schoelcherism

The final issue of *Tropiques* reprinted a public homage to Schoelcher that Césaire had delivered on July 21, 1945. Césaire began by declaring, "There is one fact on which the historians of the future will unhappily all agree: that from 1918 to 1939, democracy was very sick." In France, "everything occurred as if the republic was ashamed of its great events or its great men," including the Convention, Robespierre, and the Paris Commune.[41] During this time, Martinican democracy too was pathologically "ashamed of its origins" and sought "to erase [*escamoter*] Victor Schoelcher, as if one could conjure away [*escamoter*] this formidable ghost [*ombre*]."[42] But suggesting that the war had led to democratic awakening and renewed interest in Antillean abolition, Césaire speculated that "perhaps the Martinican people of the future will say . . .

it was these men then who through force of recognition veritably rediscovered the spirit of Victor Schoelcher."[43]

Césaire's affinity is not surprising. Schoelcher too sought to seize history through an opening provided by a constituent assembly situated in a gap between mere liberty and real freedom. Both pursued straightforward reforms with revolutionary implications. During his struggle to realize departmentalization, Césaire sought not simply to remember Schoelcher but to vitalize his project, to recognize it as contemporary, and to make it so through such recognition.[44]

Schoelcher first encountered slavery in 1829/30, while visiting Mexico, Cuba, and the United States for his family's porcelain business. This experience inspired two treatises against color prejudice and slavery, which he submitted for prize competitions sponsored by the Société des amis des noirs.[45] On his second trip to the Caribbean, in 1840/41, he documented the dehumanizing conditions in the French Antilles and studied emancipation in Haiti and the British Caribbean. His more radical writings of the 1840s followed, which demanded the immediate and unconditional abolition of slavery in the French Antilles.[46] He condemned transition periods preceding emancipation, as instituted in the British colonies, as forms of coercion violating the legal equality upon which democratic societies depended. And he rejected instrumental arguments: "whether or not slavery is useful, it must be destroyed; something *criminal* must not be *necessary*."[47] This principled position led him famously to declare, *"no colonies if they can only exist with slavery."*[48]

But Schoelcher also sought pragmatically to persuade planters that free labor was preferable to bloody slave revolt, a surer means of prosperity, and, anyway, a historical inevitability. He reminded them of slaves' "invincible desire for independence" which "now and then manifests itself in the brutal awakening of man . . . [in] open revolt . . . accompanied by fire and murder."[49] They already knew that "slavery is a volcano ready to crush [*ébranler*] their society . . . you live in a state of worry even while not wanting to admit your fears . . . you are in peril."[50] Invoking the Martinican slave uprisings of 1811, 1822, 1823, 1831, and 1833, as well as "the specter of Saint-Domingue," Schoelcher declared that only immediate emancipation could prevent "a future of catastrophes."[51] The sole question was whether emancipation would proceed in an orderly, manageable, and productive fashion or violently and chaotically. Furthermore, all interested actors would prosper from abolition: slaves would obtain freedom, whites could live without fear, property would become secure, and abolitionists could help Creoles remake the colony's economy.[52]

Schoelcher thus figured slave emancipation as the intersection of uncon-ditional principle and unquestionable interest. Reason, morality, justice, his-torical force, the will of the world's people, and the urgent desire of enslaved peoples would compel all colonial powers to abolish slavery. Ethically and prac-tically, he called for abolition to be imposed in a single decisive act of mass "spontaneous liberation."[53] Although this would "destabilize the colonies," he emphasized that the point was "to change the foundations of a society . . . to abolish slavery is, without a doubt, to carry out a revolution."[54] The challenge was to do so with minimal violence. Full and immediate emancipation would offer "all the political and material advantages of a . . . *Fait accompli,* irrevo-cable, absolute, no return possible."[55] Its revolutionary impact would then be less likely to be diluted or reversed.

Schoelcher's instrumental calculations opened onto a utopian vision of postemancipation reciprocity and solidarity. Since "blacks want to work and whites can work . . . they will mix together in the Antillean fields and from their union, we will see a new activity arise."[56] His "dream" was for Antillean territories to become a new Syracuse, where a "future alliance" of former slaves and masters might "produce great things.[57] Their felicitous location "in the middle of the ocean, all grouped between Europe and America," suggested "that one day they could constitute together a separate social body in the mod-ern world. Small independent republics, they will be confederally united by a common interest"[58] These "confederated islands" would have a "special . . . mixed [race] population . . . we can expect to see arise from these West Indies new prodigies who will surprise the universe [through] its gift to the world of enlightenment, science, and art."[59] Because such a possibility might take centuries to realize, Schoelecher's immediate aim was an Antillean social reor-ganization that would require a new relationship with metropolitan France.

Schoelcher saw legal emancipation as only the starting point for a more com-prehensive restructuring; slaves would become French citizens and colonies French provinces. This required extending to these colonial populations uni-versal suffrage, national political representation, the protection of metropoli-tan law, access to public education, and a free press.[60] Abolition would obviate "the whole arsenal of exceptional laws . . . the bastard regimes of [ministe-rial] *ordonnances,*" setting in motion a process of democratization whereby "legal assessors give way to juries, governors become prefects, *conseils coloniaux* are trans-formed into *conseils généraux de département.* Nothing from the colonial past would survive. Emancipation does not allow any of this heritage of servitude."[61]

Moreover, Schoelcher believed real emancipation depended upon new eco-nomic relations between former slaves and masters. He called for the modernization of the sugar industry, fair contracts for free laborers, land redistribution, indemnities for freed slaves, and the guaranteed right to work. He promoted an ambitious plan to transform the plantation economy into one based on smallholding cultivators. Manufacturers, small and large landholders, artisans and laborers, would be joined in a common task.[62] Nelly Schmidt identifies Schoelcher as a follower of Charles Fourier's utopian socialism, envisioning freed Antilleans forming workers' associations and agricultural cooperatives.[63] This overseas program resonated with that of social republicans for metropolitan France.

Schoelcher believed the first step toward this utopian future was already within reach. Influenced by British and American abolitionists, he wrote throughout the 1840s for antislavery periodicals, collaborated with antislavery organizations,[64] and drafted abolitionist petitions on behalf of French workers and the Society for the Abolition of Slavery, which he presented to the Chamber of Deputies.[65] When the 1848 revolution erupted, Schoelcher was touring colonial Senegal, Gambia, and Mauritania, gathering materials for a book on the slave trade in Africa. Returning to Paris to demand immediate abolition, he was appointed president of the new Commission for the Abolition of Slavery and asked by François Arago, Minister of the Navy and Colonies, to join the Provisional Government as undersecretary of state for the colonies. Warning Arago that the slaves would revolt if not freed, he drafted the abolition decree that the Provisional Government passed on April 27, 1848.[66]

Calling slavery "an attack on human dignity" and "a flagrant violation of republican dogma," the act proclaimed that "slavery will be entirely abolished in all French colonies and possessions." It prohibited "all French people . . . from possessing, buying, or selling slaves, and from participating, directly or indirectly, in any traffic or exploitation of this type" under penalty of loss of French citizenship.[67] New "Commissaires généraux de la République" would enforce abolition in Martinique, Guadeloupe, Guyane, Réunion, W. Africa, Mayotte, and Algeria; these colonies would henceforth be represented in the National Assembly.[68] Additional decrees sought to reorganize political, economic, and social life to accommodate the end of slavery.[69]

Schoelcher's first report after abolition reminded the Provisional Government that "it is not only a matter of proclaiming the emancipation of blacks. . . . Measures must be taken so that this great act of reparation of a crime against humanity [*crime de lèse-humanité*] is accomplished in the most profitable manner for those who were its victims."[70] For Schoelcher, this meant rejecting attempts to curtail freed slaves' rights or coerce their labor. Describing how, contrary to planters' predictions, emancipated blacks immediately demonstrated a desire to work and acquire land, he highlighted their "habits of order, calculation, foresight" and "a regularity of conduct . . . that surprises the magistrates. Already many have a small nest egg; all have a taste for property . . . and some have demonstrated enough intelligence to be capable, henceforth, of managing on their own sizable farms."[71]

Schoelcher repeatedly linked liberty, citizenship, and work. In 1842 he proposed legislation regulating labor conditions, defining a fixed minimum wage and standard working day, and guaranteeing workers' mobility. But it also included measures to attach freed laborers to the soil and punish vagrancy through strict five-year contracts. These would guarantee work to free blacks *and* workers to white landowners.[72] In a post-election speech to the people of Martinique and Guadeloupe, he declaimed "it is through work that you will conquer the respect of your fellow European citizens . . . [and] prove more and more how you are worthy of this name of citizen with which you have been belatedly recognized."[73]

Desiring a system of "truly free labor," Schoelcher's commission advocated to regulate worker-landowner relations, guarantee jobs and sufficient income for workers, prohibit vagabondage, create savings banks, and make education universal. Believing that adequate "encouragement and compensations" were necessary "to instill a love of order and economy,"[74] he called on the state to extend the metropolitan "national workshops" to these territories and expropriate land from planters for redistribution to freed slaves; thus, "property would be liberated at the same time that labor would be freed."[75] He condemned proposals to compensate planters for lost slaves, explaining "if France owes an indemnity . . . it is owed, without a doubt, to those who suffered from it more than to those who profited from it."[76] He called this grand plan to elevate slaves into independent proprietors a second "emancipation that must complement" mere abolition.[77]

Schoelcher hoped that legal and socioeconomic transformations would propel one another; slavery would be abolished, colonialism overcome, and overseas territories integrated into a socialist republic. But the Provisional Government refused to include representatives of agricultural workers on juries charged with arbitrating labor disputes[78] and decided to recruit African labor to the Antilles, which Schoelcher warned could re-create the slave trade "under a disguised form."[79] It also decided to replace the Commission on Abolition with a new body to compensate former slaveholders. On May 17, soon before the socialist current of the revolution was crushed by the bourgeois establishment, Schoelcher resigned from the government.[80]

In August, he decided that the National Assembly would better allow him to "defend all the consequences of the beautiful and generous revolution of 1848," including "popular sovereignty," the abolition of the death penalty, the right to work, public hospitals, free education, a rational justice system, progressive taxes, the protection of individual liberty, political and social equality, and "the fraternity of all French people and all the nations of the globe."[81] He lost the election for deputy from Paris but was later elected to represent Martinique and Guadeloupe, promising to support an indemnity law compelling landlords to pay a fair salary to cultivators and introducing tax exemptions on sugar to assure markets for the products of their labor. He also committed to "complete their assimilation to France. Purified of servitude, the colonies are henceforth an integral part of the metropole; even better, there are no more colonies, there are only overseas departments which must be ruled by the same laws as those on the continent."[82]

During the brief Second Republic, Schoelcher fought to realize abolition in the Antilles and the social vision of the 1848 revolution.[83] But his program stalled. Antillean administrators limited the scope of emancipation through new practices of censorship, surveillance, and socioeconomic regulation. The work requirement was strictly enforced and a system of tenant farming developed. Credit, indemnification, and land redistribution never materialized, nor were national workshops established overseas. Sugar production and the tax and tariff code remained unchanged. Immigrant labor was employed on the old plantations. Planters, the sugar industry, and colonial chambers of commerce resisted economic reforms while colonial administrators resisted the creation of a civil society and public sphere. In October and November 1848, the newly arrived commissars of the republic were replaced by colonial governors. Electoral fraud provoked uprisings, mass arrests, and the imprisonment of black socialists. Public safety became pretext for political repression; courts, trials, and prisons were employed as instruments of social control, especially in Guadeloupe, which in May 1850 was declared to be in a state of emergency, along with Martinique.[84]

By 1851 the revolutionary opening that Schoelcher helped to create was closed. Abolition failed to transform Antilleans into equal citizens and the colonies into proper departments governed by French common law. Nor was Antillean society reorganized through peasant cooperatives and freely associated labor. Instead, republican emancipation had created a hybrid form of colonial rule over quasi-citizens inhabiting demidepartments. This failure coincided with the more general eclipse of the revolutionary possibilities opened by 1848.

Schoelcher's utopian vision for the Antilles had been inseparable from the socialist order he hoped the revolution would create in metropolitan France. Since the 1830s, Schoelcher had collaborated with various republican clubs, journals, and militants, including socialist followers of Proudhon, Cabet, and Marx. Schmidt reports that on March 22, 1844, Schoelcher and Louis Blanc belonged to an International Committee of Democratic Propaganda that hosted a dinner for Marx, Ruge, and Bakunin.[85] As a politician Schoelcher advocated amnesty for the 1848 insurrectionists, prison reform, death penalty abolition, the right to work, public assistance,[86] universal suffrage, free and compulsory public education, a public health service, inexpensive rail transport, and new legal protections for women and children.[87] He called for a colonial declaration of human rights by European parliaments to ensure that all colonized peoples were subject to a rational and legitimate rule of law.[88] After the revolution, he corresponded with Mazzini about a unified international political organization to promote solidarity for the European-wide democratic struggle against authoritarianism.[89] And he joined his longtime republican ally Victor Hugo in advocating for a federalist "United States of Europe."[90] His commitment to revolutionizing socioeconomic relations within and between metropolitan France and the Antillean department was opposed not only by planters and metropolitan commercial interests with a stake in sugar production but by most republican politicians.

After abolition, government officials blamed a series of political uprisings in Martinique and Guadeloupe on a "Schoelcherism" they identified with anarchism and communism. But among Antilleans "Schoelcherism" signified the struggle to convert formal liberty into substantive freedom.[91] This was the Schoelcher that Aimé Césaire invoked between 1945 and 1948 during his own struggle to realize departmentalization. Césaire's invocations were untimely conjuring acts. As he later explained of his poetry, "In naming objects, it is an enchanted world, a world of *monsters*, that I make surge forth . . . a world of *forces* [*puissances*] that I summon, that I invoke, and that I convoke."[92]

The Spirit of Schoelcher

Césaire's Schoelcher differed from the domesticated icon that had been sanctified under the Third Republic. On July 13, 1948, the French state authorized Schoelcher's remains to be transferred from Père Lachaise to the Panthéon.[93] Several months earlier, Césaire, Senghor, and Gaston Monnerville participated in a centennial celebration of the abolition of slavery held at the Sorbonne. Most speakers, including Senghor and Monnerville, identified abolition as a triumph of republicanism. But Césaire refused to allow Schoelcher to be subsumed within the procedural tradition of parliamentary republicanism. Instead, Césaire identified him with a discredited tradition of revolutionary republicanism, with popular subaltern forces, including the metropolitan proletariat and the Antillean peasantry, whose 1848 insurrections ensured abolition.[94] Césaire thus *inflected* this commemoration; he claimed unrealized legacies to confront current conditions. A Parisian newspaper headline the following day declared "Incident at the Sorbonne. A Black Deputy [*deputé nègre*] Insults the French Bourgeoisie That Liberated his Ancestors."[95] Césaire's point, of course, was to question assumptions about liberation and filiation.

From Césaire's postwar vantage, Schoelcher's commitment to immediate, total emancipation was an untimely revolutionary act that challenged the dominant republican sentiment. Césaire noted the perverse nineteenth-century coexistence of Enlightenment and darkness; while European "poetry, science, and philosophy" blossomed, Africans were "hunted, tracked down, domesticated, transformed into an exportable commodity" and "branded with red irons . . . mutilated . . . hung and sold."[96] Césaire's point is that such barbarity was routinized and legitimate: "This is licit, normal. Everything is in order [*tout est dans l'ordre*]."[97] Schoelcher too was repelled by this contemporaneity of rationality and slavery. Referring to his own time, Césaire announced "we are aware of striking against institutions that, defying evolution and as if established against the current, outlive their reasons for being."[98]

Césaire recognized that the political opening for abolition was largely created by forces of popular rebellion. He cited an 1844 petition drafted by Schoelcher, wherein metropolitan workers expressed solidarity with colonial subjects by calling for immediate abolition. Césaire praised the "magnificent people of Paris" who deployed revolutionary republicanism *against* bourgeois republicans.[99] And he credited the direct action of Martinican slaves, whose rebellion anticipated the 1848 emancipation decree.[100]

But Césaire also identified Schoelcher as the rare public figure able to think beyond his own historical time by mobilizing science, philosophy, and ethics to challenge the specious pro-slavery arguments of politicians, businessmen, scholars, and theologians. He likewise noted Schoelcher's sensitivity to political timing. Whereas the 1948 commemoration identified slave emancipation as a natural development of French republicanism, Césaire contended that abolition was not inevitable; it depended on a properly timed revolutionary act. Schoelcher insisted that the Provisional Government abolish slavery immediately without deferring to a postrevolutionary assembly, which he predicted would be more concerned with reconstructing French society than with slave emancipation. Césaire saw this political urgency as inseparable from Schoelcher's belief that the 1848 revolutionaries were sovereign lawmakers who had a republican obligation to abolish, at the earliest possible instance, a criminal institution. He thus praised Schoelcher for recognizing that "to abolish slavery at this precise moment in French history required more than the vague good will of a few people, it required the revolutionary support of the will of a people and the inflexible lucidity of a political project [*une politique*]."[101]

Césaire reminded his audience that Schoelcher's lucid demand for immediate and unconditional abolition was a

> marvelous thing [*le merveille*]: these men who had climbed out of the abyss were not offered a diminished liberty; it was not a fragmented right; they were not offered an apprenticeship; they were not placed under observation, they were told: "My friends, for too long there has been an empty place at the assembly of humanity. It is yours." And in one stroke, we were offered total liberty, all rights, all duties, all enlightenment. And that indeed was the work of Victor Schoelcher.[102]

In a political instant, this dehumanized population suddenly "erupted onto the great stage of world history."[103]

Césaire also emphasized Schoelcher's commitment to building a postemancipation society, citing him as saying: "we are not proposing a one-day project . . . these are not a few vague improvements to throw at the islands like alms to a poor beggar . . . it is . . . a future to create . . . come what may!"[104] Schoelcher recognized "that to leave the *nègre* free but deprived in an anarchic head-to-head with a rich colonist would be to deliver black liberty to all the risks of a false democracy . . . where economic security does not exist, the basis of liberty is null . . . is rickety . . . it cracks and vacillates . . . [and is] crushed by its own weight."[105] Affirming Schoelcher's vision of a "second emancipation,"[106] Césaire recounted his desire "to facilitate the black proletariat's access to property and to transform the colonies into veritable peasant democracies," as well as "to transform the old colonies into French departments."[107] This lucid, revolutionary, audacious, principled, and strategic act was "a fruitful example willed to posterity."[108]

Césaire recalled that Schoelcher "tirelessly pursued the work that he had begun in 1848" with only "a single goal: to transform into real liberty, the formal liberty that he had seized for blacks from the colonial aristocracy."[109] Abolition, however, instituted new forms of labor servitude and racial domination. *Béké* socioeconomic power and property rights survived the political reorganizations, and there was no redistribution of land or wealth to former slaves. Social stratifications and racial taxonomies persisted, new processes of proletarianization emerged. Though slavery was disavowed, its legacy weighed heavily on everyday life, now organized around civic equality but suffused by fear and resentment among emancipated blacks and dispossessed whites.[110]

Schoelcher was a vocal critic of Louis-Napoléon Bonaparte and spent the Second Empire exiled in London.[111] He characterized the December 2, 1851, coup as one of the "sad days when humanity momentarily moves backward."[112] In April 1871 Schoelcher returned to the Third Republic and was elected to represent Martinique in the National Assembly. He also served on the government's Commission du Travail Colonial. But he failed to persuade the French state that abolition had to be accompanied by full citizenship, socioeconomic equality, and proper integration into a social republic.[113]

Césaire reclaimed Schoelcherian emancipation as an unrealized historical possibility. In language consistent with his Communist affiliation, he asserted that Schoelcher's incomplete efforts had paradoxically turned "the modern colonized [Antillean] into both a total citizen and a complete proletariat,"[114] an untimely contradiction that could propel a revolutionary form of departmentalization. Proclaiming "henceforth, on the shores of the Caribbean seas, the motor of history roars,"[115] he affirmed a Marxian understanding of historical transformation while challenging the idea that world history is made exclusively on the European continent. This phrasing also warned the imperial state that Antilleans were potential revolutionary subjects who would continue to shape postwar France. He declared Schoelcher a "clairvoyant" figure and "great initiator," whose "audacious act" remained relevant.[116] He insisted, "To evoke Schoelcher is not to invoke an empty ghost [vain fantôme]. It is to recall ... a man whose every word remains an explosive bullet. That his project is incomplete is only too evident."[117] Its untimely power resided precisely in its status as not yet complete: "what the decree of Victor Schoelcher brought to our fathers, the slaves of 1848, was the past repaired and the future prepared."[118]

Césaire thus reminded Martinicans of the ongoing contemporaneity of the 1848 emancipation. He called on them to emulate the freed slaves who "knew that henceforth ... they are masters of their history, for better or for worse ... by the very light of this past, they learn to consider that true emancipation is not that which is decreed, but that which man conquers for himself, that it is not behind them, but before them, and that it is up to them to prepare for it, in communion with the people of France, in the luminous wake of 1848."[119] Césaire here sought not to domesticate the memory but to mobilize the legacy of 1848, criticizing current conditions from the standpoint of Schoelcher's unrealized vision. His Schoelcher remained a "present man" with "qualities required by the seriousness of this moment."[120]

Césaire hailed Schoelcher as "the wisest man who ever took on the colonial question" and "the great initiator" whose work represents a "manual of dignity and bible of wisdom," especially valuable as "France . . . is worried about its own proper destiny, and asks itself how best to administer the thousands of men who live in what it is convenient to call the Empire."[121] Likewise, at a "moment when throughout the world the [colonial] question is no longer posed in academic terms, but with . . . machine gun fire . . . the great merit of Victor Schoelcher is . . . [his] present relevance [*actualité*]."[122] Employing radical remembrance against depoliticizing commemorations, Césaire sought to transform Schoelcher from national fetish into vital force, reminding the Parisian audience in 1948 that "it would be useless to commemorate [Schoelcher] if we had not decided to imitate his politics."[123]

This invocation constructed an implicit constellation between Schoelcher's abolition and Césaire's departmentalization. Both figures regarded legal emancipation as a catalyst for socioeconomic reorganization, through integration rather than separation, and both recalibrated political strategies as their constitutional initiatives failed adequately to address the problem of freedom. For Césaire, Schoelcher was not just a predecessor but an interlocutor, to be addressed rather than commemorated; his struggle for departmentalization was undoubtedly mediated by Schoelcher's unrealized vision.

Realizing Departmentalization

Postwar Martinique was characterized by antagonism between, on the one hand, unions, elected assemblies, and the general public and, on the other, the French state, the newly appointed *préfet*, metropolitan riot police, local gendarmes, employers, and planter elites. This spurred cycles of syndicalist mobilization, state violence, and social unrest. At stake was whether the government would extend all social laws to the overseas departments, whether Antillean workers would enjoy the same salaries and benefits of their metropolitan counterparts, and whether metropolitan funds would be used to expand social services and promote economic development. The crucial question was whether departmentalization would, in Césaire's formulation, "abolish [colonialism] through integration" or found a new system of quasi-colonial subjection.[124]

Although the French social security system had been established in October 1945, its provisions were not extended to overseas departments (DOM) until October 17, 1947.[125] Even then, only specific measures applied to the DOM, with uneven implementation. Martinicans discovered that specific metropolitan laws and benefits would have to be claimed through direct action and legislative struggle.[126]

While occupying Schoelcher's former seat as deputy from Martinique, Césaire pressured the French state to extend employment and social security provisions to the DOM. He also called for development initiatives, relating, "on the morning after the Liberation, the aspirations of Martinique, Guadeloupe, Réunion, and Guyane can be summarized by two ideas." First, "an end to the famous regime of decrees which subjected people ... to the arbitrary will of the governor." Second, "a policy of investment [*équipement*] and modernization that would allow our territories to escape the stagnation ... into which three centuries of the most mediocre policies had plunged them."[127]

On August 23, 1947, Pierre Trouille was named the first prefect to Martinique. Rather than end colonial rule, his appointment reproduced the arbitrary and authoritarian power of previous colonial governors.[128] Trouille diverted state funds, designated for schools, hospitals, day care, housing, public health, and urban cleanup, to improve the port and build an airport. He also mobilized police to restrict political expression, break strikes, punish militants, and interfere in local elections. He prohibited the mass demonstration planned to commemorate the hundredth anniversary of abolition, organized by the Municipality of Fort-de-France (Césaire's office) on April 27, 1948. When Martinicans resisted, Trouille sent police to attack the crowd and arrest its communist leaders. His government closed newspapers, fined dissidents, rounded up militants for arbitrary imprisonment, and imported Compagnies républicaines de sécurité (CRS) troops from the metropole to break up agricultural strikes. Local courts spent years trying Martinicans for crimes related to these strikes and protests. Trouille's imperial attitude and repressive tactics were maintained by his successor, Christian Laigret, who took office on March 7, 1951.[129]

Despite this repression, agricultural laborers, factory workers, and civil servants fought for the working conditions, labor protections, and social security benefits (including health, unemployment, and accident insurance, pensions, and family allocations) promised by departmentalization. Successful strikes were undertaken by dockers, cane cutters, distillery workers, metalworkers, employees of the electric utility and the Transat shipping company (Compagnie générale transatlantique), and public service workers. These last followed a thirty-three-day strike in March 1950 with the longest strike in Martinican history (65 days) in 1953. Among the victories were retirement benefits for salaried employees, employer contributions for social security benefits, pay equity for civil servants, and higher agricultural wages.[130] This mobilization was led by syndicalists, such as Victor Lamon and Albert Platon, and communists, notably Georges Gratient. Bissol and Césaire solicited the government on behalf of persecuted workers, protesters, and strikers.

Between 1946 and 1954, Césaire argued that republican legality required immediate and full implementation of departmentalization. Like Schoelcher, he employed the threat of insurrection to influence metropolitan legislators. Césaire regularly condemned the government's "negligence" and "indifference" towards the DOM and warned of mass disillusionment, social unrest, and revolutionary anticolonialism; he admonished, "we should not close our eyes and put ourselves to sleep with pretty phrases about the *oeuvre* that we accomplished in these countries in 1848 if, in 1948 or 1949, we are almost at the same point as we were in 1848."[131]

Initially Césaire blamed autocratic officials and calcified policies for this negligence and inaction. During a 1949 debate about funding public works in the DOM, Césaire declared, "we have had enough of these irresponsible administrators, of these proconsuls . . . [who] govern despotically."[132] He exhorted the state to better control prefects "chosen more for their obedience to a political party than for their competence or intelligence," who served "as the gravediggers of the French Union."[133] Using the future anterior tense, he observed that the state was creating a dangerous "contradiction . . . between the new political form that will have been given to these countries and the social, economic, and administrative reality that you will not have had the courage to modify, which will have remained colonial."[134] He warned that this "contradiction will intensify and explode before everyone's eyes. . . . I shudder at the fact that you march towards this catastrophe so unconsciously."[135] He addressed a speech to Minister of the Interior Jules Moch, criticizing French shortsightedness regarding the authoritarian regime of Pierre Trouille:

> Allow me to give you this warning. When, under the flag of assimilation and the pretext of standardization, you will have piled up injustice upon injustice, when it will be evident that instead of a true assimilation, you intend to only offer them a caricature, a parody of assimilation, then, you will provoke immense resentment in these territories. . . . You will have caused to be born in the hearts of Martinicans . . . and Guadeloupeans a new feeling that they had not known and for which you will bear historical responsibility, a sentiment whose consequences are unpredictable: you will have caused to be born among these men a . . . national feeling.[136]

In the first and second legislative sessions of the Fourth Republic, Césaire served on the committees for foreign affairs, national education, and overseas territories, for the latter leading a subcommittee, the Management of Investment Funds for the Social and Economic Development of Overseas Territories. He fought for extended retirement and unemployment benefits, accident and long-term-illness insurance, and family allocations, paying special attention to equalizing pay and benefits of overseas civil servants and to fair treatment of overseas teachers, regulation of longshoremen's working conditions, protections for agricultural cooperatives, tenants rights, and the unjust treatment of striking workers. He supported a national minimum wage applied to the Antilles, rent controls, nationalization of overseas banks, tax exemptions for overseas agricultural products, increased scholarships and funding for public works and economic modernization projects, emergency funds for victims of natural disasters, and measures to eliminate electoral fraud. He also introduced legislation to establish July 21, Victor Schoelcher's birthday, as an annual holiday in the DOM.[137]

Despite these efforts, his disillusionment mounted. In a 1953 parliamentary speech he denounced the government for having "forgotten" the law granting the DOM "abolition of [their] colonial status." They "only demanded one thing, but an essential thing . . . a new contractual status founded on nondiscrimination and equal rights between local populations and French citizens living in metropolitan France." Whereas other peoples sought to end colonialism through independence, "the aspiration of the inhabitants of the old colonies was to abolish it, yes, I said abolish, through integration." However, he explained, successive French governments "had nothing more urgent to do than empty the law of March 19, 1946 of its content, to denature and mutilate it." Thus the old colonies "became caricatures of French departments . . . because on the basis of atrocious poverty, economic stagnation, and unemployment, we have seen the specter of the old colonialism reappear, rejuvenated and fortified, with its trail of inequalities, prejudices, and oppression. . . . It is inadmissible that . . . the overseas departments constitute *départements d'exception*." Finally, "the populations of the overseas departments are resolved, come what may, to organize, to unite, to struggle until the rulers of this country finally decide to return [racial discrimination] to the museum of history."[138]

As late as February 1954 Césaire was embroiled in heated debate about extending French social insurance overseas. "How is this possible!" he thundered. "For eight years these countries have been departments and, until now, no effective application of any important social law has sanctioned this juridical transformation."[139] Departmentalization had been meant to "remedy the essential defects of an anachronistic social system that has afflicted these territories: two centuries of slavery replaced by a century of feudal capitalism! One cannot imagine a more persistent violation of the spirit of a law for which, at the time, Parliament voted unanimously."[140] He warned the assembly that the annual strikes of Martinican cane workers were the sign of "a social problem of exceptional gravity" born of "intolerable poverty," a problem that could not be ignored. He implored his colleagues to consider "the millions of people whose condition is an offense to humanity and who, if too proud to beg for some kind of pity, feel, however, authorized to claim your justice."[141]

After nearly a decade of government intransigence Césaire's analysis had shifted. He stopped criticizing the colonial attitudes obstructing departmentalization and developed a structural critique of socioeconomic inequality overseas. Defending embattled Martinican functionaries he explained that ongoing economic exploitation, antidemocratic governance, and social stratification in the Antilles was rooted in the "very structure of an iniquitous society founded on the right of some to the most hateful privileges and the shameless disregard [méconnaissance] of the rights and dignity of the many."[142] No amount of police repression, he argued, could resolve the problems created by this outmoded, illegitimate, and antirepublican system of domination. He marveled that the state remained pathologically attached to a "colonial ancien régime" that had already "expired."[143]

Césaire reminded his metropolitan counterparts that at the recent Pan-American Congress in Caracas, nineteen countries had called for immediate autonomy and eventual independence for all territories in the Western Hemisphere. The French government could not "prevent the birth of a great hope in our country,"[144] for colonialism had already been "condemned by history."[145] The only question was whether France would accommodate a free and equal overseas population or force them to create separate states.

Césaire no longer believed that the departmentalization law could abolish colonialism through integration. Although he still called for specific metropolitan laws to be applied overseas, his parliamentary interventions assumed a new tone. He began to enumerate the years of government refusal to implement the 1946 law. For years Césaire had argued that full departmentalization was necessary to alleviate poverty and social misery in Martinique. Now he suggested that departmentalization itself was their source. He concluded that departmentalization, originally a historic opening for substantive emancipation, had become an obstacle to it.

In 1948, Césaire had attributed to Schoelcher a "lucid view of the conditions of true liberty," claiming that "his grandeur is precisely in the fact that he knew not to be a prisoner of his own work, that he knew how to surpass [*dépasser*] it."[146] Césaire traced how Schoelcher's political vision evolved over time and insisted that the great abolitionist was the true progenitor of the 1946 departmentalization law.[147] One hundred years later, when departmentalization failed to ensure substantive freedom for Antilleans, Césaire similarly refused to be a prisoner of his own past creations. He too had a lucid understanding of liberty and a pragmatic approach to politics. As the radical possibilities opened by departmentalization were obstructed by the restricted regime of liberty that it actually established, Césaire revised his political project without abandoning his underlying goal: economic autonomy and political self-management within a multiracial social republic. He would quit the PCF, form an independent political party, and reject departmentalization in favor of autonomy through federalism.

From Historicity to Futurity

It might be tempting to conclude that as Césaire rejected departmentalization, his apparently moderate political program began to align more closely with his radical anticolonial writings. But I would suggest that the very claim that a text like *Discourse on Colonialism* was inconsistent with Césaire's parliamentary politics is premised on a misunderstanding of his radical hopes for departmentalization.

Césaire told biographer Georges Ngal that in 1950 he had been asked to write the article that became *Discourse on Colonialism* by a right-wing journal that assumed that because he supported departmentalization he would produce "an apology for the colonial enterprise." Instead, "What I said there, I had been thinking for a very long time. . . . I did not hold back and I said everything in my heart. It was done as a pamphlet and a bit like an article of provocation. It was . . . for me, the opportunity to say all that I had not managed to say in the tribune of the National Assembly."[148] One *could* read this recollection to mean that the *Discourse* revealed the unmentionable anticolonial convictions closest to Césaire's heart. However, the *Discourse* could also be read as revealing the radical sensibility that had always subtended Césaire's program for the abolition of colonialism through a process of transformative integration.[149]

Césaire's *Discourse* was initially provoked by France's severe response in January 1950 to political unrest in Côte d'Ivoire.[150] Occurring during the escalating war in Indochina, this event followed an anticolonial insurrection in Madagascar in 1947. Césaire's later poem "Time of Freedom," which commemorated the Côte d'Ivoire protests, indicates that he understood the violent character of the French state.[151] Whatever Césaire's limitations, he cannot be accused of being blind to or naive about colonial power.

Readers have rightly focused on the comparison in the *Discourse* between colonialism and Hitlerism. Césaire argued that Europeans were less concerned with crimes against *man* than with crimes against *white* men. Given that Europeans had tolerated colonialism for centuries, "before being the victim [of Nazism] they were its accomplice."[152] Both colonialism and Nazism entailed processes of lawful expropriation by strong nations for public purposes and were legitimized by prevailing systems of thought. Césaire thereby established a continuum linking "Western and Christian civilization," humanist ideology, bourgeois society, modern capitalism, colonial domination, and Nazism.[153] This equation allowed Césaire to argue that "between colonizer and colonized there is . . . no human contact, but relations of domination and submission that transform the colonizer into a pawn, an enforcer, an overseer, a switch and the native into an instrument of production."[154] Asserting that "colonization = thingification [*chosification*]," Césaire recounted how imperialism and proletarianization destroyed the potential of non-European civilizations which had produced democratic, cooperative, and fraternal societies.[155]

Moreover, for Césaire, colonialism dehumanized both perpetrators and victims. "The colonizer, to maintain his good conscience, gets used to seeing the other as an *animal*, learns to treat him as an *animal*, and tends objectively to transform himself into an *animal*."[156] At both the societal and the individual level, "colonization works to *decivilize* the colonizer, to *stupefy* [*abrutir*] him . . . to degrade him, to awaken in him buried instincts."[157] With every act of colonial brutality, "a universal regression occurs, a gangrene develops, a source of infection that spreads . . . poison is introduced into the veins of Europe and with slow but steady progress the continent proceeds toward savagery."[158] Thus Césaire can claim that "unable to justify itself before the bar of 'reason' or the bar of 'conscience' . . . *Europe is indefensible*."[159]

Although *Discourse*, was uncompromisingly anticolonial, it was not an absolute rejection of Western civilization from the standpoint of indigenous authenticity. Césaire developed a historical critique of European colonialism and capitalism, not a cultural critique of Europe as such; he identified potentialities immanent in both European and non-European societies. Defending himself against accusations that he was "an 'enemy of Europe' and a prophet of the return to the *pre*-European past," Césaire defied critics to find evidence that he "underestimated the importance of Europe in the history of human thought" or "claimed that there could be a *return*."[160]

We are not "either/or" people. For us, the challenge is not a utopian and sterile attempt to reduplicate but to supersede [dépassement]. We do not want to revive a dead society. . . . Nor do we want to prolong the existing colonial society. . . . We need, with the help of our brother slaves, to create a new society, rich with modern productive power and warm with ancient fraternity.[161]

Rather than reject modernity from the standpoint of primordial Africanity, Césaire imagined an alternative process of modernization whereby the communal and democratic possibilities that inhered within African civilizations could be nourished through noncoercive forms of contact with Europe. This new society could overcome colonialism and promote "true humanism—a humanism that fits the world [à la mesure du monde]."[162] The challenge was how to transcend both current colonialism and traditional society without erecting rigid boundaries between Europe and Africa or the Antilles—to find the political form that would best enable this true humanism.

For Césaire modern colonialism, like Roman imperialism, was "preparing *Disaster* and the harbinger of *Catastrophe* . . . all this wreckage, all this waste, humanity reduced to a monologue . . . [which] *cannot but bring about the ruin of Europe itself*."[163] But rather than oppose European imperialism with Antillean nationalism, Césaire petitioned Europe for a new partnership though which colonizers and colonized could save each other from subjugation by the United States, which embodied a "modern Barbarism" of "violence, excess, waste, mercantilism . . . stupidity, vulgarity, and disorder."[164] For him, American capitalism represented a "prodigious mechanization, but of man, the massive rape of everything that our already despoiled humanity still knew how to preserve . . . a machine to crush, grind, and brutalize peoples."[165] It would be a tragic error for Europe or its colonial populations to substitute one form of dehumanizing capitalist colonialism for another. The task was to find a viable alternative to European colonialism *and* American capitalism that would allow colonizers and colonized to recognize their common predicament without recourse either to the abstract humanism that authorized colonialism or the parochial nationalism that would obstruct the creation of a *true* humanism made to the measure of the world.

The *Discourse* sketched out just such an alternative, declaring that Europe's "salvation" depended on its becoming "the awakener of countries and civilizations" through a new "*nationalities* policy . . . founded on the respect of peoples and cultures."[166] This "last chance" for Europe depended on a revolutionary proletariat, "the only class that still has a universal mission, because in its flesh it suffers from all the harms of history, from all the universal wrongs."[167] Grounding his humanist program in lived particularity, like Mazzini, Césaire promoted nationalities while rejecting nationalism, calling on colonizers to act in partnership with colonized peoples to create a postimperial and culturally plural society. At that point he still hoped that departmentalization could be a means to this end.

Critics have found it difficult to reconcile the *Discourse*'s uncompromising critique of colonialism with Césaire's willingness to cooperate with the French state through the assembly. But I would suggest that this apparent contradiction between the radical pamphleteer and the moderate parliamentarian is premised on a methodological nationalism that presumptively equates colonial emancipation with state sovereignty. Of course there were tensions between Césaire's legislative initiatives and his political criticism. And his political projects were often contradictory. He was a multifaceted thinker, operating on many fronts, confronting a difficult set of imperfect political alternatives. But rather than wonder how to reconcile his anticolonial criticism and his parliamentary politics, presumed to be at odds, we could instead ask how they may have been complementary means to the same end. Both envisioned a transformed future whose political framework and cultural configuration could not yet be known.

In *Discourse* Césaire refers to French bourgeois consciousness as a "forgetting device" [*oublioir*] repeatedly unlearning what its own science had already discovered about the sophisticated character of non-European civilizations.[168] In contrast, Césaire's pamphlet remembers both the value of these civilizations and the colonial processes by which they were destroyed. It also seeks to "remember" a future that *might have been* if colonized societies had been free to realize their potentialities through peaceful reciprocal interaction with other civilizations. Césaire's pluricultural vision of a mutualist modernity without colonial domination was both a conjured future past and an envisioned world to come. This suggests that Césaire's affiliation with communism was less about Soviet orthodoxy or historical materialism than about faith in a revolutionary multitude comprising colonial peoples *and* metropolitan workers, *both* of whom had inherited the legacies of slave insurrections *and* antibourgeois revolutions. Césaire's *Discourse* was an act of cosmopolitan remembering and anticipation that worked through the ruins of a dehumanizing modernity.

Similarly Césaire's postwar poems repeatedly invoke temporal ruptures and stage dramas of genesis whether as the origins of life, the beginnings of history, or the making and ending of worlds.[169] Though rarely referencing concrete events, this is a revolutionary poetry that figures interruption, transformation, emergence, creation, and awakening. Césaire's charged poetic images tack between and, thereby, demonstrate the inextricable relations between concrete, embodied, and worldly dimensions of existence, on the one hand, and transcendent or cosmological phenomena, on the other. This is also a poetry of untimeliness where conventional distinctions between past, present, and future do not obtain; memory and futurity, reality and imagination, are dialectically entwined.

Cutthroat Sun (*Soleil cou coupé*, 1948; published in English translation as *Solar Throat Slashed*) overflows with images of living pasts that haunt, erupt into, or are conjured in a present opening. The speaker in "The Griffin" announces, "I am a memory that does not reach the threshold . . . I reascend to haunt the sinister thickness of things."[170] Another poem invokes the "Barbarity / of the dead circulating in the veins of the earth / who at times come and break their heads against the walls of our ears / and the screams of revolt never heard / which turn in tune with musical tones."[171] Insofar as haunting memories persist and the dead insist on being heard, these poems express the peculiar political temporality of the postwar period. Actors are visited, seized by, and sometimes overcome by *revenants* even as they also conjure them deliberately (as Césaire did with Schoelcher and Toussaint).

"To Africa / for Wifredo Lam" stages the actuality of transgenerational amity. It begins elegiacally by invoking an apocalyptic past of plague, famine, and mass death. The speaker enjoins a toiling peasant to "strike Anger . . . let your act be a wave that howls and regathers toward the hollow of cherished / rocks as if to perfect an island rebelling against birth / there is in the ground the scruple of a tomorrow and the burden of speech as well as silence." In this poetic image a devastated peasant's hoe scrapes ground that is the (remembered?) scene of a violent history. It is not clear whether the setting is Africa or the Antillean island against whose birth the peasant is rebelling. His ineffective cultivation becomes an act of remembering that merges with that of the poet scratching paper with pen. By the end of the poem this blurring of tenses is complete: "strike peasant I am your son . . . but the beautiful messenger ostrich . . . beckons me out of the future in friendship."[172] Here the poet's act of reaching across time to the laboring peasant as father, or recognizing in peasant labor a certain living relationship with the past and connection to a suffering history that is also the poet's own, shifts to an image of a messenger from the future (perhaps that very peasant) who greets the poet, now a past figure, in friendship.

In "Noon Knives," we glimpse the metamorphosis of anger into salvation through an imagined black revolt in Paris. "When les Nègres make Revolution they begin by uprooting giant trees from the Champ de Mars." The poet may be recalling a time before this public park became a military training ground and was an unenclosed commons of small gardens for Parisian citizens. Perhaps he conjures its past as the scene of revolutionary festivals and counter-revolutionary massacres; antagonisms obscured by its cultivated facade. The poem's imagined revolution is less a violent triumph than an arrival and reconciliation: a "solar jubilation" and a "sumptuous noon which makes me absent from this world." It is "a day for our fraternal feet / a day for our hands without rancor / a day for our breath without diffidence / a day for our faces free of shame." The poem ends with an image of revolutionary labor, simultaneously infinitesimal and infinite: "and les Nègres go searching in the dust . . . for the splinters from which mica is made as well as moons and the fissile slate out of which sorcerers make the infinite ferocity of the stars."[173] This marvelous and miraculous prospect of creating something new from a catastrophic situation with no apparent exit may be one interpretation of Césaire's statement, at once earnest and tongue in cheek, that "No circle is ever vicious."[174]

The poems in *Lost Body* (*Corps perdu*, 1950) also relate politics and time, revolutionary rupture and embodied memories, and beginnings and ends. In "Howling" the speaker announces, "My time shall come and I hail it / a time fast / and simple as the sea / in which each word shall radiate [. . .] then— the origin of time / then—the end of time / and the erect majesty of the original eye."[175] This suggestion that revolutionary transformation not only occurs *in* time but operates *on and through* time is echoed in "Summons," a poetic charter for Césaire's temporally mediated utopian politics. "Space conquered Time the conqueror / me I like time time is nocturnal / and when Space galloping sets me up / Time comes back to set me free / Time Time / oh creel without venison summoning me." In the postwar opening Césaire indeed summoned time—the spirit of Schoelcher, the future past of abolition—and was summoned by time—by historical opportunity and the preceding generations of which he was an heir. When Antilleans seemed to be conquered by the spatial organization of departmentalization, Césaire again summoned time to liberate them—by conjuring the legacy of Toussaint Louverture, like a village asleep at the bottom of a well, whose memory ascended in order to haunt the thickness of things and whose voice crashed against the walls of his ears.

SIX Federalism and the Future of France

The history of man is to make the abstract universal concrete. . . . The process is
molecular, day by day never resting, continuous. But at a certain stage, the continuity is
interrupted. The molecular changes achieve a universality and explode into a new quality,
a revolutionary change. —CLR JAMES

"Senghor" or Senghor?

In the decade following independence a reductive understanding of Senghor's
thinking and politics calcified. Images of him as a racial essentialist, servile
Francophile, and neocolonial comprador informed scholarship long after the
political conditions that generated them disappeared. Senghor is not beyond
criticism, but the uncritical way these petrified and politicized images have
been embraced obstructs the serious engagement his postwar interventions
warrant.

Consider Sékou Touré's comments on September 11, 1973. In the context
of accusations that Senegal was harboring dissidents plotting a coup against
the government of Guinée, Sékou Touré denounced Senghor and Félix
Houphouët-Boigny as "traitors to Africa" and called on Muslims across the region to "condemn these agents of imperialism, colonialism, and Zionism in
order to reduce them to nothingness."[1] Such epithets—and a tendency to
lump Senghor with Houphouët-Boigny as a conservative collaborator, usually
on the grounds that he was not a revolutionary nationalist—became common
in the postcolonial period.

Around the same time, Cameroonian philosopher Marcien Towa denounced Senghor's ideas. A generation younger than Senghor, Towa wrote a
DES thesis on Hegel and Bergson at Caen in 1960 and a doctoral thesis at

the Sorbonne on Negritude in 1969. In 1971 Towa remarked, "we cannot but notice the almost term by term correspondence between colonial racism and the framework that Senghor calls 'negritude.' Both affirm the congenital and irremediable irrationality of the *nègre*, his instinctiveness, his sensuality, his emotionality, in both cases they deduce from this convenient psychology the need for his subordination."[2] Senghor's assertions about civilizational distinctions were often dubious, but he never claimed, as Towa suggests, that black people were incapable of reason and unfit for science. Nor did he ever "invite, in the name of biological fatality, [Africans] to bow before European superiority," let alone defend "the legitimacy of colonization."[3] Noteworthy is Towa's assertion of a "perfect correspondence" between Senghor's claims about "the cognitive value of emotion and sensuality," his "vehement defense of colonization," his "opposition to any idea of independence," and his "notion of the 'complementarity' between Europe and Africa."[4] Because Senghor called for a democratic union of peoples rather than political independence, Towa could only regard him as an apologist for colonialism.[5]

Similar assumptions informed Frantz Fanon's more sophisticated and influential critique of Senghor and the Negritude project. In the opening chapter of *Wretched of the Earth*, Fanon invokes Senghor as an archetypal "colonized intellectual"—a "vulgar opportunist" and "mimic man" who instrumentalizes the voice of "the people" to whom he has no authentic connection.[6] Fanon's colonized intellectual remains slavishly attached to the "Western values . . . implanted" in his mind by the "colonialist bourgeoisie."[7] This, Fanon suggests, is why President Senghor refused to properly decolonize Senegal.[8]

In his presentation at the Second International Congress of Black Artists and Writers in 1959, Fanon challenged the assembled "bards of Negritude" for failing to recognize that "every culture is first and foremost national."[9] He claimed these intellectuals stood in an "outsider's relationship" to their people.[10] Rather than participate in "dense subterranean life in perpetual renewal," they treated culture "like a foreigner," assembling an "inventory of particularisms" and becoming preoccupied with "inert" and "mummified fragments" that were "reified" as "custom" and "tradition."[11] Fanon accused them of choosing the past over the future by neglecting present conditions and struggles,[12] specifically Algeria's demand for independence. He concluded that their conferences on "Negro-African culture" and "the cultural unity of Africa" were exercises in empty mystification.[13]

From this perspective Fanon declares, "now the moment has come to denounce certain pharisees. Humanity, some say, has got past the stage of nationalist claims. The time has come to build larger political unions, and consequently the old-fashioned nationalists should correct their mistakes. We believe on the contrary that the mistake, heavy with consequences, would be to miss out on the national stage" for "national consciousness is the highest form of culture."[14] Challenging Senghor and his federalist colleagues, Fanon argued that "national consciousness is alone capable of giving us an international dimension" and that if nation building "expresses the will of the people . . . it will necessarily lead to the discovery and advancement of universalizing values."[15] Fanon's claim that international solidarity and universal values should be mediated by the development of particular national cultures is legitimate. But on what grounds does he insist that one is the *necessary* route to the other or that any arrangement other than national independence is one in which "colonialism still lingers"?[16] These assumptions prevented him from engaging the substance of Senghor's interest in nonnational paths toward the goal that Fanon himself famously identified in *Wretched of the Earth*:

> Let us reexamine the question of man . . . of humanity in its entirety . . . let us not pay tribute to Europe by creating states, institutions, and societies that draw their inspiration from it. Humanity expects other things from us than this grotesque and generally obscene emulation . . . if we want humanity to take a step forward, if we want to take it to another level than the one where Europe has placed it, then we must innovate, we must be pioneers. . . . For Europe, for ourselves, and for humanity, comrades, we must make a new start, develop a new way of thinking, and endeavor to create a new man.[17]

Fanon *and* Senghor linked colonial emancipation to human emancipation. One treated authentic national consciousness and a sovereign national state as necessary for a new internationalism. The other began with social interdependence and cultural reciprocity as the basis for new forms of transcontinental solidarity and postnational democracy. Which would represent new thinking and which emulation? I am not suggesting that Fanon was wrong about Algerian independence. And his prescient critique of neocolonialism among independent African states was on target. But the revolutionary situation from which he wrote left him unable or unwilling to recognize real affinities between his and Senghor's radical humanist objectives; he did not address the political future that Senghor actually envisioned for Africa. The fact that this unwillingness has continued to afflict many subsequent critics is more difficult to accept. In a given situation, the identity of the supposed pharisee is not always self-evident.

Writing about the anticolonial student movement in Paris in the 1950s, Samir Amin recounts that his cohort met regularly with the older generation of African party leaders, trade unionists, and elected officials about the "burning issues of the day."[18] He recalls,

> most important of all, perhaps, was the opportunity that these meetings provided to discuss basic strategic issues. What did we want? What should be the aims of the anticolonialist struggle: independence, assimilation, or a "genuine French union" involving a more or less federal multinationalist state? Today it may seem that the only progressive option was independence, but things looked more complex at that time, especially in the period between 1946 and 1950.[19]

For these young radicals, the best political framework for African emancipation was an open question. Amin invites us to remember that

> the PCF's strategic objective, at least in 1946, was to build a "genuine" people's French Union, highly centralized and homogeneous in its social-economic organization but diverse in respect of the nations composing it—in other words, a multinational socialist state along the lines of the USSR. I do not know if that would have been feasible, but in any case it was not what history wanted to happen. It certainly would have involved economic sacrifices for the French people to help the ex-colonies catch up.[20]

Amin notes that most African leaders with whom they spoke about decolonization had "no strategic vision; they were tacticians and nothing more."[21] Whereas these matters made both Houphouët-Boigny and Sékou Touré "yawn," Senghor and his Sudanese colleague (and critic) Gabriel d'Arboussier "shared the strategic objective of a multinational state in which the former colonies would be associated with France, [d'Arboussier] believing that this would happen through socialist revolution in France, [and Senghor] that it could be achieved through gradual evolution. Curiously, therefore, Senghor was at least in this respect closer to the Communist Party than one might think."[22] Amin explains that it was only *after* this prospect of a socialist and multinational people's union was blocked by the French right that "young Africans took the initiative of declaring independence as the strategic goal."[23] Amin's memories suggest that if we are to stop rehashing shibboleths about pharisees, we need to revisit Senghor's political project from the perspective of the postwar opening and think with him about that openness.[24]

Constitutional Acts

Upon his release from the POW camp in 1944, Senghor was more interested in a career as a scholar and poet than a politician. But after the Liberation, he agreed to serve on the Monnerville Commission, a body charged by the Provisional Government with making proposals regarding political representation for colonial peoples in the upcoming Constituent Assembly. Then in October 1945, on behalf of the Senegalese section of the French Socialist Party (SFIO), he and his political mentor, Lamine Guèye, were elected to this assembly.[25]

In his first public statements Senghor exploited the opening that the Liberation had created for ending colonialism *and* transforming the republic. He leveraged de Gaulle's desire to distance ordinary French people from Vichy collaborators by invoking the political debt owed by the state to Africans who fought for the French nation during the war.[26] Senghor informed the Constituent Assembly that "bureaucrats brag about their status as *résistants* in order to resist the emancipation of overseas peoples. I ask you . . . the black troops that . . . for two years constituted the bulk of Free French Forces . . . were they too not *résistants*? For us, there is only one resistance that counts, it is the resistance against the Nazi spirit."[27] In an interview several months later, Senghor expressed his "hope that metropolitan French people, now that they have known the torments of occupation and racist measures, will better understand the iniquity of their colonial system."[28] He announced that Africans would no longer accept their status as "subjects" under "a regime of occupation" and warned "whites of our unshakeable will to win our independence . . . by any means, even violent. I do not think that France which just eliminated Hitlerian racism can reproach us for this decision."[29] Despite this warning, Senghor neither endorsed violence nor pursued national independence for African territories. Rather, he became a critic of national autarchy and a tireless advocate for federalism within a framework that would bind metropolitan and overseas societies within a new transcontinental polity.

Hopes that the colonial relationship might be reformed after the war had been raised by the Brazzaville Conference (1944). In his opening speech, de Gaulle declared "concerning the life of the world of tomorrow, autarchy would neither be desirable nor possible for anyone."[30] He thereby discouraged colonial ambitions for national independence *and* indicated that metropolitan assumptions about national sovereignty might have to be revised. The conference resolution declared that "The aims of the civilizing work accomplished by France in the Colonies, RULE OUT ANY IDEA OF AUTONOMY, ANY POSSIBILITY OF EVOLUTION OUTSIDE OF THE FRENCH IMPERIAL

BLOC; THE EVENTUAL CONSTITUTION, EVEN IN THE FAR FUTURE, OF SELF-GOVERNMENT IN THE COLONIES IS RULED OUT."[31] But this rejection of self-government was paired with a pledge that France's colonies would henceforth "enjoy great economic and administrative liberty" as they became more and more "associated with the management of public affairs in their countries."[32] Similar promises of colonial reform had been made repeatedly by the French state since the end of World War I. But the Brazzaville resolution did so in a new federalist idiom. It proposed creating a Federal Assembly that would correspond to a new French Federation. The metropolitan state was referred to as "the federating organ" which would now allocate some of its powers to the overseas territories.[33]

Subsequent struggles over the French Union would be animated by the question that the Brazzaville conference both raised and elided: Would the postwar republic be a unitary state with absolute sovereignty over juridically subordinate colonial territories? Or would it become a decentralized federal republic in which former colonies would enjoy legal equality and political autonomy as associated members?

In a 1945 article in *Esprit*, Senghor criticized the French state for retreating from the opening signaled by Brazzaville.[34] He remarked that although African soldiers had fought for France, been interned in German camps, and sacrificed their lives in the Resistance, the Liberation had been followed by "particularly eloquent silences" about African colonialism.[35] He recalled that following the conference administrators in French Africa had been instructed to institute a series of colonial reforms without waiting for a new constitution, but had not done so. He contended that there had been "no serious reform," that "the spirit of Vichy seems to still reign; a paternalist, not to say racist, spirit," and that Africans are treated "like vulgar collaborators."[36] Protesting the fact that "Negro-Africans continued to be under the 'domination' of Metropolitans and non-Africans," Senghor insisted, "we demand justice, for others and equally for ourselves."[37]

After challenging racist evolutionary theories and recounting how African literature, art, morality, religion, and social organization were deformed by nineteenth-century colonialism, Senghor declared that "the 'good Negro' is dead; the paternalists should begin mourning."[38] He elaborated,

> you asked for our cooperation to remake a France to the measure of Man and the universal. We accept, but the metropole must not delude itself or attempt to con us. *We want a cooperation of dignity and honor* without which it would only by Vichyist "kollaboration." We have had our fill of

good words—to the point of nausea . . . we now need acts of justice. . . .
We are not separatists, but we want equality in *la cité*.[39]

He concluded by outlining his hopes for a new constitutional "federation" based on "the liberty and equality . . . of peoples and races" in which the metropole will "allow autochthones themselves to modify their institutions," that there be local and federal assemblies with "deliberative" rather than mere "consultative" power, that overseas peoples be eligible for all civil service jobs with equal compensation, that Africans be protected by the same common laws and courts as Europeans, that forced labor be abolished, and that educational reforms be introduced. Senghor was clear: "we will not dissimulate, this is a revolutionary program. But either the Fourth Republic will be the heir of the First and Second Republics, and it will be revolutionary by liberating all the 'colonized' . . . or it will merely be like the Third, capitalist, imperialist, 'occupiers,' and it will risk having the revolution turn against it."[40] Acknowledging that "representatives of [capitalist] trusts" will call him anti-French, he closed by intoning that "the people of France have everything to gain [by following his plan for cooperation] but the financial powers do not."[41] This commitment to self-management, cultural autonomy, and full citizenship in a nonracial democratic polity guided Senghor's efforts to define the new union and federal republic during the Constituent Assembly.

Senghor interpreted the Brazzaville statements about federation as a charter for a new form of postimperial democracy. Most metropolitans, however, understood them in imperial terms.

An article in the same issue of *Esprit* by Robert Delavignette, "The French Union: On the Scale of the World to the Measure of Man" (dedicated to Senghor), explained how the very concept of a French Union was elaborated in March 1945. In response to Japan's seizure of Indochina, the French state offered the "Federation of Indochina" the status of "proper liberty" within a new political union, the terms of which would be specified by the Constituent Assembly. Despite Delavignette's ardent language about this "organic unity" and "new form of life" producing a "new humanism" based on civilizational cooperation and exchange, his was a vision of *cultural* solidarity. Unlike Senghor, he did not enumerate specific legal or political proposals. Moreover, he suggested that there might still be governors-general overseas and he supported the concept of "citizen of the French Union" modeled on the Roman Empire.[42]

Seemingly minor but politically significant differences separated the type of French Union proposed by the April 1946 draft of the constitution, which was rejected in a national referendum, and the union that was instituted by the October 1946 constitution.[43] The April draft declared that "France constitutes, with its overseas territories, on the one hand, and the associated states, on the other, a Union of freely consenting parties."[44] Articles extended full citizenship to all peoples of the union and allowed them to elect deputies to the National Assembly by universal suffrage. Unless otherwise stated, all French laws would apply overseas automatically; other articles allowed overseas populations to retain their particular "personal" status, so that they could be governed under local civil law codes, and provided for territorial assemblies.

Many in the assembly who approved the draft regarded the union as a way to preserve the empire and preempt national liberation movements. The idea of a French Union had first been proposed by the Provisional Government on March 24, 1945, as a desperate attempt to retain sovereignty over Indochina.[45] When, three months later, French officials signed the UN Charter, they accepted a "sacred trust" to promote self-government for colonized countries.[46] Because the union form implied that overseas territories were willing partners rather than subjugated colonies of the metropolitan state, France could claim to comply with the charter while avoiding UN restrictions regarding colonialism. Yet it was also plausible for colonized peoples to hope that this constitution, which promised full citizenship *and* local self-government within a democratic union, could lead to a postimperial polity. Despite the evident dangers of formal affiliation with a reconstituted France, especially after so many decades of false promises of reform, this federalist blueprint was broadly supported by deputies from the overseas territories and departments.[47]

On April 5 1946, when Senghor, on behalf of the Commission de la Constitution, presented the articles on the French Union for debate in the Constituent Assembly, he called the new charter an "act of faith in the Republic." He described how the revolutionary events of 1789 and 1848 led to the abolition of slavery and the recognition of colonial territories as integral parts of the republic. He recounted that they also marked the triumph of a Jacobin tradition through which assumptions about the unitary state the politics of assimilation, and universal civilization became entrenched. The French Union, Senghor suggested, would extend the emancipatory aspects of these legacies while transcending their unitary aspects through a federal system that ended colonialism, extended citizenship, and granted autonomy. This new political form would also build upon recent ethnological insights about the multiplicity and historicity of world civilizations. He quoted (without naming) philosopher Roger Caillois's *Le Rocher de Sisyphe* (1942) to conclude that "civilization and history are essentially fluid phenomena." Against the "poison of Nazism that continues to gangrene the universe" through "antagonistic imperialisms, nationalist passions, and race struggles," Senghor proffered the union as "an example for the world . . . where peoples of diverse cultures, religions, languages, and races will know how to live freely, equally, and fraternally." At the same time, he conceded that the commission was unable to resolve and so deferred the question of whether the new constitution would recognize overseas peoples as proper "French citizens" or mere "citizens of the French Union."[48]

According to historian C. Bruce Marshall, there was widespread agreement between overseas and metropolitan deputies about the shape of the proposed union.[49] This Constituent Assembly was dominated by Communist and Socialist parties who supported it as well.[50] Given colonized peoples' wartime loyalty, many French policymakers believed that the colonial relationship should be revised. This had already been expressed in a series of laws passed by the assembly in 1946. In addition to the departmentalization law there was the May 7, 1946, Lamine Guèye Law, which extended formal citizenship to all overseas inhabitants of the union, and acts that abolished forced labor, created a new system for development aid through the Fond d'investissement pour le développement économique et sociale des territoires d'outre-mer (FIDES), and strengthened territorial assemblies in the colonies.[51]

Despite this climate of consensus the draft constitution was rejected in a May 5 national referendum.[52] Between the first and second rounds of constitutional deliberations, following the June 1946 elections to a Second Constituent Assembly, the Christian-democratic Mouvement républicain populaire (MRP) eclipsed the Communists as the dominant political party.[53] Vietnam was winning its war of national liberation, and negotiations with Ho Chi Minh were faltering. Representatives of pro-colonial commercial and settler interests had formed a lobbying group, the États-généraux de la colonisation, which promoted a different kind of French Union that would protect the state's imperial authority. And de Gaulle publicly declared his opposition to a federalist union that might compromise metropolitan sovereignty over colonial territories. Legislators had earlier agreed that the articles regarding the more democratic French Union would not be revisited during a second Constituent Assembly. But these pressures led Georges Bidault, the MRP president of the Provisional Government, to support revising the plan for the French Union.[54]

Between April and September 1946, several legislative proposals circulated that would have made the union a new charter for colonialism.[55] In order to counterbalance the growing influence of pro-imperial policy and opinion makers, a group of colonial deputies still committed to the provisions of the April draft formed a parliamentary coalition called the Indépendants d'outre-mer (IOM).[56] In June 1946 this group called on France to renounce its unilateral sovereignty over colonized peoples. It proposed a plan that defined the union as "a federation of nations and peoples who freely agree to coordinate or combine their resources and their efforts to develop their respective civilizations, to increase their well-being, to perfect their democratic institutions, and to assure their security."[57] It would grant all overseas peoples full French citizenship, significant powers of self-government through local territorial assemblies selected by universal suffrage, and the ability to send democratically elected representatives to a federal Assembly of the Union.[58] But this proposal, supported by the Commission des Colonies, provoked opposition from the Provisional Government, the MRP, the Socialist Party, and Gaullist conservatives.[59]

During the September 18 debate in the assembly, Senghor argued that in order to be democratic the Fourth Republic would have to become a "true federation" or "Union of French Socialist Republics" in which former colonies would be self-governing autonomous states.[60] He distinguished this "true federalism" from the "dangerous" plans for an undemocratic "airless federalism" [fédéralisme poussif] then being promoted by reactionary lobbyists serving the "private interests" of "financial oligarchies."[61] Senghor challenged critics who argued that "black barbarians" could not participate in national politics because they were "not French,"[62] pointing out that overseas territories were legally integrated into France and that the concept of popular sovereignty required all members of a state be granted equivalent rights to fashion legislation to which they would be subject. Accordingly, he argued that the "sovereign assembly" of the French republic cannot be a mere "metropolitan assembly."[63] He explained that excluding Africans from the republican polity based on the fiction they were not French invidiously invoked culture to restrict citizenship. In contrast, he called for a democratic federation built upon the premise of cultural diversity. He simultaneously criticized monoculturalism from the standpoint of plural democracy and criticized unitary republicanism from the standpoint of cultural plurality.

Senghor's argument was based on four propositions. First, the world is composed of many distinct civilizations, "each of which places the accent on a singular aspect of the human condition." Second, every great civilization is a "cultural crucible" and "devouring factory" that requires a "constant influx of human raw materials and foreign contributions." Third, imperialism created a situation of intense cultural interaction through which metropolitan and African peoples had a historic opportunity to "fertilize" themselves. Finally,

Senghor announced, "together we will create a new civilization, whose center will be in Paris, a new humanism ... on the scale of the universe and of humanity."[64] He maintained that although empire had created the possibility for a new federal democracy, it could only be realized if "we rid ourselves once and for all of the seeds of imperialism that, at our invitation, Nazism planted within us. Hitler is dead; we must all kill the piece of him that lives within us."[65] In his view, an "equal Union of French Socialist Republics" would entail both the end of colonialism *and* the rejection of autarchy. It would require "cooperation between civilizations" as well as "active assimilation" by each.[66]

Senghor reasoned that imperialism had created relations of interdependence between metropolitan and overseas societies and established precedents for France as a multicultural nation, multinational state, or transcontinental formation in which legal pluralism was institutionalized. Given this history, a truly democratic union could be realized only through a postcolonial federation that granted both French citizenship *and* self-government to formerly colonized peoples. "The first task of our Assembly," Senghor argued, "should be ... to create local democratic assemblies" through which each overseas "country" could establish its own appropriate laws and constitution.[67] This union of peoples would require and enable civilizational reciprocity, expanding and exploding the very meaning of "France" by sublating both colonialism and unitary republicanism.

Senghor's rhetoric simultaneously veiled and expressed this transformative ambition. He characterized the union as "a familial home, where, without a doubt, there will be an elder [*un aîné*], but where brothers and sisters will truly live in equality ... For the French Union to be durable, it must ... be founded on liberty and equality, conditions of human fraternity, of French fraternity."[68] This affirmation of republican principles did not clearly betray an intention to radically alter the existing republican order—Senghor's reference to an "elder" even suggested that the metropole would be a cultural mentor or political leader. He thus appealed simultaneously to conservatives concerned with retaining the empire, moderates who wanted to liberalize colonial rule, and radicals who hoped to transform it. He reassured metropolitans that he was proposing modest measures through which to maintain overseas peoples' attachment to France and preempt revolutionary nationalism from developing. Countering the government's claim that allowing colonies to become autonomous states within a democratic union would plant "the seeds of secession," Senghor maintained that "trust generates trust and it is not the presence of certain revolutionary words ... that will provoke secession, but the nonapplication, overseas, of democratic principles."[69] But for Senghor, liberty and equality in the union could exist only within the framework of a truly democratic federation that would by definition end empire and reconstitute France as a plural republic. In other words, he affirmed the republican tradition in a radically literalist manner.

Senghor's parliamentary poetics were deliberately economical, multivalent, and allusive. Consider his invocation of the French revolutionary legislators who had argued in 1792 that overseas French nationals would have to be fully integrated into the republican polity. Senghor declared, "this is not the first time . . . that the Great Ancestors—and they are, for me also, my spiritual ancestors—give us proud lessons in democracy."[70] Here Senghor pledged fidelity to the French republican legacy while mobilizing its revolutionary tradition against the existing republican order. He thereby challenged the assumption that the republic necessarily *belonged* to white metropolitans. By suggesting that as a republican member of the French nation, he was a rightful heir to, and had a legitimate claim on, the legacy of *his* revolutionary "ancestors," he deracialized the very concept of filiation. At the same time, he offered his metropolitan colleagues a lesson in French history, reminding them that the unitary state was a contingent creation.

Much of this debate about the constitution revolved around provisions concerning citizenship, sovereignty, and consent.[71] Whereas the colonial deputies insisted that all overseas peoples be automatically granted full French citizenship, the government wanted to establish a separate citizenship of the French Union, which would grant basic civil and political rights to residents of the colonies as French nationals but would not recognize them as full citizens. The category "citizens of the union" would legalize separate electorates through a racially discriminatory double electoral college system, ensuring that a disproportionate number of white colonials would continue to be represented in the National Assembly and in local assemblies.

The IOM deputies insisted on a single electoral college system based on free and equal universal suffrage: one person, one vote. They demanded that relevant metropolitan laws be automatically applied overseas, that territorial assemblies be granted substantive governing powers over local affairs, and that overseas delegates be equally represented in a federal Assembly and Council of the Union. They proposed that these bodies be granted concrete decision-making powers over matters of common concern. In contrast, the government sought to reserve a quasi-colonial role for administrative intermediaries who would formulate special laws and thereby create an exceptional legal regime overseas. It intended to limit the powers of territorial assemblies and to restrict the union assembly to an advisory role.

Whereas the government wanted to specify the exact legal terms of union membership, the IOM warned that this would legally fix the imperial status quo. Accordingly, colonial deputies advocated for a minimal constitution that would allow the legal status of specific territories to evolve over time—whether into independent states associated with the union, autonomous states federated within it, or departments directly integrated into the metropolitan nation. The IOM argued that the final shape of the federation could be determined only *after* overseas peoples themselves, as full citizens within member states, participated directly in defining its provisions.

Similar issues fueled the debate over whether territories could decline to join the union. Imperial apologists argued that "free consent" would nullify French sovereignty, encourage overseas secession, and fuel anticolonial nationalism. In their view, it would also enable foreign powers to seize effective control of French colonial territories. In contrast, overseas representatives insisted that there could not be a true "union of peoples" without voluntary participation. They reasoned that this option would provide overseas peoples with a viable option for self-government without national independence. Moreover, they argued, voluntary consent would preempt foreign influence by ensuring overseas peoples' affiliation with a multinational France. Free consent was also necessary for France to comply with international law, as established in the UN Charter.

This last point was made by Aimé Césaire during the September 18 debate over the government's proposal to redefine the union. After invoking violent anticolonial struggles then unfolding in India, Palestine, Indochina, and North Africa, Césaire instructed metropolitan legislators that "at a moment when colonial empires are bursting apart across the world . . . for a great nation, there is no worse danger than being caught short by history."[72] He explained that when the peoples of the Antilles, Africa, Madagascar, and the Maghreb helped France "to liberate itself from servitude," they fought not merely against the German invaders but against "the spirit of violence, racism, and despotism. . . . It was, of course, a war for liberation, but also for liberty, [which is] even more beautiful than liberation."[73]

Césaire declared colonialism "contrary to the very principles of the republic that you are trying so hard to construct. How can it be! You want to erect a social and democratic republic that will not recognize any distinctions of race or color, and at the same time, you attempt to conserve, to maintain, to perpetuate the colonialist system that carries within its flesh racism, oppression, and servitude?"[74] He reminded metropolitans that the UN Charter "precisely stipulates the disappearance of colonialism. . . . France cannot move backwards. By signing that act in San Francisco on June 26, 1945, it solemnly repudiated colonialism. To ask it to go backwards would be to ask it to perjure itself before the world."[75]

Invoking the legacies of June 1848 and the Paris Commune, citing Marx and Montaigne, Césaire supported African deputies' demands that the constitution retain language about democratic self-government for overseas territories that would freely consent to join the union: "if we radically suppress the freedom to join the French Union, we will not build a new edifice but will purely and simply extend colonialism by rebaptizing it."[76] Against arguments that Africans were incapable of exercising citizenship, he marshaled ethnographic evidence for precolonial democratic traditions. To those who feared extending self-government would encourage African independence, he argued that "it is not the granting of liberty [*liberté*] that pushes colonial peoples to secession, it is the refusal of freedom [*liberté*], it is racism, it is bullying" that does so.[77] He called the government's plan a "monument of prudence" at a time when "the drama . . . the grandeur of the epoch we traverse is that it does not allow prudence to be identified with wisdom."[78] He concluded with the kind of warning that became his trademark in the assembly: "Beyond you, we are addressing the entire country. A great hope has risen among colonized peoples: the hope to see born of their suffering and sacrifices a more just world. . . . The day when these people feel that this hope was once again ridiculed" there will erupt a grave anti-French "conflagration."[79]

Césaire aligned with the IOM deputies who saw in a federal republic an opportunity to share equally in state sovereignty while also enjoying local self-government, to denationalize self-determination and to transform France into a plural democracy. But the government sought to establish quasi-federal institutions within the union in order to exclude overseas peoples from the French polity while retaining absolute sovereignty over their territories. The final draft of the constitution, prepared by the Commission des Colonies, conformed more closely to the government's hope for a federal empire than to the IOM's plan for a democratic federation. Despite the latter's objections, the restrictive plan was approved by the assembly, with communist and socialist representatives' support, on September 28, 1946. It was then ratified by the French public in the October 13 referendum, despite the fact that de Gaulle had called on the people to reject it.[80]

These debates remind us that many political actors on both the right and the left envisioned France's future in a federalist idiom. Varieties of federalist thinking traversed the political spectrum. The conflict over whether postwar France would be a national-imperial federation or a postimperial federal democracy underscores how fine the line was between the actual order and a possible alternative to it. Seemingly small distinctions between competing visions of the French Union could have been the difference between oppressive and emancipatory political arrangements.[81]

The government certainly promoted the French Union in order to legitimize a colonial arrangement. But it is important to remember that Africans who desired autonomy within a democratic federation, who hoped to reconstitute France as a federal republic, did not fail to support decolonization; they pursued a different *form* of decolonization. Unfortunately, many critics have echoed Marshall's assumption that colonial legislators who did not explicitly support national independence naively accepted France's ideological "myth of national unity." Or his suggestion that their consent to join a union was only a transitional step toward their *real* goal of independence. [82] His account reproduces the very territorial and nationalist logic that scholars of decolonization need to historicize.

From Ambiguous Union to Peaceful Revolution

The preamble of the constitution of the Fourth Republic held that

> With its overseas peoples, France forms a Union founded on the equality of rights and duties, without distinction of either race or religion. The French Union is composed of nations and peoples who place in common or who coordinate their resources and efforts to develop their respective civilizations, improve their well-being, and assure their security. Loyal to its traditional mission, France intends to lead the peoples over whom it has taken charge to the freedom to administer themselves and to democratically manage their own affairs; setting aside any system of colonization founded on arbitrary rule, it guarantees to all equal access to civil service positions and the individual or collective exercise of rights and freedoms proclaimed below.[83]

In this ambiguous formulation, neither immediate autonomy, full French citizenship, nor free consent is mentioned directly. It is not clear whether this union would create a federal democracy, a confederation of loosely allied peoples, or a paternalist framework for imperial protection.

As if to dispel fears that it might establish a decentralized federation, articles 1 and 3 affirmed "France is an indivisible secular, social, and democratic republic" in which "national sovereignty belongs to the French people." But the latter are never specified. The key provisions concerning overseas territories were in

Title VIII, which defined the French Union as an assemblage composed of metropolitan France, its overseas departments and territories, and an outer ring of associated states and territories (including semiautonomous protectorates, mandates, and territories that had separated from France, such as Vietnam). Article 62 suggests this was less a framework for federal democracy than an imperial security arrangement retaining sovereignty for the metropolitan state: "The members of the French Union place in common the totality of their means to guarantee the protection of the whole Union. The government of the Republic assumes the coordination of these means and the direction of policies appropriate to prepare and assume this protection."[84]

The constitution designated the president of the Republic as the president of the union, the latter possessing a High Council and Assembly. But complicated electoral rules would ensure the underrepresentation of overseas peoples in these bodies, and the Assembly of the Union would be simply advisory. In civil matters, French law would *not* automatically be applied overseas. In each territory a representative of the metropolitan government would be the head administrator. Territorial assemblies would be created. But their composition, powers, and whether they would be elected by universal suffrage would depend on subsequent laws. Rules governing which overseas peoples would elect representatives to the National Assembly were also deferred.[85]

Especially ambiguous were the provisions concerning citizenship. According to Article 80, "All of the *ressortissants* of the overseas territories are citizens, in the same sense [*au même titre*] as French nationals of the metropole or the overseas territories. Particular laws will establish the conditions in which they will exercise their rights as citizens." Article 81 added: "All French nationals and *ressortissants* of the French Union are citizens of the French Union which ensures the enjoyment of the rights and liberties guaranteed by the Preamble of the present Constitution." Article 82 stipulated that citizens without French civil status would be allowed to preserve their "personal" (i.e., local) legal status in civil matters.[86]

Though these articles seemed to grant overseas peoples citizenship rights equal to their metropolitan counterparts,[87] they also established a fundamental division *within* the category of citizenship between "French nationals" and "overseas *ressortissants*." It was not clear whether French Union citizenship would grant overseas peoples the same rights and freedoms as metropolitan citizens nor whether whatever rights they enjoyed overseas would be equally valid in metropolitan France.[88]

This version of the French Union thus functioned as a framework for colonial rule, despite a series of liberalizing reforms.[89] Overseas peoples enjoyed neither legal equality as individuals possessing full citizenship nor political autonomy as peoples with substantive powers of local self-government.[90] The constitution of the Fourth Republic effectively foreclosed the democratic federalist possibility that had been opened first at Brazzaville, then in the April 1946 draft constitution, and finally in the parliamentary debates over the October constitution. Yet Senghor and his colleagues insisted that the prospect of a federal democracy remained sedimented within the form of the union and its ambiguous articles. Senghor's belief in this possibility animated his public interventions between 1946 and 1958.

In 1947 Senghor criticized the "dark shadows" cast by a constitution that eliminated free consent, established a separate "French Union citizenship," and failed to include a "proper Declaration of Rights or clear provisions for autonomy of overseas territories" through local assemblies elected by universal suffrage. He also criticized the double electoral college system as a "measure of racial discrimination which allows Europeans, in fact the power of money, to oppose democratic politics."[91] He warned policymakers already concerned about losing Vietnam: "The harm can still be repaired. And it will be; because we Negro-Africans will only agree to remain in the French Union on this condition. We want neither to be dupes nor accomplices."[92] But he paired this threat of secession, with a reassurance that Africans

> are less interested in ridding ourselves of metropolitan tutelage than of the tyranny of international capitalism. . . . We are not rebels [revoltés], but revolutionaries. We want to construct a better world, better than the colonial world of yesterday, better also than our world before European conquest. We will do it through the inspiration of scientific socialism and the old African collectivism.[93]

He thus contrasts nationalists, mere rebels, to his cohort's revolutionary ambition to construct a socialist world in partnership with the former imperial power by drawing on African and European traditions. He simultaneously invoked socialism to criticize autarchic nationalism and African forms of life to criticize Eurocentric socialism.

Senghor was elected to the Constituent Assembly through the Socialist Party. Following a power struggle with Lamine Guèye, whom the Socialists ultimately backed, Senghor resigned from the party on September 27, 1948, and founded with Mamadou Dia the Bloc Démocratique Sénégalais (BDS), an independent political party. Created at a moment of political vitality and volatility in French West Africa, the BDS became a powerful political machine.[94] Public resentment over broken promises about reform was manifest in the mutiny of African soldiers at Camp Thiaroye in Senegal, the Dakar general strike in 1946, and the transcolonial railway strike of 1947/48.[95] Senegalese political culture was also charged by regular electoral campaigns. But although Senghor was implicated in local power struggles, his initiatives should not be dismissed as simply instrumental or opportunistic; they were creative political acts seeking revolutionary possibilities within existing arrangements.

This helps to explain why Senghor's "Report on Method" to the first annual BDS Congress in 1949 actually praised the October 1946 constitution for extending the revolutionary spirit of 1789 and of the abolition of slavery on "16 Pluviôse year II."[96] Senghor asserted the twentieth century was defined by "the contraction of our planet" and a new "interdependence of people" such that "the struggle of any one of them is that of all the others." This meant that "we can no longer speak of absolute sovereignty for any people, and autarchy becomes suicide." At the same time, while he supported Africans' desire to "integrate" their struggle into that of the new "global proletariat," he also warned that the latter was a mythic abstraction that ignored cultural differences and local interests.[97] He called for West Africans to "associate not . . . with a power bloc, but with a Federation of free peoples, for political and economic reasons. This is the only way today to escape the ideological grip of blocs which, with an accent of war, will leaven dictatorship."[98] Fortunately, "history has already integrated us into such a system, in the French Union of 1946."[99]

This perplexing embrace of the constitution against which he had fought makes more political sense if we recall Senghor's poetically inflected interest in immanent critique. Like Césaire's early efforts to realize the promise of departmentalization, Senghor attempted to identify provisions within the existing constitution that, if fully implemented, would radically reconstitute France. Speaking for the IOM group he called for "the concrete realization of the French Union" through "the faithful application of the Constitution . . . in letter and spirit."[100] He argued that the future of France depended on recognizing that the existing constitution already mandated a democratic union.

Senghor claimed only to be demanding small-scale "reform projects" focusing on "decentralizing and deconcentrating" the administration's power in Africa.[101] He advocated laws to democratize territorial assemblies, equalize employment opportunities, salaries, and conditions for overseas civil servants, create a new African labor code, and Africanize the public health service. He also called for "the economic coordination of the French Union" and "intelligent investment" in overseas economies through FIDES the new state development agency.[102] Yet he also maintained that through such reforms, the "Revolution of October 27 1946 could be realized peacefully, in fact."[103]

If fully applied, the constitution would elevate the imperial republic into a federal democracy.

Like Césaire, Senghor envisioned an organic movement from constitutional reforms to revolutionary transformation. Simultaneously, he recognized that legal acts could only foster colonial emancipation if social conditions and consciousness were transformed, requisite capital invested, and institutions created. He denounced the outmoded imperial trade system, or *pacte colonial*, which favored monoculture, preempted industrialization, depleted the soil, and reduced the standard of living for Africans.[104] He argued that "reciprocal economic solidarity" among "members of the French Union" was "inscribed in the preamble of the Constitution" as "one of [its] fundamental principles,"[105] and legally required the state to abolish unfair subsidies for metropolitan products, eliminate artificially deflated prices for African products, and initiate agricultural reforms, financial investments, and economic development in Africa. These, he argued, were necessary steps in "the socialist revolution intended by the Constitution of 27 October 1946."[106]

Without genuine economic development throughout the Union, Senghor claimed, Europe could not be a "third force" to counterbalance the United States and USSR in the postwar order.[107] He warned legislators that "events in Indochina prove to you that we [Africans] are France's last chance"[108] and predicted that if the government excluded them from the European Economic Community, they would secede from the republic and diminish France's stature within Europe.[109]

Further, Senghor noted, constitutional law compelled the government to include the overseas territories on an equal footing in a new European Community.[110] He explained that by joining such a community, France would transfer a degree of its sovereignty to an extranational body. It followed that because "sovereignty belongs to the French people" and since "no portion of the people, even if it be the metropole, can attribute sovereignty to itself alone," French Africa deserved full membership in a new economic community. Senghor insisted that because the term "French" in this context was "not ethnic, but political," it necessarily included overseas peoples.[111] He reasoned that if metropolitan voices can condemn African nationalists as anti-French, then "French logic calls on you to condemn as anti-French the formula of 'continental Europe.'"[112] This was a gesture of subversive fidelity that turned against itself the French state's hostility to anticolonial nationalism. Senghor declared that African deputies remained "resolutely hostile to all that is nationalism, racism, or continentalism, but we demand of our metropolitan colleagues to feel the same as we do."[113] He thereby pledged his support for France *and* indicated that "France" must be understood nonnationally; it no longer referred exclusively to white Europeans, metropolitan society, or a monocultural and unitary republic. Speaking as a loyal republican, a French citizen, and a national legislator, as well as an African member of the Union, Senghor hoped to extend the letter and logic of the existing constitution to a point of transformative rupture. This is what he meant by "peaceful revolution."

A New Charter

Recognizing that the actual French Union subordinated Africa to metropolitan authority, Senghor regularly criticized the government's refusal to apply existing law in good faith. By 1953, however, he criticized the constitution itself as legally incoherent insofar as it affirmed the singular and indivisible character of the republic even as it purported to extend autonomy to certain overseas territories in the form of "associated states."[114] Senghor argued that the unitary state was now historically outmoded. Though this "Cartesian" political paradigm, inherited from the revolution, had once allowed republicanism to combat regional particularism, he explained, it could not address the republic's present need to accommodate overseas territories democratically.[115]

Senghor contended that the unitary republic established by this constitution was politically self-undermining because it forced subject peoples to make an either/or choice between false alternatives, political assimilation or national independence. He explained that their full assimilation into the nation-state would never be acceptable to a metropolitan population frightened of being legislatively outnumbered and culturally overwhelmed. Furthermore, Africans had witnessed how "autochthonous" civilization was destroyed in the DOM through assimilation, even as Antilleans were also denied the social and economic benefits that departmentalization supposedly secured for them.[116] Conversely, he reminded Africans that in an era when even "European nations . . . feel the need to associate together within a larger community," small colonies as isolated countries could never be "truly independent." For them, independence would be "a poison gift."[117] Nevertheless, Senghor observed, the existing union was fueling nationalist sentiment among overseas peoples.[118] He warned metropolitans that if France destroyed its connections with its former colonies, it would be weakened in relation to the Cold War superpowers, the European Community, and transnational blocs such as the British Commonwealth. In his view, neither assimilation nor independence would serve either metropolitans or Africans.

Senghor concluded, "*the true solution to the problem is the Federation.* Because [it] resolves inequalities born of the colonial regime and allows, at the same time, for . . . interdependence."[119] He demanded a new constitution that would free Africans from this false alternative *and* enable postwar "France" to retain its international stature. He insisted that in this constitution, "federalism" and "confederalism" be legal rather than metaphorical terms specifying "*a political system in which States are united, on the basis of equality, by juridical relations that are freely negotiated*" and in which all "parties give their consent to the principle, the meaning, and the limits of federation."[120] The French Union had to be defined in "juridical" rather than "sentimental terms."[121]

In the mid-1950s, Senghor further specified that this new political form would be a confederal union composed of a federal republic—which would include the metropolitan state and freely consenting overseas member states—and independent associated states. Members would enjoy political autonomy over their domestic affairs. Their populations would have full citizenship and representation in a federal parliament without surrendering their inscription within customary civil law. Membership would also guarantee economic reciprocity and social solidarity with metropolitan France.[122] And believing that African territories could only be viable members of a federal republic if they were organized on a solid economic foundation,[123] Senghor insisted on their right to group themselves into local federations which would federate with the metropolitan state.[124] Colonies and protectorates that had already evolved into autonomous states (such as Vietnam, Tunisia, and Morocco) could *confederate* with the federal entity.[125] The union would thus be a federation of federations within a larger confederation.

Senghor emphasized that overseas members would be "made into States not associated *with* but integrated *into* the French republic" directly;[126] "the nation and sovereignty would derive from the French state, not necessarily from the homeland [*patrie*]."[127] This was more than a plan to extend republican liberties to overseas peoples or include them in the existing republic. Senghor's proposal would reconstitute the very form of "France" according to principles of decentralized sovereignty and legal pluralism. He even suggested changing the name of the "French Union" to "the Union," claiming "the former '*protégés*' of France, who could tomorrow be associates, would not accept the epithet 'French' . . . it would, without a doubt, wound national pride to consent to this new sacrifice."[128] Senghor surmised that "the federal idea" would "eventually make of metropolitan France one state among others, no longer the federator, but the federated, whose particular institutions would be dominated by the broader institutions of the federal State."[129] Seemingly moderate claims for political inclusion and republican equality, he hoped, would initiate a "peaceful revolution." State sovereignty would be decentralized and citizenship grounded in the polity rather than the *patrie*. The unitary republic would be transformed into a transcontinental federal democracy incorporated within a confederal union that would not even be called France.

Again, Senghor qualified this radical vision with reassurances. He conceded this was "a long term and large scope ideal" that neither metropolitan public opinion nor overseas elites were ready to accept.[130] Allowing it might take twenty years to create such a union,[131] he emphasized small-scale practical demands to strengthen local assemblies and create a new Conseil de Gouvernement in French West Africa—"light modifications" within the framework of the existing Union. But he confessed his hope that "these . . . small reforms . . . if passed and faithfully applied, will enable an apprenticeship in local democracy; combined with economic development and education, they will allow for the speedy and true realization of the Federal Republic."[132]

Here was Senghor's radically literalist strategy of making modest demands and pragmatic concessions that worked simultaneously to reassure critics, facilitate immediate reforms, and contribute to a revolutionary transformation. He warned recalcitrant legislators that if they prioritized short-term metropolitan interests over the general interest of the republic, the results would be catastrophic. "If there are no reforms," he predicted, "it will be too late in ten years,"[133] claiming that "if France continues with this blindness," Africa will respond to American propaganda concerning national independence which "would truly mark the fall [*déchéance*] of France, even worse, it would mark the triumph of a capitalism and a racism that will lead us inevitably to war . . . to the destruction of the planet and the end of hope for man."[134]

Senghor's rhetoric was well timed. Defeat in Indochina, the start of the Algerian war, and independence for Tunisia and Morocco meant West Africa's participation in the Union could no longer be taken for granted. Nationalist movements in anglophone African colonies were gathering momentum. Anticolonial unrest was manifest in Madagascar (1947), Côte d'Ivoire (1950/51), Guinea (1954/55), and Cameroon (1955–1957). A new generation of activists across West Africa was demanding self-government, whether through autonomy or independence. According to Ruth Schachter Morgenthau, this imperial anxiety pushed the government to rethink its politically repressive Africa policy and the regressive form of the French Union, making it more open to collaborate with moderate African leaders.[135]

Beginning with a 1953 congress, Senghor's IOM deputies had campaigned for the revision of Title VIII in order to transform France into the federal republic that might have been (and provide a nonnational framework for Algerian self-determination). In 1955 President Edgar Faure appointed Senghor to his cabinet as sécrétaire d'état à la présidence du conseil and was charged with rewriting the provisions of Title VIII.[136] As in 1946, a public discussion unfolded about the legal and political merits of federalism, whether as vehicle for a more democratic union or instrument of imperial rule.[137] But despite Senghor's efforts in the government, the assembly, and the press, the outcome was not what he envisioned.

This process led instead to the 1956 Loi-Cadre, which initiated a set of legal, political, and financial reforms granting French African territories a significant measure of local self-government through popularly elected assemblies and executive councils. Powers once concentrated in the colonial administration were distributed to overseas organs of representative government. But, as Morgenthau indicates, these laws attempted to decentralize and liberalize French rule in Africa without altering the unitary state defined by the 1946 constitution. The Loi-Cadre may have made a decisive step toward autonomy and independence, but it was not a serious attempt to refigure France as a federal republic. Instead, it devolved power to discrete African territories in ways that reinforced the integrity of the sovereign metropolitan state.[138]

By anticipating a postcolonial order of autarchic nations allied to a French state now reduced to its European dimension, the Loi-Cadre expressed the nationalist logic of decolonization that Senghor's interventions contested. He supported the concrete reforms introduced by the 1956 law enhancing self-government for Africans. But he did not vote for the Loi-Cadre, whose territorialist paradigm he opposed.[139]

Senghor's IOM affiliates performed poorly in the 1956 elections and lost seats to African deputies of the RDA party, whose leader, Félix Houphouët-Boigny, was invited to join the government. But leaving the cabinet afforded Senghor more freedom to advocate for a federal republic.[140] As calls for independence resonated with grassroots constituencies across West Africa, Senghor continued to resist what he regarded as the temptation of autarchy. His commitment to self-determination without state sovereignty flowed from both a timely reading of the current conjuncture and an untimely orientation to a possible future. He was not only pragmatically informing French strategists that its Africa policy was failing or Africans that independence might lead to economic decline. He was also animated by a utopian commitment to a democratic and socialist union that would allow each to realize its humanity more fully.

The Future of Eurafrique

Senghor believed that imperialism had arrived at a historical turning point. "An irresistible current is leading overseas peoples towards autonomy and independence. The problem today is not to stop this emancipation, to swim upstream against the current, but to channel it . . . to provide a constructive and juridical form for a popular sentiment [*élan populaire*]."[141] He identified federalism as the most effective form through which metropolitans and Africans could anticipate this onrushing future. In a 1955 essay Senghor established a continuum among governance, anticipation, choice, foresight, and federalism. He wrote, "to govern is to anticipate [*prévoir*] . . . to govern is to choose. In reality, choice is a function of anticipation [*la prévision*]." In his view it was easy to

> foresee [*prévoir*] that . . . in ten years, there will no longer exist "dependent peoples" . . . France must plan ahead [*prévoir*]. . . . the unitary Republic is isolated . . . collaboration is the condition of progress for both parties . . . it is because it knows how to anticipate [*prévoir*] that France will choose the solution of federalism, the only one that responds to the realities of the twentieth century.[142]

Conversely,

> A *no* [to federation] would be catastrophic for you and for us. For you because, disappointed thus, overseas peoples will advance towards total independence, despite you and against you. For us because, too weak to live in autarchy, we will turn towards one of the two superpowers, alienating precisely the liberty that we had wanted to reconquer.[143]

Playing on France's inflated sense of historical importance *and* its Cold War anxiety about national decline, Senghor argued that its principal wealth was located in "the spirit of its civilization, this spirit of liberty and humanism that makes Paris the capital of *man*." This spirit could be protected only "by realizing a French Federal Republic integrated into a confederation that extends to all five continents; by making overseas peoples not subjects but peoples freely associated with France . . . by rejecting colonialism and . . . offering this example for the admiration of the world."[144]

But Senghor also implored overseas peoples to embrace a federalist form of decolonization. He criticized the "false dilemma" between either "the uniform of assimilation" or the "iron collar [*carcan*] of total independence."[145] Nationalism would not help Africans respond adequately to economic problems such as "credit, unemployment, emigration, and raising the standard of living in underdeveloped countries."[146] Moreover, he reminded them, "the modern world does not make room for small economic *entities whose independence is a myth* if they lack sufficient resources and do not participate in a large UNION."[147] He declared, "there is no political independence without economic independence . . . without an economic infrastructure, in short, without capital—though I did not say without capitalism. There is no political independence in the illiteracy of the masses, and their education still requires capital."[148] Even cultural preservation, he noted, would require economic resources. A federal union would therefore guarantee Africans both "the democratic management of [their] affairs" and "national solidarity" in "the social and economic domain."[149]

But for Senghor, federalism was not simply an instrumental means for metropolitan aid and investment: it corresponded to a new epoch of world history. Whereas nationalism was a relic of an "old Cartesianism" historically "superseded," federalism expressed the most advanced scientific thinking based on "the principle of *complementarity*" for which "truth no longer appears as linear logic, but as dialectical. It no longer reveals itself in an autarchic monologue, it gives birth to itself through dialogue, or, better, in a colloquium."[150] Federalism (the political corollary of dialectics) and dialectics (the epistemological corollary of federalism) were the forms of a future already arrived.

Senghor believed that a democratic federation would best help metropolitans and Africans realize their fullest potential as human beings and members of civilizations. It would also create a civilization for a new era of human history. His political vision thus corresponded to a cultural project: "the ultimate goal of political economy is the development of society. But what is the development of society if not that of its civilization . . . of thought and art . . . of the creative activity through which man distinguishes himself from animals?"[151] For him, "federal institutions [were] only means in the service of *culture*," an interactive process or "colloquium" that was lived.[152] He argued that "cultural stagnation [and] racial purity, like economic autarchy, are dormant waters. A people, like an individual, needs, to live and grow, to nourish itself, to absorb and to assimilate—but through an assimilating assimilation . . . by integrating into itself those human values that are foreign to itself,"[153] asserting "all the great civilizations were formed by cultural and biological *métissage*."[154] Conversely, he believed particular civilizations forged "the patrimony of humanity" while attempting to realize themselves as fully as possible.[155] He explained, "to live as civilized people . . . is first to be oneself, by assuming one's history . . . becoming conscious of the past is the first duty of a people,"[156] yet "this past, which informs the present, is only a means to prepare one's future to come [*destin avenir*]. On cannot enclose oneself in the past nor prolong the present, because stagnation is certain death."[157]

For Senghor, "*métissage* . . . is the justification for federalism."[158] Federation was the political form commensurate with the cultural processes through which, in succession, Africans might fully develop their own civilization, a new Franco-African civilization may emerge, and the prospect of a planetary "civilization of the universal" could open.[159] He declared, "overseas peoples do not want just any 'union.' In order for the *rendez-vous* to be fruitful, it must be one of giving and receiving, one of reciprocal enrichment. It is this dynamic conception of federalism that I propose."[160] Senghor's conception of "Eurafrique" indexed just this process of cultural reciprocity within a shared political field.

The Eurafrique discourse in imperial France in the early 1950s emerged from debates over the creation of a new European Economic Community.[161] Among the proponents of a "third force" to counterbalance US and Soviet power were those in France insisting that any European Community must include the whole French Union, including its overseas territories. "Eurafrique" was one name for this entity. Others saw in Eurafrique a way to defend a threatened empire.[162] But its advocates also included the African IOM deputies in the National Assembly anxious about the future economic consequences of a European Community that might exclude their territories. As president of this group, Senghor seized the concept of Eurafrique from imperial apologists and made it more than a purely defensive and pragmatic arrangement between vulnerable Africans and a precarious France.[163]

In the legislative debate following the 1950 Schuman Declaration to create a European Community, Senghor announced to metropolitan legislators that overseas deputies would support France joining this supranational entity as long as it did so as a "Eurafrique" that was "founded upon the association and equal development of two complementary continents."[164] Following the treaty establishing the European Coal and Steel Community, he reiterated this concern while addressing metropolitan fears.[165] He informed the assembly that a "Eurafrican France with 88 million inhabitants will play its role as guide and leader [*animatrice*] of the European Union."[166] But he warned, "Eurafrique cannot be created without the consent of Africans" who "will not lend their support to a union in which the overseas countries are a means and not an end, where political and social democracy would have as its border the Mediterranean."[167] Senghor reminded his colleagues that Africans' inclusion was a constitutional obligation, since under the Fourth Republic the overseas territories were integral parts of France. He explained, "by 'Europe' we understand, generally, the states of the West and their African possessions."[168] Democracy and development in French Africa, he argued, could secure French supremacy in a new Europe.

Senghor's Eurafrique signaled a pragmatic alliance but also indexed a new political and social compact through which metropolitan and overseas peoples would enter a relationship based on reciprocity and *métissage*. In a 1955 essay joining his interwar analyses of cultural complementarity to his postwar interest in federal cooperation, he wrote that Eurafrique "can only be a marriage in which each of the partners contributes its share and its qualities—a transaction, to put it crudely. . . . Just as there are no longer master races, there is no privileged continent. Each has its grandeur and its misery, each developed a singular trait of the human condition."[169]

Senghor recounted that "the spirit of Negro-African civilization" endowed Africans with the "gift" of "wisdom, which is the art of living."[170] This joy in being flowed from a "civilization of unity in which everything is linked to everything and to oneself," the human person lives in "harmonious plenitude," and collectivity forms a life-affirming democratic community organized around public deliberation and popular consent. He believed that such joyous wisdom subtended African religion, epistemology, and aesthetics, within a humanly integrated and reconciled form of life.[171]

To Senghor, modern Europe was deformed and its existence alienated by capitalism, individualism, and scientific and technical rationality. "If the goal of politics is indeed to make it so that the greatest number of people . . . are happy . . . living a life of harmonious plenitude . . . Africa has nothing to ask of Europe."[172] He recounted that "by propagating . . . its rationalist, scientistic, materialist, and atheist civilization, its capitalist civilization, Europe disorganized . . . Negro-African civilization by drying up [its] very sources."[173] He called for a return to the vital sources of African culture to reanimate values and capacities through which a disalienated form of modern life and a new politics of human plenitude could be pursued.

This is the perspective from which to understand the invidious distinction that Senghor then made between Europe's rational, progressive, and development-oriented outlook and African repugnance to progress and indifference to change.[174] But however misguided his decision to use the primitivist discourse of midcentury colonial ethnology and administration, it was in service of a broader critical strategy. He employed this distinction to argue that metropolitan France must pursue progressive development policies to raise African standards of living. His negative evaluation of traditional Africa served a deeper critique of European colonialism and civilization which, Senghor argued, had reduced human imagination to automatism, collective organization to statism, and life to routine.[175] The "most spectacular" inventions of European "discursive reason," he explained, were

> today, in the process of destroying the very existence of men . . . far from combating our true ills, which are the egoisms of class, nation, race, or continent, European reason has made itself their docile servant. If it helped Europe to transform the world and . . . its material life, it has not transformed its *true life*, that is to say its moral life. This, rather, does not emerge from formal reason, from rational reason, but from analogic reason, which is sympathetic intuition.[176]

When he asked Europeans not to "impose their religious faith" on Africa, he referred not to Christianity but to the atheistic "faith which rests on progress and money."[177]

Senghor thereby refigured the supposed distinction between European and African civilizations as a contrast between a "centripetal" instrumental reason that serves material power by distancing and "dismantling" the object of knowledge and a "centrifugal" intuitive reason that equates knowledge with the plenitude of being through a loving and aesthetic identification with an object that it approaches. A seeming difference between rational Europe and irrational Africa thus becomes one between two types or aspects of reason, each of which was available to both. Senghor's criticism of modern instrumental reason from the standpoint of African ontology may be problematic, but his argument is more nuanced than it appears to be.[178] Rather than contrast African stasis and backwardness to European historicity and progress, he established a link between European modernization and modern social misery. Rather than contrast an emancipatory European rationalism to an oppressive African superstition, he identified an underlying relation between technical and scientific rationality and modern systems of oppression. Rather than contrast African poverty with European comfort, he contrasted a superficial understanding of material well-being to a more profound sense of human fulfillment. Rather than contrast Europeans as rational to Africans as emotional, he distinguished between two different modalities of knowing: the superficial and instrumental analytic reason of Europe and the vital and empathetic analogical reason of Africa. For Senghor, the antinomies around which modern life in *both* Europe *and* Africa were organized and impoverished could be transcended only through combined discursive-technical and intuitive-aesthetic forms of reason: when "reunited in the same person, [these complementary civilizations allow] for the realization of the whole human condition."[179]

Aesthetics held special status in Senghor's view of of disalienation: "the art object, by its very reality, creates a new world, that of tomorrow. It is thus that a new Africa is being created in the heart and spirit of our writers who, because rooted in the reality of the present, already project its roots, full of sap, into the air of the future. This world will no longer be wholly African, neither will it be only Europe; it will be a *métis* world" that "reunites complementary virtues in a dynamic symbiosis."[180] Eurafrique, both the source and product of this symbiosis, would require "a certain humility on the part of Europe. It must understand that if it has a lot to give, it has no less to receive. Only thus will be realized this Eurafrique . . . which must be the cornerstone of civilization.[181]

Senghor's Eurafrique indexed a process of reciprocal exchange through which European and African civilizations could each more fully realize their singularity *and* a new Franco-African civilization could be created. Both results would help create "the civilization of the universal."[182] Through perpetual borrowing, internalization, and adjustment Africans and Europeans could be reconciled in the service of the overarching aim of human self-realization on a planetary scale. Thus Senghor's description of Eurafrique as a "greater cultural force prepared for peace" that would exist "between the two antagonistic [Cold War] blocs, who only believe in violence."[183] Never meaning only to signal an instrumental alliance, he employed Eurafrique and federalism to reconfigure "France" itself as a multicultural and transcontinental entity. Eurafrique described the shared imperial history that bound them together and was a prospective vision of what imperial France might one day create and become.

Desacralizing Independence

In a 1957 article for *Le Monde*, Senghor argued that overseas peoples "demand less the right of independence than the right to self-determination [*autodéter-mination*]."[184] Whereas national independence could institute only a limited formal sovereignty, self-determination meant a deeper sense of existential dis-alienation and real self-management. Criticizing "the virus of independence," he stated Africans were ready to imagine a future association with France, but the metropolitan government's commitment to empire made such imaginings impossible. He declared that "*decolonization* is the first and fundamental condition of the Franco-African Community," though specifying that "institutional decolonization . . . is not a sufficient condition . . . the decolonization of minds must be accomplished first."[185] Africans needed to abandon "every inferiority complex" and develop a robust "African personality" so that they could "adapt" aspects of French civilization "to their own proper genius."[186] Likewise, French colonizers had to abandon their "superiority complex" and recognize "the colonized to be . . . rich in civilization" and "possessing all of the virtues of the human condition."[187] Senghor insisted France recognize that "there is not *a* civilization but *many* civilizations. Or, better, if there is a human civilization, it is dialectic, each continent, each race, each people of which presents us with a singular and irreplaceable aspect."[188] Decolonization was a dialogical and dialectical "gift between partners."[189]

Senghor was especially disturbed by metropolitan leftists who attacked African federalists as "separatists" or "anti-French."[190] Reminding them that many such Africans participated in the Resistance, he asserted that they embodied the authentic spirit of the French Revolution more than those metropolitans who responded to overseas peoples' struggles for self-determination by retreating into a defensive and self-defeating nationalism.[191] Simultaneously claiming and refunctioning this legacy for a new interdependent epoch, he called for the "the spirit of the Revolution" to "renew itself today in light of the science of civilizations" and realize "the pacific revolution that will give birth to the veritable Franco-African community."[192]

The following year, on the eve of the collapse of the Fourth Republic, during a debate on the Algerian War, Senghor argued that metropolitan France should compromise its sovereignty by transforming the unitary state into a federal republic, and by granting Algeria independence, after which it could choose to associate with France. But he added a caveat: "when I say 'with France,' that means within the framework of a 'French federal republic' itself integrated into . . . a Union of Confederated States."[193] He invited his metropolitan counterparts to emulate African parties that had decided to "desacralize" and "transcend" the "notion of independence."[194] He argued that the real spirit of the French Revolution could only be renewed and realized in light of a contemporary understanding of cultural multiplicity and transcontinental solidarity if the French government would abandon its commitment to a unitary state and stop resisting Algerian independence. For Africans to be "concretely decolonized" and "disalienated," they would need not only to abolish the legal fact of colonialism[195] but to transform their mental structures and transcend all notions of autarchy. Senghor thereby linked the tradition of republican fraternity to the possibilities for multiculturalism and legal pluralism that imperialism had created, calling for a new Franco-African community and a true federal union.

Anticipating Political Futures

Between 1946 and 1958, Senghor promoted a vision of federalism as a medium for decolonization that would enable self-determination while transcending national autarchy. Animating his untimely efforts was both the insight that the new French Union was an imperial facade *and* the foresight that this union *also* created the institutional infrastructure for what *could have been* a true federal democracy. Territorial legislatures and an Assembly of the Union were in place. Africans possessed French citizenship and access to French courts, enjoyed mobility to and the right to work in the metropole and a range of civil rights and social benefits. Senghor recognized in empire an alienated form of federation.[196]

Like Césaire, Senghor demanded not simply a full integration of overseas peoples with the existing nation-state but a type of integration that would reconstitute France itself. Legal pluralism, disaggregated sovereignty, and territorial disjuncture would be constitutionally grounded. The presumptive unity of culture, nationality, and citizenship would be ruptured. By taking literally the constitution's language about the Fourth Republic as a union of peoples, Senghor challenged the autarchic claims that Africans were not French and should be excluded from full participation in the national legislature, the welfare state, or the European Community. He also challenged as antirepublican any attempt to deny self-government through local assemblies to overseas peoples. Senghor exploited the seemingly simple insight that the term "French" was political, not ethnic, and that "Europe" already included French West Africa.

Senghor's pursuit of decolonization through democratic federalism stemmed from a concern with securing substantive liberty for Africans in a conjuncture marked by neocolonial capitalism, Cold War geopolitics, and an emergent European Union. But his belief that state sovereignty was *not* the most effective framework for what he called "concrete decolonization" was more than a realist concession to the existing order. It was a vision of human freedom that anticipated a world that did not yet exist. This dual orientation to present and future was reflected in his political rhetoric, which tacked between calling for modest reforms and outlining a transformative program, reassuring imperial apologists and encouraging anticolonial activists. He joined professions of loyalty to apocalyptic warnings. He affirmed republican principles whose logic disclosed a transcendent vision through which the existing empire *and* republic would be sublated.

Senghor's interventions operated in multiple registers. First, he argued that a federal partnership would serve all parties' immediate interests. It would allow metropolitan France to resist American hegemony, counterbalance the British Commonwealth, and lead a new European Community. It would provide Africans with economic resources, social protections, and political security. Cultural coexistence would allow each civilization to more fully realize its singular potential. Second, Senghor proposed that a democratic federation would create a framework through which metropolitan and overseas peoples could better realize republican self-government in "an era of interdependence." This form would allow actors to pursue freedom in relation to emerging historical conditions. It would also require and create novel cultural configurations based on civilizational reciprocity and *métissage*.

Senghor's vision also entailed an unconditional hope that envisioned a world to come. It indexed a future in which modern alienation would be overcome, political emancipation realized globally, and a "civilization of the universal" established. This register conjured a prospective process of cosmopolitan reconciliation, human self-realization, and even cosmological concordance among human, natural, and spiritual worlds—a utopianism that joined immanent critique, concrete acts, and political imagination. Grounded in existing conditions, his vision was an example of Ernst Bloch's "concrete utopia" and David Harvey's "dialectical utopia."[197]

Senghor pursued a future in which partnership with imperial France would not mean neocolonial dependency, as it typically did. He acted as if the world in which he wanted to live had already arrived and attempted to institute a political arrangement that could only succeed in it. Yet this utopian vision was matched by constitutional acts aiming to create such a world by recognizing possibilities within existing arrangements. He wagered on the future from the postwar opening and wagered on the present from a future whose contours he strained to glimpse. In that historical instant, he seemed to believe, the distance between the actual and the possible, the existing and imagined, was within reach.

But Senghor's program was also utopian in the pejorative sense of the term. He sometimes treated federalism as what Marx would call a "ready-made" solution.[198] With poetic economy, his proposals intentionally evaded numerous questions regarding institutional organs, electoral procedure, and jurisdiction.[199] He said little about the likely limitations of legal association with metropolitan France. Although he argued that this democratic federation would be consonant with other forms of solidarity, such as pan-Africanism and socialist internationalism, and despite his interest in federating autonomous states within West Africa, he did not work out the mediations between these distinct levels of African political identification. Nor is it clear whether his fed-

eration was meant to found a constitutional democracy, a system of cooperative socialism, a multinational society, or the cosmopolitan internationalism
envisioned by Immanuel Kant.[200]

To argue that Senghor was a visionary actor is not to deny that he often pla-
cated powerful constituencies, pursued personal interests, or hedged his bets.
His constitutional initiatives were bound up with party politics, power struggles, and conciliatory gestures toward the French government.[201] Colonized
peoples who struggled for state sovereignty and national independence were
not mistaken; throughout the twentieth century the national state was an un-
surpassed framework for social democracy and popular sovereignty.[202] But we
cannot preemptively dismiss as reactionary attempts to envision nonnational
forms of colonial emancipation. My argument, in other words, is directed not
toward actors who pursued national liberation but toward critics who reflex-
ively condemn those who did not.

Consider the national liberation struggle that began in colonial Algeria
in 1954. As the war unfolded, a series of proposals emerged to preempt national
independence through decentralizing forms of integration, reconciliation,
"exceptional promotion," the creation of a Franco-Muslim Community, or a
French-Algerian federation. Similarly, at the end of the war, legal plans concerning minority rights and *multicommunitaire* arrangements were designed
to protect the ethnic French community in an independent Algeria, as well as
Algerian Muslims with French nationality in the metropole.[203] These proposals may have attempted to refigure the unitary national state through experiments in legal pluralism. But they aimed to preserve colonial rule by preclud-
ing Algerian self-determination. In contrast, Senghor intended democratic
federalism to abolish colonialism. Given the conditions in Algeria, federalist
solutions could not have emancipated nonwhite populations; without a con-
current social revolution, they could only strengthen the position of the settler elite over "native" populations. In this sense, French Algeria resembled
Antillean slave colonies after the French Revolution where planter elites demanded local political autonomy in order to evade the democratic imperatives
of the Jacobin republic.

Once we remember that a given people can pursue self-management through
any number of political frameworks, we can recognize Senghor's refusal to
reduce self-determination to national liberation as a strategic choice and
principled position. He hoped that a postcolonial federation would secure
political autonomy for Africans without surrendering future membership in a
plural republic and united Europe of which they were already an integral part.
Such a form might also serve as a model and building block for a worldwide

cosmopolitan order, reconciling political universality and cultural multiplicity, popular sovereignty and legal plurality, national membership and transnational solidarity. He believed that a federal democracy could more fully realize the emancipatory potentiality of republicanism in and for the interdependent world that imperialism had helped to create.

I am *not* suggesting that Africans could have found a way to accommodate themselves to a reformed colonialism or that decolonization may not have been necessary. Nor am I suggesting that the French Union marked the end of colonial rule. It clearly did not. My point is that the immediate postwar period marked a "historical hiatus" when the gap between the actual, the possible, and the desirable was often infinitesimal yet seemingly unbridgeable. Senghor wrote from within and about this gap. His untimely reflections on a federal future also captured the attention of his old friend Aimé Césaire.

SEVEN   Antillean Autonomy and the Legacy of Louverture

A phenomenon of this kind [the French Revolution] which has taken place in human history *can never be forgotten* . . . even if the intended object behind the occurrence . . . were not to be achieved for the present. . . . For that event is too important, too intimately interwoven with the interests of humanity, and its influence too widely propagated in all areas of the world to not be recalled, when favourable circumstances present themselves, by the peoples which would then be roused to a repetition of new efforts of this kind.
—IMMANUEL KANT

Colonialism and Culture

Césaire's commitment to both departmentalization and the French Communist Party wavered after France's disastrous intervention in Indochina and the commencement of the Algerian War. The party opposed the Vietminh's and FLN's demands for national independence and backed the metropolitan government's assumption of emergency powers in Algeria in 1956.[1] Césaire shared the PFC's belief that self-determination did not *require* state sovereignty[2] but supported the FLN's revolutionary struggle for national liberation.

On January 27, 1956, at a public event organized by the Comité d'Action des Intellectuels contre la Poursuite de la Guerre en Afrique du Nord, Césaire identified "the Algerian problem" as "a particular case of a broader colonial problem."[3] Criticizing Europeans who clung to imperialism "without recognizing that its time has passed," Césaire explained that Algerians wanted "the *pure and simple abolition of the colonial regime*."[4] Above all, they needed "assurance that [they] can freely orient [their] own destiny. This means the birth or rebirth of the Algerian state, united with France by laws of friendship and solidarity, and no longer by relations of subjection and domination."[5] Césaire recognized the legitimacy of Algerian statehood but allowed that once independent, Algeria might enter a confederal relationship with a decolonized France.

Césaire further elaborated his ideas about self-determination at the First International Congress of Black Artists and Writers, held in Paris at the Sorbonne, September 19–22, 1956. Organized by the Society for African Culture, which was affiliated with the journal and publisher Présence Africaine,[6] the conference drew participants from Africa, the Caribbean, and the United States.[7] Alioune Diop, president of the society and editor of the journal, opened the conference by challenging the assumption that "culture and politics belong to two radically distinct worlds," observing "if political authority (the state) can exercise deadly pressure on culture . . . it is then certain that it is up to culture . . . to inspire politics."[8] Diop argued that black writers and artists had a responsibility to realize the universal promise of modern Western culture *and* to universalize African cultural forms; both had been debased by imperialism.[9] He declared "culture is a dialogue" among peoples and that "we others from the non-European world . . . have to spark . . . new values, and explore together the new universe born of the meeting of peoples."[10] He envisioned a black humanism available to all peoples seeking to overcome the alienating distinction between manual and intellectual labor through which ordinary people in modern society were separated from philosophical speculation and aesthetic production.[11]

Césaire similarly argued that emancipation must entail a people's freedom to fashion autonomous cultural forms and futures. Condemning colonialism for having "broken the living spirit [*élan*] of civilizations that had not yet fulfilled their promise," he insisted that the seemingly static or backward cultures ethnologists encountered were products of the "colonial situation."[12] This critique of colonial knowledge of culture engaged with anthropologists (including Caillois, Frobenius, Kroeber, Malinowski, Mauss, Mead, and Segalen) and social theorists (Hegel, Lenin, Marx, Nietzsche, Spengler, and Toynbee).

Césaire challenged the imperial "illusion" that the colonizer could substitute his own civilization for the destroyed indigenous one.[13] Because European powers never made all their own cultural resources available to colonized people, genuine assimilation was impossible and a true "transfer of civilization" would never occur.[14] And because colonialism was not a form of "civilizational contact like others," it could not lead to "a new [hybrid] civilization."[15] Citing Malinowski, he reasoned that successful cultural borrowing cannot be imposed; it must be an organic process of active appropriation. In a "living civilization," he explained, "this heterogeneity is lived internally as a homogeneity . . . the elements . . . are experienced by the consciousness of the community as their own, no different from the most typically autochthonous elements."[16] Césaire characterized this as a "dialectic of having" whereby "foreign elements become mine, have passed into my being . . . because I can organize them in my universe, because I can bend them to my needs. Because they are at my disposition and not me at theirs. It is precisely this dialectic which is refused to colonized people."[17] Césaire concluded that "the cultural situation in colonial countries is tragic"; subject peoples cannot take "historical initiative" and are deprived of "the concepts from which [they] could build or rebuild the world."[18] What could now be done?

Rejecting the false alternative between "autochthonous tradition and European civilization," Césaire called on "black men of culture" to create a "para-African culture yet to be born" that would be rooted in but surpass inherited civilizations.[19] The resulting renaissance would provide new solutions to a range of modern political, social, and economic problems. The challenge was to anticipate without predefining this configuration: "our role is [not] to construct a priori a plan for the future black culture. . . . Our role, infinitely more humble, is to announce . . . and to prepare the arrival of the one who possesses the response . . . our peoples and their creative genius, finally rid of that which fetters or sterilizes it."[20] The task of cultural creators, he announced, is to "liberate the demiurge that alone can organize this chaos into a new synthesis . . . a reconciliation and transcendence [dépassement] of the old and the new . . . [to] give voice to the peoples [and] let black people enter the great stage of history."[21]

Césaire believed that abolishing colonialism would restore this "dialectic of having." Africans and Antilleans could then develop the most singular *and* most universal dimensions of their civilizations. This dynamic process whereby the apparently foreign is lived as one's proper inheritance signals precisely the political relationship to modern France Césaire desired for Antilleans.[22]

Political Reorientation

In August 1955, the Communist Federation of Martinique withdrew support for departmentalization.[23] During the January 1956 election campaign, it demanded greater Antillean autonomy within the French Union and supported colonial peoples' right to national liberation. These elections occurred during another mass strike by agricultural workers. Simultaneously, MRP legislators in Paris were arguing that people in the overseas departments did not have a right to the same standard of living as their metropolitan counterparts.[24]

In his 1956 campaign platform, Césaire made a set of "constitutional demands that would grant to the people of Martinique a greater role in the management of its own affairs" by granting the local Conseil Général more power and making the prefect accountable to it.[25] He called for higher salaries, collective bargaining agreements, family allocations, social protections for cultivators, fishermen, and artisans, lower taxes, a public investment fund that would finance economic modernization, and the right of Martinicans to trade freely on the global market. He complained that despite economic stagnation and social misery, the government still refused to develop industry, extend credit, or implement social security laws overseas. In response, he offered a new charter for self-management,

> Because we are convinced that in such a tragic situation, salvation will not come to us from the outside, because . . . the status of Martinique is in the hands of its own children and . . . we no longer have any illusions about the feelings that the administration harbors with regard to our people, we ask that the Martinican people assume a greater role in the management of our own affairs.[26]

Looking beyond departmentalization, he proposed "a politics that is democratic in its inspiration, social in its aims, and Martinican in its means."[27]

The Communist Federation was then at the height of its power, and Césaire was easily reelected. But on October 24, 1956, he shocked his comrades by resigning from the PCF. There were neither political nor personal issues dividing him from the federation.[28] His resignation coincided with the escalation of the war in Algeria, Khrushchev's denunciation of Stalin's political crimes, and the anti-Soviet revolution in Hungary.[29] In *Letter to Maurice Thorez*, where he relayed his decision, Césaire attempted to think beyond departmentalization, based on a narrow conception of political assimilation, *and* orthodox communism, based on an abstract conception of proletarian emancipation. Neither, he suggested, was capable of resolving the current Antillean impasse.

Césaire criticized the PCF for subordinating colonized peoples' interests to workers' struggle. Its "utopian perspective" did not accord political initiative to Antilleans.[30] He desired that "Marxism and Communism be placed in the service of black peoples [*peuples noirs*]," rather than the other way around, "that the doctrine and the movement be made for men, not men for the doctrine or the movement."[31] Césaire called for a "Copernican revolution" in the anticolonial struggle,[32] announcing that black peoples, whose "hour has sounded," must make history through a self-directed movement.[33] He also endorsed a politics of solidarity with other colonized peoples engaged in a similar "struggle for justice."[34]

Disaffected with both departmentalization's republican universalism and the PCF's internationalist universalism, Césaire desired a politics that neither "buries [him] in a narrow particularism" nor forced him to "lose himself in an emaciated [*décharné*] universalism."[35] Hoping to transcend both "walled-in segregation" and "dilution in the universal," he envisioned an alternative "universal rich with everything that is particular, enriched and deepened by all particulars, by the coexistence of all particulars."[36] Césaire was clearing conceptual ground for a concrete program that would break with party ortho-doxy *and* supersede departmentalization. He implored his comrades, "we must have the patience . . . to remake that which had been unmade . . . to invent . . . our route and to get rid of already made forms, petrified forms that block our work."[37] Antillean self-management would be both the route and the destination.

Césaire's *Letter* denounced the party's failure to address Antillean struggles. But rather than challenge communist universality in the name of cultural par-ticularity, it criticized the class-centric character of the PCF's orthodox Marx-ism as provincial and divisive. Arguing against "rejecting a priori and in the name of an exclusive ideology, men that are . . . fundamentally anticolonialist," Césaire declared,

> I opt for the broader against the narrower; for the movement that places
> us elbow to elbow with others and against one that leaves us to our-
> selves; for one that gathers energies and against one that divides them
> into chapels, sects, and churches; for one that liberates the creative en-
> ergy of the masses and against one that channels and ultimately steril-
> izes [this energy].[38]

He thus renounced the party in the name of a pragmatic politics that would create solidarity across divisions of class, ideology, and geography.[39]

Leaving the PCF was a crucial step in Césaire's political reorientation.[40] In his introduction to Daniel Guérin's *Les Antilles Décolonisés* (1956), Césaire contextualized his initial support for departmentalization.[41] Declaring that, con-trary to public speculations, he had "neither feelings of guilt nor partisan ten-derness" for the 1946 law; he recalled that "in its time, it received the approval of large masses of Antillean people."[42] This meant that "if it was an error, it was not a banal error, and rather than condemn it, we need to explain it, grasp it by its roots and its extensions, indeed, [we need to grasp] phenomenologically the thought process [*la démarche de l'esprit*] that it presupposes."[43] He conjured the image of a people who "were formal citizens of a state" but only possessed a "marginal citizenship" and asked, "how can we fail to understand that their first collective step would not be to reject the empty form of their citizenship, but . . . to transform it into a full citizenship?"[44]

Césaire traced how by resolving one contradiction, departmentalization created another. Echoing Marx's "On the Jewish Question," he explained that "henceforth, equality would be total in the domain of law," but "each day, inequality would sharpen in the domain of facts . . . a terrible contradiction was developing within departmentalization . . . that could only be resolved by the negation of departmentalization."[45] This contradiction had provoked "an awakening of national sentiment in the French Antilles."[46] In a departure from his other writing, Césaire here figured departmentalization as a moment in a dialectical process leading toward national consciousness. He wrote, "progress will consist [for Antilleans] like for other colonial peoples, in passing from being swallowed by the gloomy universality of empire, to participating in the living spirit of finally individualized nations."[47]

Using Hegelian language, Césaire characterized departmentalization as a "ruse of history."[48] To preempt anticolonial nationalism, the French state had encouraged the colonized to seek "abstract equality." But because "equality will not allow itself to remain abstract," the colonized "reclaims the word" and demands substantive equality by overcoming departmentalization. This was a "surprising reversal of relations through which history transforms the naiveté of the colonized into a ruse and turns the ruse of the colonizer into naiveté."[49] This reasoning led Césaire to assert that the "national idea" is the "only reality on which it will henceforth be possible to build the future."[50] He even claimed, like Mazzini and Fanon, that the nation always serves as "the mediation of liberty," concluding that while Guérin's proposal for an Antillean Federation might be realized in the future, it was presently unrealistic. Given the realities of 1956, the "task of our generation," is to build particular Antillean nations.[51]

Césaire comes closer here to a nationalist position than in any of his postwar writings. But we should note that he understands Antillean national sentiment as a conjunctural product of departmentalization's untimely colonial character, not as an inevitable outcome: "this swinging between a past that we do not want and a present that we cannot accept because it does not accept us."[52] Nor despite his affirmation of national consciousness, does he relate it necessarily to state sovereignty. Above all Césaire sought a framework through which to avoid "dilution in the universal" and "walled-in segregation." This introduction therefore is notable less for its qualified nationalism than its opposition to departmentalization. It was part of the process through which Césaire decided that "cooperative federalism" would evade the pitfalls of both communist mediated assimilation and nationally mediated state sovereignty.

Federal Autonomy

On November 7, 1956, Pierre Aliker created a Comité Aimé Césaire, which circulated a call by Césaire for the people of Martinique to establish an autonomous political organization. In response, the Communist Federation expelled him. Césaire returned to Fort-de-France and delivered a public address to 15,000 supporters.[53] Many of his communist colleagues defected to join him, and Communist Federation candidates were widely defeated in the next municipal elections. In September 1957 the declining federation separated from the PCF and reconstituted itself as the Parti Communiste Martiniquais. It insisted that Martinique met the criteria of a nation and called for Martinican self-government in alliance with Marxist-Leninist parties and movements worldwide.[54] In March 1958, Césaire and Aliker founded the Parti progressiste martiniquais.[55] The PPM became an immediate electoral force and the organizational vehicle through which Césaire, its president, and his circle would pursue autonomy as self-governing regions of a larger federal state.[56]

In Martinican public discourse "autonomy" was sometimes used in a narrow sense. Césaire himself initially identified the PPM's program as an *alternative* to both assimilation and "autonomy"—by which he seems to have meant political independence or an economically self-sustaining Martinique. At its Third Congress in 1967, when the PPM officially declared its support for "autonomy," it meant something like the British conception of home rule: an autonomous state with sovereignty over local affairs within the framework of a larger confederation with the former imperial power. This conception of autonomy is notably different from the PPM's earlier program for autonomy within a federal union (1958–67).[57]

The most comprehensive outline of Césaire's federalist program is in his Report to the Constitutive Congress of the PPM (March 22, 1958), titled "For the Transformation of Martinique into a Region within the Framework of a Federated French Union." Césaire recounts that until 1945 socioeconomic isolation had allowed Martinique a certain autonomy. Then when "this status became a fetter on the development of Martinique and an obstacle to our progress," the "idea of departmentalization" was "born."[58] Césaire maintained that "if one day the regime created by departmentalization, thanks to the very progress due to departmentalization, in its turn appears as an obstacle, nothing, that is to say, no fetishism will prevent it from being reconsidered to make room for a regime that will not only be the negation of two previous regimes, but their transcended and enriched form."[59] The historical perspective that departmentalization had been only a provisional instrument for colonial emancipation allowed Césaire to challenge both critics who denounced departmentalization as "a failure of imagination" and uncritical defenders who made it "taboo" to rethink the 1946 law.[60]

Césaire sympathized with those supporters of departmentalization who argued that separation from France would be socially and economically disastrous. He observed, "given the present state of things, to pass from departmentalization to autonomy would be to provoke the dismantling of our social laws and to carry out an attack on our workers' standard of living... omni-lateral autonomy, would be, in the current state of things, an autonomy of poverty [misère]."[61] Yet he recognized that political assimilation was itself a source of Antillean impoverishment. He believed that economic development would require industrialization, protective customs barriers, and the right to trade freely on the world market, but metropolitan self-interest led the French state to block such measures. Moreover, he argued, because the high cost of equivalent salaries, labor protections, and social security benefits for Antilleans would require a reduction in metropolitan standards of living, the socioeconomic dimensions of the 1946 law would never be implemented.[62]

Césaire criticized departmentalization as an overly centralized system; policies concerning Martinique were "decided in" and "imposed by Paris." He cited Proudhon's belief that political assimilation "entails the risk of tyranny."[63] And he criticized the "cultural and human" effect of departmentalization as a "process of depersonalization" that "denatures" social groups by denying their distinctiveness.[64] He observed that this system, which "attacks the very vitality of the country," is responsible for "the malaise of a people who feels that it is no longer responsible for its own future [sort], and only plays the role of an extra in a drama of which it should be the protagonist."[65] In his view, independence for Martinique would be economic suicide while full assimilation through departmentalization was neither possible nor desirable. He concluded that "however difficult it is, Martinicans must be able to look this truth squarely in the face" and "adapt our behavior to the situation."[66]

Césaire identified "the federal idea" as the only "true synthesis."[67] He criticized attempts by socialist legislators, such as his Martinican colleague Paul Symphor, to reform rather than abolish departmentalization though the "chimera" of "adapted assimilation."[68] And he reassured those who feared separation that federalism would not end financial support from the metropolitan state.[69] He declared that "the federal idea is not a bastard compromise between assimilation and autonomy, but a third term that, in the dialectic, overcomes the antinomy... only the federal idea, which is the opposite of separation and at the same time the opposite of assimilation, allows us to resolve correctly the Antillean problem."[70]

As an autonomous region within a federal union of peoples, Antilleans would enjoy the political equality and economic solidarity demanded by proponents of assimilation as well as the self-government and cultural autonomy proclaimed by critics of departmentalization. Césaire declared, "without prejudging a future evolution, it seems to me that the notion that, at the present moment, would best recover the field of our singularity, would be the word region."[71] He invoked the Italian constitution which treated Sicily and Sardinia as distinct "regions" enjoying governmental autonomy yet receiving state economic development funds, and maintained that "in recommending a similar status for the Antilles, we are not slipping into utopia . . . there exist precedents and other models."[72] Like Camus and Arendt, Césaire challenged assumptions about "realistic" versus "utopian" programs:

> only a federal system provides a reasonable solution to the constitutional difficulties that assail us. But the [typical] Martinican, enemy of utopia, poses the question: Isn't all this a chimera? Does this have any chance of seeing the light of day? I do not hesitate: to the very extent that total assimilation appears to me to be a chimera, the federal idea seems to be realizable.[73]

Césaire explicitly identified with the federalist position that had been developed by Senghor and his parliamentary allies, reminding supporters that this shift would realign Martinique with other peoples struggling to end colonialism through "the transformation of the Unitary French Republic into a Federal French Republic."[74] He lamented that "departmentalization established a rupture between us and progressive Africans," but predicted that "support for the federal idea would give us more power by placing us on the same terrain of demand and combat as our African brothers and French progressives."[75] He concluded with a declaration that if the PPM can transform

> the Overseas Departments into federal regions . . . we will have succeeded in allying our double concern to remain linked to France and to be good Martinicans, and without falling into a separatism that would kill us, we will have triumphed over another separation as well, which would eventually prove to be mortal, the separation of man from himself.[76]

We should distinguish Césaire's dialectical account of the movement from colonialism to federalism via departmentalization from a vulgar historical materialism that posits necessary transformations or fixed stages of development. He attended to how dynamic contradictions within a particular social formation in a given conjuncture created conditions for its overcoming. But his pragmatic commitment to intervene strategically into present arrangements while remaining open to unknown future possibilities was precisely about the contingency of political acts rather than the necessity of historical evolution. By pushing Martinicans to recognize the failure of departmentalization, he emphasized that they faced a historic opportunity to assume responsibility for making history.

Césaire regarded federalism as the most promising framework at that moment through which Martinique could achieve economic self-reliance, social solidarity, self-government, and cultural dignity. Earlier, he had hoped that departmentalization would reawaken the future past of Schoelcher's utopian vision of abolition. Now, through federalism, he sought to revitalize the unrealized emancipatory promise of his original program for departmentalization. He also acknowledged that the future could not be "prejudged." If federalism failed or conditions changed, it too must be overcome. He never faced that decision: his project to redefine Martinique as an autonomous region within a reconstituted federal republic was never realized.

Constitutional Crisis

Césaire's long report was reprinted in weekly installments by *Le Progressiste*, the official PPM newspaper, between July 5 and August 2, 1958. By then the Algerian War had evolved into a broader conflict that toppled the Fourth Republic.[77] On May 13 supporters of French Algeria staged a coup d'état in Algiers and called for de Gaulle to return to power to defeat the nationalist insurgents and keep Algeria French. Metropolitan fears that rightist imperial forces would stage a coup in Paris created broad support for de Gaulle to resolve the crisis. On June 1 he was invested as head of state by the National Assembly and granted special powers to rule by decree for six months and draft a new constitution.[78]

De Gaulle presented this unconstitutional assumption of state power as an act of public service. It was a piece of political theater nearly as striking as the apparent self-liberation of Paris that he had staged in 1944.[79] This new historical hiatus allowed de Gaulle to create the strong executive state he had always wanted. But it also allowed African and Antillean legislators to lobby for a constitution that would finally remake France as a decentralized democratic federation.

On May 25, under the heading "Paris or Weimar?" *Le Progressiste* criticized the antirepublican way the Fourth Republic was dissolved. It reprinted articles from the metropolitan press that denounced the Algerian coup as fascistic and ran a piece outlining the difference between a genuine federal state and a merely decentralized unitary state.[80] Subsequent issues promoted "a progressively decentralized, flexible, and nuanced federal union."[81] Pierre Aliker wrote,

> our current departmental status must be replaced in the new constitution by new provisions that will transform this false department which we now are into an authentic region enjoying, within the framework of a renovated French Union, a large degree of autonomy which will allow Martinicans to take hold of their own problems [*à bras le corps*].[82]

Césaire warned de Gaulle that history would condemn him for not having resolved the contradictory "diarchy" whereby France was ruled simultaneously by different authorities in Paris and Algiers.[83] He called on contemporaries to reread Schoelcher's arguments that political crises rooted in social inequality could not be resolved through military force.[84] Nor, he added, could de Gaulle's Roman models resolve the contradictions of a class society.[85]

Despite such criticism, the PPM ultimately supported de Gaulle's return to power, hoping the constitutional crisis might compel him to create a federal republic. In an August 1958 article, Césaire cited Marx, Engels, Lenin, Proudhon, and Bakunin to claim that federalism marked an advance over traditional bourgeois parliamentarianism. "At the present moment," he maintained, "federalism constitutes the only form of relation that could prevent the French Union from sinking into either chaos or tyranny." Because the union was "traversed by the nationalism of renascent peoples [and] local particularisms, conditions exist which would make a Federative Republic a 'step forward'— the only, and only decisive one, now possible."[86]

But the constitution for a Fifth Republic, which replaced the French Union with a new French Community, was not what the PPM desired. Césaire denounced it as "a missed opportunity." He related, "the Overseas Territories expected General de Gaulle, alas, from the bloody and smoking ruins of Empire, to found a community of free peoples. But we must say that the General has retreated from this great plan."[87] The proposed constitution created only a facade of federalism while preserving the unitary state and failed to define a new legal status for the DOM. Césaire predicted this shortsightedness would turn the Antillean relationship with France "rotten or bitter."[88]

Césaire was especially concerned about provisions allowing the new republic to treat the departments as second-class and semicolonial territories. According to Article 73, "the legislative regime and administrative organization of the overseas departments can be the object of adaptive measures required by their particular situation."[89] This ambiguous provision was read by many as a progressive measure to grant departments more local autonomy. But it would also allow the state to undermine hard-won legal equality. Césaire informed the Martinican public that "the remedy is perhaps worse than the illness, because in reality what they offer us is simply a return to a regime that we know well, to a regime against which our ancestors spent their time struggling, *the regime of special laws and exceptional decrees.*" Césaire argued that if Martinicans wanted to avoid "these old ruts," they needed "to refuse the stupid dilemma: *assimilation or secession* . . . [and] to have the courage to inaugurate a new . . . federal system." Announcing that the time had come either "to imagine or to die," he pleaded, "while there is still time let us therefore imagine a system that fulfills rather than compromises [peoples'] personalities; that coordinates initiatives rather than paralyzing them; a system that would be a bundle of living liberties rather than the superimposition of lazy resignations beneath the stick of a dismal bureaucracy."[90]

At a mass rally in Fort-de-France on September 8, Césaire called on Martinicans to vote no on the referendum.[91] Camille Darsières, a longtime PPM militant and close associate of Césaire's and Aliker's, recounts that Césaire then traveled to Paris to communicate these concerns to the government and negotiate concessions for the DOM.[92] He met with de Gaulle, his chief of staff, Georges Pompidou, and his minister of state, André Malraux.[93] These luminaries reportedly promised Césaire that this constitution was only a first step and that under the Fifth Republic Martinique would have a local assembly with greater substantive power, would receive significant development funds, and could exercise effective autonomy (through Article 73) by adapting metropolitan laws.[94]

At a second rally in Fort-de-France on September 20, Césaire reversed himself and called for a yes on the referendum. He hosted Malraux who reassured the crowd that the government understood its concerns and would support its demands for local autonomy and economic investment. The day before the referendum Césaire defended his new position in an essay titled "Hold the Ground Already Won" [*Tenir le pas gagné*], a quote from Rimbaud's poem "Adieu," in which the speaker acknowledges the failure of his art and imagination and returns to the harsh "*cité*" of worldly reality.[95] Césaire explained that despite its flaws, the proposed constitution was "a great contract . . . of fraternity, aid, and mutual comprehension" within which Martinique's status could still evolve: "between the mystical *yes* and the mechanical *no* . . . there is room for a third path, the yes of reason, the yes of hope, the yes of vigilance."[96]

Césaire's policy reversal on the referendum disappointed many observers. A sympathetic Darsières relates having been bewildered by the party's sudden support for the constitution but also recalls that the constitution met the PPM's minimal conditions of allowing Martinique to adapt national law to its own particular conditions and transform its legal status if it desired.[97] (Article 86 allowed members of the French Community to hold local referenda on independence. As independent states they could remain members of the French Community.[98]) Ernst Moutoussamy, a Martinican communist, accused Césaire of being seduced by Gaullism.[99] Nevertheless, and despite the determined opposition of the Martinican Communist Party, the September 28 referendum was approved by a landslide there and in the rest of France.

Césaire may have shared the ambivalent mix of resignation and humility expressed by Rimbaud in "Adieu." The speaker abandons dreamy skies to enter the decaying *cité*. He feels shame about his failure to invent new worlds but is resolved to move beyond an illusory existence and reengage "with glowing patience" a debased but real world. Rimbaud's poem traces the relation between worldly embodied and spiritual-aesthetic realms, as if one can be reached only by way of the other. Perhaps Césaire decided that the best way to transcend departmentalization was by passing through the existing political situation. Perhaps he believed that the imperfect constitution did not have to correspond to his imaginative ideal as long as it provided a pathway toward a different political order

Césaire's attempt to conjugate the actual and desirable followed Rimbaud's exhortation to hold ground already won: French citizenship, economic subventions, and the legal possibility of transforming Martinique into a self-governing collectivity within the French Community. Césaire also believed that Martinicans themselves needed to act if they wanted substantive autonomy within this new legal framework. In his campaign flyer for the November 23, 1958, elections to the first Assembly of the Fifth Republic, which marked his own ambivalent return to the *cité*, he explained that Martinicans who voted yes "must now give a form to the Republic, give it life, give it a direction. In sum, it must be oriented." Electing him would "accentuate the process of decolonization that, happily, has been inaugurated by the government."[100]

Césaire again pledged "to improve the standard of living of the Martinican people and to assure the modernization of our country" through full employment, "rational industrialization," better salaries, extension of the guaranteed national minimum wage to the DOMs, higher family allowances, and low-cost housing. He insisted that they "play a greater role in the management of their own affairs and that local elected officials be granted power to adapt metropolitan laws to local circumstances."[101] Yet these much-reiterated demands indicate that Martinique's departmental predicament persisted in a largely unchanged form.

Armand Nicolas reports that after a visit there in April 1958, a representative of the Ministy of Overseas Departments observed a "deep and generalized malaise" concerning "the insufficient participation of local populations and their elected officials in the management of their own affairs."[102] Césaire continued to inform his metropolitan colleagues of declining purchasing power, rising costs of living, low wages, high taxes, limited credit, unfair preferences for metropolitan civil servants, unequal pay for overseas functionaries, the selective implementation of social benefits, widespread unemployment, and the French state's refusal to make economic and social investments there.

On December 20, 1959, three nights of rioting in Martinique began after an automobile with a white metropolitan driver struck a black man on a scooter. The prefecture deployed CRS units, which attacked civilians. In response, police stations were burned and car windows smashed; three protestors were killed and many more wounded and arrested. On December 24 the Communist-led Conseil Général condemned police brutality, demanded economic reforms, and called for Martinique's departmental status to be modified in favor of greater autonomy. The metropolitan government sent planes with army reserve units and prepared battleships with helicopters and armed vehicles for deployment. By December 29 an agreement was reached between the minister of Overseas Departments, Jacques Soustelle, and Martinique's parliamentary deputies. The government agreed to defer a plan to recruit immigrant agricultural workers and raised the minimum wage 5 percent. Although the riots were officially blamed on communist agitators, the government feared they might signal separatist sentiments. A report from the prefecture determined that the CRS had committed regular abuses in recent years and contributed to a racially charged and socially tense atmosphere on the island. The ministry proposed using Article 73 to grant more power to Antillean assemblies. These events also led the PPM to endorse the Conseil Général's motion to revise Martinique's legal status.[103]

Whereas the Conseil Général and the Martinican Communist Party had immediately supported the rebellion, Césaire was in Paris when it erupted. As in the 1940s, he denounced the police repression and insisted on fair treatment for arrested protesters. But despite his mass popularity and the PPM's electoral successes, the 1959 uprising indicated that Césaire was slipping out of sync with popular sentiment; ordinary Martinicans were uncertain that substantive self-management and socioeconomic improvement would be possible under the Fifth Republic. Césaire's postwar trajectory was haunted by this challenge of coordinating legal initiatives through democratic procedure and direct action through mass protest.

The Art of Decolonization

The responsibilities of cultural elites during decolonization was the subject of Césaire's presentation at the Second Congress of Black Writers and Artists, held in Rome March 26–April 1, 1959, nine months before these riots broke out. He argued that although colonialism was "morally finished" and had "lost its historic assurance," decolonization was "not automatic . . . [it] is never the result of a 'fiat' by the conscience of the colonizer. It is always the result of a struggle, always the result of a push. Even the most peaceful of them is always the result of a rupture."[104] To this end, the "man of culture" should work "to hasten the maturation of popular consciousness without which there can never be decolonization."[105] Warning that "all decolonizations are not equal," Césaire suggested that writers and artists must ensure that "colonial structures" were "destroyed, extirpated in the true sense of the word, that is to say, torn out by their roots." Implicitly invoking Schoelcher, he declared, "that is why true decolonization will be revolutionary or will be nothing."[106]

Césaire paid special attention to revolutionizing structures of cultural domination. He reminded listeners that "the struggle against colonialism is not finished . . . just because imperialism will have been militarily defeated."[107] Because he believed empire depended on a distinction between colonizers as cultural producers and colonized consumers, he identified a distinctive role for artists and writers. They had a "duty," in his view, "to reestablish the double continuity ruptured by colonialism . . . with the world . . . [and] with ourselves."[108] He identified these "men of truth" as "re-introducers of our people to the world . . . re-inventers of solidarity amongst ourselves . . . soldiers of unity and fraternity."[109] Then he temporalized his argument: "And it is not only solidarity in space that black writers and artists reestablish, it is also . . . historical continuity."[110]

Invoking Senghor, Césaire observed that because "imperialism divided history" by distinguishing between a before and after of colonialism, it "balkanized" the time of overseas peoples.[111] He called on black artists to "reestablish . . . reaffirm or reinvent" this broken historical continuity. Underscoring the political significance of this temporal operation, he explained that when Sékou Touré declares he is the descendant of Samory, "it is not a matter of puerile genealogical vanity" but a way of saying "I assume [the legacy of] Samory."

This gesture "reestablishes history" and "puts things back in their place."[112] By repairing spatial solidarities and historical continuities, black cultural producers could elevate colonized populations into autonomous historical actors.

Césaire also called on black cultural producers to make art and literature "sacred . . . by raising the particular situation of our peoples to the universal."[113] He contended that "artistic creation" could "restore the social body shaken by the colonial shock in its capacity to resist" by "reconnecting [the people] to history, by hoisting them to a plane that is precisely that of the future."[114] But these creators had "a human duty" even more profound than their "particular duties" because "finally, there is a question that no man of culture can escape, regardless of his country or his race, which is the following: 'What kind of world are you preparing for us?'" In language that recalled both Mazzini's Holy Alliance and Sartre's interpretation of the Liberation, Césaire related black self-determination to human self-realization:

> By articulating our effort with the effort of the liberation of colonized peoples, by struggling for the dignity of our peoples, for their truth and for their *recognition*, it is by definition for the whole entire world that we fight, to liberate it from tyranny, from hatred, and from fanaticism . . . we want a rejuvenated and re-balanced world, without which nothing will have any meaning . . . not even our struggle today . . . not even our victory tomorrow. Then and only then will we have been victorious and our final victory will mark the advent of a new era. We will have contributed to giving a meaning . . . to the most overused yet most glorious word: we will have helped to found a universal humanism.[115]

For Césaire art was a privileged medium of true decolonization and decolonization a creative act through which black self-determination could bring forth a new era of human history.

The poems Césaire published in *Présence Africaine* between 1955 and 1959, collected in the volume *Ferrements*, explored this relation of art, politics, and time. They reestablish spatial solidarities by aligning with popular rebellions and radical actors; they restore temporal solidarities by calling upon past spirits and claiming historical legacies. These poems also exhibit the density, opacity, humor, violence, expressive power, and awesome erudition that had come to characterize Césaire's modernist aesthetic. They were political not only due to anticolonial content but because they were subversive creative acts, singular and refractory artifacts that confounded categories and resisted reduction.

"Memorial for Louis Delgrès" (1959) conjured the legendary black general who had confronted the French invasion force sent by Napoleon to Guadeloupe in 1802. After several days of resistance against General Richepanse's troops, which were charged with reoccupying the territory and reintroducing slavery, Delgrès refused to surrender. His army of former slaves retreated to a mountain fort in the town of Matouba. On May 28, 1802, they set fire to their armaments, creating an explosion that killed themselves and many of their adversaries. Richepanse then reinstituted slavery in Guadeloupe. Simultaneously, General Leclerc was waging war against a revolutionary army of freed slaves led by black and mulatto generals (Louverture, Dessalines, Christophe, and Pétion) in neighboring Saint-Domingue.[116]

Césaire's poem is framed by two epigraphs. The first notes that Delgrès was born in Martinique and recounts that during the siege of Matouba, he was spotted on the ramparts of the fort playing a violin to encourage his troops. The second, from a proclamation that President Dessalines made to the Haitian public on April 28, 1804, describes Delgrès as a "magnanimous warrior." These epigraphs relate revolutionary anticolonialism to art, drama, and generosity. They establish geographical connections among Martinique, Guadeloupe, and Haiti and historical continuity among Delgrès, Dessalines, and Césaire.

"Memorial" begins with a speaker confessing to being "forever haunted" and "always obsessed" by the image of a fist surging up to break through a blanket of fog.[117] He declaims, "Louis Delgrès I say your name / and lifting out of silence the pedestal of this name / I hit the precise thickness of night / with an ecstatic hive of fireflies."[118] Here historical memory produces poetic illumination, and poetic evocation illuminates history. Césaire implies that Delgrès's act of resistance was significant because it overturned the illusion of historical determination—destiny—upon which the system of colonial slavery depended: "then History hoisted on its highest pyre / the drop of blood of which I speak / where the strange rupture of destiny / came to be reflected as in a deep parage."[119] "Parage," denoting both lineage and inherited rank, was used in feudal law to refer to an individual's share of an inheritance or to the system of land tenure in which an inheritance is divided equally among brothers.[120] This image suggests that Delgrès's "notable leap" toward death was at once a claim on his rightful inheritance (dignity, agency, autonomy) and a legacy that future generations could rightfully inherit.

The poem celebrates Delgrès's creative and courageous ability to confront history and confound destiny, to rupture the historical continuum that subtended colonial domination. We read: "O Violent Breaker Disconcerter / I sing the hand which disdained to skim / with the long spoon of days the cane juice / boiling of the great vat of time."[121] Césaire's Delgrès condemned not only slavery but the temporal order that seemed to condemn him to it. The poet recalls that Delgrès's revolutionary refusal to be reduced to his labor power confounded or disconcerted the expectations and categories upon which colonial slavery depended. Likewise, Césaire's poetry is a disconcerting practice that confounds colonial expectations.

By figuring Delgrès's revolutionary act as a temporal refusal, "Memorial" affirmed the possibility of alternative futures neither historically ordained nor foreseen before the hero's dramatic gesture. When the speaker says "I call for a liana that grows on the palm tree / (for it is our obstinate future on the trunk of the present)," he invokes the prospect of a hybrid or grafted future that Delgrès's act enabled.[122] Suggesting the hubris of defying time, the speaker calls Delgrès "an Icarus by investiture" who "hollowed out of the ash's path the phosphorous wound of an unfathomable source."[123] Perhaps it is this link between destruction and illumination that allows the poet to assert that Delgrès is "here in this sap and this blood inside this evidence / at the four corners of the islands, meandering us." Figured as the "supple multitude of the imperishable body," Delgrès is at once universal and particular, abstract duration and the concrete tradition of popular rebellion.[124]

"Memorial" concludes with an image of disjointed time, where Delgrès's past and the Antillean future intersect through his remembered legacy: "So/ constructor of the heart in the soft flesh of mangrove trees / today Delgrès / in the hollow of intersecting paths / taking up this name outside the maremmas / I proclaim you and in any future wind / you the buccinators of a distant vintage."[125] Delgrès's untimely presence is mediated by the song of the poet proclaiming his name. This poetic act mirrors the political act of this "vintage," or highly valued, "buccinator," the muscle that forms the wall of the human cheek. It follows that Césaire refers to Delgrès as a "trumpeter"—one announcing a different relation between Antillean peoples and historical time. "Buccinator" also links the transgenerational trumpet sound of Delgrès's act and the poem that trumpets it and sings his name.

This Delgrès resembles the self-sacrificing and equally absolutist Rebel, the protagonist of Césaire's earlier dramatic poem *Et les chiens se taisent* (And the Dogs Were Silent, 1946), who also demanded freedom at the price of death.[126] Both figures may therefore seem to diverge from Césaire's own political practices; he was neither a political absolutist nor a revolutionary leader of a popular insurrection. Yet "Memorial" was not simply a poem about a slave rebellion. Delgrès was a *free* man who refused to *return* to a state of domination already overcome. "Memorial" thus dramatizes the intolerable prospect of recolonization *after* emancipation. In this respect, despite the evident differences between revolutionary Guadeloupe in 1802 and the Department of Martinique

in 1959, Delgrès's gesture likely resonated with Césaire's understand
Antillean predicament. Césaire too confronted the prospect of h'
versal and political foreclosure: the French state was recolonizing
while Africa was being decolonized. Like Delgrès, Césaire confr
timely movement from freedom back to domination through a process
seemingly reversed the supposedly unidirectional flow of progressive history.
These reversals and regressions brushed against the emancipatory grain of their
respective times (i.e., the Atlantic revolutions and decolonization).

Césaire's 1946 play-poem about the Rebel was abstract and decontexualized.
It could be read as referring to New World slavery, colonial domination, the
condition of peoples of African descent in the modern world, the liberation
of France, postwar alienation, or even the human condition generally. Its classical structure and underspecified setting contributed to its broad allegorical
power. In contrast, "Memorial for Louis Delgrès" was an elegy for a historical
actor. This poem marked a new round of engagement by Césaire with Antillean history. As in 1946, Césaire confronted the problem of colonial emancipation through the optic of nineteenth-century slave emancipation. But as
his present conditions changed, so did his historical reference points. When
struggling to realize the potential of departmentalization in the 1940s, he had
conjured the spirit of Schoelcher and the 1848 abolition of slavery. But as departmentalization shifted from a medium of emancipation to an obstacle, Césaire's pursuit of federal autonomy was now mediated by Toussaint Louverture's struggle for black self-determination in Saint-Domingue.

From the Spirit of Schoelcher to the Legacy of Louverture

On July 19, 1958, Césaire published a short piece in *Le Progressiste* in which he
related,

> I am in the habit, every year as July 21 approaches, of rereading Schoelcher.
> And each time . . . I marvel at his contemporary relevance [*actualité*].
> Schoelcher, old Schoelcher as they called him in his time, the maniac
> [*l'homme à marottes*], is living, more than ever living. His frock coat may
> have aged, but not his ideas. And Schoelcher is always before us.[127]

"Devant," a spatial term, rather than "avant," a temporal term, signals Schoelcher's
untimely power to remain "before" his descendants, facing them rather than
preceding them. Césaire invoked this untimely maniac to criticize the maniacal
"colonels" then prosecuting the Algerian War "who over the body of the anes-
thetized republic, contemplate reshaping with a sword the face of France." He

writes, "from the depth of his tomb, it is Schoelcher who shouts to them . . . to find a form of social organization that guarantees to each citizen in exchange for his labor, the development and satisfaction of his needs."[128]

Césaire suggests more generally that Schoelcher's reflections may help contemporary leaders to recover the real meanings of seemingly evacuated political categories.

> Freedom, Justice, Humanity, these great ideas that we thought discredited and that we wanted to discredit . . . by qualifying them as utopian or for 1848ers, these ideas, because the world has suffered for having allowed them to be invaded by rust, the world has again learned to cherish them. Idealism never had such freshness or flavor than since through Hitler to Rakosi and passing through Stalin, history became the terrible prize of "realists" . . . it is not peoples who need to be re-taught Schoelcher, because peoples are instinctually Schoelcherist. It is governments. And Schoelcher would without a doubt be, and better than Machiavelli, an excellent tutor of princes.[129]

Refiguring the relationship between realism and utopia, Césaire sought, in a radically literalist fashion, to reclaim, derust, and reanimate seemingly decrepit ideas. Yet in 1958, it was likely Schoelcher's commitment to self-surpassing political experiments rather than his specific program for emancipation through assimilation that spoke to Césaire; less his plan for success than his way of negotiating failure.

We saw that Schoelcher never realized his aim of converting legal abolition into sociopolitical equality by transforming the Antillean colonies into French departments.[130] Schoelcher's abolitionist politics had first been forged during his 1841 voyage to independent Haiti.[131] Then when the emancipatory potential of 1848 had been foreclosed, he again turned his attention to Saint-Domingue. On July 27, 1879, Schoelcher was invited to give a talk in Paris on Toussaint Louverture as part of an effort by Thomas-Prosper Gragnon-Lacoste to raise funds to construct a memorial tomb for Toussaint in Bordeaux, where his ashes remained.[132] This talk laid the foundation for Schoelcher's 1899 historical monograph on Toussaint.[133]

For Schoelcher, the revolution in Saint-Domingue had demonstrated that history could be redirected and a new society created when enslaved blacks transformed themselves into an autonomous political force. But Schoelcher also mourned Toussaint's descent into despotism as a tragic betrayal of republican principles. He contended that there remained "too much of the old slave in Toussaint for him to believe that labor could be obtained without coercion."[134] Throughout Schoelcher's life, he regarded Toussaint as both an icon of black freedom and an example of how revolutionary leaders can abandon emancipatory ideals. Writing about Haiti when his own struggle for Antillean emancipation had reached an impasse, Schoelcher projected his past hopes and present despair onto Toussaint's dramatic public life. Likewise, Césaire turned to the legacy of Louverture after the emancipatory potential of departmentalization had been foreclosed.

As discussed, Césaire first visited Haiti in 1944.[135] He recalled being struck by the cautionary example of "a country that had conquered its liberty . . . its independence, and which I saw was more miserable than Martinique."[136] During this stay Césaire began writing a play about Toussaint Louverture.[137] But deciding that he had "taken the wrong road" and that the work was "too historic," he turned it into something more "mythic and magic," with a "Dionysian spirit."[138] Toussaint became the Rebel and the initial play evolved into *And the Dogs Were Silent*. Césaire did not return to Haitian history until the late 1950s. It is no accident that his writing of *Toussaint Louverture: The French Revolution and the Colonial Problem* coincided with his embrace of cooperative federalism.[139] Working through Louverture's confrontation with the problem of freedom helped him reorient his own emancipatory project.

Like Schoelcher, Césaire attended to the immensity of Louverture's achievements and the impossibility of his enterprise, to his manifold failures and the ever-unrealized possibilities for black liberty and human emancipation that his interventions opened. But whereas Schoelcher could neither understand nor forgive Toussaint's authoritarian rule, Césaire interpreted this dictatorship circumstantially, as compelled by a revolutionary crisis, and argued that Louverture chose to sacrifice himself as a political act addressed to future generations.

Since May 1794 Toussaint Louverture had fought as a general in the Revolutionary French army. But as tensions developed between him and the Directory government, he was ready to defend black liberty *against* the metropolitan republic. As commander-in-chief of the Saint-Domingue army he concluded peace with the British and negotiated trade agreements with England and the United States. These would ensure commercial partners and an arms supply in case of war with France. Believing that political autonomy required economic self-sufficiency, he invited white planters to reclaim their property and cooperate with his regime. He also issued proclamations requiring freed slaves to return to plantations and work for wages. Toussaint expelled Gabriel Hédouville, the ranking representative of the metropolitan government, from Saint-Domingue and defeated the forces of André Rigaud, his former ally and leader of a free colored army in the south. Finally, he reconquered Spanish

Santo Domingo, unifying the territory and denying easy entry to the French army.[140]

In these ways Toussaint pragmatically prepared for war and consolidated his authority over an autonomous regime he ruled as a military governor.[141] But these were also performative gestures through which he *acted* like a head of state before the general population, potential rivals, the metropolitan government, the international community, and even future generations. A turning point in his relationship with the French republic arrived with Napoleon Bonaparte's November 9, 1799, coup d'état, which toppled the Directory. The 1795 constitution had defined French colonies as "integral parts of the Republic" and "subject to the same constitutional law."[142] But Bonaparte's December 13, 1799, constitution now declared that colonies would be governed by "special laws."[143] Toussaint recognized that this government, influenced by planters and the maritime bourgeoisie, hoped to restore prerevolutionary colonial rule and perhaps even reinstate slavery. In response, he convened a Constituent Assembly composed of elite white and free colored representatives from each department to draft a legal charter for his regime.[144]

Whereas Bonaparte deployed "special laws" to segregate and subordinate the overseas territories, Toussaint used similar logic to ground self-government in a republican idiom.[145] In an announcement to the population of Saint-Domingue, his Constituent Assembly explained that Bonaparte's constitution had "degraded the dignity of free men" and "forced them to accept laws that they did not fashion and to which they did not consent."[146] The assembly assured the public that a new "local constitution" would create "appropriate laws" according them the "rights you possess by nature."[147]

Toussaint's May 10, 1801, constitution declared slavery "forever abolished" in the territory.[148] It stipulated that "all men, regardless of color, are eligible for all employment . . . [with] no distinctions other than those based on virtue and talent . . . the law is the same for all."[149] This commitment to legal equality was also linked to an affirmation of self-determination: "the colonial regime is determined by laws proposed by the Governor and rendered by . . . [the] Central Assembly of St-Domingue."[150] Article 28 designated Toussaint Louverture governor "for the remainder of his glorious life."[151] Broad military, executive, financial, and legislative powers were concentrated in this position. The state could regulate free speech, political dissent, civic organizations, peasant mobility, religious faith, "social virtues" and "family bonding" as well as "professions regarding public mores, public safety, health, and wealth of its citizens."[152] Toussaint's belief in the economic foundation of liberty were expressed in articles on property as "sacred and inviolable," the binding character of land leases, and the rights of absentee owners to retain title to their colonial properties.[153] On the grounds that "the colony . . . cannot suffer the least disruption in its works of cultivation," the strict system of labor discipline would continue. Article 76 indicates that the spirit underlying these provisions was more radically republican than liberal democratic: "any citizen owes service to the land that nourishes him or in which he was born for the maintenance of freedom, equality, and property, whenever the law calls upon him to defend them."[154]

The 1801 constitution joined formal equality and the rule of law to a revolutionary dictatorship. It established Toussaint as the leader of a self-governing republic that enjoyed de facto territorial sovereignty (at the expense of popular sovereignty). Schoelcher may have called it "nothing less than an act of independence" rendering French sovereignty "purely nominal,"[155] yet it clearly defined Saint-Domingue as a "colony, which is part of the French empire, but ruled under particular laws."[156] In it, "all men are born, live, and die free and French."[157] Toussaint proposed a novel political arrangement: Saint-Domingue would be a self-governing constitutional state within the French empire.

The assembly charged Toussaint with "sending the present constitution to be sanctioned by the French government" but declared that due to the colony's "perilous situation" and the "unanimous wishes pronounced by the inhabitants of Saint-Domingue, the Chief General is henceforth invited, in the name of public good, to proceed with its execution."[158] The whole point of this constitution was that the government's legal legitimacy and positive laws derived only from the people of Saint-Domingue. Yet the constitution also sought authority from the metropolitan government to enact itself. We see how the Constituent Assembly could both criticize metropolitan rule *and* claim to be "guided by the ardent desire . . . to prove their attachment to the French government"[159] and how Toussaint "had the generosity, the courage, to take the reins of an abandoned and defenseless colony" *in order to* "spread respect for the French name."[160]

Toussaint acted as both a sovereign head of state and a servant of the French republic. He enacted both roles when he charged his white French adviser, Colonel Vincent, to deliver the already promulgated constitution to Bonaparte. Vincent reportedly asked him, "what could the French government now do [in Saint-Domingue] given that there are no provisions within the constitution that allow it to either appoint or send any [officials] to the colony?" When Toussaint suggested that "the government will send commissioners to speak with me," Vincent corrected him, "better yet ambassadors."[161] Toussaint also entrusted Vincent with a letter informing Bonaparte that he had convened "a central assembly which could define the future of Saint-Domingue through wise laws, based on the customs of the population . . . I submitted to their desires. This constitution was welcomed by all classes of citizens with transports of joy." He presented this as a fait accompli—"the final touches have just been made to this project"—but still requested "the sanction and approval of my government," assuring Bonaparte that his endorsement would also provoke "transports of joy" in "citizens of all classes." Underscoring his status as a government functionary, he addressed it from "Toussaint-Louverture, general in chief of the army of Saint-Domingue, to citizen Bonaparte, First Consul of the French Republic . . . 27 Messidor year IX of the single and indivisible French Republic."[162]

Despite Toussaint's desire for Saint-Domingue to remain a French territory, Bonaparte responded, "the constitution that you have created includes many good things but also contains elements that are contrary to the dignity and the sovereignty of the French people, of which Saint-Domingue is a part."[163] He acknowledged that Toussaint had been left without metropolitan help to fight the enemies of the revolution, to end the civil war, and establish the rule of law. But he warned,

> now that circumstances have so happily changed, you will be the first to render homage to the sovereignty of the nation that counts you among its most illustrious citizens. . . . Any other conduct would be irreconcilable with our conception of you. It would result in your losing your numerous rights as well as the recognition and benefits of the Republic and would open [*creuserait*] beneath your feet a chasm that, in swallowing you, could contribute to the misfortune of these brave *noirs* whose courage we love and whose rebellion we would regretfully be obligated to punish.[164]

Bonaparte then relates his decision to send "citizen Leclerc" to Saint-Domingue to assume the post of "Captain General, as the ranking official [*premier magistrat*] of the colony. He is accompanied by sizable troops to spread respect for the sovereignty of the French people."[165] Bonaparte would later recall, "we considered [Toussaint] a rebel the instant that he published his constitution."[166]

Yet Toussaint continued to solicit Bonaparte's endorsement. He complained to Vincent, "I did good . . . why has the government never wanted to recognize this and write to me? If I was white, no praise would be beneath me; being *nègre*, perhaps I deserve even more."[167] Toussaint implored a prominent Creole who was fleeing to France to again plead his case:

I will send letters to the First Consul by you. . . . Tell him about me, tell him how prosperous agriculture is, how prosperous is commerce. . . . It is according to all I have done here that I ought and that I wish to be judged. Twenty times I have written to Bonaparte, to ask him to send Civil Commissioners, to tell him to dispatch hither the old colonists, whites instructed in administering public affairs, good machinists, good workmen: he has never replied. . . . I want . . . to make him see that in ruining me he ruins the blacks—ruins not only San Domingo but all the western colonies. If Bonaparte is the first man in France, Toussaint is the first man in the Archipelago of the Antilles.[168]

We see here that Toussaint regarded himself as the First Consul's partner *and* counterpart.[169] Laurent Dubois notes how closely aspects of Louverture's regime resembled the colonial system Bonaparte desired in Saint-Domingue, except that cultivators would not be enslaved and administration would be in the hands of an autonomous and largely black elite. He argues that only Bonaparte's racism can explain his rejection of Toussaint's experiment.[170]

Note that Toussaint's commitment to partnership with imperial France was neither a sign of passivity nor pacificism. When war became the only way to defend liberty and autonomy, he shifted from negotiation to confrontation. In February 1802 he informed General Dessalines that until the rainy season, when yellow fever would decimate French troops, "our only resources are destruction and fire. . . . Remember that the land bathed in our sweat must not provide our enemies with the least sustenance. . . . Shoot everyone en route, throw the bodies and the horses into the rivers; destroy and burn everything, so that those who come to return us to slavery will always meet before their eyes the image of hell that they deserve."[171]

Their soldiers indeed employed guerilla tactics, including burning the countryside and retreating from frontline encounters. By spring 1802 Toussaint's troops had almost defeated French forces. But one of his most powerful generals, Henri Christophe, defected to the French and Toussaint decided to negotiate peace with Leclerc who guaranteed general liberty for blacks. The following month, despite warnings of a plot against him, Toussaint met with a French general who had him arrested and deported to France. He died on April 7, 1803, of an untreated illness in a cell in Fort de Joux in the Jura mountains. There he was isolated, kept under strict surveillance, malnourished, denied medical attention, and eventually forbidden to write.[172]

James suggested that Toussaint's devotion to the French republic led to this "untimely and cruel death."[173] He observed that Toussaint had faced a "truly tragic" dilemma[174] and noted that "Toussaint was attempting the impossible."[175] Yet James also thought he had deceived himself about French intentions to reestablish slavery, hesitated when resolute action was necessary, lost touch with his allies, and alienated popular support.[176] In James's view Toussaint's "total miscalculation of . . . events" led to an "inevitable catastrophe."[177] His military interventions were "daring" and "tireless," but his politics "lagged behind events" and "the black revolution had passed him by."[178] James regarded Toussaint's efforts to "negotiate . . . the new relation with France" as "ruinous . . . revolutionary policy" and identified the May 1802 cease-fire as marking the moment Toussaint lost the allegiance of Dessalines, who then led the black masses to independence.[179]

But according to what metric had the revolution passed Toussaint by? Was his strategy trapped in the past or did it anticipate the future? Were his political acts born of misrecognition or the result of a canny reading of the political present? Were they motivated by a devotion to France or by a commitment to transcontinental federation as the best way to protect emancipation and autonomy for Saint-Domingue at that time?

Césaire also criticized Toussaint's failure to communicate clearly the threat posed by the French invaders and the rationale for his actions. He suggested that in 1801 Toussaint mistakenly acted *as if* it were 1794, as if the magic phrase for mobilizing people was still *general liberty* rather than *independence*, as if Leclerc was Hédouville, all "without recognizing that the situation was fundamentally different. The consequences were serious."[180] But Césaire also credited Toussaint with an acute understanding of the political present. He argued that Toussaint had sacrificed himself to protect black emancipation, buying time so Dessalines could defeat Leclerc when the time was right. He interpreted Toussaint's decision to walk into the ambush as "his last, and without a doubt one of his most fruitful political acts."[181]

When Césaire referred to Louverture as "the Precursor," he was not only identifying him as the avatar of anticolonial revolution.[182] Césaire was also recognizing him as a patient and visionary political strategist, ever mindful of long-term aims. Césaire's Louverture made sacrifices in the present, including his own life, to ensure his people's future freedom. He demonstrated an ability to "reconvert his politics," adopting new positions that corresponded more adequately to changing circumstances.[183]

Throughout the long struggle that began with the slave uprising in 1791, Toussaint pursued arrangements that would ensure the greatest liberty for his people given the existing political landscape. Such concerns led him to fight French revolutionaries before joining them against enemies of republicanism, then to propose a novel form of colonial autonomy within an imperial federation, and finally to confront France directly.[184] Beneath these apparent reversals, Toussaint's goals remained consistent: general liberty, economic independence, and political autonomy. Given the imperial order that would face postemancipation Saint-Domingue, Toussaint believed a formal partnership with France could best ensure these objectives, which his 1801 constitution sought to institutionalize.[185] He concluded that historical developments had made it possible—perhaps necessary—for Saint-Domingue to be a self-governing and economically independent partner of France. Among them were the transnational interdependence that characterized the French imperial economy, the republican sensibility of the revolutionary Atlantic, and the de facto territorial sovereignty the slave rebellion had allowed him to seize.

Toussaint's constitution aimed both to formalize the existing state of affairs and initiate a revolutionary transformation. The political arrangement he envisioned and enacted would have fundamentally reconfigured the colonial character of Saint-Domingue, the imperial relation between France and the colony, the republican character of the French nation-state, and the national character of the republic. It would have undermined the racist norms governing the existing capitalist, imperial, and interstate systems. These factors led Napoleon to destroy Saint-Domingue rather than sanction the autonomy of a society of freed slaves led by a black general.[186]

The historically possible system that Toussaint envisioned proved to be politically impossible. His untimely intervention was out of sync with both French national and imperial norms and the separatist wishes of his militant soldiers and slave rebels. The latter distrusted his willingness to collaborate with white planters and officials. Perhaps knowingly, Toussaint's constitution provoked the confrontation with Napoleon that led to his own untimely death, the demise of his political experiment, and Haitian independence. When all signs indicated that his dream of a federal partnership was foreclosed and that Napoleon wished to reinstitute slavery in Saint-Domingue, Toussaint was willing to engage in brutal war to defend emancipation and autonomy. Yet until the end, he insisted that he served the French republic, that Saint-Domingue remained a French colony, and that self-rule within an imperial framework would best serve both parties.[187]

Toussaint's attempt at an unprecedented federal partnership exemplified the paradox characteristic of strategic-utopian projects. It would have created an alternative set of arrangements only possible in a world that had already been transformed in precisely these ways. But in many ways Toussaint's utopian republic already existed. By 1801 he *had* created a new society in Saint-Domingue composed of emancipated blacks whom he governed (albeit as a revolutionary dictator) without the intercession of French officials. This autonomous black state *was* economically self-sufficient. Its plantation exports allowed it an interdependent relationship with imperial France even as it concluded independent commercial and diplomatic treaties with neighboring colonies and states.[188] Louverture's regime was an actually existing impossibility, his constitution a concrete or enacted utopia. By acting as if the future had already arrived, his initiative hastened its arrival. It performed the impossible, reshaping the present and addressing itself to a future that it anticipated by preceding, foreseeing, enacting, and calling forth.

Louverture was indeed a "precursor" whose precedent and spirit remained present to figures such as Schoelcher and Césaire. Césaire contended Toussaint's constitution anticipated forms of dominion and commonwealth 150 years ahead of their time.[189] But just as Césaire had to liberate Schoelcher's legacy from the official republican commemoration of abolition, Louverture's legacy had to be disentangled from mythic narratives that fixed him as the father of Haitian independence. Memories of Louverture, of course, never disappeared. His stature only grew during the nineteenth century as the specter of the Haitian Revolution haunted French policymakers and inspired peoples of African descent.[190] But the revolutionary and utopian specificity of Louverture's constitutional initiative was often obscured.

Haitian independence helped create the appearance of a necessary equivalence among anticolonialism, political emancipation, and national independence. This conflation was later reinforced by activists and scholars who viewed the Haitian Revolution through the lens of twentieth-century anticolonialism. Commentators often interpreted Toussaint's refusal to declare national independence as a failure to do so; his commitment to partnership with France has been criticized as poor judgment, false consciousness, or instrumental duplicity. Césaire's postwar projects for decolonization suffered these same accusations and should be situated within Louverture's lineage.

But to claim that Césaire's turn to federation was mediated by the legacy of Louverture is not to suggest that he simply imitated the Precursor. Césaire enacted a range of sometimes ambivalent identifications. His engagement with Haitian history informed his strategic orientation to politics and his programmatic writings about "true" decolonization as a revolutionary overcoming of colonialism with indispensable political, socioeconomic, cultural, and psychic dimensions. He conjured the revolution in Saint-Domingue as a portentous precedent for the Antillean revolution he warned would come if France continued to treat the departments as colonial possessions.[191] Yet the

Haitian Revolution also functioned for Césaire as a projective object through which he could act out a desire for the anticolonial revolution that might never come in postwar Martinique.[192]

Césaire resolutely embraced Louverture's legacy as a clairvoyant political strategist. Like Toussaint's, Césaire's project also required patience, negotiation, and self-sacrifice.[193] Historical transformations also compelled Césaire at crucial junctures to rethink his strategy, abandon earlier positions, and formulate new programs of action. Both figures separated self-determination from state sovereignty, recognizing that imperialism itself had created conditions for overcoming colonial subjection through transcontinental partnership. Both proposed seemingly modest adjustments to existing arrangements that could hopefully transcend them, even as such revolutionary changes would largely affirm an already emerging set of relations.

Césaire's desire to transform the Antilles into an autonomous region within a decentralized federation was undoubtedly refracted through the legacy of Toussaint Louverture, whom he regarded as a contemporary, just as he had Schoelcher ten years earlier. But as it became clear that France was not going to be reconstituted as a federal union under de Gaulle, the scale and scope of Césaire's political ambitions narrowed. He focused less on the form of the French state than on changing Martinique's legal status. Making the same claims on the metropolitan government year after year, he played his part in a Sisyphean political drama. Its absurd and tragic quality was sharpened by the fact that Césaire had reversed course at the eleventh hour and agreed to support the 1958 referendum on the basis of a promise and a hope against which he had to have known better. This too was the backdrop for his engagement with Toussaint as a self-sacrificing utopian realist, revolutionary federalist, and untimely visionary whose seemingly impossible program may have been addressed to a future that he could not prejudge.

Untimely Demands or Untimely Vision?

Césaire's public interventions under the Fifth Republic played with the untimely character of politics, and the political character of time, in the age of decolonization. His repetitive addresses to the National Assembly spoke about time running out for the French empire. In June 1960, during a debate about the omnibus *loi-programme* for the Overseas Departments, he rehearsed a series of demands concerning banana prices, tobacco quotas, lack of credit, the trade deficit, the threat posed to Martinique by the European Common Market, and the troubling extension of the powers of prefects in the Antilles.[194] But he quickly shifted registers, announcing, "We are in the age of decolonization . . . you cannot decolonize Africa and recolonize the Antilles. This is why I ask the government to revise the status of Overseas Departments and to seek . . . a new formula that reconciles both their attachment to France and their legitimate desire for autonomy."[195] He assumed a future standpoint from which to criticize the Antilles as untimely objects and the metropolitan government as an untimely actor: "Monsieur Minister, we are in a moment of historical acceleration. . . . These structural reforms, I pray to you, undertake them quickly . . . while there is still time so that . . . in a future that can suddenly be upon us you will perhaps not be led, you or your successor, to say melancholically . . . Alas, if only I had known."[196]

In a subsequent debate over the 1961 budget for the DOMs, Césaire denounced a politically repressive decree that allowed Antillean prefects to expel any civil servant whose "behavior was judged to trouble public order." Given the discretionary power it accorded to unelected officials without defining what acts were punishable, Césaire remarked: "In truth, your law is a sort of royal and imperial decree [loi de majesté, a loi de bas empire]."[197] He then repeated his untimely warning: "So, Monsieur Minister, you see how I was right last July when I spoke of colonial nostalgia among certain parties! . . . At the moment when the French government, in Africa, is removing the last colonial governors, you use this measure to offer them to the Antilles. We will not thank you for this gift!"[198] Once again Césaire underscored the relative modesty of Antillean demands for autonomy and added, "believe me, dear colleagues . . . henceforth, you cannot afford to make a single political mistake in the Antilles."[199]

Yet Césaire continued to call for a political arrangement that would preserve relations of "mutual trust, comprehension, and fraternity" between the metropole and Antillean territories.[200] During a December 1, 1960, parliamentary debate, he reiterated the "need . . . to create something new." Rather than another inadequate fiscal reform, he declared, the Antillean territories need "above all a political reform that would allow them to protect their market, reanimate their economy, and infuse their populations with new energy, a political reform that would, within the framework of a reasonable autonomy, allow the Antilles to think through their own problems and to define their own solutions." He concluded, "present us with a good political reform . . . while there is still time," or Antilleans will create a separate state.[201] He predicted that France's "liberty-killing acts [libérticides]" would provoke "the explosion of a people whose rights and hopes have been scorned."[202]

Césaire's threat was not phantasmatic. Since the riots of December 1959, public order and democratic liberties in Martinique had been shaken by rebellion and repression. The impasse of Antillean decolonization was being acted out in the theater of the streets. Public demands to redefine Martinique's legal status mounted through pressure exercised by the Communist Party of Martinique and the PPM, local assemblies, trade unions, lycée students, and expatriate Antilleans in the metropole.[203] In response, the metropolitan government attempted to destroy anti-French and separatist tendencies among communists, radicalized students returning from the metropole, and outside agitators. In January 1960, Alain Plénel, a progressive education inspector who had criticized state violence during the 1959 riots, was recalled to Paris. The prefecture seized and censored communist newspapers and arrested party militants.[204]

In the National Assembly, Césaire denounced the October 15 ordinance that allowed prefects to expel public employees whose behavior was deemed to trouble public order. Unions and civil servants mounted street protests. Yet between 1960 and 1963 prefects proceeded to expell numerous functionaries, especially teachers, from the DOM. They seized supposedly subversive political writings, regulated or banned many foreign publications, censored television broadcasts, prohibited public meetings, dissolved political groups, fined or jailed critics of the regime, refused visas to foreigners suspected of radicalism, and required that civil servants be vetted by the Ministry of Overseas Colonies. On March 24, 1961, gendarmes fired on a crowd of striking agricultural workers in Lamentin, killing three and wounding twenty-five.[205] The government sought to introduce reforms that would assuage public anger and improve living conditions. But insufficient development funds, a failed attempt at land reform, and only token educational improvements did not alter the political and economic conditions that fueled public resentment. In the early 1960s, the French government encouraged the large-scale migration of Antilleans to the metropole and enlisted Antillean youth to rebuild and settle in Guyane. These schemes confirmed that the state wanted only to restore public order and displace rather than address Antillean structural problems.[206]

In "Crisis in the Overseas Departments or a Crisis of Departmentalization?" (1961), Césaire observed that French officials, along with public opinion, recognized the enduring "Antillean problem" only when compelled by instances of violent social unrest. By ascribing such incidents to a local "malaise," they reduced the "Antillean problem" to a generic "social problem" related to overpopulation, land shortage, lack of industry, or a backward economy.[207] Césaire insisted this malaise was actually symptomatic of a pervasive *political* crisis in the Antilles: "the truth is that . . . the crisis of the Overseas Department is nothing but a crisis of departmentalization itself."[208] He remarked that "in a world fully involved in decolonization, the French Antilles remain . . . one of the rare colonial territories."[209] He defined colonies as "dominated" and "alienated" countries whose very existence is a "someplace else," an "over there," or an "outside." Assimilation was never fully applied to Antillean social and economic domains, and departmentalization was "an obstacle . . . to economic progress," a "mystification" and "form of domination" that kept these countries dependent on metropolitan France and preempted independence movements.[210]

Césaire declared: "today . . . the hour for agonizing revision has arrived . . . the artificial regime of departmentalization cannot last." He continued, "the Antillean revolution has already begun" as "people frustrated by being denied the right to govern themselves and denied the power to orient their own future [*destin*], people who have been denied their own selves, are awakening to a new demand: *autogestion* and recovery of their own personalities."[211] Since the Antillean problem was a colonial problem, its only solution was decolonization. Accordingly, the "path of the future" was that these territories be allowed to group themselves into a Guyanese-Antillean federation through which to administer their own affairs.[212]

Although Césaire called for departmentalization to be replaced with a new regime of autonomy, he still did not equate self-management with state sovereignty. In 1962 he was unequivocal: "departmentalization is centralization, and centralization, in this domain, is paralysis, it is tyranny, it is arbitrary rule, it is the death of local initiative and the death of local liberties."[213] But he remained committed to a federal vision of decolonization that was "simple and clear: a social demand, an economic demand, a political demand . . . summed up succinctly in our triptych: Work—Industrialization—Self-Management [*autogestion*] within a French institutional framework."[214] And several years later, when running for reelection: "henceforth all paths to the future and for . . . progress pass through the autonomy of Martinique, an autonomy that has nothing to do with independence, but an autonomy that while maintaining us within the French framework will allow us, ourselves, at least, to manage [*gérer*] our own affairs."[215]

Césaire's public interventions between 1956 and 1962 indicate that he was imagining a form of decolonization that transcended the alternative between departmentalization and national independence. He was not too timid to commit to independence, nor was he prevented from doing so by false consciousness about France's real intentions. We should take Césaire at his word when he declared his desire to create "something new." Whatever its limitations, Césaire's political project carefully confronted freedom as a problem. Like Senghor, he called for a political form that did not yet exist for a world that had not yet arrived. He identified within French history revolutionary traditions of populism, socialism, and self-management that could be linked to figures like Schoelcher and Louverture. Through the politics of radical literalism, Césaire hoped to fashion an elevated form of postimperial republicanism that would transvalue the very idea of France.

This program was utopian insofar as it could be realized only in a world that was already postnational and realist insofar as it was based on existing conditions and institutions. Césaire's interventions were animated by critical foresight and revolutionary anticipation, yet with full knowledge that historically possible projects might be politically impossible. He acted as if such a future was within reach and might arrive at any moment. Here was a dialectic of the possible and the impossible, the timely and the untimely, wherein each disclosed, inhered within, and helped to realize the other. By pursuing an impossible vision systematically, he revealed what might have been possible in the present; by seizing the present possible, he glimpsed what seemed to be an impossible future.

Césaire's vision of decolonization was addressed as much to prospective heirs as to contemporaries. But its futurity was inseparable from its historicity, from the long-term lineage that linked Louverture's constitution, Schoelcher's abolitionism, Césaire's departmentalization, and Senghor's federalism. He engaged history not to mourn lost pasts but to awaken living potentiality. The temporal dimensions of Césaire's postwar interventions show us that the period 1945–62 cannot simply contain the history of decolonization. These earlier figures and eras persisted as postwar entities, not simply memories but vital spirits, durable legacies, and effective forces. Historiography must grapple with the very real way that the 1790s and 1840s were immediate historical contexts, were present and presents, for the period 1945–60.

The Drama of Decolonization

Césaire's historical inquiry into the revolution in Saint-Domingue led him to reflect more deeply on historicity as well—on the plasticity of time, noncontemporaneity, and the politics of futurity. These temporal issues subtended his political acts and were motifs within his art. After writing his book on the historical drama of Toussaint, Césaire's aesthetic attention shifted to writing tragic dramas in which the relation between politics and time took center stage.

Césaire identified an affinity between the imperial dramas of the 1790s and the 1950s (as he had between those of 1848 and 1946). Throughout his book on Toussaint, he suggested that slave emancipation and decolonization were not only *like* one another but were *linked* to one another as scenes in the long-term drama of black modernity. He identified Saint-Domingue as the "first country in modern time to have posed . . . in all its social, economic, and racial complexity, the great problem that the 20th century has exhausted itself trying to resolve: the colonial problem. The first country where [this problem] unknotted itself [*s'est dénoué*]."[216] He regarded Caribbean history as an arena of epochal "unknotting" without dramatic resolution, historical *dénouage* without *dénouement*. The story of exile, enslavement, emancipation, and self-management among New World blacks was ideal material for tragic drama, and theater an ideal medium through which Césaire could attempt to work through their tragic predicament. In a 1967 interview with Nicole Zand in *Le Monde*, Césaire explained, "My theater is the drama of blacks [*Nègres*] in the modern world."[217]

Césaire's postwar poetry, criticism, and political interventions often employed theatrical metaphors. Whether speaking about the revolution in Saint-Domingue, emancipation in 1848, or decolonization, he referred to blacks becoming historical actors by storming the stage of world history. There they would either restore a historical continuity that colonialism had broken or refuse what had been presented to them as their historical destiny, partly by awakening pasts and anticipating futures. Césaire often spoke about blocked openings, tragic reversals, and untimely regressions. His political practice, which sought to enact seemingly impossible arrangements, was itself informed by dramatic logic and theatrical strategy. It is not difficult to imagine why Césaire regarded the writing and staging of political plays as a medium for engaging the politics of freedom and the problem of time.

Césaire's playwriting should be understood in relation to a broader postwar move from avant-garde poetry to experimental theater as a site of formal innovation and politically engaged aesthetics. Through the optics of cruelty, absurdity, epic, dialectics, or life, figures such as Artaud, Beckett, Brecht, Camus, and Sartre regarded theater as a privileged medium through which artist and public could reflect on and transform social relations and political structures. Radical theater would allow antirealist aesthetics and social criticism to inform one another; it would overcome both the reductive tendencies of mimetic political art and the depoliticizing tendencies of avant-garde art.

During this period of Antillean impasse, Césaire published four plays: *And the Dogs Were Silent* (1956), *The Tragedy of King Christophe* (1963), *A Season in the Congo* (1966), and *A Tempest* (1968). *The Dogs* and the adaptation of Shakespeare's *Tempest*, written at the suggestion of the director in Paris who had staged his earlier plays, were more abstract than the middle two plays, which staged actual historical events. And whereas *The Dogs* and *A Tempest* represent acts of anticolonial revolt, the plays about Christophe and Lumumba focus on the drama of decolonization, the problem of freedom *after* emancipation. They also engage the relationship between freedom and time.

Césaire wrote *The Tragedy of King Christophe* between 1959 and 1961, while he was completing his history of Toussaint.[218] Christophe was a former slave who became one of Toussaint's leading generals during the revolution. His fellow general Jean-Jacques Dessalines was the first ruler of independent Haiti in 1804. Two years later Christophe and the mulatto general Alexandre Pétion conspired to mount a coup against Dessalines, who was assassinated on October 17, 1806. After a contested presidential election that found Christophe victorious, the presidency was stripped of substantive power and an armed struggle began. Eventually the new nation was divided, with Pétion as president of a republic in the south and Christophe ruling a kingdom in the north. The latter became an authoritarian dictator obsessively concerned with labor discipline, territorial security, and international legitimacy. His compulsion to create a lasting legacy, for himself and for Haiti, even at the price of the people's liberty was famously expressed in an obsession with building a grandiose palace in Sans-Souci and a mountaintop fortress known as the Citadel. Faced with the prospect of a popular insurrection at home and invasion by Pétion from the south, Christophe killed himself on October 8, 1820.[219]

Whereas Césaire's historical essay examined Toussaint's self-sacrificing attempt to ensure emancipation, this tragic play treated Christophe's self-undermining and megalomaniacal attempt to create a sovereign state in northern Haiti under monarchial rule. Through Christophe, Césaire explored the painful dilemmas of postcolonial leaders who attempted to found free societies. In a 1963 interview, he explained, "Decolonization? Yes. But after? I deliberately allowed for this ambiguity."[220] In 1967 he related, "King Christophe incarnates negritude confronted by . . . the passage from dependence to independence and responsibility."[221] The play was first performed at the Salzburg Festival in 1964. It was staged by Jean-Marie Serrau, an acclaimed Brechtian director who also collaborated closely with Césaire on his next two plays. Financial challenges prevented it from being performed in France until May 12, 1965.[222]

Within a year after *King Christophe*'s metropolitan debut, Césaire published *A Season in the Congo*, which portrayed the demise of Patrice Lumumba, an event that had recently unfolded on the stage of international politics.[223] Between June 1960 and January 1961, the world community witnessed what looked like an epic struggle between popular democracy and power politics in the Congo. Lumumba, the freely elected prime minister, was prevented from exercising sovereign power by a combination of antidemocratic forces, including secessionist provinces, political rivals, white settlers, the Belgian state, the US government, and the UN. Finally, during a desperate trip where he attempted to gather national support for his legitimate government after a coup orchestrated by General Mobutu, Lumumba was captured by political rivals. He was transported to his enemies in Katanga province, then led by the secessionist leader Moïse Tshombe, and executed by an extralegal death squad that included Belgians and Congolese.[224]

A Season in the Congo was first performed on March 20, 1966, in Brussels, at a time when Lumumba's death, for which Belgian authorities denied responsibility, remained highly controversial. Serreau then staged a production of it first at the Venice Biennale in September 1967 and in Paris the following month.[225]

The protagonists of both plays are self-sacrificing visionaries who fail to secure a possible but untimely form of colonial emancipation. Each is compelled by historical circumstances to inhabit a tragic predicament and choose among unacceptable alternatives. Neither is as lucidly pragmatic as Césaire's Toussaint was about the situation or its likely outcome. In all three cases, I would suggest, Césaire was less interested in these figures as tragic individuals than in the world-historical circumstances that conditioned their attempts to convert formal liberty into substantive freedom after the end of colonial rule. Césaire treated Toussaint as an exemplary figure whose predicament and choices offered clues about how his twentieth-century descendants might confront the problem of freedom. Césaire's Christophe and Lumumba confronted dilemmas similar to Toussaint's. But their one-sided approaches to colonial emancipation, statist for one and populist for the other, also provided insight into the tragic dimension of decolonization as it was then unfolding historically.

These plays were theatrical meditations on a problem that Césaire spent his life confronting: the deep structural tension within the project of self-determination for colonized peoples between state sovereignty and popular sovereignty. In contrast to the Rebel who sacrificed himself through an act of revolutionary revolt, his Christophe and Lumumba gave their lives to doomed programs for postcolonial freedom *after* the end of empire. *King Christophe* staged the fatal danger of territorial without popular sovereignty. *A Season in the Congo* staged the fatal danger of popular without territorial sovereignty. In these plays, each form of sovereignty is both necessary for and a threat to the other; without some balance between them, genuine self-determination cannot be established.

By the time he wrote his Lumumba piece, Césaire had decided cooperative federalism would be the best way to institutionalize self-government in
Martinique. This arrangement, he believed, would allow Antilleans to avoid
both Christophe's obsession with protecting national frontiers and maintaining domestic security and Lumumba's faith that foreign agents would act according to their self-proclaimed ethical values and political norms. Federal
autonomy would guarantee popular sovereignty for Antilleans while forcing
"France" to recognize them as citizens of a state constitutionally bound to treat
them according to concrete national law rather than the unenforceable ethical norms of international principles.

In these plays, Christophe and Lumumba are preoccupied with historical
and political temporality. Neither has enough time. Each seeks to accelerate
history in order to overcome disabling legacies and "catch up" with a world
that their people, through slavery and colonialism, helped create. And their
political preoccupations are future-oriented: Christophe's with constructing a
permanent edifice that would ensure the duration of Haitian emancipation, Lumumba's with creating precedents that would prevent future African strong-
men from disregarding popular democracy and national welfare. Lumumba
believed that at stake in decolonization was not only freedom for Africans but
the future of democracy.

Césaire's Christophe was a former slave who understood how easily emancipation could be reversed. Accordingly, he devoted his life to ensuring the
future of Haitian sovereignty. As for Lumumba's greatness, Césaire later
explained:

> Lumumba is a revolutionary insofar as he is a visionary. Because, in re-
> ality, what does he have before his eyes? A miserable country. . . . The
> grandeur of Lumumba was to sweep aside all of these realities and to see
> an extraordinary Congo that is still only in his mind, but which will be-
> come a reality tomorrow. And Lumumba is great, through this, because
> there is always a beyond [au-delà] for him.[226]

His Christophe was haunted by the past, while his Lumumba foresaw a future
haunted by his historical present. Both were concerned with overcoming and
creating living legacies. Their present experiences were refracted through vital
pasts and fateful futures. Similarly, Césaire's contemporary audiences were
compelled to recognize these pasts in their present. By setting up a historical constellation that linked Christophe's Haiti, Lumumba's Congo, and the
postwar Antilles, Césaire used theater to explore conventional assumptions
about how past, present, and future relate to one another.[227] He reminded his

audience that untimeliness was both a problem that decolonization had to confront and a possible resource that could subtend political struggle and sustain political imagination.

Finally, these plays underscored the theatrical dimension of politics itself. For Césaire politics were as much about *showing* something as they were about doing something. His political plays showed audiences that poetry may act on the world directly and politics may conjure imaginary possibilities. His theater was not merely a matter of creating a more explicitly political or timely art; it provided another medium through which he could explore the intimate relationship between politics and aesthetics.

This commitment to politics as theater and theater as politics may be compared to Jacques Rancière's reflections on the affinity between the aesthetics of politics and the politics of aesthetics. For him, politics and art are radical not when they treat progressive subjects or contain revolutionary messages but when they are able to reconfigure the "the distribution of the sensible," the dominant norms governing what can be shown and said, seen and heard. Both politics and aesthetics are capable of creating new subjects, subjectivities, and sensibilities. Any act, political or aesthetic, that reveals the underlying truth that neither birth nor wealth nor education give one group the natural authority to rule another is radical. Rancière emphasizes that aesthetic politics and political art stage or enact a scandalous equality, recognizing precisely what Césaire's plays and political acts revealed—that politics is an art of demonstration, a serious performance, a staging of transformative possibilities.[228]

Césaire's political plays do not merely recount the tragic dilemmas that Christophe and Lumumba confronted. They also stage a political scandal by treating Christophe and Lumumba as subjects of tragic drama, Haiti and Congo as scenes of world-historical events, and Antilleans and Africans as world-making actors on the stage of global history. Césaire and his fellow overseas deputies embodied and enacted a similar scandal in the National Assembly, the sacral theater of republican politics, where their existence challenged the idea that any social group possessed an inherently greater title to govern than any other. They demonstrated the truth of Rancière's claim that democracy is the rule of "anyone at all."

Reading Rancière with Césaire invites us to question the assumption that radical politics must occur in the streets through direct action and that parliamentary acts are necessarily reformist and moderate. The crucial issue is not where politics occur but what transformations they can effect. Either direct action or parliamentary politics may introduce revolutionary change or reproduce existing relations. Historically, radical constitutional initiatives and popular social movements have typically required one another for revolutionary openings to be converted into regimes of freedom. On one level, Césaire clearly understood this dialectical relationship between legal initiatives and direct action. He regularly stressed that the abolition of slavery in 1848 would not have occurred without the pressure posed by ordinary Antilleans. His eloquent interventions in the National Assembly regularly invoked the specter of revolutionary upheaval if metropolitan promises were again broken and Antilleans' trust violated. Yet he devoted himself to party building, election campaigns, parliamentary politics, and municipal administration. He never created a social movement that could have helped realize his ambitious political vision for the Antilles, France, and the world. Rather than institute seemingly unimaginable possibilities in a disjunctive present, his untimely vision would have to be recognized by the future actors to whom it was also addressed.

EIGHT

African Socialism and the Fate of the World

When all economic misery and pain has vanished, laboring humanity has not yet
reached its goal: it has only created the *possibility* of beginning to move toward its real
goals with renewed vigor. Now culture is the form of the idea of man's humanness.
And culture is thus created by men, not by external conditions. Every transformation
of society is therefore only the framework, only the possibility of free human
self-management and spontaneous creativity. —GEORG LUKÁCS

Léopold Senghor regarded federalism and socialism as inseparable elements
of a decolonization that would operate on an imperial scale by transforming
overseas *and* metropolitan territories. He shared Césaire's interest in identifying unrealized potentiality within devalued or deformed African *and* European traditions that could be reclaimed and refunctioned. This orientation
informed his attempt to find in Marx's writings, socialist politics, and African
culture resources for an anticolonialism that could transcend the mechanical
materialism and political instrumentalism that he identified within existing
socialism. Scholarly discussions of Senghor's federalism are often separated
from those of his socialism. Because his postwar interventions have typically
been interpreted from the perspective of his later presidency, his commitment
to African socialism is often regarded as a superficial or opportunistic state ideology rather than a considered engagement with Marx's writings.[1]

Marxism as Critique of Socialism

As we saw, Senghor pursued self-determination without state sovereignty on
two fronts: the National Assembly and the Bloc Démocratique Sénégalais. If
the assembly was the primary stage on which Senghor articulated his program

for nonnational decolonization, the BDS was the institutional organ through which he sought to realize it.

On September 27 1948, Senghor resigned from what he saw as a corrupt and hypocritical Socialist Party (SFIO). This public and performative act followed a power struggle with the established Lamine Guèye faction of Senegalese socialists, whose support was based primarily on coastal urban elites and citizens of the Four Communes.[2] In his letter of resignation to Secretary General Guy Mollet, Senghor asked, "Since when has opportunism become a socialist virtue?"[3] In language similar to that which Césaire later addressed to the PCF, Senghor criticized the SFIO's poor voting record on colonial issues: "The truth is that the party . . . sacrifices principles to electoral results, Marxist ethics and socialist action to tactics . . . [it] uses overseas territories not as an end but as means." Senghor related that his decision caused "a great rending of my heart and mind."[4] For his aim was not to abandon socialism but "precisely to realize it."[5]

In October 1948 he cofounded the BDS party with Ibrahima Seydou Ndaw and Mamadou Dia.[6] His older colleague N'Daw was a colonial army veteran, peanut farmer, and political activist in Kaolack and Sine-Saloum who had close ties to rural cultivators and Muslim marabouts. Dia was a pious schoolteacher whose political career Senghor had helped launch. He became Senghor's principal ally and adjutant until 1962. Dia had been raised in a Senegalese village near Thiès and attended Koranic school as a young child. After receiving a degree at the competitive École William Ponty he worked as a teacher and school director before being elected, with Senghor's support, to the Assemblée du Conseil Général on the Socialist ticket in 1946. He quickly aligned with Senghor in the rift with the Guèye faction of the Senegalese SFIO. He shared Senghor's desire to create a party whose socialist program was more directly grounded in African peoples' distinctive cultures and conditions with special attention to the needs of rural populations.[7]

Regarding BDS activities, Senghor was primarily concerned with metropolitan interventions and the party's larger political vision, while Dia assumed responsibility for local Senegalese politics and the party's economic program.[8] But Dia too participated in French national politics. In 1948 he was elected to represent Senegal in the French Senate, where he served until being elected a deputy in the National Assembly in 1956. In 1953 he became the secretary general of the Coordinating Committee of the IOM group of federalist legislators.[9] During his time as a parliamentarian in Paris, Dia studied geography, law, and political economy. He belonged to a cohort of Third World students, which included Samir Amin, strongly influenced by François Perroux's ideas about global economic development.[10]

Dia was especially interested in reorganizing Senegalese social relations on the basis of producers' cooperatives.[11] Like Senghor, he hoped to link a socialist program for local self-management and humane economic development to the transformation of imperial France into a federal democracy. He promoted economic liberation through African unity as well as a vision of mutual and complementary development on a global scale that would promote worldwide solidarity and a community of united nations. Like Senghor, he believed that to combat neocolonialism African peoples needed to overcome territorial nationalism and regroup themselves into larger federal formations.[12]

Morgenthau describes how Senghor and Dia shifted power away from established Senegalese socialists by building the BDS into a broad coalition of rural farmers and fishermen, lower-level civil servants, and marginalized city dwellers. The party consolidated its electoral base through alliances with Muslim marabouts, local chiefs, regional and ethnic associations, trade unions, veterans, schoolteachers, professional associations, Catholic missions, and European commercial interests.[13] The BDS presented itself as an alternative to the established coastal elites while distancing itself from the more militant forms of syndicalism and anticolonialism then developing across urban West Africa.[14]

Senghor identified the BDS as an organ of "the masses of peasants and laborers" and denounced the Socialist Party in Senegal as an instrument of the urban bourgeoisie and rural feudal authorities.[15] Whereas they could only offer "favors, decorations, promotions, at best nominal citizenship," the BDS promised "structural reforms that alone could make real the rights inscribed in the Constitution."[16] Senghor supported measures for broader suffrage, a labor code, municipal autonomy and local assemblies, workers' accident compensation, and the reform of agricultural cooperatives and credit systems.[17]

The BDS "condemned violence and revolt as means" to socialist transformation.[18] It paired "the peaceful solution" of constitutional change, namely "the institution of a French Federal Republic," with a "realist conception" of the economic challenges facing colonial Senegal.[19] Rather than abolish relations of capitalist production altogether, it sought to eliminate *le colonat*, an exploitative variant of sharecropping, and regulate colonial capitalism.[20] Senghor explained, "a powerful modern economy, can only be constructed upon a prior accumulation of capital. The task is to impose social responsibilities upon capital and to limit its profit margins to a reasonable level."[21] Senghor placed his hopes for responsible accumulation on agricultural cooperatives, which, following Dia, he believed would "resolve the triple question of credit, production, and commercialization."[22]

After forming the BDS, Senghor began to write directly about Marx and African socialism.[23] Many of the positions he developed over the coming years were already present in a 1948 essay "Marxism and Humanism."[24] There Senghor challenged attempts by left Catholics and orthodox Soviets to reduce Marxism to economism, positivism, or atheism.[25] He argued that although Marx criticized Hegel's speculative idealism, he never intended to replace it with a vulgar materialism. Rather, Marx's point was that consciousness cannot be grasped apart from the specific conditions and concrete lives in which it is embodied. Senghor acknowledged that Marx posited an objective reality that exists independently of human consciousness but insisted that Marx's analysis was not confined to observable facts. Structurally, Marx "sought to seize the surreal that subtends [apparent] phenomena." He argued that Marx's dialectical method emphasized the "reciprocal action" that linked material conditions to spiritual acts in a relation of "spiral and equivocal causality."[26]

For Senghor, Marx's dialectical method also served an ethical project centered on the critique of alienation. In his reading, Marx demonstrates that capitalist production based on private property did not only create "de-realized" and "depersonalized workers." It produced a dehumanizing condition of "disequilibrium," whereby workers became alienated from their labor, individuals from the collectivity, and humans from their own essential being.[27] To this, Marx counterposed a conception of human freedom based on a distinction between *individual liberty*, the bourgeois right to private property, and *personal* liberty, "the possibility of the development of individual faculties" through community. This social form of "personal" freedom would transcend alienating oppositions between objectivism and subjectivism as well as materialism and idealism. The full human capacity of all individuals could then be realized by reconciling labor and capital, man and himself, and human and natural worlds.[28]

Senghor argued that for Marx, the aim of socialist revolution was not only to end labor exploitation and class antagonism and to create a more equitable distribution of goods. Marx's attempt to reground productive capacity in social reappropriation also sought to establish a "new order" that would ensure "the blossoming of the person's intellectual and spiritual life."[29] Elsewhere Senghor argued that revolutions did not necessarily require seizing the state violently. He reminded BDS militants that for Marx, social revolution meant above all "the transformation of the world by and for man" and "the establishment of the order of the human condition."[30] Senghor mobilized Marx to emphasize the spiritual dimension of human freedom that he believed could neither be reduced to the individual liberty celebrated by liberalism nor the material well-being fetishized by traditional socialists.

Senghor attempted to reconcile what he regarded as Marx's ethical humanism with the Christian "personalism" developed by the Thomist philosopher Jacques Maritain. He quotes Maritain: "humanism . . . tends essentially to render man more truly human . . . in leading him to participate in all that could enrich him in nature and in history [so that] man develops the virtualities contained in himself, his creative forces and the life of reason, and works to make the forces of the physical world the instruments of his liberty."[31] This, Senghor asserted, was precisely Marx's project one hundred years earlier.

Senghor also contended that Marx's expansive vision of personal freedom was inseparable from his dialectical philosophy, writing,

> Marx . . . proposes neither a doctrine nor a system, but . . . a method of action in the service of total man, which excludes all totalitarianism, all fixity because man always remains to be realized. Marxism is not a catechism . . . it implies a continual process of overcoming [*dépassement*]. . . . It is dialectical . . . in truth, there is no definitive state: everything is movement, struggle, change.[32]

Senghor speculated that humans would even one day surpass communism. In short, he attempted to detach Marx's philosophical humanism from actually existing socialism, whether embodied in European parties or the Soviet state and to reclaim Marxism as a standpoint both from which to criticize actual socialist parties and to craft an independent socialism for postimperial Africa.

African Socialism

"Marxism and Humanism" was guided by the question Senghor would address directly in a series of "Reports on Method" prepared for the annual BDS party congresses: why Marx's critique of capitalism was relevant to the task of understanding African alienation. Senghor noted that social stratification in Africa was less a function of class exploitation than colonial and racial subjugation.[33] In colonial Africa, he argued, workers were actually elites and peasants the real proletariat.[34] But despite these differences, he believed, Marx's critique of European capitalism related directly to African societies insofar as they remained subject to the parasitic commercial capitalism of the *pacte colonial*.[35] Because imperialism had created deep bonds between metropolitan and overseas territories, Africa was an integral part of the "Europe" that Marx analyzed.[36]

Senghor later developed a critique of the *pacte colonial* as a system of asymmetrical exchange that violated the principles of economic solidarity enumerated in the preamble of the constitution of the Fourth Republic. He argued that French state planning, which underwrote a reign of cartels and trusts, perverted socialism and destroyed any prospect of African industrial development or self-sufficiency.[37] He insisted this system be abolished through syndicates and cooperatives. But he maintained that overcoming alienated labor in Africa would not only entail "returning to the colonized his land [and] product" but also his "soul."[38]

Senghor believed that Marx's dialectical method and ethical project could be applied to particular African societies, which might pursue distinct roads toward socialism. Citing Marx's 1881 exchange with Vera Zassoulitch on rural communes in Russia, Senghor insisted that as an agrarian society, Africa already practiced the kind of social production and solidarity that Marx envisioned.[39] He explained to party cadres that by defending the distinctive "Senegalese and African man" the BDS was following Marx's methodological and ethical focus on "the whole human" [*l'homme integral*].[40]

But in order to reclaim Marx for Africa, Senghor had to confront religiosity, which he called "the very sap of Negro-African civilization."[41] He insisted that Marx's purported atheism was only a conditional rejection of Christianity, which had been deformed by capitalism into an ideological rationalization for systemic social misery.[42] He argued that whereas European atheism was founded upon the "myopic logic" of "classical rationalism," Marx's work actually rejected this "rational logic." It attended to the surreal phenomena subtending the apparent reality that was the domain of empirical science. Marxism, Senghor liked to explain, was a "*dialogue* between reason and the real."[43] He claimed that Marx recognized among different peoples the existence of a plurality of "reasons" that did not always assume the particular rationality of the *cogito*.[44] He often quoted Marx's claim in his 1843 letter to Arnold Ruge that "reason has always existed, but not always in a rational form."[45]

Senghor believed that Marx's support for the emancipation of the total person was consistent with religion's fundamental aims and values. Senghor thus denounced "atheistic" socialist parties as "churches" guilty of quasi-religious dogmatism that contravened the original spirit of Marx's writings. He maintained that African spiritualism directly embodied Marx's "integral humanism."[46] And he contended that Christianity and Islam in Africa also promoted revolutionary socialist aims by challenging "all sorts of despotisms" in order to "[restore] human dignity."[47] To denounce religion from the standpoint of socialism, Senghor suggested, was therefore to "slip from a practice to a doctrine, from a method of action to a metaphysics or even a philosophy of history."[48] Referring to orthodox socialism, he wrote, "At this moment when atheist parties have become churches and live their faith, we must be careful not to forget religion as the source of will. For us, it is not a question of making the party into a religion, but of supporting it with our religion."[49]

Senghor stated that socialism was not a doctrine but a method and that African religion promoted socialist methods by combining will and act with vital energy and popular emotion. He wrote, "our religions insist precisely on the fact that the will is forged through the act. We acquire faith by praying and practicing charity." Similarly, he explained "one becomes a [socialist] militant worthy of the name through syndicalist action, cooperative action, in study groups, conferences, organization, and propaganda." For Senghor, African religion and socialism intersected in this focus on concrete practice over abstract doctrine, which was "the only way that we can abolish [*supprime*] 'the existing state of things,' the only way that we can create a *revolution, which is nothing other than a permanent transformation of the world, by and for man.*"[50] Senghor instructed party members that "we can quite legitimately be socialists while remaining believers."[51]

This faithful socialism would require the BDS to organize cooperatives and syndicates. Senghor observed that "syndicalism, that is to say, worker direct action" required "courage and communitarian faith among its militants."[52] Through such political work, he declared, the party would "begin to model the socialist face of the *cité* of the future."[53] Here he seems to suggest that African socialists should not only shape their own future polity but enact a *cité* to come through an anticipatory politics that could guide socialist transformation globally.

Senghor's ideal African socialism would integrate politics, ethics, and religion. He explained to party members in 1953,

> It is not a question of collapsing or confusing politics and religion, of assigning one to the role of the other. *Politics*, as you know, is not exactly a religion, not even a philosophy—nor either a science. It is an art, the art of administering *la Cité*. It does not aim to discover and give the absolute truth. It is the art of using a method which, by ceaselessly corrected approximations, allows the greatest number [of people] to lead a more complete and happy life because it conforms more closely to the *human condition*. Politics is an active humanism. But because this is so . . .

it must be integral to and found itself upon an ethics. And religion still remains the most solid foundation of ethics.[54]

In order to be authentically socialist and authentically African, the BDS had to undertake a political project rooted in vernacular religious ethics. But Senghor was not only arguing that African socialism be founded on local forms of religiosity. He was suggesting that such a religiously inflected socialism might more fully embody the unrealized spiritual and humanist potentiality in socialism's original promise.

Senghor's African socialism posited a relation whereby politics revealed the truth about religion and religion the truth about politics.[55] Each disclosed the end toward which the other should strive. Within Senghor's schema, doctrinaire socialism and atheism were dogmatic materialist religions focused more on "church" power than human dignity. His vision implied that politics became more political when routed through religion and religion more religious when routed through politics. For Senghor, authentic politics, like religion, addressed itself to transcendent potentiality. And authentic religion, like politics, addressed itself to worldly possibility. Senghor thus developed a critique of religious absolutism from the standpoint of Marxian dialectics and a critique of vulgar Marxism from the standpoint of religious ethics. These were also immanent critiques: of religious absolutism from the standpoint of humanist and worldly currents within religious tradition and of mechanical materialism from the standpoint of Marx's attempt to overcome the dehumanizing opposition between subjectivity and objectivity. Senghor thereby challenged fixity and foundationalism whether expressed in religious or political idioms. He envisioned *religion without dogma* and *socialism without orthodoxy*. His objective was religious humanism and secular transcendence.[56] And neither, for Senghor, could be separated categorically from realist calculation and strategic politics. His revolutionary hope was tethered to a gradualist program of concrete acts, social reforms, and constitutional adjustments.

Identifying "Cartesianist Jacobinism" as a "French deviation," Senghor argued that the BDS party would "return socialism to its first vocation . . . that of coexistence and interdependence."[57] Because original socialism had a "federalist tendency," he explained, his aim was to create "a balance which is local autonomy within union."[58] Strategically, this meant that "syndicalism because socialist is anti-autarchic" and must, in the spirit of "Eurafrican cooperation," "federate itself" within an "international organization."[59] In his view, autarchic solutions to the global problem of capitalist alienation could not succeed. The BDS should both focus on African specificity and support socialist internationalism through close alliances with other working classes, democratic movements, and subordinated peoples.

But Senghor was also claiming that economic self-management and humane development of the total person could best be pursued within the framework of a postcolonial federation.[60] As in Proudhonian mutualism, Senghor considered socialism and federalism to be two sides of the same coin.[61] "Economic relations between the metropole and the overseas territories," he explained in 1954, "would cease to be dictated unilaterally. We would no longer be satellites of the metropole, our economy would thus be complementary and not a supplement."[62] He instructed party organizers that federalism, socialism, and religion were "interdependent . . . acts of the trilogy [which] form a single drama, that of the *human condition*."[63] As he recounted, "using the method of socialism . . . we discovered federation as the only solution to our problem and *to that of France*."[64] In other words, socialism required federalism and federalism would renew socialism; together they would resolve Africa's local problems, its problems with France, and France's own problems.[65] In the Cold War era, Senghor suggested, France and Africa would each need socialism, federalism, and each other.

Decolonizing France, Redeeming the World

Senghor called neither for France to decolonize Africa nor for Africa to liberate itself, but for Africans to *decolonize France*. African socialism would play a vanguard role in a process whereby the imperial republic would be elevated into a plural democracy. In turn, this transcontinental formation could serve as the elemental unit for an alternative global order. Senghor's socialism-federalism-religion trilogy would promote African singularity, Franco-African *métissage*, and "the civilization of the universal." This federation would allow members to pursue the dreams of human solidarity and reciprocity proclaimed by various currents of postwar internationalism. Once again, he believed that if colonial emancipation were to institute a new era of human solidarity, it could best do so by inventing a sociopolitical form that did not yet exist for a world that had not yet arrived.

Operating on imperial, international, and global scales, Senghorian decolonization sought to inaugurate a new epoch of world history through a process of interdependent overcoming. Colonial capitalism would be superseded by cooperative socialism. Illiberal empires would become postnational federations. International conflict would be displaced by civilizational rapprochement. Cold War antagonism would be transcended. Marxism and spiritualism would be reunited, ethics and politics reintegrated, multiplicity and democracy reconciled. This was a redemptive vision of African-led decolonization as planetary salvation. In the spirit of Marx, Senghor developed a critique of national sovereignty from the standpoint of human emancipation, rather than a critique of colonial domination from the standpoint of national sovereignty.[66]

Senghor's position proceeded from the postulate that because true alienation was moral as well as economic, emancipation could not focus exclusively on material well-being. African socialism would have "to return man to himself."[67] The aim was not merely to raise Africans' standard of living but to restore to them their "reason to live." He argued that African socialism must start with but also surpass "economic realities."

> Because *the real* is not wholly contained by these realities. Economic alienation is only one aspect, an instrument of our veritable alienation, which is in the moral domain. . . . It is good to raise the standard of living for the masses, but the very life of man, his dignity, is not in his *standing* [English in original]. . . . It is in the vigor of his spirit and in his taste, his sense of beauty, it is in his conscience and his creative activity. In our struggle against the resurrection of the *pacte colonial*, let's guard ourselves against conflating means and ends. "To live" let's protect ourselves from "losing the reason to live."[68]

European socialist parties, he explained, had failed precisely because they inverted means and ends, focusing on material improvement rather than moral liberation, economic rather than cultural development, and superficial rational rather than the deeper spiritual and aesthetic dimensions of human being.

Senghor described culture as "the most powerful means of revolutionary action," as it "illuminates consciousness" and "[transforms] the world . . . for the blossoming of the person."[69] Because he believed that "an action, to be fruitful, must be nourished by thought" and that "action is first of all will" or "energy of the soul," cultural practices and products could be revolutionary media.[70] He blamed the failure of the Second International on its desiccated rationalism, suggesting that even early Soviet communists recognized that socialism could succeed only if rooted in popular culture, the élan vital of a people, and "the immense energy of faith."[71] He denounced party-dictated socialist realism as violating the spirit of Marx's thinking by restricting free artistic expression, instrumentalizing creativity, and presenting an impoverished conception of social reality.[72]

Senghor was less interested in rejecting socialism than in *realizing* it, by returning to its Marxian sources, via Africa, in order to overcome its existing incarnations. He instructed BDS cadres that "the failure of socialists is not a failure of socialism."[73] He directed them to return to "the works of Marx . . . not to recite them, like the Bible, or the Koran, like a *dogma*, but to recuperate from them their spirit, their living and vivifying substance." Marx, he explained, recognized that "man, to be fully human, must escape his alienation by capital and be a *creator* of beauty."[74]

According to Senghor, culture had "a double objective: to satisfy immediate physical needs . . . but above all to satisfy the spiritual exigencies of life in society . . . [which] essentially is nourished by . . . art." Such art leads "man to commune with men, [and] all men with all the forces of nature," making "him more free by allowing him to *realize* himself."[75] African art, Senghor argued, expresses what he regarded as Marxian aims insofar as it was

> about . . . leading the people to participate in the collective life of the *cité* . . . [it is] precisely not [meant] to satisfy animal needs, but these needs being satisfied, to give life [*faire vivre*]. . . . It is about creating a communion of men . . . with the vital forces of other men, and through this, with the cosmic forces of the universe. . . . In short, it is a matter of transforming our spiritual life by integrating it within social life to make it more intense because more human.[76]

Senghor figured black art as a medium of human and cosmic reconciliation through which Africans could revitalize Marxism and redeem socialism. In turn, an ethical and vitalist socialism rooted in African culture, aesthetics, and religiosity would save Europe, which had been alienated by an instrumental rationality that reduced the human person to material utility, confused standard of living with reason for living, and perversely inverted human means and ends. Senghor thus reminded his Senegalese supporters that "Black Africa's art and literature remain our most precious heritage. They are necessary in the world at a moment when Western and Eastern European technical reason risks transforming men into robots, worse, of annihilating humanity."[77]

Senghor maintained that European "discursive reason" was only "a method, an instrument" that provided "practical recipes for utilizing nature" to improve material existence. But, he argued, such scientific and technological rationality could not be used to "perfect ourselves." Referring to European reason, he asked,

> Aren't its inventions, of which thermonuclear engines are only the most spectacular, in the process of destroying the very existence of man like the miracles of the sorcerer's apprentice? . . . far from combating our true

evils, which are the egoisms of class, nation, race, or continent, European reason has made itself the docile servant of them. If it has helped Europe transform the world and, as Karl Marx wanted, its material life, it has not transformed its true life, that is to say, its moral style.[78]

The *moral* transformation of *true life*, Senghor argued, required the kind of "analogic reason" or "sympathetic intuition" that he believed subtended both Marx's thinking and African ways of being, knowing, and making.[79] He thus criticized existing socialist parties from the dual perspective of Marx's actual writings and "labor in precolonial Africa," which was "a rite and source of joy by the grace of rhythm and song."[80] These were not nativist gestures meant to reify incommensurable differences between Europe and Africa but a reminder to each that their postcolonial prospects, both spiritual and material, depended on the other. He believed that Europe and Africa could help one another to develop in ways that would facilitate worldwide human self-realization within the civilization of the universal.

Senghor's African socialism contained numerous tensions. Consider his celebration of Marx's dialectical method and critique of alienation, which identify immanent contradictions leading to crises within capitalist societies, versus his assertions about reciprocity, interdependence, and social solidarity *without* overcoming capitalist social relations. His invocations of popular spirit, collective emotions, and syndicalist action versus his reformist faith in constitutionally driven societal transformation through legal reforms. His emphasis on democratic and cooperative self-management versus his alliances with conservative power brokers across Senegal and in Paris. His pragmatic belief in socialist federalism as the best solution for African decolonization at that moment versus his tendency to imply that federalism was an intrinsic human good. His federalist convictions about mutualism as the basis for socialism versus his statist interest in planning and development. Senghor's proposals also implied future problems that he never addressed concerning ownership of natural resources, capitalist polarization, and structural economic dependence.

But such tensions do not warrant treating Senghor's project for a socialist-federalist form of decolonization as a charter for the territorial nationalist logic it forcefully challenged. Such an interpretation is possible only if his socialism is separated from his federalism or reduced to the political ideology of a national state rather than recognized as a utopian project born of sustained reflection on the prospects for self-determination under late-imperial conditions. Senghor's vision was partly based on an immediate concern with how best to promote moral and material development in the postwar world. He did not treat socialism and federalism as doctrinal or dogmatic ends in themselves; whether they would be the best paths to decolonize Africa, to reconstitute France, and to create a new global order would depend on the situation.

As historical conditions changed, so did Senghor's conception of African socialism. From roughly 1948 to 1956 he attempted to recuperate Marx's writings in order to challenge economic determinism and mechanical materialism, to produce an immanent critique of actually existing socialist parties, and found an independent African socialism. But he then began to use African socialism to criticize Marxism itself, which, in an about-face, he accused of economism, determinism, and atheism. This shift was conditioned by the declining prospects for a federalist decolonization for West Africa

The Territorial Trap

With the passage of the Loi-Cadre in 1956, significant administrative powers devolved to local organs of African government.[81] By vesting authority in separate territorial assemblies, the new system bypassed the "federal" administrative infrastructure that already existed in French West Africa, thereby undermining prospects for political unity across the region.[82] The Loi-Cadre set the stage for a conflict between African "territorialists," who supported separate national governments, and "federalists" who wanted a multinational African government. Félix Houphouët-Boigny, in Côte d'Ivoire, was the most vocal public advocate of territorialism; Senghor and Dia were leaders of the regional federalist movement.[83]

Despite their opposition to territorialism, Senghor and Dia responded to the Loi-Cadre by creating a larger political organization through which to govern Senegal under this new system. In 1956 the BDS neutralized many of its critics (communists who had defected from the Senegalese RDA, socialists who had defected from the SFIO, and regionalists in the Movement for Cassamance Autonomy) by joining with them in a new Bloc Populaire Sénégalais. The BPS then won overwhelming victories in the local March 1957 elections. Socialist supporters of Lamine Guèye and Ousmane Socé Diop, had largely coalesced around a new Parti Sénégalais d'Action Socialiste. But in April 1958 the BPS co-opted this urban elite by merging with the PSAS to create the Union Progressiste Sénégalais. The UPS, co-led by Senghor and Guèye, then absorbed other independent socialist parties and the Senegalese section of the RDA. N'Daw, Dia, Guèye, and Diop all assumed official posts in the semiautonomous Senegalese government; Senghor happily remained a party leader.[84]

Through these flanking maneuvers, Senghor and Dia created a broad-based coalition. They also regarded the UPS as an instrument for organizing a wider West African federalist movement that could counteract the territorialist RDA. In July 1958, the UPS led efforts to organize a unity conference in Cotonou under the auspices of the Parti du Regroupement Africain (PRA). Although Senghor served as president of the PRA, its more radical delegates dominated the meeting. Against his and Dia's opposition, they passed a resolution that called for immediate independence from France.[85]

These intersecting conflicts—between territorialists and federalists and between advocates of autonomy within a union and those who supported independence—were played out during the debates around de Gaulle's 1958 constitutional referendum. At stake was whether overseas territories would choose to become members of the Fifth Republic's new Communauté Française. The PRA militants who supported the Cotonou resolution called for a "no" vote while party leaders campaigned for a "yes" vote. Senghor, Dia, and Guèye believed that the proposed community offered the best hope for federalist reforms. When de Gaulle toured West Africa to campaign for his constitution he was denounced by Sékou Touré in Guinea and was confronted in Senegal by crowds of protestors demanding independence. Senghor and Dia were both in Europe at the time. For better or worse, their position triumphed; every French West African territory except Guinea voted yes in the referendum.[86]

The new constitution held that "the Republic and the peoples of the Overseas Territories who, by an act of free determination . . . institute a Community . . . founded on the equality and solidarity of the peoples that compose it."[87] Its member states would "possess autonomy . . . administer themselves and freely and democratically manage their own affairs." The larger community government would be responsible for foreign policy, defense, money, strategic raw materials, justice, higher education, and telecommunications.[88] The constitution stipulated that "there only exists one single citizenship [status] in the Community" for all of its inhabitants.[89] As we saw, Article 73 allowed for distinct legal regimes to evolve overseas through "adaptive measures necessitated by their particular situation."[90] Similarly, Article 74 recognized that "the Overseas Territories . . . have a particular organization that takes into account their proper interests within the ensemble of the interests of the Republic."[91]

But we also saw that de Gaulle's constitution did not transform France into a true federal union.[92] Senghor and Dia were criticized by sectors of their own constituencies for supporting it.[93] Senghor explained that he and Guèye, who were members of the Comité Consultatif Constitutionnel that drafted the document, told de Gaulle they would support the constitution if West African territories could join the community as a multinational federation and if they were free to decide later to convert autonomy into independence.[94] Senghor thus claimed responsibility for Article 76: "Overseas Territories . . . can become either Overseas Departments of the Republic or, whether or not grouped together, Member States of the Community," and Article 86: "the transformation of the status of a member state of the Community can be democratically demanded, . . . according to the same procedures, a member state of the Community can become independent."[95]

Senghor argued that his support for the community was not a renunciation of the principle of African independence per se but an "unequivocal" affirmation of "the unity of French-speaking Negro-African territories."[96] He recounted that his yes vote "essentially had a political meaning . . . we voted for the Constitution, not necessarily for the government of the Republic, let alone for General de Gaulle."[97] He added that "since the Loi-Cadre, which balkanized the federations of AOF and AEF," there had developed across West Africa a new desire "among the elites . . . to reconstitute the two federations and to promote them into Federal States."[98] In short, he insisted that he essentially voted *for federalism.*

But Senghor now equivocated around the question of independence. He had long argued that autonomy within a federal union would be a better framework for African decolonization than national sovereignty. He also believed that a range of solutions to the problem of freedom could coexist in the community. Accordingly, he called on the French state to recognize Algeria's and Guinea's independence and to embrace them as partners within a postcolonial "commonwealth."[99] Yet, he also declared that joining the community "was only a means to realize *independence* for black Africa."[100] Was Senghor renouncing his support for a federal union with metropolitan France? Was he pandering to separatist constituents? I suggest this was a resigned concession to what he began to regard as the inexorable force of the nationalist vector of decolonization. He explained, "whether we celebrate or deplore it, the fact remains, the 20th century is one of overseas nationalisms. The dependent peoples of Asia and Africa are animated by the same will to national independence. A Frenchman can hardly reproach them for this. It was France that started it all." He recounted how during the revolutionary wars of the 1790s France "inoculated" Italy, Germany, Russia, and the Balkans with a "nationalist virus" and how this "European epidemic" then spread through Asia and Africa. Senghor remarked, "it is vain to struggle against History."[101]

In these debates Senghor often temporized, contradicted himself, and disregarded his own role in the historical processes he criticized. He was clearly politically maneuvering. But he was also adapting his program to new circumstances and narrowed options. His opposition to national autarchy and territorial "balkanization" never wavered. But as the possibility of transforming France into a democratic socialist federal republic diminished, he rescaled his hopes for federalism and socialism.

Under the Fifth Republic the "federal" administration of AOF effectively ceased to exist. The constitution created a territorialist system of separate overseas governments confederated with the metropole. The community did not establish executive organs at the regional level through which Africans could exercise their new autonomy. In April 1959, the French state formally dismantled the AOF system. This move prepared a future where African peoples, whether as autonomous territories or independent states, would be divided along national lines. Each government would negotiate a separate bilateral relationship with metropolitan France. The ongoing Algerian War and the punitive treatment of Guinea after its "no" vote also undermined the credibility of France's claim to have created a democratic community of peoples. Across French West Africa demands for independence by radical parties, trade unions, and young educated urbanites gathered strength. Against this backdrop, Senghor pragmatically shifted his efforts to "the realization of a 'multinational confederation' with France" by creating a federal African state that could join the community.[102]

In Senghor's view both Houphouët-Boigny's desire for African countries to join the French Community as autonomous nations and Sékou Touré's desire for them to separate from France as independent states were equally misguided forms of "balkanization."[103] Accordingly, he and Dia joined forces with the Sudanese political leader Modibo Keita to create a multinational socialist federation within Africa.[104] Although Keita was a member of the Sudanese section of the RDA, he was an antiterritorialist advocate of African unity. But he was a more orthodox socialist than Senghor and believed in a strong state. In January 1959, they convened a meeting in Bamako. Representatives from Senegal, Sudan, Haute-Volta, and Dahomey agreed to organize themselves into a new federal state that would be an autonomous member of the French Community. But Houphouët-Boigny pressured Dahomey and Haute-Volta to withdraw from the plan. Senghor and Keita still cofounded a new Mali Federation composed of Senegal and Sudan and governed by the Parti de la Fédération Africaine (PFA). This state formally established itself as a member of the community on April 4, 1959, with Keita as president and Dia vice-president. The following September, the Mali Federation exercised its constitutional right to request independence, which was granted on June 20, 1960. Disagreements soon developed between the partners about whether each territory would remain semiautonomous or would merge into a unified state. These differences were compounded by Sudanese fears about Senegal's hegemony and Senegalese resistance to Sudan's interference in its internal affairs. By August the federal partnership dissolved, and Senegal and Sudan (henceforth called Mali) became independent nation-states.[105]

Political Reorientation

Between 1956 and 1960 Senghor acted instrumentally to co-opt adversaries, neutralize critics, and build a party machine whose influence he hoped to project across French West Africa. His objectives also shifted from demanding an intercontinental federation to supporting an international confederation, then to creating a sovereign federal state, and finally accepting a national state. These shifts marked the unraveling of his postwar vision. But even when independence seemed to be the unavoidable dénouement of decolonization, he remained a forceful critic of nationalism and still tried to conjugate federalism, socialism, and universal civilization.

Senghor did not begin to reflect seriously on the category of "nation" or emphasize "confederation" until his dream of reconstituting France as a federal republic had been foreclosed. Even then he criticized the illusion of nominal independence and affirmed his commitment to multinational interdependence. Consider his 1959 Report to the PFA, which engaged the question of nation building by positing an ascending chain linking *patrie*, nation, federation, and confederation. According to this quasi-Kantian vision, each entity would be more fully realized in its specificity through participation in the larger entity that encompassed it even as the overall progression led toward greater freedom, universality, and humanity. In Mazzini-like reasoning, this universal freedom and humanism would be grounded in and inseparable from the ongoing existence of particular peoples, countries, nations, and states. Even during the time of the Mali Federation, when he abandoned plans to reconstitute France as a federal republic, Senghor continued to search for a political form that would correspond to his vision of concrete universalism and rooted cosmopolitanism.

Observing that "the most powerful states today are federal states," he surmised that "France's weakness is perhaps its excessive centralization."[106]

Distancing Mali from the Jacobin paradigm, he pledged to "resist one of the temptations of the nation-state, which is the standardization of persons across countries [*patries*] . . . the impoverishment of persons, their reduction to robot individuals, their loss of sap and juice."[107] In his view, "the superiority of the federal state over the unitary state" was based on its recognition that "wealth is born from the diversity of persons and *patries*, from their *complementarity*."[108] Senghor reasoned that "only democracy . . . will allow the Negro-African to realize himself" and asserted that "our democracy will be *federal* . . . local diversities, by virtue of their complementarities, will enrich the Federation. Inversely, the Federation will preserve diversities."[109]

He invoked Proudhon's belief that "the only way to reduce the tyranny of the state and conjure away its maladies" was through the federalist "decentralization and deconcentration of . . . economic and political institutions."[110] He also pointed to Yugoslavia as a model for a "federal structure" that could be extended from the state to "regional and communal collectivities" and encompass "social and economic domains."[111] And given that "the interdependence of race, continents, [and] nations" was the "reality of the twentieth century," Senghor argued, "real independence" required "a development plan" that "cannot even be thought, let alone realized within the narrow limits of a national territory."[112] He quoted François Perroux's claim that "today, for all nations, the real powers through which sovereignty is exercised are a function of effective alliances and coalitions."[113]

But in a departure from his earlier thinking, he also promoted federalism as a statist vehicle for "rational and dynamic planning."[114] He called for "a strong democracy and planned economy" devoted to "open socialism" within "federal states."[115] Citing the recent volume, *The Third World*, edited by Georges Balandier, he informed students and labor leaders that they would have to cooperate with state policies to minimize public expenditures, accept French aid, and solicit private investments.[116] For these reasons, he declared, "the Federation . . . is our primary framework. But a Federation integrated into a larger ensemble, the Community, and associated with an even larger ensemble, the European Common Market."[117]

Senghor bolstered this position by again citing Perroux's critique of "nationalisms obsessed with the allure of juridical sovereignty":

> common terms . . . such as sovereignty, independence, autonomy, collective will, the will of the state—can no longer be used interchangeably. . . . A territorial sovereign state . . . is neither the necessary, nor obviously, the sufficient condition for an ensemble of populations to manage

[*disposer*] itself, to discover or rediscover the values of its own civilization, or increase its capacity to produce and its standard of living.[118]

Senghor contended that members of the French Community, including the Mali Federation, were already "*independent* in the etymological sense of the word." For "independence is essentially non-dependence in one's decisions" and "we are still, at all moments, free to choose the path of our destiny."[119] He explained that "for a jurist, independence is a *form* not a reality . . . an independent state is one that is recognized as such internationally . . . one that possesses the external signs of sovereignty."[120] He elaborated, "a merely nominal independence is a false independence. It can satisfy national pride, but it does not abolish the consciousness of alienation, the feeling of frustration, the inferiority complex, since it does not resolve the concrete problems facing the underdeveloped countries: to house, clothe, feed, cure, and educate the masses."[121] For him real independence was not a function of state sovereignty. But was he suggesting that autonomy within the community was a preferable arrangement or a preliminary step towards independence? It is difficult to know whether by wavering he was conceding to popular demands, recognizing an unstoppable historical movement, or hedging his bets until conditions disclosed whether the Mali Federation would best flourish as an autonomous member of the community or as an independent state.

Senghor called for "the transformation of "the Community into a Multinational Confederation," which, he reminded supporters "had always been our common ideal."[122] He argued that participation in such an entity would ground rather than compromise Malian sovereignty and strengthen rather than weaken African unity.[123] "Horizontal solidarity within Africa," he explained, "will be created bit by bit, by beginning at the beginning, with economic and cultural relations, while vertical solidarity between us and our metropoles will be transformed without breaking. Neither race wars not continental wars will allow us to establish [*consolider*] Peace."[124] Note his use of the term *consolider*: to strengthen through joining and unifying; this is a verbal form of solidarity.

Finally, Senghor linked this call for a federal state within a multinational confederation to his enduring dream of universal civilization and planetary reconciliation.

> *Man* remains our ultimate concern, our *measure*. . . . A people that refuses to show up at the *rendez-vous* of History, that does not believe itself to carry a unique message, this people is finished and should be consigned to a museum. The Negro-African will not be finished before even having

begun. Let him speak and, above all, act. Let him bring, like leaven, his message to the world. To help create the Civilization of the Universal.[125]

Senghor thereby suggested that the "civilization of the universal" was the ultimate aim of his socialist federalism. Attempting to transcend the conventional opposition between universalism and particularism, he figured African civilization as making a signal contribution to the planetary tapestry of human civilization as well as acting as a messenger and *hostie* that would help to redeem the modern world by, in some sense, Africanizing—by which he also meant humanizing—Marxism, socialism, and humanity itself.

Of course, Senghor himself did not advocate a multinational confederation until after it became clear that his earlier program to decolonize France by transforming it into an intercontinental federation had been foreclosed. The distinction between federation and confederation for Senghor was significant. It was only at this late date that he called for France to "transform the Community into a *Commonwealth* à la française," a "Franco-African Confederation" that former colonies would "agree to enter" as "independent states."[126] Whether or not he acknowledged it at the 1959 PFA Congress, the shape of Senghor's plan for a "great intercontinental ensemble" had changed.[127]

African Socialism as a Critique of Marxism

As Senghor recalibrated his initial program for federalism, he also modified his thinking about African socialism. Earlier, he had reclaimed Marx as a standpoint from which to criticize actually existing socialism. Now he used African socialism to criticize Marx. In the 1959 Report to the PFA, he pledged "to rethink the founding texts [of socialism] in relation to Negro-African realities."[128] He observed that Marx's relevance for contemporary Africa was limited by his inability to foresee important twentieth-century developments. These included the capitalist state's capacity to integrate the labor movement through social legislation and a communist revolution that made the state into "an all-powerful soulless monster, suppressing the natural freedoms of the human person, and drying up the sources of art, without which there is no longer a reason to live."[129] Senghor added that Marx was able to envision neither the importance of colonialism for worldwide capitalist development nor the tendency of the Western working classes to identify with imperial states rather than act in solidarity with colonized masses.[130]

Senghor continued to praise Marx's insights about human emancipation. He traced a continuity between Marx's earlier writings about alienation and his theory of reification in *Capital*. In both cases, he believed, Marx demonstrated that when the worker was separated from the product of his labor he became alienated from his own humanity as a free "creator."[131] In his view, "Marxian analysis" demonstrated that "it is all Western civilization, machine civilization, factory civilization that is reified."[132] Marx's aim, according to Senghor, was to restore a "natural balance" whereby "man will stop being dominated by his products and dominate them. He will institute the rational because planned, organization of production.... Thereby man will rediscover his place and his role in the universe. And the reign of *freedom* will then succeed that of *necessity*."[133] Here Senghor shifts from using Marx to praise man as a creator of beauty to idealize him as a rational planner.

Senghor noted that Marx was able to recognize both "the grandeur and misery of man in and through labor" under capitalism. "From master of his tool, he becomes master of the world. But at the same time ... he separates himself from the world and from himself." Senghor suggested that this "vision of man" was "no less deep or true than that of the greatest philosophers. It recalls the vision of Pascal."[134] He explained, "beyond economic 'appearances,' [Marx's thought] plunges into the human realities that create them. For a *factual* vision of things, Marx substitutes a profound vision of human requirements. This is a new humanism, new because it is *embodied* [*incarné*]."[135] For Senghor, this conception of a concrete and embodied humanism, at once worldly and transcendent, continued to mark a crucial point of affinity between his and Marx's thinking.

Senghor claimed that "Marx's ambition, and his paradox, has always been to express ... the dignity of man and his spiritual needs without recourse to metaphysics, morality, or religion, not even philosophy."[136] Yet, he argued, Marx was only able to do so "in the name of a certain human *interiority* or transcendence that supersedes man."[137] According to Senghor, the concept of *praxis* allowed Marx to then shift focus "back from God to man, from the transcendent to the immanent."[138] Earlier, Senghor would have embraced this attempt to overcome the oppositions between immanence and transcendence, matter and spirit, and materialism and idealism. Now he used it to accuse Marx of having "an equivocal conception" of man and the universe.[139] Senghor asked, "what is religion if not the bond that unites man to the world?"[140]

Senghor then extended to epistemology his suggestion that Marx was disavowing the transcendent bases of his own thinking. On the one hand, he praised Marx's dialectical understanding that "subject and object are only two aspects of a single reality."[141] He noted that if Marx recognized the human mind as a type of matter, it was not matter as conceptualized by "the so-called exact sciences" but the human and social matter of a given century—the nineteenth, of a given place—western Europe. It is complex, made of the reciprocal reactions on one another of infrastructure and superstructure, economic and cultural facts, things and men. It is a matter made up of contradictions, in a state of perpetual becoming. It is matter animated by *dialectical* movement.[142]

However, Senghor also argued that in his analysis of capitalism "Marx reverts . . . to an old conception of mechanical materialism and seems to deny the active role of the subject in knowledge. He turns into a positivist . . . against his dialectical method . . . he opted for a strict *determinism*."[143] But Senghor does not support this assertion.

Senghor had become concerned with recuperating dialectics from what he now characterized as Marx's one-sided materialism, positivism, and determinism. He did so partly through a vitalist claim that neither Hegel nor Marx invented this idea of "perpetual *becoming*."[144] He wrote,

As Heraclitus already noted more than 2,000 years ago, things, like beings, are perpetually in a state of becoming. Within themselves they contain . . . inner contradictions that . . . will bring about their destruction, more exactly, their transformation into new syntheses or symbioses, new realities.[145]

Skipping forward, Senghor also noted that "the dialectic is employed by the most effective philosophical and scientific methods of today, including existentialism, phenomenology, psychoanalysis."[146] In a gesture that anticipated the direction his thinking would soon move, Senghor invoked the Jesuit priest and paleontologist Pierre Teilhard de Chardin, who claimed to have found a "synthesis of the Christian 'God' above and the Marxist 'God' of the future [*en-avant*]."[147] This postulate, Senghor explained, allowed "believers" to "retain the positive contributions of socialism" through "the dialectical method" but also "legitimizes our faith."[148]

Senghor framed this discussion with a surprisingly categorical statement: because "no social realities, especially cultural realities, can be reduced simply to the 'class struggle,'" he informed PFA supporters, "we are . . . engaged in the critique of 'dialectical materialism.'"[149] Yet Senghor had never before read Marx as reducing social reality to the class struggle. He seemed to conflate Marx's writings with the orthodox socialists and communists that he formerly criticized from the perspective of these writings. He still praised Marx's "philosophy of humanism, economic theory, [and] dialectical method."[150] He affirmed the European traditions of "syndicalism, planning, federalism, and mutualism, which come to us from French idealist socialists—Saint-Simon, Proudhon, and Fourier."[151] But Senghor was now at pains to distinguish Marxist humanism and utopian socialism, which the PFA embraced, from actually existing state socialism. He criticized Leninism's "univocal" materialism and determinism, and Stalinism for abandoning Marx's revolutionary commitment to "human dignity and . . . freedom."[152] He condemned Soviet communism for pursuing American-style capitalist development.

Senghor was equally critical of the American "regime of liberal capitalism and free enterprise," for endorsing racial segregation and elevating "material success to the status of a lifestyle."[153] Like many postwar reformists, Senghor declared, "We stand for a middle course, for a *democratic socialism*, which goes so far as to integrate spiritual values, a socialism which ties in with the old ethical current of the French socialists."[154] He also invoked contemporary French Marxists, including Henri Lefebvre, Pierre Fougeyrollas, and Edgar Morin, who criticized the Communist Party for subordinating the person to the class and hiding "reality behind the screen of ideology."[155] Senghor asserted that following the French Revolution and the revolution of Marxism, "a third revolution is under way, in reaction against capitalist and communist materialisms, that will integrate moral, if not religious values with the political and economic contributions of the two great revolutions. In this revolution, peoples of color, including Negro-Africans, must play their role; they must contribute to the construction of the new planetary civilization."[156]

This understanding of socialism as an ethical and spiritual project for human realization resonated directly with his understanding of African forms of life. Citing European ethnologists, he elaborated:

> Negro-African philosophy, like socialist philosophy, is existentialist and humanist, but it integrates spiritual values . . . for the Negro-African, the 'vital forces' constitute the fabric of the world . . . animated by a dialectical movement. . . . Negro-African society is collectivist, or, more exactly, communitarian, because it is composed of a *communion* of souls more than an aggregate of individuals . . . we had already realized socialism before the European presence . . . we have a vocation to renew it by helping it to restore its spiritual dimensions.[157]

Senghor is arguing that socialism was a useful framework for African development because it confirmed and complemented already existing, but suppressed, tendencies in Africa. But he was also suggesting that African civilization had the capacity and responsibility to renew socialism by restoring to it the lost moral, cultural, and spiritual dimensions that were part of Marx's initial humanism.

In his 1959 presentation to the Second International Congress of Black Artists and Writers, Senghor argued that Marx showed that "the economy only determines society through certain mediations—races, families, groups of all sorts" and "superstructures react back on infrastructures in the same way that the latter do on the former." This process, Senghor explained, animates "the *dialectical* movement of History at the end of which erupts [*jaillit*] the freedom of Man." He cautioned that this was not a mechanical or predetermined process, explaining that the socialist "method is only a framework. It is up to us, in particular, to discover the mediations and to define their roles. It is, in fact, a question of *explaining Man by man*." This was possible, in Senghor's view, because African social institutions and cultural traits "carry within them *human values of universality* even as they are specifically black [values]."[158] Senghor, in other words, postulated a concrete, embodied, and incarnate African humanism that was at once situated and universal.

As he had done repeatedly since the 1930s, he outlined "Negro-African" civilization's specific forms of consciousness and knowledge, its particular ontology and conception of religion, its characteristic social organization and institutions, its conceptions of property and labor, its ethical orientation, and its approach to aesthetics. This was another attempt to reconcile African singularity, European modernity, and universal humanity. He again stressed how an alienated humanity could more fully realize itself by learning, or remembering, the lessons that African civilization could teach about modes of being, knowing, relating, and creating. He wrote,

> in black Africa, art is not only *social*, but *vital*. It accompanies and accomplishes activities of *production* . . . not only material production, but also spiritual production. . . . Art is vital because *production*, in the material sense, is the first expression—in time—of Man: his *generic* activity. But, beyond this material production, art expresses . . . the interior life by which he essentially distinguishes himself from the animal. The materialist Karl Marx affirmed this truth. . . . Only Man can dream and express his dream in works that transcend him [*le dépasser*]. And in this domain, the *Nègre* is king. Thus the exemplary value of Negro-African civilization and the need to decrypt it in order to found a new humanism upon it.[159]

This was familiar territory for Senghor. The difference was that now he related this distinctive vision of an "incarnate" African humanism to his specific historical conjuncture to emphasize the indispensable cultural and spiritual dimensions of decolonization.

He remarked, "new autonomous or independent States are being born in black Africa . . . But . . . what will black peoples do with their recovered liberty? For it is evident that freedom without consciousness is worse than slavery."[160] Senghor contended that as important as parliamentary democracy and socialism certainly were, such institutions could not create "real independence, not only of peoples but also of persons."[161] And he reminded black intellectuals who considered religion to be an outdated and regressive form of consciousness that "religion, whatever it may be, more generally *faith*, is as necessary for the soul as bread, rice, or millet are for the body. . . . The challenge is not to suppress religion, nor to replace it; it is to assign it to its true place and to refine it by making of it one of the elements of humanism today."[162]

Like Césaire, he assigned writers and artists "a primary role in the struggle for decolonization," instructing them that

> *Man* must be the center of our preoccupations. One does not construct a modern State for the pleasure of constructing. The action is not an end in itself. We must therefore protect ourselves from a will to power that defines the State, that crushes *Man* beneath the State. It is, in fact, about creating the black man within a humanity marching towards its *total realization* in time and space.[163]

For Senghor, the task was not merely to found independent states but to create a new man who could remake the world and redeem, by realizing, humanity. Whether he maintained this critical relationship to state power is a different story.

From Marxian Dialectics to Vitalist Metaphysics

When state sovereignty for Senegal became inevitable, Senghor's writings became at once more philosophically dense and less politically innovative. His efforts to complement Marx's thinking devolved into a theoretically cruder attempt "to carry [Marx's dialectical] logic to its ultimate consequences in order to complete and, let us dare say, correct" it.[164] Now positing a break between Marx's earlier philosophical writings and the political economy of *Capital*, Senghor claimed that Marx's dialectical materialism was trapped within a form of superficial discursive rationality. Breaking with his earlier analysis, he situated Marx within an abstract and deterministic philosophical tradition that accepted the subject-object distinction (which he traced back through

Kant, Spinoza, and Descartes to Aristotle). Senghor added that Marx's understanding of world history placed too much emphasis on the class struggle, his conception of internationalism depended on a fictive solidarity between metropolitan working classes and colonized masses, and his vision of human freedom neglected the cultural and spiritual dimensions of disalienation.[165]

On these grounds Senghor argued that Marxism could *not* adequately address the concerns of African societies where, he instructed the youth wing of the PFA, people traditionally lived "in communion . . . with the solidary forces of the whole universe: the living and the dead, men and animals, plants and pebbles."[166] Nor, for Senghor, could Marxism meet the twentieth-century demand for a "panhumanism" rooted in the realities of global "interdependence."[167] Referring to Marxism as a "dehumanized humanism" based on an "inhuman metaphysics" and an "atheistic materialism," Senghor concluded that Africans would "betray Marx by using, as such, the Marxian dialectic, without changing a comma."[168]

Citing philosopher Gaston Bachelard's epistemological claim that "a new situation always requires a new method," Senghor turned to non-Marxian currents of antirealist philosophy that, in his view, rejected the subject-object distinction and developed lived, practical, and participatory ways of knowing the world.[169] He regarded such approaches as more able than either classical rationalism or dialectical materialism to grasp the underlying essence of things as they really are, without trapping them in logical categories. Among the European thinkers that Senghor invoked to develop this vitalist approach to African socialism, including Kierkegaard, Bachelard, Merleau-Ponty, and Maurice Blondel, he engaged most deeply with Pierre Teilhard de Chardin and Gaston Berger.[170]

In his 1962 Seminar for Political Cadres of the Senegalese Progressive Union, Senghor wrote, "socialism is essentially a *politics*, that is to say, the art of governing men in a given society, by harmoniously organizing their relations. The object of socialism is thus not the economy, as too many Marxists today believe, but concrete living man, in his totality, body and soul."[171] He cited Lefebvre to affirm that Marx himself had hoped to transcend "economic man."[172] But he argued that Marx's aim was actually realized more successfully by Teilhard de Chardin who "plunges beyond the appearance [*apparition*] of man" and "studies the human phenomenon, progressing from apparently inanimate matter until the Omega Point (God), traversing the critical thresholds of the Biosphere (life) and Noosphere (thought)."[173]

Senghor embraced Teilhard's evolutionary belief that supraindividual forces "have accelerated the process of socialization, through . . . the symbiosis of different civilizations. This explains how, before our eyes, the Civilization of the Universal is actually being built."[174] He explains that for Teilhard, techno-scientific processes of "co-reflection" on an international scale are leading humanity towards a state of "more-being [*plus-être*]."[175] Out of this "movement of *panhuman convergence*," Senghor contends, "the planetary civilization will be born, a symbiosis of all particular civilizations."[176] This process, he explains, is propelled "not by a causal push from behind, but by a final attraction from ahead."[177] Senghor interprets Teilhard to say that humanity coheres through a "personalized *center* that attracts towards itself all human centers in order to make them flourish, by organizing them, this is the famous *Omega Point*. It is *God*. It emerges dialectically as the result of *orthogenesis*, from the cosmic drift [*dérive*] of Man."[178] In language that is at once Christian, Hegelian, and vitalist, Senghor concludes, "in the middle of this twentieth century, we are therefore pushed—or more precisely, drawn [*aspiré*]—toward the Center of centers, this ultraconsciousness of consciousnesses, which is God . . . the ultimate aim of our progress."[179] But Senghor also figures this forward and upward propulsion as a worldly and human affair. "Since Marx, since the decline of capitalism and the emergence of socialism, we are only at the beginning of the era of ultrareflection, which must lead us from well-being to more-being before we consume ourselves in God. First, we must construct the earth, our earth."[180]

Senghor praises Teilhard for recognizing that "beyond material well-being, spiritual more-being—the blossoming of the soul: of intelligence and the heart—is . . . the ultimate aim of human activity."[181] He also defines this goal as love. Senghor explains that "humans, having satisfied their animal needs, their *well-being*, through democracy and planning, can then, in union, which is Love, realize their *more-being*. It is this Love-Union that can be found at the ordinal center of art, morality, and religion."[182] Democracy, socialism, and communism, according to Senghor, all failed in the quest for "totalization and socialization without depersonalization . . . because they sacrifice the part to the whole, the person to the collectivity." Since the latter was "thought only as a technical organization," he asserted, social integration was pursued through "constraint and violence" rather than nonviolent "human love" and "love of the Super Person."[183]

Senghor relates this conception of love to efforts by both phenomenology and "Negro-African gnosiology" to transcend the opposition between matter and spirit.[184] According to Senghor, Teilhard resolved this opposition through a "dialectical revolution" which recognized that there is not spirit [*esprit*] and matter, but Spirit-Matter . . . only one single energy, which presents itself in two aspects. One, *tangential energy*, is that of physicists and chemists. It links minute particles [*corpuscules*] to one another materially. The other, *radial energy*, psychically links centers of consciousness one to the other. This second type of energy should be considered the "primary stuff of things."[185]

Senghor concludes that this "new dialectic does not contradict that of Marx but only deepens and completes it by removing from it any trace of one-sided determinism [*unilateralité*]."[186]

Teilhard figured this long-term movement toward panhuman convergence, planetary civilization, and cosmic reconciliation as a self-propelled organic process. Senghor agreed. But he also believed that African socialists must play an active role in accelerating and orienting it through a rational and humane approach to development and planning. His thinking about the medium-term future was informed by Gaston Berger, who he contends was influenced by Teilhard's evolutionary theory and Blondel's conception of action-oriented thought.[187]

Senghor refers to Berger's conception of "la prospective" as a "science of the future" that makes a crucial distinction between "operative time," which is "the time of action," and "existential time," which is "the time of poets . . . whose fabric is anxiety."[188] He quotes Berger's claim that "prospective reflection "makes us seize the future as such, with its complexity, mobility, risks, and surprises."[189] This "prospective" orientation seeks to "seize," in the sense of anticipating, and orienting action toward, a future that it cannot predict. As much an ethical as a technical operation, it is concerned not only with what might happen but with what *should* happen. Senghor explains, "beyond economic facts, *la Prospective* attaches itself to human facts" by placing "man at the heart of our problems—often man as a means, but always as an end."[190] Senghor declares, "we have been practicing La Prospective without realizing it. No doubt because, like Berger, we are Senegalese."[191]

These were not merely abstract considerations for President Senghor. As a head of state he was charged with fostering Senegalese social welfare. Before, he had related his future-oriented conception of African socialism to a federalist utopia of decentralized self-management. Now he related "prospective" thinking to a statist utopia of humanist development. Whereas he once used Marxian dialectics to criticize instrumental reason, he now instrumentalized vitalist phenomenology for "good planning," which, "as the organization of a more human future, must be prospective. It must rest on an analysis of the situation in Senegal, on the scientific inventory of our economic and social data."[192]

Equally surprising was Senghor's claim that such planning will "awaken 'dormant energies.' To combat prejudices, routine, inferiority complexes, and the spirit of fatalism. In a word, we must awaken the national consciousness to the call of *Négritude*."[193] Did his shift from Marxism to phenomenology, from dialectical ethics to vitalist metaphysics, from federalism to statism, from poetic anticipation to technological planning, from intuitive knowledge to scientific data, also signal a shift to nationalism or nativism? Although the relative emphasis he placed on either cultural specificity or human solidarity varied, I would suggest that his commitment to embodied humanism, situated universalism, and concrete cosmopolitanism persisted.

Senghor concluded this 1962 address by indicating that "prospective" planning also had a transcendent dimension rooted in ancient religiosity. As with socialism, he sought to recuperate the radically ethical, universal, and humanist core of early Christianity and Islam against their later "inevitable crystallizations."[194] He asserts that "Jesus was a *revolutionary*. In his sermons, he challenged Roman morality—that of the colonizers—and the ancient Law of Israel. Born poor, he had a predilection to support the poor and oppressed of all races and religions."[195] Similarly,

> Mohammed proposes first to perfect the Arab community. . . . But beyond that, like Jesus, he aims at all men. He works for the establishment of a *new society*, for the birth of a *new man*. Mohammed thus reveals himself to be an *emancipator of women*, contrary to what the average European believes. Like Christianity, Islam introduces *universal* values into human society.[196]

For Senghor Christianity and Islam were revolutionary projects for planetary social justice. He even suggests that Marxism "is a Christian reaction to the embourgeoisement of historical Christianities. Several of its ideas, including the concept of *alienation*, have their source in Christian theology."[197]

Senghor figured early Christianity as a cosmopolitan movement whose openness and vitality were eventually undermined by the development of European rationality:

> the Apostles and their successors had very soon felt the need to use *Greek culture* which was then the most advanced. It was necessary, sine qua non, for the effective propagation of Christianism. Already, abandoning Hebrew and Aramaic, St. John wrote his gospel in Greek. It was only

after the invasion of Western Europe by Germans, the *barbarians*, that Christianism assumed the role of the guardian of the science and technology of Greco-Roman civilization. . . . The scholasticism of the Middle Ages . . . was truly a *method of open discussion*, of research.[198]

Senghor contends that it was after the collapse of Scholasticism that a Greek conception of the cosmos was replaced by a Christian mathematical philosophy.[199]

Senghor suggests that from within the Roman empire, early Christianity defined itself and changed the world precisely through linguistic borrowing and cultural *métissage*. By extending and reworking aspects of Greco-Roman civilization these Christians forged a singular form of life that was at the same time a cosmopolitan universalism. By adapting and, in some sense, realizing a Greek conception of the cosmos, it practiced a cosmopolitanism that was simultaneously Christian, Roman, Greek, and universally human, but *not* grounded in scientific or technological rationality. Nor was this ethic of cosmopolitanism rooted in Western European culture. It arrived there and was instituted in Christian universities through medieval Scholasticism before being ruined by mathematical reason and lost through modernity and to moderns.

This story is not simply an exercise in golden-age nostalgia. It is a critique of Christian modernity from the standpoint of ancient Christianity, and of European rationality from the standpoint of Mediterranean cosmology. It challenges ideological assumptions about the supposed equivalence of European territory, mature Christianity, and humanist thinking. It undermines civilizational narratives that posit modern Europe as the direct descendent of ancient Greece. This story is also an allegory for the relationship between imperial entanglement, African renaissance, and the planetary reconciliation that Senghor spent his life pursuing. More concretely, he also implies that this cosmopolitan legacy can now be reawakened by African socialism through African forms of knowing and being. In his view, African civilizations nourished precisely the human and spiritual values embodied in this ancient ethic, in part through transcultural borrowing and mixture. Senghor thus concludes,

> For we Senegalese, the task is therefore clear. Not to neglect, in the construction of our Socialism and the execution of our Plan, the *spiritual means* contained within our religions. To return to their sources and return to these religions their *meaning*, their *interiority*, that which Feuerbach called . . ."the immediate liaison between the individual and the universal." For this is the meaning of *re-ligion*: a liaison, through the reciprocal integration of subject and object, of Man and the Universe. . . .

This is what, for many years, we have been doing by integrating social-ism with *Négritude*.[200]

We see here that even after Senegalese independence, Senghor called on African socialism to identify, reawaken, and elevate lost possibilities that he believed remained crystallized within Marxism and socialism, early Christi-anity, and African civilizations. In his view, a culturally grounded and spiritu-ally oriented "prospective" approach to planning would not only foster Sen-egalese national development. It would also help to realize a cosmopolitan humanism and a cosmological universalism that could contribute to recon-ciliation and redemption at the level of the species and the planet. Even after Senghor's vision of self-determination without state sovereignty was blocked, his thinking about state politics, African socialism, and universal civilization remained animated by an untimely attempt to anticipate worlds to come. He still hoped to awaken immanent possibilities condensed within outmoded objects.

But we can also see that when Senghor became president he increasingly related dialectics to a vitalist evolutionary process rather than to an ethical po-litical project. As the prospect of a federalist form of decolonization was fore-closed, the emphases of his thinking shifted from the human and historical to the organic and cosmological. His African socialism finally *did* become a legit-imizing state ideology, which he deployed instrumentally to authorize plan-ning, party rule, and national unity, and to marginalize critics and minimize dissent.[201] His presidential invocations of *Négritude* also often functioned to justify politically unpopular and even socially conservative state practices.

The tension between Senghor's commitment to producers' cooperatives, self-management, and decentralized power, on the one hand, and statism, na-tional unity, and social peace through alliances with conservative forces, on the other, ultimately erupted in his fateful confrontation with Dia in 1962. As Dia, who was then prime minister of Senegal, sought to implement a more radical version of cooperative socialism in postcolonial Senegal, Senghor was worried about its potential to alienate powerful interests, including Muslim organizations and French commercial houses, whose political support and financial investment he courted.[202] Senghor's decision to imprison his longtime lieutenant for supposedly planning a coup d'état surely marked the collapse of Senghor's postwar vision of African socialism as a program for redemptive decolonization and human emancipation.[203]

Poetic Power

Janet Vaillant rightly suggests that Senghor prefigured his ambivalent relation to state power in his dramatic poem "Chaka," which was first published in *Présence Africaine* in 1951 and later included in *Ethiopiques* (1956).[204] Written in the form of a play, it stages the passion of Shaka Zulu, the real life warrior king and legendary hero of epic poetry, whom Senghor presents as a Christ figure.[205] The play-poem is set in the moments before Chaka's death, after his half brothers have mounted a coup d'état and left him "nailed to the ground with three spears, ready for the howling void." Chaka calmly intones, "Yes, here I am between two brothers, two traitors, two thieves. . . . Here I am brought down to earth. How bright it is, the Childhood Kingdom! And this is the end of my passion."[206]

The first act, or "song," is meant to be accompanied by "sonorous funeral drums." It stages an antagonistic dialogue between Chaka and the white colonizers with whom he had collaborated. They debate Chaka's legacy as a leader who unified his people and built a powerful state through conquest and coercion. A White Voice tells Chaka that he is "a poet . . . a smooth speaker . . . a politician!"[207] Chaka replies that he "killed the poet" and is "only a man of action, a man alone, and already dead."[208] A Seer reminds Chaka that "power is not secured without sacrifice, absolute power requires the blood of the most beloved."[209] In this play, the poet-politician is indeed torn between his love for his fiancé, Nolivé, whom he killed, and his love for his people, who were confronted with foreign enemies.

Senghor's Chaka defends his use of political violence even as he is haunted by his own violent acts. The White Voice taunts him with accusations: "They wanted a warrior and you were nothing but a butcher . . . power was indeed your goal."[210] Chaka protests that he had to make sacrifices for the greater good: "Like a careful landowner, I brought an axe to dead wood, I lit a fire in dry brush. They were ashes for sowing in winter."[211] He refigures wars of conquest against fellow Africans as resistance to British colonialism. "Forests cut down, hillsides ruined. . . . And the people . . . dying of hunger. . . . Could I remain deaf to such scornful suffering?"[212] He pleads that he regarded power as only "a means. . . . Oppression is the only thing I hate. . . . It is not hatred to love one's people. . . . I wanted all men to be brothers. . . . Each death was my death. Harvests to come and the stone for grinding such white flower from black tenderness had to be prepared."[213] But however much Chaka insists that his means justified his ends, he is also haunted by his past crimes. A spectral voice that is at once faraway and inside himself laments that even a "condemned man is accorded a few hours of forgetting."[214] This longing to forget betrays the ethic of the leader who takes responsibility for his actions as well as the vocation of the poet who remembers, narrates, and commemorates.

The second "song" is accompanied by "lively drums of love" and stages a call and response between Chaka and a Chorus just before his death. He has now left the domain of politics and returned to the kingdom of poetry where he hallucinates a reunion with the fiancé whose murder he had wanted to forget. The Leader of the Chorus announces, "It is the moment of rebirth [*re-naissance*]. . . . The poem is ripe in the garden of childhood, it is the hour of love . . . in the minute that precedes."[215] To his ghostly Nolivé, Chaka sings, "Oh, my fiancé, I've waited so long for this time / So long have I grieved for this night of love without end, suffered so much, so much. . . . For such a long time I spoke in the solitude of endless palavers. . . . Against my vocation. Such was the ordeal [*épreuve*] and the purgatory of the Poet."[216] Here the murderer presents himself as a victim, a poet forced, against his vocation, to waste his time in parliamentary deliberation. Or is this the lament of the man of action forced to inhabit the world of words, a poetic purgatory?

This passion play ends with the dying Chaka celebrated as a martyred messiah, a political leader and poetic creator who has sacrificed himself to liberate his people and redeem humanity. The Chorus refers to him as "the Anointed," and its Leader sings

> You are he who is Gifted with a Wide Back, you carry all the black-skinned peoples. . . . You are the athlete and your cloth [*pagne*] has fallen. . . . You are the slender dancer who creates the rhythm of the tam-tam . . . the creator of words of life / The poet of the Kingdom of Childhood . . . And we stand here at the gates of the Night, drinking the ancient stories . . . We will not sleep, Ah! we do not sleep while waiting for the Good News.[217]

The Chorus shouts, "Death to the politician, and long live the Poet!"[218] In response Chaka seems to agree even as he recasts the poet as a self-abnegating creator of political possibilities: "I am the pirogue that splits the river, the hand that seeds in the heavens, the foot in the belly of the earth . . . the stick that plows by beating the drum . . . Let this great sonorous battle, this harmonious struggle . . . continue to last! But no, I will die waiting . . . From the drums let there rise the sun of the new world."[219] The Leader of the Chorus confirms that Chaka's sacrifice for his people has been universally redemptive: "White dawn, new aurora that opens the eyes of my people . . . dew, that awakens the sudden roots of my people . . . There the sun at its zenith over all the peoples of the earth."[220] Does this mean that Nolivé's political murder is thereby justified by the Good News that does indeed arrive?

Senghor transformed the pitiless Shaka Zulu of historical legend into an ambivalent poet-politician and *hostie noire*. This dramatic poem enacts many of the dilemmas that Senghor as a man of politics confronted concerning the proper balance between private and public, means and ends, action and thought, present and future, pragmatic strategy and ethical vision. It is also a parable about the relationship between politics and poetry, instrumental action and aesthetic imagination, timely intervention and the untimely magic of memory, dreams, and legacies.[221]

In his own acts, Senghor had long demonstrated the affinity between politics and poetics. But in "Chaka" he seems to return to his earlier fear that a career in politics was antithetical to the poetic vocation. It expresses an ambivalent relationship to power and anticipates the haunting compromises that Senghor would make as a leader. But it would be a mistake to believe that such later developments disclose the covert truth that had always existed beneath the veneer of Senghor's postwar vision of African socialism—as if he had always intended to use it instrumentally to aid his ascent to power and to rationalize his actions as president. In fact, Senghor's growing statism after independence had less to do with the underlying motivation of his African socialism than with the troubling ways that he responded to the foreclosure of federalism as a viable political option.[222]

Scholars have yet to attend adequately to Senghor's conviction that real decolonization must operate on an imperial scale by transforming overseas and metropolitan societies simultaneously, that Africans should explode and redeem France by reconstituting it as a democratic socialist federal republic, that socialism, federalism, and decolonization in Europe and Africa had to be integrated within a single transformative project whose aim was not only African liberation or European redemption but planetary reconciliation and human realization.

Critics typically counterpose a gradualist like Senghor to the "real" radicals of the African independence movement. Of course the political differences between Senghor and revolutionary nationalists, socialists, and pan-Africanists were significant. But are there grounds for automatically privileging the moderate versus revolutionary taxonomy as the crucial axis of comparison and understanding? Alternative inquiries might attend to the difference between those who supported politics of autarchy and the politics of interdependence or between territorialist and planetary optics. Such perspectives might allow us to recognize Senghor as one among various types of postwar internationalists, all of whom elaborated distinct solutions to a common concern with looming neocolonialism. Our focus could then shift from criticizing the supposed contradiction between Senghor's revolutionary rhetoric and his reformist practices to examining the tension between dialectical-historical and vitalist-metaphysical tendencies within his postwar initiatives.

It might be useful to recall that while territorial nationalists like Sékou Touré and pan-Africanists like Kwame Nkrumah sought to improve Africa's position in the postwar interstate system, Senghor dreamed of transforming that system itself through new political forms that superseded state sovereignty. Whereas they hoped to replace colonial capitalism with African socialism in new nations or regional associations, Senghor believed that a socialist decolonization that did not also seek to revolutionize *metropolitan* societies could never succeed. We don't have to agree with his specific proposals to appreciate how this insight might invite us to rethink decolonization in far-reaching ways. Just as Senghor identified immanent potentialities within the multifaceted French Union, perhaps we can identify unrealized political potential within his plan to decolonize France through African socialism.[223] His attempt to end colonial imperialism *and* transcend territorial nationalism should be considered a moral and utopian project whose "ambition," in Gandhi's legendary formulation, was "much higher than independence."[224] Rather than dismiss him as a failed revolutionary nationalist, perhaps we should revisit him as a flawed postnational visionary.

Thinking *with* Senghor about African socialism—taking seriously his cosmopolitan ruminations about postnational democracy and his cosmological reflections on planetary reconciliation—allows us to conjure the history of a decolonization that might have been. To suggest that his unrealized future past warrants our attention is not to say that it would have resolved the problem of freedom. I am not proposing that we convert to Senghor's theologico-political program. But we should try to recognize the work that it sought to do. The point isn't that his version of African socialism would have redeemed humanity. But it is worth examining why Senghor claimed that it might. The obscured past of Senghor's unrealized future may also illuminate our present predicament, which is defined partly by the collapse of the Bandung project, the resurgence of resource imperialism, the supposed inability to imagine socialist alternatives to a seemingly unsurpassable neoliberal capitalism, and the democracy deficit of our postnational constellation.[225] If we inhabit the future that Senghor both feared and anticipated, we may now be able to recognize more clearly his exhortation to supersede empire by creating political forms through which to "desacralize" national independence as the necessary form for self-determination.

NINE   Decolonization and Postnational Democracy

The pluralistic world is thus more like a federal republic than like an empire or a kingdom. However much may be collected, however much may report itself as present at any
effective center of consciousness or action, something else is self-governed and absent
and unreduced to unity. —WILLIAM JAMES

The world-historical transformation known as "decolonization" was simultaneously an emancipatory awakening of peoples and a heteronomous process
of imperial restructuring. Most actors and agencies on both sides, however,
believed that territorial national states would be the elemental units of the postwar order. Former imperial powers, the United States, the UN, and the majority of non-European peoples whose social worlds had been brutally deformed
by imperialism shared the assumption that self-determination meant state
sovereignty.

I have argued that Senghor's and Césaire's refusals to reduce decolonization to national independence derived from their convictions about the difference between formal liberation and substantive freedom. Each proposed
plans to reorganize his society, reconstitute France, and remake the global order.
But neither adequately tethered his transformational vision to a dynamic social
movement through which it could be realized. Both supervised political parties that, although seeking to channel popular demands, failed to express a
people's will, except in narrowly electoral terms. They each led massively popular
political organizations whose constituencies felt little commitment to their leaders' most cherished aims.

This disconnect between constitutional initiatives and direct action was
rooted equally in strategic blindness and untimely insight. Césaire and Senghor

were canny political actors. Yet each gradually lost touch with the growing conviction among the global dispossessed that political independence was a necessary prerequisite for emancipation from colonial rule. But their inability to identify and inflect mass sentiment was also tied to an unwillingness to do so. Pragmatically, they believed that autarchic national solutions could not adequately address the problem of colonial freedom in an epoch of global interdependence. Ethically, they believed that the history of imperial entanglement allowed them to claim the legacies, resources, and rights supposedly reserved for metropolitans.

Césaire celebrated the long history of popular insurgency through which Antilleans had shaped history; he wrote explicitly about the dialectic of direct action and constitutional acts upon which radical transformation depended. Yet the PPM became an institutionalized political machine, controlling the levers of departmental government in Martinique and municipal government in Fort-de-France. While calling for a new regime of autonomy to transcend departmentalization, Césaire also made a series of accommodations with the French state. To many younger autonomists, nationalists, trade unionists, and communists, he represented the status quo in a context of socioeconomic decline for ordinary Antilleans.

Though speaking on behalf of ordinary Africans, Senghor rarely acknowledged the importance of direct action for any project to radically transform mentalities, social relations, and political practices. He retained a vanguardist conviction, adapted from the American New Negro movement, that a subaltern social group's most educated, talented, and privileged members had a duty to lead their consociates toward a better life. Like Césaire, he assigned a special role to writers and artists who would creatively anticipate different ways of being (free). Politically, he idealized the democratic process, trusting that radical constitutional change and progressive social policies could lead to a peaceful societal revolution. As a leader, he was less concerned with harnessing the power of social insurgency to build a new socialist society than with maintaining a balance between political dispute and public peace. His commitment to consensus through incorporation prevented him from understanding that his postwar political projects could be realized only if propelled by mass movements. He too became identified as an entrenched boss of a political machine.

Whether Césaire's and Senghor's untimely acts were "failures" is debatable: the criteria for evaluation are hardly self-evident. I have tried to prepare the ground for such a debate by attending to the complexity and specificity of their political, critical, and aesthetic visions and practices. In contrast to conventional historical methodology that instructs researchers to look behind actors' statements for what "actually" happened, I suggest that a deep understanding of events requires close attention to what was actually said. An assumption that their writings were primarily instrumental and should be measured against their empirical effects forecloses the opportunity to let their thinking illuminate the problems they confronted and those that we have inherited. Rather than rush to judge Césaire's and Senghor's acts against existing political metrics, we should consider how their political legacies might unsettle inherited assumptions about success and failure, ends and means, revolutionary and reformist, utopian and realist, progress and regress.

African Regression

This is not the place to evaluate Senghor's mixed presidential record. But it is worth noting how after Senegalese independence, he moved from acting like a *philosophical* pragmatist, rejecting a priori formulas for reaching desirable ends, to acting like a *political* pragmatist, leading through compromise and governing through the incorporation of, rather than confrontation with, adversaries.[1]

Vaillant describes how after breaking with Dia, Senghor's priorities shifted from promoting rural self-management to funding national infrastructure. His policies focused on maintaining the allegiance of educated civil servants, government functionaries, and powerful Muslim brotherhood organizations. He had originally crafted a constitution featuring a robust parliamentary system with a strong prime minister and weak president. But after imprisoning Dia, he changed the constitution, introducing a strong presidential regime in which government officials reported directly to him. This authoritarian drift coincided with national economic decline. Senghor never diversified Senegal's groundnut economy, which depended on an unpredictable international commodities market. He counted increasingly on French development aid, technical experts, and private investments. Senghor's government passed policies favorable to French companies, became a reliable ally of the French state, and avoided displeasing powerful provincial marabouts. His failures to meet popular expectations through effective development programs eroded public support for Senghor's regime by the 1970s.[2]

But Vaillant also recounts how Senghor sought, from 1976, to rehabilitate himself through democratic reforms and a more liberal constitution. Trade unions, political parties, and a free press were legalized, the public sphere revived, and open elections were held. Moroever, despite several constitutional crises, Senghor's state was never exceedingly violent, and he was the first African leader to voluntarily relinquish power. As president, Senghor's cosmopolitan convictions were redirected into promoting federal organizations within Africa and a dubious program for *francophonie* internationally. He continued to celebrate cultural *métissage* and the civilization of the universal.[3]

But I have warned against treating Senghor's flawed presidency as the optic through which to regard his earlier speech and acts regarding federal democracy and African socialism, as if he had always acted opportunistically to put himself into a position to rule a sovereign state. An independent Senegal marked not the realization but the eclipse of his untimely vision for decolonization. Rather than condemn Senghor as a failed national president, we should remember his warning that the form of freedom promised by territorial nationalism for African peoples was bound to fail. Many critics have argued—perhaps rightly—that Senghor was never as radical as he maintained. But Senegal's difficult road following independence suggests we also ask what might have been if Senghor's program for self-determination without state sovereignty had been realized.

Following his imagined framework, African *sans papiers* in metropolitan France would not be foreigners demanding hospitality but citizens whose rights of mobility, family reunification, social security, and political participation were legally protected. Africans would not be outsiders appealing for economic aid from a *foreign* French state nor targets of dehumanizing humanitarianism. Violations of their human rights could be adjudicated in a federal justice system rather than depend on the weak ethical norms of international law or the good will of powerful nations. West African peoples would be integral members of an expanded European Union. Imagine what Senghor might have felt when his volume *Nocturnes* (1961) received an international poetry prize for *foreign* authors writing in French.

I am not suggesting that Senghor's program to reconstitute France as a democratic socialist federation would have necessarily led to a happy outcome. But there are no a priori grounds for dismissing it as any less plausible than the territorial national solutions to colonial freedom the world did embrace. The nationalist logic of decolonization created isolated states easily influenced by the French government through separate bilateral agreements over security, aid, and trade relations. In the 1970s France developed the criminal system of neocolonial control over African states that became known as *la françafrique*. Forming corrupt alliances with authoritarian rulers of antidemocratic governments, France exerted direct financial and military pressure on nation-states it treated as quasi-colonial outposts with protected markets for French business interests. *La françafrique* was maintained not only by the Ministries of

Defense, Foreign Affairs, and Overseas Cooperation but by a corrupt extralegal network of spies, covert operatives, mercenaries, arms dealers, and corporations, especially oil companies. These cynical alliances functioned to repress democracy and maintain economic dependence in these African societies. Even when they led to greater development aid, foreign investment, and military protection, the system primarily enriched African elites and sustained French geopolitical power rather than improve the lives of peasants or workers.[4]

While the French state treated African nations as if they were still overseas possessions, it began to treat the growing population of African immigrants and citizens in metropolitan France as unwelcome foreigners. Between 1945 and 1973 African nationals, primarily from Mali, Mauretania, and Senegal, were recruited to work in French factories and housed in state-constructed hostels. The flow of these workers was propelled by the high labor demand in France created by the postwar economic boom, then by declining living conditions in West Africa, and finally by the desire to reunify families separated through labor migration. By the late 1960s provisional labor migrants had become a settled population of immigrants and second-generation citizens. After the economic downturn in the early 1970s, when the French government no longer permitted legal immigration from overseas, all denizens of African descent—whether citizens, legal immigrants, or undocumented illegals—endured more severe forms of republican racism and social stigmatization.[5]

In the 1980s climate of growing xenophobia, the French state revised its nationality laws. French-born children of foreign nationals no longer received automatic citizenship, family reunification policies were suspended, illegal immigrants were regularly arrested and deported. Everyday surveillance and harassment of Africans residing in France, especially in the *banlieues*, intensified against the backdrop of vitriolic public debates about national identity, republican values, multiculturalism, French decline, and colonial nostalgia. As extreme-right political parties with explicit anti-immigrant platforms received larger percentages in municipal, parliamentary, presidential, and European elections, mainstream republican politics became more hostile to immigrant communities. Another set of restrictive anti-immigrant measures, the Pasqua Laws, were passed in the early 1990s.[6]

In this context, a politicized movement of undocumented African immigrants launched a series of public protests, culminating in the occupation of the Église Saint-Bernard by hundreds of Senegalese and Malians demanding legalized status; police stormed the church and expelled the protesters, some of whom were then deported.[7] In the same context, Nicholas Sarkozy, then Interior Minister of the Chirac government, launched a campaign to militantly police immigrant neighborhoods; he famously referred to unruly youths who protested his policies as scum that should be hosed away. This attitude helped fuel the massive October 2005 uprisings in the *banlieues*.[8] These began with the deaths of two teenagers, one of African and the other of North African descent. They were electrocuted while attempting to hide in a power substation when, after playing soccer with friends, they were chased by police looking for robbery suspects. Weeks of rioting followed across France, focused especially on the destruction of cars and public buildings; the government declared a state of emergency.

In an inflammatory speech in Agen on June 25, 2006, Sarkozy linked neoliberal self-help ideology, anti-immigrant nationalism, and the insistence that France owes neither apologies nor debts for its colonial past. After suggesting that immigrants making political claims on the state were parasites, dwelling pathologically in the past and living on the labor of others, he declared that those who did not love France or were not willing to work should leave.[9] In his 2007 speech in Dakar, Sarkozy acted as if France were still an imperial power and Senegal a colonial territory. He identified Africans as primordial beings outside the framework of modern history.[10]

Recent debates about whether the state should "repent" for its colonial past, not to mention the February 23, 2005, law sponsored by Sarkozy requiring public schools to teach French students about the positive aspects of French colonialism, illustrate that the history of interpenetration and interdependence that had made African peoples integral parts of a "French" social formation has long been forgotten or disavowed, like the Algerian Muslims who were French citizens, the Harkis who served France during the Algerian War, and African veterans of the two world wars, long denied their rightful pensions by the French state.[11] The French government's recent plan for a Mediterranean Union would function less as intercontinental confederation than as a neoliberal trading bloc, aggravating the economic asymmetry between France and its former Maghrebian colonies.[12] From this perspective, the nationalist logic of decolonization has contributed to dispossession; state sovereignty has neither been a recipe for self-determination in postcolonial Africa nor a guarantor of basic rights for Africans in the metropolitan postcolony.

Antillean Experiments

Formally, the French DOM are less sovereign than politically independent African nations. To many they appear frozen in a relationship of colonial dependency. Yet some aspects of the postnational political arrangements that

Senghor and Césaire had envisioned for the postwar period have gradually and quietly developed in Martinique, Guadeloupe, and Guyane.

Soon after de Gaulle's election in 1958, hopes for a new regime of autonomy faded. Under the Fifth Republic, economic decline, social dependence, and cultural alienation—corresponding to a surge of Antillean labor migration to the metropole—fueled political resentment in Martinique.[13] The left, which had formerly supported departmentalization, now fought to revise the territory's legal status. Autonomists, represented by Césaire's PPM and the Martinican Communist Party, sought a new regime of self-government without complete separation from France.[14] Nationalist organizations in the 1970s demanded full political independence[15] but failed to attract a mass following. Césaire, by contrast, became the most powerful politician in Martinique. But Gaullist policies during the 1960s and 1970s allowed the conservative right in Martinique to derail all attempts at autonomy. Entrenched departmentalists manipulated fears that any change in legal status would be a first step toward independence, warning that France would abandon its DOM and that Martinique's economic security, social protections, and acquired rights would disappear.[16]

This political diagram changed in May 1981, when, following François Mitterrand's presidential election, Césaire declared a moratorium on the PPM's efforts to change Martinique's legal status.[17] This decision to collaborate with the metropolitan state was inspired by the socialist government's policy of decentralization, through which substantial administrative powers devolved to organs of local governance in the DOM. Decentralization officially sanctioned the regional "right to difference" and funded Antillean cultural associations, media outlets, and programs to support diversity and raise consciousness.[18] The 1980s and 1990s were decades of vibrant cultural reclamation, featuring vigorous debates among metropolitan and overseas Antilleans over cultural authenticity, whether refracted through *négritude*, *antillanité*, or *créolité*.[19] From the late 1990s, this culturalist turn converged with a growing preoccupation with the historical memory of slavery, colonial violence, and anticolonial struggles in Martinique. Debates unfolded over official commemorations and the state's historical responsibility for past harms perpetrated against Antillean peoples.[20]

In Martinique there emerged a broad political consensus that traversed classes and ideological positions, combining the rejection of cultural assimilation, an affirmation of regional specificity, and a commitment to integration within the French republic. Popular support for a distinct cultural "nation" grew, while the prospects of state sovereignty virtually disappeared.[21] But accommodation is not stagnation; the challenge of integrating the Antilles into the national state had always entailed pragmatic improvisation and adaptation. In Martinique the laws of the republic and its administrative forms were often reworked through a series of derogations, adjustments, and local preferences based on the specific conditions and needs of this Caribbean territory.[22] Departmentalization has entailed neither a straightforward process of cultural assimilation to the French nation nor political assimilation to the unitary republic. Automatic statements about neocolonial dependence in the Antilles ignore the peculiar political arrangement that has emerged over the past sixty years in the DOMs.

Martinican political scientists Justin Daniel, Fred Constant, and Fred Reno have demonstrated that departmentalization has enabled the formation of a distinct and autonomous juridicopolitical system that does not simply mirror its metropolitan counterpart and that allows for a large degree of independent maneuvering. Simultaneously, departmentalization created a system of economic and political subordination, and decentralization in turn opened the way to local clientelism, party factionalism, and identitarianism. Yet Martinique has also developed a substantial degree of political autonomy and cultural integrity without sacrificing full citizenship and social protections within a democratic French republic. The system recognizes Martinican geographic and cultural specificity while allowing for movement and mixture. It also legally protects the deep ties linking Antilleans to metropolitan society, the republican polity, and European history.[23] This unofficial movement toward legal pluralism and administrative diversity within a decentralized and multicultural French republic is further complicated by the peculiar status of the Antillean departments in the European Union, as well as by their growing commitment to membership in a broader Caribbean region.[24]

This existing Martinican system, having displaced, not just reproduced, some of the precepts of unitary republicanism, suggests the realization of some of Césaire's initial hopes for departmentalization. But we cannot grasp Césaire's legacy only by examining the failures and successes of departmentalization. We must also consider departmentalization in relation to the broader vision and spirit of engagement that animated Césaire's political projects. We must engage his legacy not only in terms of the departmentalization that came to be but in terms of the postimperial federation that might have been.

To inquire into Césaire's legacy is to seek the residues and resonances of his commitment to confront colonial emancipation as an open-ended problem for which state sovereignty was not the presumptive solution. His spirit is thus present in projects seeking to convert formal liberty into substantive freedom by restructuring rather than rejecting the juridicopolitical partnership between the overseas departments and a French republic of which Antilleans have always been an integral part and on which they have enduring legal, material, and moral claims. We should not automatically associate Césaire's legacy with the Antillean nationalists and independentists seeking to extend Negritude's rejection of cultural assimilation without pursuing its corresponding cosmopolitan political project. These Antillean culturalists have developed a separatist orientation that has often led them to criticize republicanism and universalism as foreign, hypocritical, or illusory. A fixation on cultural authenticity has generated a politics of identitarian and communitarian *ressentiment* and revendication. For these critics, departmentalization signals *only* cultural assimilation and colonial alienation. Their leaders have also expressed hostility toward Antilleans settled in metropolitan France and discriminatory xenophobia toward immigrants from other Caribbean countries.[25]

Perhaps more appropriate is to recognize Césaire's legacy in other currents of pragmatic politics unfolding along paths the poet-politician originally traced in the postwar period. An organization, such as the Conseil Représentatif des Associations Noires—a federation of black French civic associations founded after the 2005 *banlieue* uprising by Patrick Lozès, a French citizen whose family was originally from Benin—extends Césaire's lifelong attempts to create bonds of solidarity among Africans and the Antilleans in the metropole. On the legislative front, Christiane Taubira, a longtime parliamentary deputy from Guyane and now minister of justice under François Hollande, extends Césaire's postwar struggle to compel the French state to honor its historical debts to the former slaves through full citizenship and social equality. Serge Letchimy succeeded Césaire as mayor of Fort-de-France, deputy from Martinique and president of the PPM. He has extended Césaire's project to create conditions for postcolonial freedom in Martinique through economic development, cultural autonomy, and democratic self-management.[26]

It is also important to recognize other heirs to Césaire, perhaps less visible but enacting his legacy in fundamental ways. In contrast to the politicians with whom they are often allied, these intellectuals approach Antillean politics with an experimental and future-oriented sensibility that rejects a priori formulas for postcolonial freedom and Antillean sociability. In contrast to the nationalist and independentist figures whom they criticize forcefully, they are cosmopolitans committed to a postracial republicanism and multicultural democracy within a reconfigured France. They include Guadeloupean novelist Daniel Maximin, Martinican political scientist Justin Daniel, and sociologist Michel Giraud, a metropolitan of Guadeloupean descent.[27]

These thinkers begin with a forceful critique of French racism, cultural assimilation, and the failures of departmentalization. They support the need to recognize Antillean distinctiveness and local autonomy. But they also deplore how cultural claims have overwhelmed, evacuated, or co-opted political space in the Antilles since the 1980s. They reject any communitarian retrenchment that would close off the Antilles from France or Europe or from its Caribbean and American neighbors. Regarding cultural authenticity and the DOM legal status as political distractions, they do not believe that integral nationalism, let alone state sovereignty, will magically bestow development or democracy on Antillean peoples. Instead, they suggest that Antillean self-management, French citizenship, and transnational interdependence may require one another.

Impatient with facile rejections of republicanism or universalism as Eurocentric, these thinkers suggest that support for full French citizenship honors the legacy and condenses the struggles of their slave and activist ancestors who pursued republican liberty and equality against the white plantocratic right, which had long supported autonomy from the French state to protect *béké* racial hegemony in the Antilles. This is the perspective from which these thinkers can understand political assimilation as expressing an enduring demand for social equality rather than the simple wish for cultural assimilation. Like Césaire, they attempt to universalize republican universality by deracializing it. They challenge its presumptive link to whiteness, France, or Europe even as they also root it in the particular history, conditions, and politics of the Antilles. Their writings suggest that the republican project is an indispensable element of their own heritage even as Antillean freedom struggles are also indissociable aspects of France's republican patrimony. For them, the overseas departments constitute the "cutting edge" of French republicanism, expressing its deepest values and prefiguring its future forms.[28] Rather than focus on the protection of an idealized Creole culture in the Caribbean, they conceive the radical possibilities of the creolization of France itself. They recognize that democracy and development in the DOM will continue to require intercultural dialogue, reciprocity, and *métissage*, as well as political negotiation and partnership.

In short, these thinkers highlight the underlying link between postcolonial freedom and postnational democracy.[29] They embrace the political potential that may inhere in the imperfect kinds of experiments in legal pluralism, administrative decentralization, and shared sovereignty that historical conditions have compelled French Antilleans to pursue. Of course, they criticize the paradoxes, contradictions, and impasses that circumscribe Antillean public life, challenging the persistence of French racism and structural inequality. But they also embrace the DOM as improvisational laboratories, where plural-ist, autonomist, federalist, and confederalist arrangements with the French republic, the Caribbean region, and the European Union can be worked out as the only viable path toward a social democratic or democratic socialist fu-ture under current historical conditions.

Césaire was not naive about the imperial underpinnings of the French Union. Likewise we should recognize the limitations of departmentaliza-tion. But just as Césaire's pragmatic interventions were guided by utopian real-ist insights into what the French Union could possibly become, we might now imagine how existing departmentalization may point beyond itself toward a form of plural democracy whose prospective realization Césaire had already envisioned. As in Césaire's account of Toussaint, the Caribbean functions as an exemplary scene of colonial modernity. And as in revolutionary Saint-Domingue, black French actors in the overseas departments must grapple with a series of refractory dilemmas and unsatisfying alternatives. But just because there may be no way out does not mean that there is no way forward.[30] To wit, the massive forty-four-day general strike launched in Guadeloupe by the Ly-annaj Kont Pwofitasyon (LKP) in January 2009, which delinked anti-imperial rebellion from demands for political sovereignty.[31] Césaire's Caribbean may serve not only as a symptom of tragedy but as a democratic prophecy. His and Senghor's visions of self-determination without state sovereignty, legacies that they inherited and willed, should surely count as a fecund source for an effec-tive history of our present through which to glimpse a possible future.

Postnational Democracy

Jürgen Habermas argues that in the modern period, "the phenomena of the territorial state, the nation, and a popular economy constituted within national borders formed a historical constellation in which the democratic process as-sumed a more or less convincing institutional form. . . . The idea that societies are capable of democratic self-control and self-realization has until now been credibly realized only in the context of the nation-state."[32] However, "develop-ments summarized under the term 'globalization' have put this entire constel-lation into question."[33] He identifies the current "postnational constellation" with the impossibility of assuming that "the unified citizens of a democratic community are able to shape their own social environment and can develop the capacity for action necessary for such interventions to succeed."[34]

The current situation thus presents the same structural dilemma that Sen-ghor and Césaire confronted in the postwar opening. Changing historical

conditions have challenged the long-standing assumption that territorial sovereignty is the necessary framework for political freedom. These include the
close of the Cold War, the dismantling of social welfare states, the failure of
Bandung development states, and the transformation of slum dwellers, immigrants, and stateless refugees around the world into permanent surplus populations.[35] For larger masses of people, decisions by distant, invisible, or unac-
countable actors circumscribe their life chances without any mechanisms for
redressing harms, let alone participating in defining desirable futures.

Responsibilities for global governance are ceded to unelected international bodies, transnational organizations, technical experts, and private
corporations. The world community seems unable to create frameworks for
self-management adequate to the transnational scale through which decisions
about global politics, human futures, and environmental sustainability must
be made. Formal independence cannot guarantee substantive freedom in most
postcolonial societies. Yet the options for North-South partnership are typically restricted either to neocolonial patron-client relations or to neoliberal
free-trade zones. Facing the reality that territory, people, and government
will not organically align, states increasingly create or accept legal diversity
within their borders. But such exceptional regimes have not been elevated into
plural democracies that link singularity and self-management to citizenship
solidarity and social equality for politically autonomous or legally distinct
communities.

Étienne Balibar discusses "a growing gap between the [transnational] level
on which a large number of private practices and social relations are now organized . . . and the framework of the majority of public institutions (and in
any case the state) which remains fundamentally national."[36] He explains,

> these difficulties . . . cannot be overcome without a radical recasting of
> the relations between people and sovereignty, citizenship and commu-
> nity: in short, without a new conception of the state . . . what is nec-
> essary here is . . . the invention of new institutions . . . for the public
> sphere . . . far from determining an "end of politics," in either a techno-
> cratic or apocalyptic sense, globalization in fact carries with it a need to
> recreate politics.[37]

Remarkably, he surmises that "there are few precedents for this in history, other
than, precisely, the transition from city-states to empires, and from empires
to nations."[38]

Given this predicament, which echoes the dilemma created by decolonization as I have outlined it, "either the social state and social citizenship will

have to be completely dismantled, or citizenship will have to be detached from its purely national definition so that social rights with a transnational character can be guaranteed."[39] For under contemporary conditions

> *all* political communities . . . are *communities of fate* . . . where heterogeneous people and groups have been "thrown together" by history and economy in situations where their interests or cultural ideals cannot spontaneously converge, but also cannot completely diverge without risking mutual destruction.[40]

The only just solution is that individuals and groups "must be recognized as citizens any place . . . they 'happen' to live and therefore work." Like Arendt, Balibar equates "permanent access" to such citizenship as a necessary condition for access to humanity.[41]

Habermas and Balibar identify a crucial challenge: how to fashion political forms that link the democratic participation and socioeconomic solidarity that were once (at least partially) enabled by citizenship in a national polity to the supranational scales and planetary demands of our political present? This raises additional questions. Can—*should*—the kind of goods signified by cosmopolitan ethics, human rights, world citizenship, or global democracy be grounded in concrete political formations through which such abstractions could be realized? If so, what are the constitutional alternatives to either an outmoded national or an implausible global state? What political arrangements could induce individuals and communities to sacrifice, share risk, and support redistribution to other humans as if they were fellow members of a socialist democracy, mutualist cooperative, or intentional community? Is it possible to ground new forms of postnational solidarity without recourse to universal abstractions (e.g., natural law, universal reason, human rights) or concrete loyalties (e.g., family, territory, nation)?

The paradox identified by Kant and Arendt persists: universal rights for humans have only ever actually existed within the framework of particular national states for circumscribed groups of citizens. This is the same problem the postwar generation faced: how to pursue the humanist promise of democratic universalism without transforming peoples into populations and political actors into merely existing humans and passive objects of normalizing interventions.

Contemporary actors and thinkers have offered various responses to this task of grounding self-determination and human emancipation at this historical conjuncture. Many progressive voices call for political arrangements to accommodate cultural multiplicity and legal plurality, regional autonomy and rights of hospitality, denationalized citizenship and disaggregated sovereignty. International lawyers debate whether the right of self-determination can be applied to minority populations within states.[42] Movements across Latin America seek to constitutionalize autonomy for indigenous peoples.[43] The 1996 constitution of South Africa articulates state and customary law through institutional arrangements promoting novel forms of legal pluralism.[44] Many critics of the Israeli occupation are attracted to various "one-state solutions" that break with the territorial logic of national sovereignty that long governed the Palestinian liberation struggle.[45] In response to rising European xenophobia, proposals have emerged to separate citizenship from community by guaranteeing rights of hospitality, political participation, work, and mobility for immigrants or refugees living in so-called foreign national states.[46] Regionally, reformers seek to transform the confederal European Union into an actual democratic federation of peoples.[47]

Others believe that new forms of postnational democracy would require a transnational public sphere, global civil society, cosmopolitan law, or world constitution. Like Kant, they dream of rationalizing international conflict by subordinating power politics to legal procedures and democratic deliberation. World constitutionalists argue that the global system, already circumscribed by international legal rules, is effectively a constitutional order to which all actors with international legal personality are subject. They either regard the UN Charter as a de facto world constitution or would like to elevate it into one.[48] Others seek to create new institutional frameworks through which systems of cosmopolitan law, world citizenship, and global democracy could be realized.[49]

In contrast are realist and pragmatic international legal thinkers influenced by Carl Schmitt and Michel Foucault. They seek to democratize international politics by accepting, even embracing, the existing system of fragmented, incoherent, and conflictual international laws, rules, customs, and norms that are constantly being produced by a wide range of public and private agents (lawyers, politicians, bureaucrats, technical experts, economic interests). David Kennedy, for example, argues that the plural and decentered condition of international law will allow a greater number and variety of actors to intervene progressively on the stage of world politics. He criticizes as illusory the desire of world constitutionalists and cosmopolitans to create a unitary, coherent, and stable system for global law and democracy. Preferring global governance without world government, he insists that a more democratic system would have to better understand, in order to confront on its own terms, the existing system whereby international legal arrangements are formulated below and outside traditional systems of laws and right by administrators and experts, formally and informally, through rules, principles, standards, and norms that operate in the background of public power.[50]

Other advocates of postnational democracy are equally suspicious of any desire for a coherent global law or world state. But they recognize the need for political forms through which to democratize governance and ground cosmopolitanism on a transnational scale. They imagine constitutional arrangements that would recognize plurality, diversity, and fragmentation within decentralized polities. Their aim is to link the strong solidarities afforded by citizenship in national states to deterritorialized and disaggregated forms of sovereignty. They envision postnational frameworks that can reconcile singularity and mutuality, multiplicity and equality, autonomy and universality. Rejecting the axiom that political communities must be grounded in shared identities, forms of life, or affective patriotism, they envision regional economic confederations, multinational constitutional states, and continent-sized federal democracies.[51]

We do not have to have faith in parliamentary democracy, procedural politics, or the rationality of constitutional right to recognize the importance of the problems these various proposals are confronting. Democratic thinking for these times would, I believe, benefit from engaging their attempts to imagine rights without states, governance without government, citizenship without community, sovereignty without territory, democracy without ethnicity. Conversely, recent calls for renewed approaches to radical democracy, communism, and anarchism must also be engaged even if their tendency to elide questions of global governance and political form sometimes signals a troubling lapse regarding a pressing problem that cannot be wished away.[52]

In short, the task of radical democracy today resembles that which Arendt identified in the Cold War epoch, when she called for a political order that could transcend the existing law of nations so that humanity itself, not sovereign states, could guarantee rights for all humans as humans. Aimé Césaire and Léopold Senghor provided flawed but provocative solutions to precisely this problem when they attempted to invent novel frameworks that could link political universality and cultural multiplicity, democratic equality and legal plurality, autonomy (for peoples) and solidarity (as humans), popular sovereignty and planetary interdependence, humanist and cosmopolitan norms with mutual responsibility and socialized risk.

Negritude Redux

Current efforts to envision postnational democracy are the unwitting heirs of postwar attempts to invent forms of self-determination without state sovereignty. In the flash between the "no longer" of late colonialism and the "not yet" of the Cold War order, Césaire and Senghor hoped to institute political frameworks that could secure their peoples' status as free humans without either grounding that freedom in national autarchy or relying on the weak ethical mandates of humanitarianism or human rights. The postwar opening did not only resemble our own transitional moment. It created the very order whose unraveling is the source of many of the political dilemmas that we now face. To think historically about our political present, we need therefore to question, rather than reproduce, the territorialist logic of decolonization; we should also examine the overdetermined processes through which postwar possibilities were foreclosed. And like Césaire and Senghor we can seek to awaken potentialities condensed within outmoded emancipatory projects. We inhabit the future that they anticipated. The unraveling of the postwar arrangements that they resisted also makes their moment differently legible in a new "now of recognizability." This allows us to fashion, between the postwar epoch and our own, a historical constellation whereby each can illuminate the other as well as the obscured connections between them.

Thinking *with* Césaire and Senghor means engaging a future that might have been. I am not suggesting that their answers can be applied to our times. Their specific proposals would no longer make political sense. But the problems they identified—concerning the relation of state sovereignty to human freedom or the prospects for self-management, plural democracy, and human solidarity in an interdependent world—persist. Their utopian realist thinking, at once concrete and world-historical, still resonates. But we can only begin to recognize their future past, let alone hear their transgenerational call to possible heirs, if we unthink entrenched assumptions about Negritude as a nativism, decolonization as national independence, and the postwar period as the Cold War order that came to be rather than an opening in which a range of nonnational political experiments were envisioned and enacted.

Although neither was a systematic thinker, Senghor and Césaire made contributions to critical theory that extend beyond the often circumscribed fields of anticolonial discourse or postcolonial studies. For example, they developed radically literalist orientations to humanism and universalism. They did not merely challenge Europeans for failing to extend these concepts to Africans and Antilleans. Nor did they reject them as provincial European constructs imposed on the world. Rather, they criticized these concepts for being abstract, disembodied, and unmediated. They did not reject humanism or universalism as such, only their actually existing liberal, republican, and socialist forms. Accordingly, they imagined a type of decolonization that would transcend the alternative between abstract humanism and territorial nationalism, while retaining the universalism of the former and the pluralism of the latter. They tried to invent political forms that would allow metropolitan and overseas peoples to recognize their entangled history and build a common future without recourse either to the ideological humanism that had authorized colonialism or the parochial culturalism that would obstruct the translocal solidarities required by postwar emancipation. In other words, they attempted to ground political solidarity on historical intersections rather than either abstract humanity or cultural identity. Thus my suggestion that they were concrete cosmopolitans. Césaire and Senghor did not simply praise cosmopolitanism as an ethical orientation or sociohistorical condition. They engaged it at the level of political form; they pursued cosmopolitan *projects* through which to surpass the alternatives of humanist universalism and culturalist nationalism. They identified within a heteronomous imperial history relations of interdependence, mutuality, and reciprocity from which they could try to craft new forms of transcontinental democracy and human solidarity.

Their works help us to recognize how imperialism itself created conditions, in alienated form, for the kind of decentralized governance, legal pluralism, and disaggregated sovereignty that now seem both urgent to institute and difficult to reconcile with republican universalism.[53] A deeper understanding of their interventions, as well as the postwar opening from which they acted, allows us to situate within a longer tradition recent efforts by subaltern communities in postcolonial France to transcend the old political calculus by refusing simply to either embrace or reject French nationality or the republican tradition. These include undocumented West Africans, third-generation Maghrebians, Islamic civic associations, Muslim women, Guadeloupean trade unionists, Martinican "negropolitans," and postcolonial soccer players, as well as women and gay militants for parliamentary *parité* and civil unions.[54] When viewed through the lens of either republican orthodoxy or the nationalist logic of decolonization, such gestures to transvalue citizenship, membership, and political subjectivity often confuse left critics. But when thought in relation to both the imperial nation-state that Senghor and Césaire confronted and the politics of radical literalism that they practiced, such attempts to transcend the alternatives between assimilation and separatism become legible. They too are unwitting heirs to Senghor's and Césaire's seemingly outmoded commitments to concrete universalism and embodied humanism.

But if we want their insights to deepen our understanding of either the postwar opening or our post–Cold War present, we need to recognize that they were concerned not only with expressing black subjectivity or advocating African or Antillean interests. They were planetary thinkers who were concerned with the relation between decolonization, human redemption, and the future of the world. To think with Césaire and Senghor about the problem of freedom helps point beyond the limitations of an anticolonial nationalism and postcolonial criticism that, for understandable reasons, has largely focused on singularity, incommensurability, and untranslatability. Scholars often identify Senghor and Césaire as ambivalent precursors or moderate counterpoints to *really* radical Third World thinkers and actors. Perhaps our new "now of recognizability" and different "distribution of the sensible," can allow us to enter into a new dialogue with these untimely figures whose attempts to call for and call forth seemingly unimaginable futures can be seen and heard afresh.[55]

But their reflections on self-determination, federal democracy, and human emancipation become legible only if we recognize them as postwar thinkers of the postwar conjuncture. Thus my call, with this book as a modest and imperfect contribution, to decolonize intellectual history, to deprovincialize African and Antillean writing, to deterritorialize social thought, and to globalize critical theory. One approach to these tasks would be to unearth new sources in order to bring to light repressed and marginalized forms of subaltern thought. I have tried, rather, to break through the crust encasing iconic intellectuals, such as Senghor and Césaire, who are more frequently talked about than listened to, more likely to be invoked instrumentally than read closely. Whether or not my specific interpretations are persuasive, I hope that my engagement with their interventions induces readers to revisit their writings and reconsider their legacies. Thinking with them about their world and ours may be a step toward producing histories of our "now" that treat pasts present and futures past as social facts linked to innovative if imperfect political acts that anticipate seemingly impossible alternatives to existing arrangements.

I have tried to show that critical history should attend directly to untimely phenomena which often confound existing approaches to contextualization, frameworks for analyzing change, and categories for distinguishing among tenses. The proleptic writings of Césaire and Senghor, like Toussaint, Schoelcher, and Marx, seem to proceed according to Frederic Jameson's suggestion that "utopias in fact come to us as barely audible messages from a future that may never come into being."[56] They also call to mind Benjamin's inverse injunction to listen carefully for "a sort of theological whispered intelligence dealing with matters discredited and obsolete."[57] Césaire and Senghor did precisely this when they identified within an already superseded empire the elements of an unprecedented federal democracy. They were aesthetic actors and political poets who resembled Kafka insofar as he, in Adorno's view, "sins against the ancient rule of the game by constructing art of nothing but the refuse of reality. He does not directly outline the image of the society to come—for in his as in all great art, asceticism toward the future prevails—but rather depicts it as a montage composed of waste products which the new order, in the process of forming itself, extracts from the perishing present."[58] In this spirit, we now can regard Senghor's and Césaire's own unrealized programs for self-determination without state sovereignty as discredited and obsolete matters, waste products of a perishing present, from which new futures might be imagined.[59]

If we are to grasp untimely political objects, thinking itself must be recognized as an untimely operation situated at the intersection of the actual and imagined, the possible and impossible, the immanent and transcendent, the remembered and the anticipated. Political thinking is often a matter of stolen glimpses across epochal divides. In Adorno's terms, "the only philosophy which can be responsibly practiced in face of despair is the attempt to contemplate all things from the standpoint of redemption. . . . Perspectives must be fashioned that displace and estrange the world, reveal it to be, with its rifts and crevices, as indigent and distorted as it will appear one day in the messianic light."[60] Likewise, political action is often a matter of blind leaps illuminated by flashes of untimely insight. As Césaire toward the end of his life explained to an interviewer, "I have no ambitions about finding a solution. I do not know where we are going, but I know that we must charge ahead. The black man must be liberated, but he must also be liberated from the liberator."[61]

CHRONOLOGY

1791	A slave revolt in Saint-Domingue leads to the Haitian Revolution.
1794	The National Assembly abolishes slavery in French colonies.
1799	NOVEMBER 9 (18 BRUMAIRE) Napoléon, leading a coup d'état, replaces the Directory with the Consulate government.
1801	JULY Toussaint Louverture promulgates a constitution for Saint-Domingue. DECEMBER Napoléon's General Charles Leclerc leads an invasion force to Saint-Domingue.
1802	MAY Louis Delgrès leads an army of freed blacks in the failed battle of Matouba against reimposition of slavery in Guadeloupe.
1803	APRIL Toussaint Louverture dies in prison in France.
1804	JANUARY 1 Haiti becomes independent under Jean-Jacques Dessalines.
1811	Henry Christophe becomes king of northern Haiti.
1828–1830	Victor Schoelcher travels to Cuba and the United States, after which he publishes his first abolitionist writings.
1840–1841	Schoelcher travels to the French and British Caribbean colonies and Haiti.

1848	FEBRUARY
	Revolutions break out in France and elsewhere across Europe.
	APRIL
	The Provisional Government abolishes slavery in France's colonies.
	JUNE
	Popular uprisings in Paris look to protect the social gains of the revolution.
	DECEMBER 2
	Louis Napoléon is elected president of the Second Republic.
1851	DECEMBER 2
	Louis Napoléon's coup d'état ends the Second Republic.
1871	MARCH
	The Paris Commune.
	Returned from exile, Victor Schoelcher is elected to represent Martinique in the National Assembly under the Third Republic.
1889	Schoelcher publishes *Vie de Toussaint Louverture*.
	Henri Bergson publishes his first book, *Time and Free Will: An Essay on the Immediate Data of Consciousness*.
1893	Schoelcher dies.
1905	Jean-Paul Sartre is born in Paris.
1906	JANUARY 12
	Emmanuel Levinas is born in Kovno, Lithuania.
	OCTOBER 9
	Léopold Sédar Senghor is born in Jaol, Senegal.
	OCTOBER 14
	Hannah Arendt is born in Linden, Germany.
1913	JUNE 26
	Aimé Césaire is born in Basse-Pointe, Martinique.
	NOVEMBER 7
	Albert Camus is born in Mondovi, Algeria.
1914	Blaise Diagne is elected to represent Senegal in the French National Assembly.

1918	Ernst Bloch publishes *The Spirit of Utopia*.
1924	Césaire enters Lycée Schoelcher in Fort-de-France.
	André Breton publishes *Manifesto of Surrealism*.
1925	Alain Locke publishes *The New Negro* anthology.
	Walter Benjamin submits his thesis on *The Origins of German Tragic Drama*.
	JULY Frantz Fanon is born in Martinique.
1926	Senghor transfers from the Catholic Libermann Seminary to the lycée in Dakar.
	Marcel Mauss founds the Institut d'Ethnologie.
1927	Martin Heidegger publishes *Being and Time*.
	Benjamin begins working on *The Arcades Project*.
1928	Senghor enrolls in Lycée Louis-le-Grand in Paris on partial scholarship.
1929	Claude McKay publishes *Banjo*.
1931	Césaire enters Lycée Louis-le-Grand.
	Senghor enters the Sorbonne, where he studies French, Latin, and Greek; writes a thesis on "Exoticism in Baudelaire"; and attends courses in ethnology and African linguistics at the Institut d'Ethnologie and the École Pratique des Hautes Études.
	First issue of *La Revue du Monde Noir* is published by Paulette Nardal.
	Emanuelle Mounier founds the journal *Esprit*.
	Theodor Adorno delivers "The Actuality of Philosophy" at University of Frankfurt.
1932	Senghor obtains French citizenship; returns to Senegal to visit his family. *Légitime Défense* published by René Ménil, Étienne and Thélus Léro, and Jules Monnerot.
	Bergson publishes his final book of philosophy, *Two Sources of Morality and Religion*.
1933	Senghor becomes president of the West African Students Association in Paris.

Leo Frobenius publishes *History of African Civilization.*

Walter Benjamin goes into exile in France.

1934   Galandou Diouf is elected to represent Senegal in the French National Assembly.

Léon-Gontran Damas is sent by Marcel Mauss and Ministry of Education on a study mission to Guyane.

Gaston Bachelard publishes *Le nouvel esprit scientifique.*

1935   Senghor obtains an *agrégation* in linguistics; becomes professor of Latin and Greek at the Lycée Descartes in Tours.

Césaire enters the École Normale Supérieure, where he writes a thesis titled "The Theme of the South in the Negro-American Poetry of the United States."

W. E. B. DuBois publishes *Black Reconstruction in America.*

MARCH

Senghor, Césaire, and Damas publish *L'Étudiant Noir.*

1936   Césaire begins writing *Cahier d'un retour au pays natal* on a trip to Yugoslavia.

Jacques Maritain publishes *Humanisme intégral.*

1937   JULY
Césaire marries Suzanne Roussi.

Damas publishes *Pigments.*

SEPTEMBER
Senghor delivers public lectures on culture and education to the chamber of commerce in Dakar, West Africa, and at the International Congress on the Cultural Evolution of Peoples in Paris.

1938   Damas publishes *Le Retour de Guyane.*

C. L. R. James publishes *The Black Jacobins.*

1939   JUNE
Damas publishes "Misère noire" in *Esprit.*

JULY
Senghor publishes "Culture and Empire" in *Charpentes* and, later the same year, "What the Black Man Contributes" in an edited volume.

AUGUST
First version of Césaire's *Cahier* is published in *Volontés*.

SEPTEMBER
Senghor transfers to the Lycée Marcelin-Bertholot and is then called up for military service.

DECEMBER
Césaire returns to Martinique to teach French and classics at the Lycée Schoelcher.

Sartre publishes *Nausea*.

1940   Marc Bloch writes *Strange Defeat*

Benjamin writes "On the Concept of History."

Arendt writes letter to Eric Cohn-Bendit on "The Minority Question."

MAY–JULY
Germany invades France; the armistice divides French territory into a German-occupied and a free zone, the latter with its capital in Vichy; before dissolving itself, the National Assembly invests Marshal Pétain as head of state.

In London Charles de Gaulle becomes leader of the Free French government in exile; in Chad Félix Éboué declares his support for it.

1940–1942   Senghor is interned in German prisoner of war camps within France.

1940–1943   Martinique is governed by the pro-Vichy Admiral Robert.

1941   APRIL
The first issue of *Tropiques* is published.

Césaire meets André Breton and Cuban painter Wifredo Lam in Fort-de-France.

Japan occupies French Indochina.

1942   Senghor, released from his POW camp, resumes teaching; pursues doctorate on African linguistics and oral poetry.

Camus publishes *The Stranger* and *The Myth of Sysiphus*.

1943   Fanon leaves Martinique to fight with Free French forces in Europe.

Simone Weil publishes "The Colonial Question and the Destiny of the French People."

Sartre publishes *Being and Nothingness*.

1944   JANUARY
Brazzaville Conference.

Senghor replaces Maurice Delafosse as chair of African Languages at the École nationale de la France d'outre-mer.

Senghor returns to Senegal on a research grant; is asked by Lamine Guèye to run for a seat in the Constituent Assembly.

MAY
Bréton publishes "Un grand poéte noir," on Césaire, in *Tropiques*.

JUNE
Murder of Marc Bloch by Gestapo.

AUGUST
The Allied forces liberate Paris.

SEPTEMBER
Césaire travels to Haiti to lecture and teach; presents "Poetry and Knowledge" at the International Congress of Philosophy.

NOVEMBER
African soldiers mutiny at Camp Thiaroye, Senegal.

Max Horkheimer and Theodor Adorno publish *Dialectic of Enlightenment*.

1945   Senghor is appointed to the Monnerville Commission.

MAY 8
The war in Europe ends; Algerian uprising in Sétif and Guelma.

MAY 27
Césaire is elected mayor of Fort-de-France.

JUNE 25
The UN Charter is signed.

AUGUST 17
Indonesian independence is declared.

SEPTEMBER
Ho Chi Minh declares the Republic of Vietnam independent of France; war with France begins.

OCTOBER
Senghor and Guèye are elected deputies from Senegal to the Constituent Assembly as Socialists, and Césaire is elected a deputy from Martinique as a Communist; the French social security system is established; Sartre and Simone de Beauvoir found *Les temps modernes*. Senghor

publishes "Defense of Black Africa," "Views on Black Africa," "Assimilate, Don't Be Assimilated," and *Chants d'Ombre*.

Sartre presents "Existentialism is a Humanism" in Paris.

Maurice Merleau-Ponty publishes *Phenomenology of Perception*.

1946   JANUARY
A general strike occurs in Dakar.

MARCH 19
Law on departmentalization passes.

APRIL 5
Forced labor is abolished in French West Africa.

APRIL 19
The proposed constitution for the Fourth Republic and a proposed French Union are rejected in a national referendum.

MAY 7
Loi Lamine Guèye extends French citizenship to members of the French Union.

SEPTEMBER 12
Senghor marries Ginette Éboué.

OCTOBER 13
The revised constitution for the Fourth Republic is approved in a referendum.

OCTOBER 18
Félix Houphouët-Boigny convenes the Bamako Congress, founds the Rassemblement Démocratique Africain party.

NOVEMBER
Senghor and Césaire are elected to the National Assembly.

Camus publishes "Neither Victims, Nor Executioners" in *Combat*.

Césaire publishes *Les armes miraculeuses*.

1947   *Présence Africaine* is founded under Alioune Diop's direction.

Damas publishes *Poètes d'expression française, 1900–1945*.

Revised editions of Césaire's *Cahier* are published in French and English.

Marx's 1844 manuscripts are published in *La Revue socialiste*.

Camus publishes *The Plague*.

Henri Lefebvre publishes *Critique of Everyday Life.*

Merleau-Ponty publishes *Humanism and Terror.*

MARCH
A mass uprising takes place in Madagascar.

APRIL
De Gaulle founds the Rassemblement du peuple français.

MAY
Communists dismissed from the French government.

AUGUST
India and Pakistan become independent; Pierre Trouille is named prefect in Martinique.

OCTOBER
The West African railway strike is declared.

1948   Senghor publishes *Hosties Noirs* and *Anthologie de la nouvelle poésie nègre et malgache,* including a preface by Sartre.

Césaire publishes *Soleil Coup Coupé* and edits Victor Schoelcher's *Esclavage et colonisation.*

MARCH
Senghor publishes "Marxism and Humanism."

APRIL
Senghor, Césaire, and Gaston Monnerville deliver speeches celebrating the hundredth anniversary of abolition.

OCTOBER
Senghor resigns from the French Socialist Party.

Senghor and Mamadou Dia found the Bloc Démocratique Sénégalais; Senghor creates the Indépendants d'outre mer group in parliament.

Léon-Gontran Damas is elected a deputy to the National Assembly from Guyane.

1949   Monnerville organizes the transfer of the remains of Victor Schoelcher and Félix Éboué to the Panthéon in Paris.

The Consultative Assembly of the Council of Europe convenes in Strasbourg.

1950   JANUARY
Civil servants strike in Martinique.

Césaire publishes *Corps perdu* and *Discourse on Colonialism.*

The French government's suppression of unrest in the Ivory Coast leads the RDA to split with the French Communist Party.

MAY
The Schuman Declaration on European cooperation is issued.

1951   The European Coal and Steel Community is created.

Georges Balandier publishes "La situation coloniale."

Adorno publishes *Minima Moralia: Reflections from a Damaged Life.*

Arendt publishes *Origins of Totalitarianism.*

Camus publishes *The Rebel.*

1952   Senghor serves as French representative to the Assemblée Consultative du Conseil de l'Europe.

Damas publishes *Graffiti.*

Fanon publishes *Black Skin, White Masks.*

1953   Fanon accepts a post as psychiatrist at Blida-Joinville hospital in Algeria.

A sixty-five-day-long civil service strike occurs in Martinique.

JULY
The Cuban revolution begins.

1954   MAY–JULY 7
Viet Minh forces defeat the French; Indochina wins independence; the Geneva Agreement partitions North and South Vietnam.

NOVEMBER 1
The Algerian Front de Libération Nationale (FLN) initiates a war of independence against France.

1955   Pierre Teilhard de Chardin publishes *The Human Phenomenon.*

FEBRUARY 23
Senghor is appointed to the cabinet of Edgar Faure; armed rebellion begins in Cameroon.

APRIL
Bandung Conference convenes.

1956   The definitive edition of Césaire's *Cahier* and *Et les chiens se taisaient* is published by Présence Africaine.

Damas publishes *Black-Label.*

Senghor publishes *Ethiopiques*.

Fanon resigns from the French civil service to join FLN; writes for *El Moujahid* from exile in Tunisia.

JANUARY
Césaire joins the Comité d'Action des Intellectuels contre la Poursuite de la Guerre en Afrique du Nord.

FEBRUARY 25
Nikita Khrushchev denounces Stalin at the Communist Party congress.

MARCH
Morocco and Tunisia become independent.

JUNE 23
Loi-Cadre extends autonomy to West African governments.

JULY 26
In Egypt Gamal Abdel Nasser nationalizes the Suez Canal; Israel, Britain, and France attack in response.

SEPTEMBER 19–22
First International Congress of Black Writers and Artists in Paris convenes; Senghor presents "The Spirit of Civilization, or the Laws of Negro-African Culture"; Césaire presents "Culture and Colonization"; Fanon presents "Racism and Culture."

OCTOBER 23
A popular revolution erupts in Budapest.

OCTOBER 24
Césaire resigns from the French Communist Party.

NOVEMBER 4–9
The USSR's forces crush the Hungarian revolution.

NOVEMBER 7
Pierre Aliker creates the Comité Aimé Césaire in Martinique.

1957   The Treaty of Rome creates the European Economic Community.

Martinican Communist Party is created.

Senghor marries Colette Hubert.

JANUARY–SEPTEMBER
The battle of Algiers is fought.

MARCH
Ghana becomes independent.

1958   Arendt publishes *The Human Condition.*

Gaston Berger publishes "L'attitude prospective."

MARCH 22
Césaire, Aliker, and Aristide Maugée found the Parti Progressiste Martiniquais (PPM).

MAY
The Fourth Republic collapses as a result of the political crisis in Algiers; the National Assembly grants emergency powers to de Gaulle.

OCTOBER 4
A new constitution establishes the Fifth Republic; all members of
French Union vote to join the new French Community except Guinea,
which becomes independent under Sékou Touré.

DECEMBER 21
De Gaulle is elected president of the new Fifth Republic.

1959   Fanon publishes *Year Five of the Algerian Revolution.*

JANUARY
The Cuban revolutionary forces succeed.

MARCH
The Second International Congress of Black Writers and Artists is
convened (Rome); Senghor presents "Constructive Elements of a
Civilization of Negro-African Inspiration"; Césaire presents "The Man
of Culture and His Responsibilities"; Fanon presents "Reciprocal Bases
of National Culture and Liberation Struggles."

APRIL 4
The Mali Federation is created.

DECEMBER
Riots and state repression occur in Martinique.

1960   Césaire publishes *Ferrements.*

JUNE 20
The Mali Federation achieves independence.

JUNE–JULY
Patrice Lumumba is elected prime minister of Congo; when the new
country's province of Katanga secedes, the UN sends troops.

SEPTEMBER 5
Senghor is elected president of Senegal following the dissolution of the
Mali Federation.

Mamadou Dia publishes *Nations africaines et solidarité mondiale.*

1961   Senghor publishes *Nocturnes* and *Nation et voie africaine du socialisme.*

Césaire publishes *Cadastre* and *Toussaint Louverture: La révolution française et le problème colonial.*

Fanon publishes *Wretched of the Earth.*

Arendt begins reporting on Adolf Eichman trial in Jerusalem.

Levinas publishes *Totality and Infinity.*

FEBRUARY 11
Lumumba is assassinated.

SEPTEMBER
Senghor addresses the UN General Assembly.

1962   Senghor publishes *Pierre Teilhard de Chardin et la politique africaine.*

MARCH
Signing of the Evian Accords ends the Algerian War.

APRIL
A national referendum approves self-determination for Algeria.

JULY 3
Algeria becomes independent.

DECEMBER
Senghor accuses Dia of plotting a coup and places him in prison for twelve years.

1963   Césaire publishes *La tragédie du Roi Christophe.*

1964   Senghor publishes *Liberté 1.*
La tragédie du roi Christophe is performed at the Salzburg Festival.

1966   Césaire publishes *Une saison au Congo;* the play is performed in Brussels.

Damas publishes *Névralgies.*

APRIL
Senghor hosts the First World Festival for Black Arts in Dakar.

1968   Student protests take place at the University of Dakar.

1969   Césaire publishes *Une Tempête.*

1971	AUGUST
	At the Morne-Rouge Convention, the Communist parties of Marti-
	nique, Guadeloupe, Guyane, and Réunion call for autonomy.

| 1973 | Senghor publishes *Lettres d'hivernage*. |

| 1976 | Senghor democratizes the Senegalese constitution; pays a state visit to |
| | Martinique. |

| 1978 | JANUARY 22 |
| | Damas dies in Washington, DC. |

| 1979 | Senghor publishes *Élégies majeures*. |

| 1981 | DECEMBER |
| | Senghor steps down as president of Senegal. |

1981	Édouard Glissant publishes *Le discours antillais*.
	Césaire announces a PPM moratorium on efforts to change Martinique's
	departmental status.

| 1982 | Césaire publishes *Moi, laminaire*. |

| 1983 | Senghor is elected to the Académie française. |

| 1993 | Césaire leaves the French National Assembly. |

| 1998 | The 150th anniversary of the abolition of slavery celebrated in Paris. |

2001	Césaire steps down as mayor of Fort-de-France.
	MAY 10
	The Taubira Law, recognizing the slave trade as a crime against human-
	ity, is passed in France; public schools are required to teach the history
	of slavery.
	DECEMBER 20
	Senghor dies.

2005	FEBRUARY 3
	A law is passed requiring French schools to teach students the "positive"
	aspects of French colonial activities; the law is later overturned.
	NOVEMBER
	Riots in French *banlieues* follow police killings of unarmed African
	youths.

2007	JULY 26
	President Sarkozy delivers a racist speech at the University of Dakar.

2008	APRIL 17
	Césaire dies.

2009	JANUARY 20
	A 44-day general strike in Guadeloupe begins.

2011	APRIL
	A plaque commemorating Césaire is placed in the Panthéon in Paris.

NOTES

CHAPTER 1. *Unthinking France, Rethinking Decolonization*

1 I borrow the felicitous phrase from Thomas Holt's magisterial *The Problem of Freedom*.

2 This emphasis on what might have been differs from the focus on reconciliation, rehabilitation, stabilization, and unifying commemoration of the war in Tony Judt's *Postwar*. For criticism of Judt's privileging memory over possibilities and not directly engaging decolonization, see Geoff Eley, "Europe after 1945," 195–212.

3 After serving in the Resistance during the war, Léon-Gontran Damas, the third founder of the Negritude movement, represented Guyane in the French National Assembly, where he headed a commission to investigate France's violent repression of protests in Côte d'Ivoire in 1950. After leaving electoral politics he conducted research for UNESCO, traveled widely in Africa and the Americas, and taught at Georgetown and Howard universities (Racine, *Léon-Gontran Damas*, 31–54).

4 I distinguish between "globe" or "global" and "world," "worldness," or "becoming worldwide," as connoted by the French *mondialité* and *modialisation*. See Lefebvre, "The Worldwide Experience," 274–89, and Nancy, "Urbi and Orbi," 31–55.

5 Cf. Henri Lefebvre's dialectic of the possible-impossible, or how alternative forms of life may be recognized within actually existing arrangements: *Introduction to Modernity*, 68, 125, 348.

6 Gary Wilder, *The French Imperial Nation-State*.

7 The concrete cosmopolitanism of Paul Gilroy and Achille Mbembe and the radical humanism of Edward Said may be situated in a lineage including Senghor and Césaire. See Gilroy, *Postcolonial Melancholia*; Mbembe, *Sortir de la grande nuit*; Said, *Humanism and Democratic Criticism*; and Alessandrini, "Humanism in Question," 431–50.

8 This has been the case for world-systems theorists, historians of British empire, and diplomatic historians. See Amin, *Re-Reading the Postwar Period*; Arrighi, *Long Twentieth Century*; Gallagher and Robinson, "Imperialism of Free Trade," 1–15; Louis, *Imperialism at Bay*; Louis and Robinson, "Imperialism of Decolonization," 462–511; Hopkins, "Rethinking Decolonization," 211–47; Connelly, *A Diplomatic Revolution*; and Lawrence and Logevall, *The First Vietnam War*.

9 Marseille, *Empire Colonial*; Cooper, *Decolonization and African Society*; LeSueur, *Uncivil War*, 36–54; Shepard, *Invention of Decolonization*.

10 See Lawrence and Logevall, *The First Vietnam War*; Amin, *Re-Reading the Post-war Period*, 105–7; Connelly, *A Diplomatic Revolution*; De Witte, *Assassination of Lumumba*; Luard, *History of the United Nations*, vols. 1 and 2. On US implication in decolonization as a process of imperial restructuring, see Louis and Robinson, "Empire Preserv'd"; Arrighi, *Long Twentieth Century*, 269–99, Smith, *American Empire*; Louis and Robinson, "Imperialism of Decolonization," 462–511; Kelly and Kaplan, *Represented Communities*, 1–26.

11 See also Wilder, "Response Essay."

12 Wilder, "From Optic to Topic," 723–45.

13 See also Wilder, "*Eurafrique*"; "Untimely Vision," 101–40; "Regarding the Imperial Nation-State"; and "Unthinking French History," 125–43.

14 On the concepts of imperial formation and imperial social formation, see Inden, *Imagining India*, 29–32; Sinha, *Colonial Masculinity*; Stoler, McGranahan, and Perdue, *Imperial Formations*.

15 See Wallerstein, *Unthinking the Social Sciences*.

16 LaCapra, *History and Criticism*, 71–94.

17 Adorno, "Notes on Kafka," 151. Adorno exemplifies this orientation to criticism, when he argues, "the fulfillment of [capitalism's] repeatedly broken exchange contract would converge with its abolition; exchange would disappear if truly equal things were exchanged; true progress would not be merely an Other in relation to exchange, but rather exchange that has been brought to itself." Adorno, "Progress," 159.

18 Senghor's and Césaire's postwar thinking differed in many respects. For example, Césaire was more interested in popular insurgency and less interested in religion than Senghor. Césaire was more concerned with Antillean history and Senghor with African civilization. Césaire devoted more time to writing poetry and Senghor to writing about aesthetics. But I seek to challenge a commonplace attempt to recuperate Césaire as the radical thinker of the pair and dismiss Senghor as essentialist or comprador. In fact, during the postwar era their thinking intersected in ways that transcended these intellectual stereotypes. We need to question the stakes of this transferential investment in embracing one and vilifying the other. For iterations of this tendency, see Arnold, *Modernism and Negritude*; Burton, "Ke Moun Nou Ye?," 5–32; Miller, *French Atlantic Triangle*, 325–30; and Jones, *Racial Discourses*. This splitting is largely shaped by a preoccupation with essentialism, which obscures a fuller engagement with each thinker's work in relation to their times and ours. See Scott's incisive critique of the "metaphysics of antiessentialism" within postcolonial theory: Scott, *Conscripts of Modernity*, 2–8, and *Refashioning Futures*, 3–15.

19 Scholarship is finally moving beyond focusing on Negritude as a (progressive or conservative) form of identitarian cultural nationalism or Africana philosophy that either helped or hindered struggles for national independence. Recent work reconsiders Senghor and Césaire as political thinkers in relation to broader fields of philosophy, critical theory, and aesthetics, and takes seriously their attempts to refigure universalism, humanism, and cosmopolitanism. Not enough work, however, integrates their thought and acts in the domains of politics, criticism, theoretical reflection, and aesthetics.

20 In contrast, Diagne captures the dialogical and convergent quality of their engagement with modernist thought by suggesting that Senghor could "find his language"

in Bergson's, which was as much a matter of resonance, citation, and inflection as of mechanical influence: Diagne, "Bergson in the Colonies," 126.

21 Vitalist strands of Senghor's and Césaire's thinking intermingled with many others, all of which were reworked within a multifaceted project that might be thought as a variant of "romantic anticapitalism." See Lukács, "The Old Culture," 21–30; Löwy, "Marxism and Revolutionary Romanticism," 83–95; Sayre and Löwy, "Figures of Romantic Anti-Capitalism," 42–92; on Marcuse's "left Heideggerianism," see Wolin, *Heidegger's Children*, 135–72.

22 Their postwar thinking may be read in relation to Lefebvre's 1947 argument in *Critique of Everyday Life*.

23 Chakrabarty, *Provincializing Europe*.

24 Chakrabarty, *Provincializing Europe*, 47–8, 101–12.

25 Chakrabarty, *Provincializing Europe*, 20.

26 Chakrabarty, *Provincializing Europe*, 255.

27 Buck-Morss, "Universal History," and "The Gift of the Past," 173–85.

28 LaCapra, *History and Criticism*, 139–42.

29 See Benjamin, *Origin of German Tragic Drama*, 27–56; Adorno, "Actuality of Philosophy," 23–39, and *Negative Dialectics*; Buck-Morss, *Origin of Negative Dialectics*; Wolin, *Walter Benjamin*, 90–106.

30 Habermas, "Postnational Constellation."

31 In Adorno's words: "Instead of achieving something scientifically, or creating something artistically, the effort of the essay reflects a childlike freedom that catches fire, without scruple, on what others have already done. . . . Its concepts are neither deduced from any first principle nor do they come full circle and arrive at a final principle" ("The Essay as Form," 152).

32 Scott, *Conscripts of Modernity*, 41.

33 Scott, *Conscripts of Modernity*, 56, 209.

34 Kosellek, *Futures Past*.

CHAPTER 2. *Situating Césaire*

1 Marx, *Capital*, 873–930.

2 Marx, "On the Jewish Question," 211–41, and "Concerning Feuerbach," 421–23.

3 Marx, *Capital*, 931–40.

4 See ch. 1, n. 1.

5 DuBois, *Black Reconstruction in America*, 219, 380.

6 DuBois, *Black Reconstruction in America*, 634, 187.

7 James, *The Black Jacobins*. See also Dubois, *Avengers of the New World*. On Toussaint facing a tragic predicament, see Scott, *Conscripts of Modernity*.

8 On the Haitian Revolution's "revolutionary universalism," see Nesbitt, "The Idea of 1804," 6–38.

9 Dubois, *Haiti*, and Gary Wilder, "Telling Histories," 11–25. For further discussion of the "counterplantation" system, see Casimir, *La culture opprimé*.

10 Forsdick, "Situating Haiti," 17–34; Nesbitt, "Troping Toussaint," 18–33.

11 Dubois, *Avengers of the New World*; Fick, "French Revolution."

12 Dubois, *Colony of Citizens*.

13 Schmidt, *Victor Schoelcher*; Girollet, *Victor Schoelcher, abolitionniste*.

14 On colonial domination in nineteenth-century Martinique, see Constant, *La retraite aux flambeaux*; Cottias, " 'L'oubli du passé' "; and Perina, *Citoyenneté et sujetion*.

15 Confiant, *Aimé Césaire*, 37, 27.

16 Confiant, *Aimé Césaire*, 164, 284–85, 287.

17 Confiant, *Aimé Césaire*, 276–77.

18 Recent scholarship on Césaire has begun to move beyond the narrow frame of earlier debates about negritude and identity. For efforts to reconsider his political legacy that resonate with my own, see Giraud, "De la négritude a' la créolité," 373–401; William, "Aimé Césaire"; Nesbitt, "Departmentalization," 32–43; Daniel, "Aimé Césaire," 24–33; Hale and Véron, "Aimé Césaire's Break," 47–62; Constant, "Aimé Césaire," 34–42; Edwards, "Introduction," 115–25; Nesbitt, "The Incandescent I," 121–41; Walsh, *Free and French*. For recent work on the multifaceted character of Césaire's thinking, see Price and Price, "Shadowboxing," 3–36; Davis, *Aimé Césaire*; Dash, *The Other America*, 63–81; Kelley, *Freedom Dreams*, 157–94; Edwards, "Aimé Césaire," 1–18; Miller, *French Atlantic Triangle*, 219–22, 325–40; Hiddleston, "Aimé Césaire," 87–102. I would have benefited from the work that has appeared since 2009 before I had drafted these chapters on Césaire.

19 Confiant, *Aimé Césaire*, 92.

20 Attempts to resist this splitting in order to develop a more nuanced understanding of the relationship between different aspects of Césaire's oeuvre include Gavronsky, "Aimé Césaire," 272–80; Rosello, " 'Césaire Effect,' " 77–91; Reno, "Aimé Césaire," 19–23; Hale and Véron, "Is There Unity?," 46–70.

21 See also Wilder, "Aimé Césaire," 121–23.

22 See James, *Pragmatism*, Dewey, *The Essential Dewey*; Hook, *Pragmatism*; Rorty, *Consequences of Pragmatism*; Menand, *Pragmatism*; West, *American Evasion*; Menand, *Metaphysical Club*; Bernstein, *Pragmatic Turn*.

23 Gilroy notes a long tradition within the Black Atlantic of conjoining a (pragmatic) "politics of fulfillment" and a (utopian) "politics of transfiguration" in ways that transcend conventional distinctions between politics, ethics, and aesthetics (Gilroy, *Black Atlantic*, 37–39).

24 Dewey, *Public and Its Problems*, 202.

25 Dewey, *Public and Its Problems*, 203.

26 I discuss this at length in *The French Imperial Nation-State*. For accounts of the interwar milieu of black Paris when Césaire and Senghor came of intellectual age, see Dewitte, *Les mouvements nègres*; Fabre, *From Harlem to Paris*; Stovall, *Paris Noir*; Sharpley-Whiting, *Negritude Women*; Edwards, *Practice of Diaspora*; Genova, *Colonial Ambivalence*; and Boittin, *Colonial Metropolis*.

27 First published in *Volontés* in 1939, it was revised, with significant postwar additions, for publication in New York and Paris in 1947, before being revised again for the definitive 1956 version published by Présence Africaine. See Hale, "Two Decades, Four Versions," and Almeida, "Les versions successives," 35–90.

28 Wilder, *The French Imperial Nation-State*, 281–90.

29 Leiner, "Entretien avec Aimé Césaire," x.

30 Macey, *Frantz Fanon*, 69.

31 Leiner, "Entretien avec Aimé Césaire," viii.

32 Fanon, "West Indians and Africans," 21–22. I analyze Fanon's *Black Skin, White Masks* as a complex repetition and rewriting of Césaire's *Notebook* in Wilder, "Race, Reason, Impasse," 31–61.

33 Macey, *Frantz Fanon*, 78–90. After the war Robert was sentenced to ten years' hard labor for his collaboration. On how his regime dispossessed blacks and persecuted communists with the explicit support of the Catholic Church and white settler community and implicit support of the United States, see Baptiste, "Le régime de Vichy," 1–24. For an overview, see Jennings, *Vichy in the Tropics*, 90–104.

34 On Suzanne Césaire (née Roussi), see Sharpley-Whiting, *Negritude Women*, 80–104, and Wilks, *Race, Gender*, 107–40. Her writings are collected in Césaire, *Le grand camouflage*. René Ménil was a Martinican educator, poet, and anticolonial activist who contributed to the earlier surrealist-communist collection of poetry and criticism *Légitime Défense* (1932) and helped found the Martinican section of the French Communist Party (1938) and the Martinican Communist Party (1957). He later denounced Negritude's culturalism from a materialist perspective. See Ménil, *Tracées*.

35 Ménil, "Pour une lecture critique," xxvi. In this retrospective essay, written under the signs of Althusser and Bachelard, Ménil criticizes the idealism, romanticism, and metaphysical tendencies underlying the essays on culture and aesthetics in *Tropiques*.

36 Leiner, "Entretien avec Aimé Césaire," viii.

37 Lettre du Lt. de Vaisseau Bayle, chef de service d'information, au directeur de la revue Tropiques, Fort-de-France, 10 mai 1943, in *Tropiques, 1941–1945*, xxxvii.

38 Lettre du Lt. de Vaisseau Bayle, xxxviii.

39 Réponse de Tropiques to Lt. de Vaisseau Bayle, Fort-de-France 12 mai 1943, signed Aimé Césaire, Suzanne Césaire, Georges Gratiant, Aristide Maugée, René Ménil, Lucie Thésee, in *Tropiques, 1941–1945*, xxxix.

40 Aimé Césaire, "Presentation," *Tropiques* 1, 5 (April 1941): 5, in *Tropiques 1941–1945*.

41 Césaire, "Presentation."

42 Césaire, "Presentation."

43 "Fragments" was published two years later with minor variations as "Les pur-sang" ("purebreds," "thoroughbreds") in *Les Armes miraculeuses*.

44 Translation by Clayton Eshelman and Annette Smith in *Aimé Césaire: The Collected Poetry*, 101.

45 Arnold, *Modernism and Negritude*, 88.

46 Aimé Césaire, "Fragments d'un Poème," *Tropiques* 1, 9 (April 1941): 9, in *Tropiques, 1941–1945*.

47 Suzanne Césaire, "Léo Frobénius," *Tropiques* 1 (April 1941): 27, 30–1, in *Tropiques, 1941–1945*.

48 Suzanne Césaire, "Léo Frobénius," 35.

49 Suzanne Césaire, "Léo Frobénius," 35, 36

50 Suzanne Césaire, "Malaise d'une civilization," *Tropiques* 5 (April 1942): 43.

51 Suzanne Césaire, "1943: Le Surréalisme et nous," *Tropiques* 8–9 (October 1943): 14–18, in *Tropiques, 1941–1945*.

52 Suzanne Césaire, "André Breton," *Tropiques* 3 (October 1941): 34.

53 Suzanne Césaire, "André Breton," 6.

54 Suzanne Césaire, "1943," 16–17.

55 Suzanne Césaire, "1943," 18.

56 Suzanne Césaire, "1943," 18.

57 René Ménil, "Naissance de notre art," *Tropiques* 1 (April 1941): 60

58 Ménil, "Naissance de notre art," 59–60.

59 Ménil, "Naissance de notre art," 58.

60 Ménil, "Situation de la poésie," *Tropiques* no. 11 (May 1944): 131, in *Tropiques, 1941–1945*.

61 Ménil "Naissance de notre art," 59–60.

62 René Ménil, "Introduction au Merveilleux," *Tropiques* 3 (October 1941): 15, in *Tropiques, 1941–1945*.

63 Ménil, "Situation," 130.

64 Ménil, "Naissance de notre art," 61–62.

65 Ménil, "Situation," 127.

66 Ménil, "Situation," 129. Cf. Ernst Bloch, the "not yet conscious." Bloch, *Principle of Hope*, 114–42.

67 Ménil, "Situation," 130.

68 Ménil, "Situation," 131.

69 Ménil, "Situation," 131.

70 Breton, "Martinique charmeuse de serpents," 120. This voyage is famously described by Claude Lévi-Strauss in *Tristes Tropiques*, 17–30.

71 Leiner, "Entretien avec Aimé Césaire," vii.

72 *Tropiques* published two pieces by Pierre Mabille: "Le royaume du merveilleux," 4 (January 1942), and "La jungle," 12 (January 1945). For an example of how his interests intersected with those of the *Tropiques* circle, see Mabille, *Le Merveilleux*.

73 Véron, "Césaire at the Crossroads," 434. One of the Haitian students in his modern poetry course was René Depestre. Fonkoua, *Aimé Césaire*, 93–94.

74 Césaire, *Nègre je suis*, 56.

75 *Travaux de la Congrès international*.

76 Césaire, "Poésie et connaissance." I analyze this piece at length in Wilder, *The French Imperial Nation-State*. Quotes are from the translation of "Poetry and Knowledge" by A. James Arnold (Césaire, "Poetry and Knowledge," xlii–lvi). Other pieces by Césaire in *Tropiques* that prefigured many of the themes and strategies of "Poetry and Knowledge" include "En guise de manifeste littéraire" (*Tropiques* 5, Apr. 1942), "Isidore Ducasse, Comte de Lautréamont" (*Tropiques* 6–7, Feb. 1943), and "Maintenir la poésie" (*Tropiques* 8–9, Oct. 1943). "En guise" reappeared in the second published version (1947) of Césaire's *Cahier*. Almeida, "Les versions successives."

77 Césaire, "Poetry and Knowledge," xlii, lv.

78 Césaire, "Poetry and Knowledge," xlii–xliii.

79 Césaire, "Poetry and Knowledge," xlii.

80 Césaire, "Poetry and Knowledge," xliv.

81 Césaire, "Poetry and Knowledge," xlvii–xlviii.

82 Césaire, "Poetry and Knowledge," xlix.

83 Césaire, "Poetry and Knowledge," xliv, liv.

84 Césaire, "Poetry and Knowledge," li.

85 Césaire, "Poetry and Knowledge," li.

86 Césaire, "Poetry and Knowledge," lii. He later wrote that "the image connects the object; by showing me its unknown side . . . it no longer defines its being, but its potentialities." Césaire, "La poésie," 5. Césaire linked immanent critique and transcendence through the term *dépassement*, which he uses to index a superseding, exceeding, overflowing, overtaking, overflowing, outrunning, surpassing, or going beyond. While resonating with the meaning of overcoming, transcendence, or sublation, it signals more of a process than an event or rupture. This concept informed his orientation to language, aesthetics, and politics.

87 Césaire, "Poetry and Knowledge," liii.

88 Césaire, "Poetry and Knowledge," liv.

89 Césaire, "Poetry and Knowledge," l.

90 Césaire, "Poetry and Knowledge," liv.

91 Césaire, "Panorama."

92 Césaire, "Panorama," 8.

93 Césaire, "Panorama," 9.

94 Césaire, "Panorama," 9.

95 Césaire, "Panorama," 9–10.

96 Césaire, "Panorama," 10.

97 Césaire, "Panorama," 10.

98 Césaire, "Panorama," 7.

99 Césaire, "Panorama," 10.

100 Arendt, "Preface," 14.

101 Leiner, "Entretien avec Aimé Césaire," xiv–xv.

102 Leiner, "Entretien avec Aimé Césaire," xii.

103 Cf. the concept of "refunctioning" in Brecht, "Modern Theater," and Benjamin, "Author as Producer."

104 Freud, "The Uncanny," 217–56.

105 Leiner, "Entretien avec Aimé Césaire," xix

106 Leiner, "Entretien avec Aimé Césaire," xxiii–xiv.

107 Leiner, "Entretien avec Aimé Césaire," xviii.

108 Leiner, "Entretien avec Aimé Césaire," viii.

109 For the use of "untimeliness" as a strategy of critique, see Nietzsche, *Untimely Mediations*, and Brown, "Untimeliness and Punctuality." For works that engage untimely processes in ways that resonate with mine, see Ross, *May '68 and Its Afterlives*; Buck-Morss, *Dreamworld and Catastrophe*; Scott, *Conscripts of Modernity*; and Price, *Convict and the Colonel*. For contrasting vitalist uses of the term, see Grosz, *The Nick of Time*; and Connolly, *Pluralism*.

110 Such states of temporal indistinction call to mind Bergson's characterization of "pure duration" as qualitative multiplicity, nonlinear intensity, nonspatial simultaneity, and concrete interpenetration. Bergson, *Time and Free Will*.

111 Cf. Nietzsche's "the eternal recurrence of the same," through which he exhorts readers to treat their lives as if every moment would have to be repeated and reexperienced forever; Nietzsche, *The Gay Science*, 273–75, and *Beyond Good and Evil*, 35–76.

112 This orientation to metahistory differs from Hayden White's inquiry into the rhetorical practices through which historical "truth" is produced; White, *Metahistory*.

113 Kosellek, *Futures Past*, 1–3, 11. Scott develops Kosellek's formulation of "futures past" in a different direction to mean futures that were envisioned in earlier epochs and have now been superseded, either because they were actually realized or because they are no longer politically viable or relevant. Scott, *Conscripts of Modernity*, 23–57.

114 Kosellek, " 'Space of Experience,' " 255–76.

115 Kosellek, "Historia Magistra Vitae: The Dissolution of the Topos into the Perspective of a Modernized Historical Process," in *Futures Past*, 26–42.

116 Kant and Hegel each struggled to reconcile precisely this contradiction between history as human contingency and providential purpose. Kant, "Universal History," and Hegel, *Introduction*.

117 Kosellek, " 'Space of Experience,' " 255–76.

118 Kosellek, " 'Space of Experience,' " 269.

119 Kosellek, "History, Histories, and Formal Time Structures," in *Futures Past*, 95, 99.

120 Kosellek, "Neuzeit: Remarks on the Semantics of Modern Concepts of Movement," in *Futures Past*, 246.

121 Kosellek, " 'Space of Experience,' " 266. Cf. Bloch, "Nonsynchronism."

122 Kosellek, "History, Histories," 95.

123 Kosellek, "History, Histories," 95.

124 Kosellek, " 'Space of Experience,' " 258.

125 Kosellek, "Perspective and Temporality: A Contribution to the Historiographical Exposure of the Historical World," in *Futures Past*, 142.

126 Kosellek, " 'Space of Experience,' " 260.

127 For recent memory studies that focus on the French empire, see Bahloul, *Architecture of Memory*; Cole, *Forget Colonialism?*; Hargreaves, *Memory, Empire, and Postcolonialism*; Smith, *Colonial Memory*; Vergès, *La mémoire enchaînée*; Miller, *French Atlantic Triangle*; Reinhardt, *Claims to Memory*; Rothberg, *Multidirectional Memory*.

128 See, e.g., Yerushalmi, *Zakhar*; Nora, "General Introduction"; Rousso, *The Vichy Syndrome*; Friedlander, *Memory, History*, and *Probing the Limits*; LaCapra, *Representing the Holocaust*; *History and Memory*; *Writing History*; and *History in Transit*; Postone and Santner, *Traumatic Realism*; Judt, "House of the Dead," 803–31.

129 This is the conception of time willed to moderns in the West by Aristotle, Newton, and Kant. Aristotle, "Physics," 289–90; Newton, *Principia*, 1–12, Kant, *Critique of Pure Reason*, 67–84.

130 Halbwachs, *On Collective Memory*, 40.

131 Halbwachs, *On Collective Memory*, 39.

132 Halbwachs, *On Collective Memory*, 169.

133 The writings of Yerushalmi, Nora, and Rousso express a tension between conceptualizing memory, following Halbwachs, as a social construction, on the one hand,
and following Bergson and Freud, in terms of untimely duration and haunting
power. Yerushalmi, *Zakhor*; Nora, "General Introduction," 1–20; and Rousso, *The
Vichy Syndrome*.

134 Benjamin, *Arcades Project*, 474.

135 Benjamin, *Arcades Project*, 917.

136 Benjamin, *Arcades Project*, 464. He discusses dialectical images further on 10, 462–
4, 473–75. See also Tiedemann, "Dialectics at a Standstill," 929–45; and Richter
Thought-Images.

137 Marx, *Capital*. Marx's attention to the untimeliness of modern capitalism may also
be found in his discussions of commodities as congealed time, the recursive character of circulation as a process of eternal return, the domination of living by dead
labor in production, and the repeating cycles of reproduction and transformation
that characterize accumulation. On the latter, see Postone, *Time, Labor*.

138 Freud, *Beyond the Pleasure Principle*. See the elaborations of Freud's conception
of "afterwardness" and "deferred action" in Laplanche, "Time and the Other," and
"On Afterwardness," 234–65; Laplanche and Pontalis, "Deferred Action," 111–14.

139 Marx wrote, "It is not a matter of drawing a great dividing line between past and
future, but of carrying out the thoughts of the past." Marx, "Ruthless Criticism,"
15. On the "not yet conscious," see Bloch, *Spirit of Utopia*, 187–203, and *Principle of
Hope*, 114–77.

140 Freud, *Interpretation of Dreams*, 651.

141 See Benjamin, *Origin*, 27–56; Adorno, "Actuality of Philosophy," 23–39.

142 Adorno, *Negative Dialectics*, 19, 28, 52, 163.

143 Benjamin, "Surrealism," 181.

144 Benjamin, "Surrealism," 179, 182.

145 Benjamin, *Arcades Project*, 462.

146 Benjamin, *Arcades Project*, 462.

147 Benjamin, *Arcades Project*, 463.

148 Benjamin, "Concept of History," 397.

149 Benjamin, "Paralipomena," 402.

150 Benjamin, "Concept of History," 396.

151 Benjamin, "Concept of History," 396.

152 Benjamin, "Paralipomena," 402.

153 Benjamin, "Paralipomena," 403.

154 Benjamin, "Concept of History," 397.

155 Benjamin, "Concept of History," 397, 395.

156 Benjamin, "Concept of History," 395.

157 Benjamin, "Concept of History," 397.

158 Benjamin, "Paralipomena," 402.

159 Benjamin, "Paralipomena," 405.

160 Benjamin, "Paralipomena," 407.

161 Benjamin, "Paralipomena," 405.

162 Bloch, "Nonsynchronism," 22–38; Bloch, *Spirit of Utopia*.

163 Bloch, *Principle of Hope*, 14–17, 114–65, 195–222, and Nietzsche, *Philosophy of the Future*.

164 Arendt, *Life of the Mind*, 205.

165 Arendt, *Life of the Mind*, 206.

166 Arendt, *Life of the Mind*, 205. This understanding of the present as an "extended now" resembles Bergson's notion of "duration" as a qualitative multiplicity, densely layered with persistent pasts and already present futures that are producing a perpetual present at every instant. Bergson, *Time and Free Will*, 75–139, and *The Creative Mind*, 1–86.

167 Arendt, "The Gap," 13.

168 Arendt, "The Gap," 14.

169 Arendt, "Home to Roost," 270.

170 Arendt, "The Gap," 14.

171 Arendt, "The Gap," 4–5.

172 Arendt, "The Gap," 6.

173 Arendt, "The Gap," 6.

174 Arendt, "The Gap," 6.

175 Arendt, "The Gap," 6.

176 Arendt, "The Gap," 4; emphasis added.

177 Arendt, "The Gap," 3. This essentially is the theme of Albert Camus's political allegory of the Occupation, *The Plague*.

178 Bloch, *Strange Defeat*.

CHAPTER 3. *Situating Senghor*

1 Césaire, "Discours" (1976), 542.

2 Césaire, "Discours" (1976), 542, 543.

3 Césaire, "Discours" (1976), 543.

4 Césaire, "Discours" (1976), 543.

5 Césaire, "Discours" (1976), 543.

6 See Courtois, "Le noisetier."

7 Césaire, "Discours" (1976), 544–45.

8 Césaire, "Discours" (1976), 545.

9 Césaire, "Discours" (1976), 545.

10 Césaire, "Discours" (1976), 545.

11 Senghor, "La Négritude," 96.

12 Senghor, "La Négritude," 98. On the internal connection between Senghor's epistemology and aesthetics, see Diagne, *Léopold Sédar Senghor*.

13 Senghor, "La Négritude," 95.

14 Senghor, "La Négritude," 105.

15 Senghor, "La Négritude," 108.

16 Senghor, "La Négritude," 109.

17 Senghor, "La Négritude," 107.

18 Senghor, "La Négritude," 107.

19 Senghor, "La Négritude," 106–7.

20 Senghor, *La poésie de l'action*, 107.

21 Senghor, *La poésie de l'action*, 59–60.

22 Senghor, *La poésie de l'action*, 18–19, 60, 79, 107.

23 Senghor, *La poésie de l'action*, 81.

24 Senghor, *La poésie de l'action*, 82–84.

25 Senghor, *La poésie de l'action*, 83.

26 Senghor, *La poésie de l'action*, 85.

27 Senghor, "Le message de Goethe," 83.

28 Senghor, *La poésie de l'action*, 84.

29 Senghor, *La poésie de l'action*, 84.

30 Senghor, *La poésie de l'action*, 84.

31 Senghor, *La poésie de l'action*, 85.

32 Senghor, *La poésie de l'action*, 85.

33 Senghor, *La poésie de l'action*, 85–86.

34 Senghor, *La poésie de l'action*, 86.

35 Senghor, *La poésie de l'action*, 86.

36 I discuss *Chants d'Ombre* in *The French Imperial Nation-State*, 208–13.

37 The formulation *hosties noires* plays with the French "*hôte*," which means at once "host" and "guest," giver and receiver.

38 Senghor, "Poème liminaire," 56.

39 Senghor, "Poème liminaire," 56.

40 Senghor, "Prière," 68.

41 Senghor, "Prière," 70.

42 Senghor, "Prière," 71.

43 Senghor, "Prière," 71.

44 Senghor, "Au gouverneur Éboué," 74.

45 Senghor, "Camp," in *Poèmes*, 75.

46 Senghor, "Camp," 76.

47 Senghor, "Assassinats," in *Poèmes*, 77.

48 Senghor, "Chant de printemps," in *Poèmes*, 87.

49 Senghor, "Aux soldats négro-américains," in *Poèmes*, 89–90.

50 Senghor, "Lettre à un prisonnier," in *Poèmes*, 83.

51 Senghor, "Lettre à un prisonnier," 83.

52 On the Thiaroye mutiny, see Mann, *Native Sons*, 116–19.

53 Senghor, "Thiaroye," *Poèmes*, 90–91.

54 Senghor, "Prière de paix," *Poèmes*, 92, 93, 94.

55 Senghor, "Prière de paix," 94.

56 Senghor, "Prière de paix," 94.

57 Senghor, "Prière de paix," 94.

58 Senghor, "Prière de paix," 92.

59 Senghor, "Prière de paix," 94.

60 Senghor, "Prière de paix," 95.

61 Senghor, "Prière de paix," 96.

62 Senghor, "Prière de paix," 95.

63 Senghor, "Prière de paix," 96.

64 Senghor, "L'apport," 142–43.

65 Cf. the distinction between "victor's justice" and "survivor's justice" in Mamdani, *When Victims Become Killers*, 270–73. See also Krog, *Country of My Skull*.

66 Senghor, *La poésie de l'action*, 84.

67 Sankalé, "L'aîné du Quartier Latin," and Vaillant, *Black, French, and African*, 179–81. On the colonial student milieu in Paris during the wars, see Wilder, *The French Imperial Nation-State*, 149–200.

68 A. F. Amorin, "Foyer de Paris," *Chronique des Foyers* 1 (July 1, 1943), 24.

69 "Tableau de notre activité générale en 1942–43, Cercle d'études culturelles des étudiants coloniaux de Paris," *Chronique des foyers* 1 (July 1, 1943), 26–28.

70 Kothj Barma, "L'Étudiant de la France d'Outre mer," *Chronique des foyers* 1 (July 1, 1943), 4.

71 I discuss these two essays in Wilder, *The French Imperial Nation-State*, 232–54.

72 Senghor, "Le problème culturel," 11.

73 Senghor, "Le problème culturel," 14.

74 Senghor, "Le problème culturel," 14.

75 Senghor, "Le problème culturel," 14.

76 Senghor, "Ce que l'homme," 293.

77 Senghor, "Ce que l'homme," 295

78 Parker, Mills, and Stanton, *Mythology*, 128.

79 Senghor, "Ce que l'homme noir apporte," 314.

80 Delavignette was prominent among the interwar "colonial humanists," who had believed that the French empire should be regarded as a supranational political formation. Senghor's thinking developed in dialogue with Delavignette, who himself celebrated Senghor as a model of the bicultural sensibility that he believed the empire was making possible. See Wilder, *The French Imperial Nation-State*, 76–148.

81 Senghor, "Vues sur l'Afrique noire," 57.

82 Senghor, "Vues sur l'Afrique noire," 57.

83 Senghor, "Vues sur l'Afrique noire," 58.

84 Senghor, "Vues sur l'Afrique noire," 58.

85 Senghor, "Vues sur l'Afrique noire," 59.

86 Senghor, "Vues sur l'Afrique noire," 64. Senghor later makes a similar argument about transcending "the false antinomy *assimilation-association*" in "Le problème de la culture," *Journées d'études des Indépendants d'Outre-Mer* (July 1950), reprinted in *Liberté 1*, 96.

87 Senghor, "Vues sur l'Afrique noire," 44–45.

88 Senghor, "Vues sur l'Afrique noire," 65.

89 Senghor, "Vues sur l'Afrique noire," 84.

90 Senghor, "Vues sur l'Afrique noire," 85.

91 Senghor, "Vues sur l'Afrique noire," 86.

92 Senghor, "Vues sur l'Afrique noire," 96.

93 Senghor, "Vues sur l'Afrique noire," 97.

94 Senghor, "Vues sur l'Afrique noire," 97.

95 Senghor, "Vues sur l'Afrique noire," 97–98.

96 Senghor, "Vues sur l'Afrique noire," 79.

97 Senghor, "Vues sur l'Afrique noire," 105.

98 Senghor, "Vues sur l'Afrique noire," 105. ENFOM was the Grande École (previously the École Coloniale) that trained colonial administrators by teaching them indigenous languages, history, geography, and ethnology, as well as colonial law and administrative science.

99 Senghor, "Vues sur l'Afrique noire," 105.

100 Senghor, "Vues sur l'Afrique noire," 106.

101 Senghor, "Vues sur l'Afrique noire," 18.

102 Senghor, "Vues sur l'Afrique noire," 29.

103 Senghor, "Vues sur l'Afrique noire," 29–30.

104 Senghor, "L'apport de la poésie nègre," 141.

105 Senghor, "L'apport de la poésie nègre," 142–43.

106 Senghor, "Comme les lamantins," 159–60.

107 Senghor, "Comme les lamantins," 168.

108 Senghor, "Comme les lamantins," 166.

109 Senghor, "Comme les lamantins," 160.

110 Senghor, "Comme les lamantins," 162.

111 Senghor, "L'apport de la poésie nègre," 136.

112 Senghor, "L'apport de la poésie nègre," 142.

113 Senghor "Comme les lamantins," 159.

114 Senghor, "Comme les lamantins," 167.

115 Senghor, "Comme les lamantins," 167.

116 Senghor, "Comme les lamantins," 167.

117 Senghor, "Comme les lamantins," 165.

118 Senghor, "Comme les lamantins," 160.

119 Derrida, "Hostipitality," 385–86.

120 Derrida, On Cosmopolitanism, 34, 39.

121 Derrida, On Cosmopolitanism, 44.

122 Derrida, "Hostipitality," 387.

123 Derrida, Of Hospitality, 25, 27.

124 Derrida, On Cosmopolitanism, 16–17.

125 Derrida, On Cosmopolitanism, 125.

126 Derrida, On Cosmopolitanism, 125. See also Levinas, Otherwise Than Being, 11–15, 111–12, 116–29, 136–40, 151.

127 Derrida, Of Hospitality, 147, 149.

128 Derrida, On Cosmopolitanism, 5–23.

129 Derrida, On Cosmopolitanism, 20, 22.

130 Derrida's various reflections on "democracy to come" may be found in The Other Heading, "Force of Law," Specters of Marx, Politics of Friendship, Archive Fever, and Rogues.

131 Levinas attempts to introduce law, politics, and justice into his ethical framework through the concept of "the third." But his understanding of the ethical relationship and justice itself as nonreciprocal, incompatible with reciprocity (which he conflates with the abstract interchangeability of humans), is not easy to reconcile with the egalitarian logic of democratic politics. Levinas, Totality and Infinity, 298, 300; "Peace and Proximity," 168–69; and Otherwise Than Being, 157–62.

132 Rancière, *Disagreement*.

133 Levinas, *Totality and Infinity*; and *Otherwise Than Being*, 244–47, 11–14, 93–97, 140–62.

134 In this respect Derrida's "democracy to come" diverges from Rancière's conception of democracy as the staging of the egalitarian principle, as the title of any at all to govern any other, or as the part of no part.

135 I am indebted to discussions with Uday Singh Mehta on the often tense relation between radical politics and radical ethics.

136 It is important to remember that Senghor also inhabited the field of postwar social thought out of which Levinas's and Derrida's thinking developed. He was born the same year as Levinas who was a naturalized French citizen who also spent the war interned in a German POW camp. This was a formative intellectual experience during which Levinas developed an orientation to ethics, alterity, and temporality that would deeply inform his postwar writings. On Levinas's early formation as a thinker in relation to National Socialism, see Caygill, *Levinas and the Political*, 5–50. On the Christian sources of his ethics of alterity, see Moyn, *Origins of the Other*.

137 Mauss, *The Gift*.

CHAPTER 4. *Freedom, Time, Territory*

1 This dramaturgy also meant that only white troops were permitted to march into Paris despite the multiracial character of the French army, which included a sizable number of troops recruited from the colonies; see "Paris Liberation." On colonial troops during the war, see Mann, *Native Sons*.

2 Charles De Gaulle, "Discours de l'Hôtel de Ville de Paris, 25 août 1944," available at http://www.charles-de-gaulle.org/pages/1-homme/accueil/discours/pendant-la-guerre-1940–1946/discours-de-1-hotel-de-ville-de-paris-25-aout-1944.php.

3 Sartre, "Liberation of Paris," 164.

4 Sartre, "Liberation of Paris," 161

5 Sartre, "Liberation of Paris," 161.

6 Sartre, "Liberation of Paris," 163.

7 Sartre, "Liberation of Paris," 164.

8 Sartre, "Liberation of Paris," 164.

9 Compare with Kant's discussion of the French Revolution as the kind of event that forever changes world history by instilling in spectators a new sense of human possibility, regardless of its immediate success or failure. Kant, "Contest of the Faculties," 182–85.

10 Arendt, *On Revolution*, 110–30.

11 Arendt, "The Gap," 5.

12 Arendt, "What Is Freedom?," 152.

13 Arendt, "What Is Freedom?," 147.

14 Arendt, "What Is Freedom?," 164.

15 Arendt, "What Is Freedom?," 166. Emphasis added.

16 Arendt, "What Is Freedom?," 167.

17 Arendt, "What Is Freedom?," 168.

18 Arendt, "What Is Freedom?," 169.

19 Arendt, *Life of the Mind*, 207.

20 Arendt, *Life of the Mind*, 208.

21 Arendt, *Life of the Mind*, 204, 206, 207.

22 Arendt, *On Revolution*, 32–33, 35.

23 Lefebvre, *Critique of Everyday Life*, 6.

24 Camus, "Combat Continues," in *Camus at Combat*, 11.

25 Camus, "From Resistance to Revolution," in *Camus at Combat*, 13.

26 Programme du Conseil National. Its platform included the nationalization of industry, energy, utilities, and banks, the creation of producers' cooperatives and guarantees concerning the "right to work."

27 Beauvoir, *Force of Circumstance*, 4.

28 Sartre, "Liberation of Paris," 163.

29 Merleau-Ponty, "War Has Taken Place," 150.

30 Merleau-Ponty, "War Has Taken Place," 151.

31 Merleau-Ponty, "War Has Taken Place," 151.

32 Merleau-Ponty, "War Has Taken Place," 151.

33 Merleau-Ponty, "War Has Taken Place," 151. Cf. Ranciére, *Disagreement*, on the distinction between politics and police and the chronic risk of politics devolving into police.

34 Merleau-Ponty, "War Has Taken Place," 150. Even nonrevolutionary centrists, like the philosopher Yves Simon, an anti-Marxist Christian democrat who was a disciple of Jacques Maritain, argued immediately after the war that a renovated French democracy should incorporate a number of socialist insights and innovations and move beyond the liberalism that produced atomized individuals, social inequality, and spiritual alienation. Simon. *Community of the Free.*

35 Aron, "Révolution et rénovation," 158.

36 Aron, "Révolution et rénovation," 135–47.

37 Camus, "From Resistance to Revolution," 12–13.

38 Camus, "The Blood of Freedom," in *Camus at Combat*, 17.

39 Camus, "The Democracy to Come," in *Camus at Combat*, 27.

40 Camus, "From Resistance to Revolution," 13.

41 Camus, October 1, 1944, in *Camus at Combat*, 55.

42 Camus, "From Resistance to Revolution," 13.

43 Camus, February 16, 1945, in *Camus at Combat*, 172.

44 Camus, February 16, 1945, 172.

45 Camus, February 16, 1945, 172.

46 Camus, February 16, 1945, 173.

47 Camus, "Neither Victims nor Executioners," in *Camus at Combat*, 274.

48 Camus, "Neither Victims nor Executioners," 266–67.

49 Camus, "Neither Victims nor Executioners," 267.

50 Camus, "Neither Victims nor Executioners," 268.

51 Camus, "Neither Victims nor Executioners," 268.

52 Camus, "Neither Victims nor Executioners," 268.

53 Camus, "Neither Victims nor Executioners," 268.

54 Camus, "Neither Victims nor Executioners," 269.

55 Camus, "Neither Victims nor Executioners," 269.

56 Camus, "Neither Victims nor Executioners," 270. Emphasis added.

57 Camus, "Neither Victims nor Executioners," 261.

58 Camus, "Neither Victims nor Executioners," 270.

59 Camus, "Neither Victims nor Executioners," 264.

60 Camus, "Neither Victims nor Executioners," 264, 265, 271.

61 Camus, "Neither Victims nor Executioners."

62 Camus, "Neither Victims nor Executioners," 272–73.

63 Camus, "Neither Victims nor Executioners," 273.

64 de Gaulle, "Discours de Bayeux."

65 Mann, *Native Sons*; Weinstein, *Éboué*.

66 de Gaulle, "Discours de Brazzaville."

67 Weil, "Colonial Question," 106, 107.

68 Weil, "Colonial Question," 112.

69 Weil, "Colonial Question," 117.

70 Weil, "Colonial Question," 117–18.

71 Aron, *Memoirs*, 143, 194, 232.

72 Aron, *L'Âge des empires*.

73 Maier and Hoffmann, *Marshall Plan*, 70–102; Judt, *Postwar*; DeGrazia, *Irresistible Empire*, 336–75; Nord, *France's New Deal*, 145–214.

74 Hilderbrand, *Dumbarton Oaks*. Churchill feared that China, led by Chiang Kai-shek, which was to have a seat on the council, was too dependent on the United States. Including France among the so-called great powers, he believed, would check American plans to dismantle European empires and provide a continental bulwark against the Soviet Union.

75 Hilderbrand, *Dumbarton Oaks*, 17–68.

76 Charter of the United Nations, ch. XI: Declaration Regarding Non-Self-Governing Territories, Article 73, available at http://www.un.org/en/documents/charter /chapter11.shtml. On the trusteeship system, see Luard, *History of the United Nations*, vol. 1, 58–62, and vol. 2, 144–60.

77 Charter of the United Nations, Article 2 (7). See also Luard, *History of the United Nations*, vol. 1, 62–63. On debates over UN jurisdiction in French North Africa, see Luard, *History of the United Nations*, vol. 2, 75–103. On the instrumentalization of the United Nations by the Algerian National Liberation Front, see Connelly, *A Diplomatic Revolution*. On British attempts to prevent the United Nations from considering the Mau-Mau Rebellion, see Cleary, "Myth of Mau Mau," 227–45.

78 Duiker, *Ho Chi Minh*; Marr, *Vietnam 1945*; Jennings, *Vichy in the Tropics*, 130–61; Brocheux and Hémery, *Indochina*. Jennings argues that the Japanese allowed French Vichy authorities a relatively free hand in governing the colonies.

79 Tonnesson, "Franklin Roosevelt," 63–8.

80 Tonnesson, "Franklin Roosevelt," 56–73.

81 Duiker, *Ho Chi Minh*, 285, 330–31, 353–56.

82 David Marr reports that after the March 1945 coup by the Japanese, de Gaulle sent orders to French ground forces "to maintain a physical presence in northern Indo-

china at any cost, thus symbolizing the persistence of French sovereignty." Marr, *Vietnam 1945*, 61.

83 Duiker, *Ho Chi Minh*, 356–98.

84 Marr, *Vietnam 1945*, 309.

85 Marcel Bigeard was captured by Germany in 1940, parachuted into France in 1944 to join the resistance army, and led a colonial paratrooper battalion in Indochina. Jacques Massu served with the Free French forces in Chad and Libya before taking part in the French invasion of Saigon in September 1945. Fall, *Street without Joy*, 62–63. Duplay et al., *Cultured Force*, 267–99.

86 Fall, *Street without Joy*, 31.

87 Nicolas, *Histoire de la Martinique*, 100.

88 Callard, "Republic of Bourguiba," 18.

89 Thomas, "Colonial Violence," 45–91.

90 Bey, *Syria's Quest*; Zisser, *Lebanon*.

91 Kent, *From Madagascar*; Tronchon, *L'insurrection malgache*.

92 Shipway, "Madagascar," 72–100.

93 Cooper, " 'Our Strike,' " 81–118.

94 For an overview of metropolitan party politics, French plans for imperial reconstruction, and the war in Indochina, see Thomas, "French Imperial Reconstruction," 13–51.

95 Rioux, *Fourth Republic*.

96 Rioux, *Fourth Republic*; Duroselle, "Turning-Point," 302–28.

97 On the consolidation of the *dirigiste* welfare state and the failure of a more radical form of postwar social democracy, see Kuisel, *Seducing the French*, and Nord, *France's New Deal*.

98 UN Resolution 1513, 67.

99 UN Resolution 1513, 66.

100 UN Resolution 1513, 66.

101 UN Resolution 1513, 67.

102 UN Resolution 1513, 67.

103 UN Resolution 1513, 67.

104 UN Resolution 1513, 66. Emphasis added.

105 UN Resolution 1513, 67.

106 UN Resolution 1541, 29.

107 UN Resolution 1541, 29.

108 UN Resolution 1541, 29, 30.

109 Portugal in particular argued that because constitutionally its territories in Africa, India, and East Timor were officially overseas provinces, they were not subject to international regulation. UN Resolution 1542, 30.

110 UN Resolution 1654, 65.

111 MacMillan, *Paris 1919*, 3–49.

112 MacMillan, *Paris 1919*, 3–35, Mazower, *No Enchanted Palace*, 28–103, Smith, *American Empire*, 139–80. Supporters of the league also included international lawyers and left proponents of world government or European federation. See Woolf, *International Government*, and *Framework*; Wilson, *International Theory*; Wells, *Shape of Things*; Franck, "France."

113 Covenant of the League of Nations.

114 Articles 12, 13, 14, Covenant of the League of Nations.

115 Article 10, Covenant of the League of Nations.

116 Wilson, "Fourteen Points," 404. Emphasis added.

117 Wilson, "Fourteen Points," 407.

118 Wilson, "Fourteen Points," 406.

119 Wilson, "Appeal for the Support of the League of Nations at Pueblo, Colorado," in *Essential Writings*, 413.

120 MacMillan, *Paris 1919*, 11.

121 Manela, *Wilsonian Moment*, 109–34, 41–43.

122 Manela, *Wilsonian Moment*, 36–43.

123 Lenin, "Right of Nations," 167.

124 Lenin, "Right of Nations," 166.

125 Lenin, "Right of Nations," 164.

126 Lenin, "Continuation of the Notes," 164, 722.

127 Lenin, "Continuation of the Notes," 724.

128 Berman, " 'Alternative Is Despair,' " 1797.

129 Berman, " 'Alternative Is Despair,' " 1874.

130 Berman, " 'Alternative Is Despair,' " 1842.

131 Hick, *New World Order*, 177–78.

132 For an legal critique of the mandate system, see Anghie, *Imperialism*, 115–95.

133 A notable exception was the 1947 plan for the partition of Palestine; see Berman, " 'Alternative Is Despair,' " 1795–8, 1898–1903.

134 Joint Statement by Roosevelt and Churchill. On the global significance of the Atlantic Charter, see Borgwardt, *New Deal for the World*.

135 Smith, *American Empire*, 374–418.

136 Hilderbrand, *Dumbarton Oaks*.

137 Article 1.1, Charter of the United Nations and Statute of the International Court of Justice, Article (San Francisco, 1945), 3.

138 Article 2.1, Charter of the United Nations, 3.

139 Article 2.4, Charter of the United Nations, 3.

140 Article 2.7, Charter of the United Nations, 3.

141 Manela has demonstrated how self-determination became a powerful idiom for anticolonial mobilization in Egypt, India, China, and Korea in the 1920s and 1930s. Manela, *The Wilsonian Moment*, 55–136.

142 Smith, *American Empire*, 374–418.

143 Arrighi, *Long Twentieth Century*, 278.

144 Arrighi, *Long Twentieth Century*, 274–88.

145 Mazower, *No Enchanted Palace*.

146 Article 2.7, Charter of the United Nations, 3.

147 Article 2.7, Charter of the United Nations, 3.

148 Article 76b, Charter of the United Nations, 15.

149 On the UN trusteeship system, see Anghie, *Imperialism Sovereignty*, 115–95.

150 Louis and Robinson, "Imperialism of Decolonization," 462–511.

151 Louis and Robinson, "Empire Preserv'd." On how Britain manipulated the USA into assuming leadership in the anticommunist war in Vietnam, see Lawrence, "Forging the 'Great Combination,'" 105–29.

152 Smith, *American Empire*, 405.

153 Young-Bruehl, *Hannah Arendt*.

154 Arendt, "Minority Question," 127.

155 Arendt, "Return of Russian Jewry," 175.

156 Arendt, *Origins of Totalitarianism*, 267–302.

157 Arendt, *Origins of Totalitarianism*, 174.

158 Arendt, "Minority Question," 130.

159 Arendt, "Minority Question," 128–29.

160 Arendt, *Origins of Totalitarianism*, 292.

161 Arendt, *Origins of Totalitarianism*, 300.

162 Arendt, "A Christian Word," 160, and "Reconciliation of Peoples," 261.

163 Arendt, "Confusion" (*Aufbau*, Aug. 14, 1942), *Jewish Writings*, 169. See also *Origins of Totalitarianism*, 291.

164 Arendt, *Origins of Totalitarianism*, 298. Emphasis added. She reproduces Kant's reasoning in "Perpetual Peace" when she adds: "Furthermore this dilemma would by no means be eliminated by the establishment of a 'world government'" (298).

165 Arendt, "Minority Question," 129.

166 Arendt, "Minority Question," 130.

167 Arendt, "Minority Question," 130.

168 Arendt, "Minority Question," 130.

169 Arendt, "Minority Question," 132.

170 Cf. the unrealized plan by Judah Magnes, Martin Buber, and Hannah Arendt to invent a binational state form in Palestine. Buber, "The Bi-National Approach"; Magnes, "Solution through Force," "Toward Peace," and "Report on Palestine"; Arendt, "Jewish-Arab Question," 193–98, and "Peace or Armistice," 423–50.

171 Kant, *Philosophy of Law*, 7.

172 Kant, *Philosophy of Law*, lx, 73.

173 Kant, "Perpetual Peace," 117.

174 Kant, "Perpetual Peace," 102. See also Kant, *Philosophy of Law*, 102–3, 109.

175 Kant, "Perpetual Peace," 103.

176 Kant, "Perpetual Peace," 104.

177 Kant, "Perpetual Peace," 104.

178 Kant, "Perpetual Peace," 102.

179 Kant, "Perpetual Peace," 102, 104. See also *Philosophy of Law*, 103, 109.

180 Kant, "Perpetual Peace," 113. See also *Philosophy of Law*, 109.

181 Kant, "Perpetual Peace," 105.

182 Kant, *Philosophy of Law*, 68.

183 Kant, "Perpetual Peace," 106.

184 Kant, *Philosophy of Law*, 110.

185 On the limited and conditional character of Kant's right to hospitality, see Derrida, *On Cosmopolitanism*, 19–46.

186 For Carl Schmitt, this interstate order was both cause and consequence of a system of European public international law and a Eurocentric spatial order for the world. Schmitt, Nomos *of the Earth*. On the Congress of Vienna, see Nussbaum, *Concise History*.

187 On the debate over whether these sectional assemblies were movements for revolutionary federalists, bourgeois moderates, or provincial counterrevolutionaries, see de Francesco, "Popular Sovereignty," 74–101; Hanson, "Federalist Revolt," 335–55.

188 Dubois, *Avengers of the New World*, 60–90.

189 Fontana, "Napoleonic Empire," 116–28; Pagden, "Fellow Citizens," 28–46.

190 See Collier, "Nationality," 37–64; Fitzgerald, "Introduction"; Rodríguez O., "Emancipation of America," 131–52; and Arana, *Bolivar*. Significant but not surprising, the legacy of Bolívar's internationalist vision for Latin American independence reappeared in public debate during the postwar period and decolonization. See Kunz, "Idea of 'Collective Security,'" 658–79.

191 Mazzini, "Holy Alliance," 117–18.

192 Mazzini, "Holy Alliance," 118–19, 126.

193 Mazzini, "Holy Alliance," 126.

194 Mazzini, "Holy Alliance," 128–29.

195 Mazzini, "Nationality and Cosmopolitanism," in *Cosmopolitanism*, 57, 58.

196 Mazzini, "Concerning the Fall of the Roman Republic," in *Cosmopolitanism*, 48–50.

197 Mazzini, "Humanity and Country," in *Cosmopolitanism*, 53.

198 Mazzini, "Humanity and Country," 58.

199 Mazzini, "Nationality and Cosmopolitanism," 61.

200 Mazzini, "Humanity and Country," 56.

201 Mazzini, "Holy Alliance," 126.

202 Mazzini, "Humanity and Country," 54.

203 Mazzini, "Humanity and Country," 54.

204 Mazzini, "Humanity and Country," 55.

205 Mazzini, "Humanity and Country."

206 Mazzini, "Nationality and Cosmopolitanism," 59.

207 Proudhon, *What Is Property?*, 216.

208 Proudhon, *What Is Property?*, 216. He opposed the absolutist forms of authority associated with European monarchs and the Catholic Church but was equally suspicious of orthodox socialists and revolutionaries. For his critique of communist "association," see Proudhon, *General Idea*, 75–99.

209 On Proudhon's social theory, see Woodcock, *Pierre-Joseph Proudhon*.

210 Proudhon, *Du principe fédératif*. See also Woodcock, *Pierre-Joseph Proudhon*, 209–49. He prophesizes that "the twentieth century will open the era of federations" (109) and envisions a time when "the [idea of a] Republic of peoples can finally overcome its mysticism [and realize itself] in the concrete form of a federation of federations" (93).

CHAPTER 5. *Departmentalization and the Spirit of Schoelcher*

1 Césaire, "Cahier d'un retour," 31. This line was first published in "En guise de mani-feste littéraire," *Tropiques*, no. 5 (Apr. 1942): 10, and this section was later added to the 1947 edition of "Cahier."

2 Fanon, *Black Skin, White Masks*, 39. On Césaire's oratory, see Gavronsky, "Aimé Césaire"; Hale, "Littérature orale," 173–86; Constant, "Aimé Césaire," 35–36.

3 Arendt, *Human Condition*.

4 Nicolas, *Histoire de la Martinique*, 84–90. Nicolas was himself an active Martini-can Communist, a generation younger than Césaire. See Ménil, "In Memoriam," *Tropiques*, nos. 6–7 (Feb. 1943), for his eulogy for Jules Monnerot.

5 Nicolas, *Histoire de la Martinique*, 90–97.

6 Nicolas, *Histoire de la Martinique*, 90–97.

7 Nicolas, *Histoire de la Martinique*, 97–100.

8 Césaire, "Georges-Louis Ponton, Gouverneur de la Martinique," *Tropiques*, no. 12 (Jan. 1945): 154–55, in *Tropiques*.

9 Nicolas, *Histoire de la Martinique*, 95–99.

10 Nicolas, *Histoire de la Martinique*, 98.

11 In 1944 he wrote to Henri Seyrig that he agreed to run for office to prevent the election of "a foul coalition" of former Vichyists. Quoted in Véron, "Césaire at the Crossroads," 440.

12 Toumson and Henry-Valmore, *Aimé Césaire*, 99.

13 Fonkoua, *Aimé Césaire*, 89. On a Communist Party questionnaire that he filled out when he was elected deputy, Césaire noted that in 1935 he had been a member of the ENS cell of the Jeunesses communists in Paris. Fonkoua, *Aimé Césaire*, 97

14 Nicolas, *Histoire de la Martinique*, 104–11.

15 Quoted in Nicolas, *Histoire de la Martinique*, 105.

16 PCF Pamphlet, 1946, quoted in Arnold, *Modernism and Negritude*, 174.

17 Nicolas, *Histoire de la Martinique*, 111.

18 See Constant, *La retraite*, and Miles, *Elections and Ethnicity*.

19 Nicolas, *Histoire de la Martinique*, 111–12. On the widespread Martinican belief that France might become a socialist society, see William, "Aimé Césaire," 320; Sablé, *Transformation*, and *Les Antilles*. Samir Amin also recalls that departmentaliza-tion was pursued by Antillean communists against right-wing colonial apologists. Amin, *Life Looking Forward*, 71.

20 On Vergès and the Réunion Communist Party in relation to departmentalization and autonomy, see Gauvin, "Le parti communiste de la Réunion," 73–94, and Vergès, *Monsters and Revolutionaries*, 72–184.

21 Rapport, séance du 26 février 1946, JORF, Documents de l'Assemblée, no. 520, 519.

22 Rapport, 519.

23 Rapport, 520.

24 Rapport, 520.

25 Rapport, 520.

26 Rapport, 520.

27 Rapport, 520.

28 Rapport, 519, 520. This likely referenced international norms regarding self-determination institutionalized in the UN Charter with American support.

29 Rapport, 520.

30 Rapport, 520.

31 Rapport, 520.

32 Césaire, "Discours à la Première Assemblée nationale constituante, 20 décembre 1945," www.assemblee-nationale.fr/histoire/aime-cesaire/discours-20dec1945.asp.

33 Césaire, Debate, March 12, 1946, JORF. Débats de l'Assemblée Nationale Constituante, no. 23 (Mar. 13, 1946): 662.

34 Césaire, Debate, March 12, 1946, JORF, 662.

35 Vergès from Réunion and Bissol from Martinique each elaborated their territory's 300-year history of entanglement with metropolitan France, the ensuing bonds, feelings of unity, and practices of solidarity as arguments for their immediate and total integration as departments. Vergès placed special emphasis on Réunion's multiracial population and Bissol on his own working-class origins and "the merit of realizing the wishes formulated by Victor Schoelcher since 1848." Debate, March 12, 1946, JORF, 663–64.

36 Ministère des finances, Commission des Territoires d'outre-mer, séance du vendredi 8 mars 1946.

37 For the debate between Valentino on the one hand and Césaire and Monnerville on the other concerning the centralization of power, see JORF, Débats de l'Assemblée Nationale Constituante, no. 25 (March 15, 1946): 752–55. On Valentino's wartime resistance and internment under the Robert regime, see Baptiste, "Le régime de Vichy," 4–5.

38 Gaston Monnerville, March 14, 1946, JORF, Débats de l'Assemblée Nationale Constituante, no. 25 (March 15, 1946): 754.

39 Nicolas, Histoire de la Martinique, 116–20.

40 Quoted in Nicolas, Histoire de la Martinique, 116.

41 Césaire, "Hommage à Victor Schoelcher," 229.

42 Césaire, "Hommage à Victor Schoelcher," 229.

43 Césaire, "Hommage à Victor Schoelcher," 230.

44 For his position on abolition and political initiatives, see Schmidt, Victor Schoelcher, and Girollet, Victor Schoelcher. For a general account of French abolitionism, and a collection of primary documents see Schmidt, Abolitionnistes de l'esclavage.

45 Schoelcher, L'esclavage des Noirs, and Abolition de l'esclavage.

46 His programmatic writings of this period include Schoelcher, Des colonies françaises, Colonies étrangeres, and Histoire de l'esclavage.

47 Schoelcher, Des colonies françaises, 384.

48 Schoelcher, Des colonies françaises, 385.

49 Schoelcher, Des colonies françaises, 375–76.

50 Schoelcher, Des colonies françaises, 375.

51 Schoelcher, Des colonies françaises, 377, 381.

52 Schoelcher, Des colonies françaises, 372–73.

53 Schoelcher, Des colonies françaises, 372.

54 Schoelcher, *Des colonies françaises*, 369.

55 Schoelcher, *Des colonies françaises*, 372–73.

56 Schoelcher, *Des colonies françaises*, 372–73.

57 Schoelcher, *Des colonies françaises*, 213.

58 Schoelcher, *Des colonies françaises*, 213–14.

59 Schoelcher, *Des colonies françaises*, 213–14.

60 Schoelcher, *Des colonies françaises*, 412.

61 Schoelcher, *Des colonies françaises*, 412–13.

62 Schoelcher, *Histoire de l'esclavage*, 375–81.

63 Schmidt, *Victor Schoelcher*, 55–56.

64 Schmidt, *Victor Schoelcher*, 15–41, 63–70. See Schoelcher, *De la petition des ouvriers*, and "Petition pour l'abolition," in Schmidt, *Abolitionnistes de l'esclavage*, 877.

65 Schmidt, *Victor Schoelcher*, 15–41, 63–70. Schoelcher analyzes the debates in the Chamber of Deputies on April 24 and 26 on petitions for abolition of slavery in Schoelcher, *Histoire de l'esclavage*, 135–46.

66 Schmidt, *Victor Schoelcher*, 99–110; Girollet, *Victor Schoelcher*, 26–28.

67 Décret d'abolition de l'esclavage, 381–82.

68 Décret d'abolition de l'esclavage, 382.

69 Schmidt, *Victor Schoelcher*, 99–110; Girollet, *Victor Schoelcher*, 26–28.

70 Schoelcher, "Premier rapport," 376.

71 Schoelcher, "Premier rapport," 377.

72 Schoelcher, *Des Colonies françaises*, 400–407.

73 Schoelcher, "Aux élécteurs de la Guadeloupe et de la Martinique," September 29, 1848. Reprinted in Schmidt, *Victor Schoelcher*, 385.

74 Schoelcher, "Premier rapport," 378–79.

75 Schoelcher, "Premier rapport," 379.

76 Schoelcher, "Premier rapport," 378.

77 Schoelcher, "Premier rapport," 378.

78 Schmidt, *Victor Schoelcher*, 103–10.

79 Schoelcher, "Deuxième rapport." Reprinted in Schmidt, *Victor Schoelcher*, 380.

80 Schmidt, *Victor Schoelcher*, 117–19.

81 Schoelcher, "Profession de foi." Reprinted in Schmidt, *Victor Schoelcher*, 383–84.

82 Schoelcher, "Aux élécteurs." Reprinted in Schmidt, *Victor Schoelcher*, 385–86.

83 Schmidt, *Victor Schoelcher*, 63–148; Girollet, 23–28, 392–95, 398–99. Girollet explains that Schoelcher sought to reform and humanize but not abolish French colonialism in other parts of the empire. Girollet, *Victor Schoelcher*, 276–352.

84 Schmidt, *Victor Schoelcher*, 114–19, 122–27, 133–46. Schoelcher's reflections on this process of foreclosure are included in Schoelcher, *La Verité*. For his critique of this repression, see Schoelcher, *Le Procés de Marie-Galante*, and *Protestations*.

85 Schmidt, *Victor Schoelcher*, 61.

86 Schmidt, *Victor Schoelcher*, 110–12.

87 Girollet, *Victor Schoelcher*, 133–71.

88 Césaire, "Hommage à Victor Schoelcher," 234.

89 Schmidt, *Victor Schoelcher*, 113.
90 "Victor Schoelcher (1804–1893). Une vie, un siècle. L'esclavage d'hier à aujourd'hui," www.senat.fr/evenement/victor_schoelcher/engagements.html (accessed July 11, 2011). For Hugo's speech on August 21, 1849, at the Congrès international de la paix de Paris, see Rolland, *L'unité politique*.
91 Schmidt, *Victor Schoelcher*, 128–37.
92 Césaire, "La poésie," 5.
93 They were transferred, along with Félix Éboué's remains, in an elaborate national ceremony on May 26, 1949.
94 Césaire, "Discours prononcé," 23–33. For a closer reading of this speech, see Wilder, "Race, Reason, Impasse," 31–58.
95 Toumson and Henry-Valmore, *Aimé Césaire*, 107.
96 Césaire, "Discours prononcé," 23.
97 Césaire, "Discours prononcé," 23.
98 Césaire, "Discours prononcé," 23.
99 Césaire, "Discours prononcé," 25. For his remarks on popular revolution, see Césaire, "Hommage à Victor Schoelcher," 232. On the 1844 workers' petition, see Schoelcher, *De la Pétition des ouvriers*.
100 Césaire, "Victor Schoelcher et l'abolition," 17–21. Schmidt recounts that by the time the commissars of the Republic reached Martinique and Guadeloupe on June 3 and 4, 1848, colonial governors had already abolished slavery there following slave uprisings in Saint-Pierre Martinique (May 20–22). Fear of a general revolt led Governor Rostoland to abolish slavery in Martinique on May 23 and Governor Layrle to do so in Guadeloupe on May 27. Schmidt, *Victor Schoelcher*, 117.
101 Césaire, "Victor Schoelcher et l'abolition," 67.
102 Césaire, "Hommage à Victor Schoelcher," 233.
103 Césaire, "Hommage à Victor Schoelcher," 232.
104 Césaire, "Hommage à Victor Schoelcher," 234.
105 Césaire, "Hommage à Victor Schoelcher," 235.
106 Schoelcher's evolving political vision may be traced through his writings in *Esclavage et colonisation*.
107 Césaire, "Victor Schoelcher et l'abolition," 47.
108 Césaire, "Victor Schoelcher et l'abolition," 73.
109 Césaire, "Victor Schoelcher et l'abolition," 47.
110 Cottias, "'L'oubli du passé,'" 293–313; Perina, *Citoyenneté et sujetion*, 16–28.
111 His critique of the coup d'état and of Bonapartist politics emphasizes their untimely power to cause history to move in reverse. See Schoelcher, *Histoire des crimes*.
112 Schoelcher, *Histoire des crimes*, vii. During the Paris Commune he called on militants to reconcile with the forces of order and end the civil war. Schoelcher, "Proposition d'une ligue de la paix," 395–97.
113 See the discourses and articles collected in Schoelcher, *Polémique coloniale*, vols. 1 and 2. On the specificity of "colonial democracy" in Martinique under the Third Republic, see Constant, *La retraite aux flambeaux*, 27–66.
114 Césaire, "Victor Schoelcher et l'abolition," 49.
115 Césaire, "Victor Schoelcher et l'abolition," 49.

116 Césaire, "Hommage à Victor Schoelcher," 233–34.
117 Césaire, "Victor Schoelcher et l'abolition," 49. Césaire referred to Schoelcher as the figure whom Grégoire had prophetically called forth to continue the still incomplete work of abolition that Grégoire had initiated during the French Revolution. Césaire, "Discours d'inauguration," 429.
118 Césaire, "Victor Schoelcher et l'abolition," 73.
119 Césaire, "Discours prononcé," 33.
120 Césaire, "Victor Schoelcher et l'abolition," 61.
121 Césaire, "Hommage à Victor Schoelcher," 232–34.
122 Césaire, "Victor Schoelcher et l'abolition," 71.
123 Césaire, "Discours prononcé," 28. See also Césaire, "Victor Schoelcher et l'abolition," 71.
124 Quoted in Moutoussamy, *Aimé Césaire*, 54. This volume republishes extensive portions of Césaire's postwar parliamentary and political discourses.
125 See, www.legislation.cnav.fr/textes/ord/TLR-ORD_4510_04101945.htm. On the French state's reluctance to implement social legislation in the overseas departments, see François-Lubin, "Les méandres de la politique sociale," 73–83.
126 On the refusal by the metropolitan state and overseas business interests to implement the social dimensions of departmentalization, see Dumont, "La quête de l'égalité," 82–90.
127 Césaire, Assemblée nationale, July 4, 1949, JORF. *Débats parlementaires,* no. 68 (July 5, 1949): 4141.
128 Nicolas, *Histoire de la Martinique,* 139–41.
129 Nicolas, *Histoire de la Martinique,* 141–50.
130 Nicolas, *Histoire de la Martinique,* 151–65. On the disaffection, racial polarization, and strikes in 1950 and 1953, see Dumont, "La quête de l'égalité," 90–96.
131 Césaire, Assemblée nationale, July 4, 1949, 4140.
132 Césaire, Assemblée nationale, July 4, 1949, 4141.
133 Césaire, Assemblée nationale, July 4, 1949, 4141–42.
134 Césaire, Assemblée nationale, July 4, 1949, 4141.
135 Césaire, Assemblée nationale, July 4, 1949, 4141.
136 Césaire, Assemblée nationale, July 11, 1949, JORF, no. 75 (July 12, 1949): 4571.
137 For Césaire's propositions and interventions during this time, see www.assemblee-nationale.fr/histoire/aime-cesaire/tables_nominatives.asp#28nov1946 (accessed August 3, 2011), as well as the lengthy excerpts from Césaire's parliamentary speeches in Moutoussamy, *Aimé Césaire*, 34–54.
138 Césaire, Assemblée nationale, June 10, 1953, JORF, no. 83 (June 11, 1953): 3006–7.
139 Césaire, Assemblée nationale, February 11, 1954, JORF, no. 7 (Feb. 12, 1954): 182.
140 Césaire, Assemblée nationale, February 11, 1954, 182.
141 Césaire, Assemblée nationale, February 11, 1954, 183.
142 Césaire, Assemblée nationale, March 26, 1954, JORF, no. 28 (Mar. 27, 1954): 1318.
143 Césaire, Assemblée nationale, March 26, 1954, 1318.
144 Césaire, Assemblée nationale, March 26, 1954, 1318.
145 Césaire, Assemblée nationale, March 26, 1954, 1317.
146 Césaire, "Victor Schoelcher et l'abolition," 47.

147 Césaire, "Victor Schoelcher et l'abolition," 27. When Césaire later advocated for autonomy, he criticized the right for retrospectively recuperating Schoelcher as a departmentalist (*JORF*, Assemblée nationale, 2e séance, Dec. 17, 1982, 8489–90).

148 Ngal, *Aimé Césaire*, 238–39.

149 *Discours sur le colonialisme* was first published in June 1950 by Éditions Réclame before a widely read second edition was published by Présence Africaine in 1955. Toumson and Henry-Valmore, *Aimé Césaire*, 136.

150 Toumson and Henry-Valmore, *Aimé Césaire*, 140.

151 Césaire, "Time of Freedom," 321. This poem originally appeared in Césaire, *Ferrements*. On the events in Côte d'Ivoire, see Benot, *Massacres coloniaux*, 148–49.

152 Césaire, "Discours sur le colonialism," 362.

153 Césaire, "Discours sur le colonialism," 363.

154 Césaire, "Discours sur le colonialism," 368.

155 Césaire, "Discours sur le colonialism," 368.

156 Césaire, "Discours sur le colonialism," 367.

157 Césaire, "Discours sur le colonialism," 362.

158 Césaire, "Discours sur le colonialism," 362.

159 Césaire, "Discours sur le colonialism," 359.

160 Césaire, "Discours sur le colonialism," 370.

161 Césaire, "Discours sur le colonialism," 376.

162 Césaire, "Discours sur le colonialism," 397.

163 Césaire, "Discours sur le colonialism," 397.

164 Césaire, "Discours sur le colonialism," 399–400.

165 Césaire, "Discours sur le colonialism," 400–401.

166 Césaire, "Discours sur le colonialism," 401.

167 Césaire, "Discours sur le colonialism," 401.

168 Césaire, "Discours sur le colonialism," 401.

169 Davis suggests that following *Les armes miraculeuses* (1946), Césaire matured as a lyricist whose poetry became less "ardent," more economical and meditative, but also more prophetic: "mantic as well as necromantic" (*Aimé Césaire*, 93, 125, 103). Arnold posits a movement from the "dazzling revelation," "special illumination," and "explosive aggressiveness," of *Les armes* to the prophetic, apocalyptic, eschatological, and demiurgic voice in the following two collections. *Negritude and Modernism*, 125, 191–251. Neither links these temporal orientations to Césaire's political projects.

170 Césaire, "The Griffin," in *Aimé Césaire: The Collected Poetry*, 171.

171 Aimé Césaire, "Barbarity," in *Aimé Césaire: The Collected Poetry*, 213.

172 Aimé Césaire, "To Africa/for Wifredo Lam," in *Aimé Césaire: The Collected Poetry*, 197.

173 Aimé Césaire, "Noon Knives," in *Aimé Césaire: The Collected Poetry*, 201.

174 Aimé Césaire, "Non-Vicious Circle," in *Aimé Césaire: The Collected Poetry*, 217.

175 Aimé Césaire, "Howling," in *Aimé Césaire: The Collected Poetry*, 223.

CHAPTER 6. *Federalism and the Future of France*

1 Lewin, *Ahmed Sékou Touré*, 31.

2 Towa, *Léopold Sédar Senghor*, 115.

3   Towa, *Léopold Sédar Senghor*, 97.

4   Towa, *Léopold Sédar Senghor*, 97.

5   For thoughtful arguments against dismissive readings of Negritude by Towa, Albert Franklin, Stanislas Adotevi, Paulin Hountondji, and Wole Soyinka, see Irele, *Négritude Moment*, 95–162, 213–28.

6   Fanon, *Wretched of the Earth*, 13.

7   Fanon, *Wretched of the Earth*, 11.

8   Fanon, *Wretched of the Earth*, 10.

9   Fanon, *Wretched of the Earth*, 151, 152, 154.

10 Fanon, *Wretched of the Earth*, 159.

11 Fanon, *Wretched of the Earth*, 159, 160

12 Fanon, *Wretched of the Earth*, 168.

13 Fanon, *Wretched of the Earth*, 170.

14 Fanon, *Wretched of the Earth*, 170.

15 Fanon, *Wretched of the Earth*, 179, 180.

16 Fanon, *Wretched of the Earth*, 180.

17 Fanon, *Wretched of the Earth*, 239.

18 Amin, *A Life Looking Forward*, 69.

19 Amin, *A Life Looking Forward*, 70.

20 Amin, *A Life Looking Forward*, 71.

21 Amin, *A Life Looking Forward*, 72.

22 Amin, *A Life Looking Forward*, 72. D'Arboussier, a communist member of the RDA, wrote an early critique of Negritude as a reactionary form of culturalist thinking that conditioned generations of polemicizing against Senghor. D'Arboussier, *Une dangereuse mystification*.

23 Amin, *A Life Looking Forward*, 72, 73.

24 For recent reconsiderations of Senghor as a political thinker, see Vaillant, *Black, French, and African*; Genova, *Colonial Ambivalence*; Atlan, "Senghor député," 71–81; Diouf, "Léopold Sédar Senghor," 171–89; and Cooper, "Provincializing France"; "Alternatives to Empire"; *Citizenship between Empire and Nation*. My research on Senghor's political projects has proceeded in parallel to Cooper's. His book was not available at the time of writing. For recent work that rereads Senghor's writing in relation to a broader field of philosophy and critical theory, see Eze, *Achieving Our Humanity*; Kebede, "Negritude and Bergsonism"; Diagne, *Léopold Sédar Senghor*; Jones, *Racial Discourses*; and Thiam, "Beyond Bergson's Lebensphilosophie."

25 Vaillant, *Black, French, and African*, 196–204.

26 On de Gaulle's resistance myth, see Rousso, *Vichy Syndrome*.

27 Assemblée nationale constituante, 21 mars 1946, *Journal Officiel de la République Française (JORF)*. Débats de l'assemblée nationale constituante, no. 29, March 22, 1946, 947. On how African elites instrumentalized the Occupation, see Ginio, *French Colonialism Unmasked*.

28 Senghor, Interview with *Gavroche*, 17.

29 Senghor, Interview with *Gavroche*, 17–18.

30 de Gaulle, *Discours et messages*, 373.

31 La conférence africaine française, 35; full capitals and "self-government" in English in original.

32 La conférence africaine française, 35.

33 La conférence africaine française, 35–36. See also Morgenthau, *Political Parties*, 38–39, and Marshall, *French Colonial Myth*, 102–15.

34 Senghor, "Défense de l'Afrique noire," 237.

35 Senghor, "Défense de l'Afrique noire," 238.

36 Senghor, "Défense de l'Afrique noire," 238, 239.

37 Senghor, "Défense de l'Afrique noire," 238.

38 Senghor, "Défense de l'Afrique noire," 247.

39 Senghor, "Défense de l'Afrique noire," 247.

40 Senghor, "Défense de l'Afrique noire," 248.

41 Senghor, "Défense de l'Afrique noire," 248.

42 Delavignette, "L'Union française," 228, 230, 233. The entire March 24, 1945, text of Minister of Colonies Gacobbi is reprinted here.

43 On the legislative debates over the shape of the French Union and Community under the Fourth and Fifth Republics, see Cooper, *Citizenship*. On African legislators during this period, see Benot, *Les parlementaires africains*.

44 Quatrième République, Projet de constitution.

45 Marshall, *French Colonial Myth*, 189–207. Arguments for the French Union as a method of retaining by reforming the empire may be found in Devèze, *La France d'Outre-mer*, as well as in *Revue juridique et politique de l'Union française* (from 1947), *Union française et parlement: Une politique de démocratie et de progrès* (from July 1949), *Chronique d'Outre-mer: Études et informations* (from January 1952).

46 Marshall, *French Colonial Myth*, 181–89.

47 Ho Chi Minh was willing to negotiate membership of an autonomous Vietnam in a democratic French Union. Duiker, *Ho Chi Minh*, 353–98. Ferhat Abbas, leader of the Union démocratique du manifeste algérien (UDMA), expressed support for federal autonomy at the time. Marshall, *French Colonial Myth*, 156–62, 230–34.

48 Senghor, "Rapport supplémentaire."

49 Marshall, *French Colonial Myth*, 208–27.

50 Marshall, *French Colonial Myth*, 144–46; Lewis, "The MRP," 276–314. On parliamentary politics and political parties under the Fourth Republic, see Pickles, *France*, and Hoffmann, "Paradoxes," 90–98.

51 Marshall, *French Colonial Myth*, 218–27; Morgenthau, *Political Parties*, 42–43; Chafer, *End of Empire*, 64–65.

52 According to Marshall, the voting public was less opposed to the plan for the French Union than to the idea of a Communist-led government. Marshall, *French Colonial Myth*, 150. The majority of the overseas population who were not citizens but supported the April constitution were excluded from the referendum. Marshall, *French Colonial Myth*, 170–72.

53 Lewis, "The MRP," 276–314.

54 Marshall, *French Colonial Myth*, 149–52, 172–79, 189–207; Morgenthau, *Political Parties*, 44–48.

55 These included proposals by the États-généraux de colonisation, the Gaullist Rassemblement des gauches republicains (RGR) coalition, and the MRP. Marshall, *French Colonial Myth*, 172–79, 245–56; Morgenthau, *Political Parties*, 44–48.

56 Morgenthau, *Political Parties*, 93–108, 301–8. See accounts by Guèye, *Étapes et perspectives*; Sissoko, *Coups de sagaie*; and Atlan, "Senghor député."

57 Quoted in Marshall, *French Colonial Myth*, 229.

58 Marshall, *French Colonial Myth*, 229–30. Morgenthau argues that the IOM deputies did not form a coherent political party with clear constituencies in their home countries. Morgenthau, *Political Parties*, 83–86, 306–7. Many overseas deputies, including Senghor, were criticized in Africa for collaborating with the colonial government. Vaillaint, *Black, French, and African*, 197.

59 Marshall, *French Colonial Myth*, 274, 276–78. Edouard Herriot, of the Gaullist RPR group, warned the assembly that "France would become the colony of its former colonies." Cited in Marshall, *French Colonial Myth*, 253.

60 Senghor, Assemblée nationale constituante, 18 septembre 1946, *JORF*, no. 94 (Sept. 19, 1946), 3791.

61 Senghor, Assemblée nationale constituante, 3792.

62 Senghor, Assemblée nationale constituante, 3791.

63 Senghor, Assemblée nationale constituante, 3790. Senghor invoked as his "spiritual ancestor" Jean-François Merlet, the pro-abolitionist legislator who on August 18, 1792, argued that a representative government in which all citizens share sovereignty must include colonial deputies in the National Assembly. Senghor, Assemblée nationale constituante, 3791.

64 Senghor, Assemblée nationale constituante, 3791.

65 Senghor, Assemblée nationale constituante, 3791.

66 Senghor, Assemblée nationale constituante, 3792, 3791.

67 Senghor, Assemblée nationale constituante, 3792.

68 Senghor, Assemblée nationale constituante, 3792.

69 Senghor, Assemblée nationale constituante, 3792.

70 Senghor, Assemblée nationale constituante, 3791.

71 This debate over the form that the French Union would assume included interventions by overseas deputies Ferhat Abbas (Algeria), Sourou Migan Apithy (Dahomey), Aimé Césaire (Martinique), Yacine Diallo (Guinée), Lamine Guèye (Senegal), Gaston Monnerville (Guyane), Raset Ravoahangy (Madagascar), Lambert Saravane (Pondicherry, India), Léopold Senghor (Senegal), Fily-Dabo Sissoko (Soudan), Jean-Félix Tchicaya (Congo). Senghor, Assemblée nationale constituante, 3785–892. On the African deputies, see Guillemin, "Les Élus," 861–77. On these legislative deliberations, see Cooper, *Citizenship*.

72 Césaire, Assemblée nationale constituante, 18 septembre 1946, *JORF*, no. 94 (September 19, 1946), 3795.

73 Césaire, Assemblée nationale constituante, 3795.

74 Césaire, Assemblée nationale constituante, 3795.

75 Césaire, Assemblée nationale constituante, 3795.

76 Césaire, Assemblée nationale constituante, 3797.

77 Césaire, Assemblée nationale constituante, 3797.

78　Césaire, *Assemblée nationale constituante*, 3797.

79　Césaire, *Assemblée nationale constituante*, 3797.

80　Marshall interprets that October vote as a rejection of de Gaulle (*French Colonial Myth*, 151). On these deliberations, see Morgenthau, *Political Parties*, 41–54, and Lewis, "The MRP." Contemporary accounts include Devèze, *La France d'Outre-Mer*; Guèye, *Étapes et perspectives*; and Sissoko, *Coups de sagaie*. For de Gaulle's public addresses concerning the Fourth Republic, see de Gaulle, *Discours et messages*, 5–37.

81　Other currents of metropolitan public opinion supported a more progressive type of federal French Union. See, e.g., Delavignette, "L'Union française," 214–36; Durand et al., *L'Union française*; Alduy, *L'Union française*.

82　See also Crowder, "Independence as a Goal," 287.

83　*Constitution du 27 octobre 1946*.

84　*Constitution du 27 octobre 1946*.

85　Morgenthau, *Political Parties*, 50–53. On the political and legal structure of the French Union, see Deschamps, *L'Union française*.

86　*Constitution du 27 octobre 1946*.

87　Here the text was consistent with the Loi Lamine Guèye, passed on May 7, 1946, which declared all inhabitants of the overseas territories to be "citizens on the same basis as French nationals of the metropole" while allowing that future laws would specify how their citizenship rights could be exercised. Marshall, *French Colonial Myth*, 222. On this law, see Crowder, "Independence as a Goal," 287, and Cooper, *Decolonization*, 302–17.

88　For metropolitan discussions of the contradictions of colonial citizenship under the Fourth Republic, see Deschamps, *L'Union française*; Lampué, *L'Union française*; Lampué, *La citoyenneté*; Godineau, *L'Union française*; and Borella, *L'Évolution politique*. For more recent discussions of the October constitution, see Marshall, *French Colonial Myth*, 295–30; Morgenthau, *Political Parties*, 41–54; Coquery-Vidrovitch, "Nationalité et citoyenneté," 296–304; and Cooper, *Citizenship*. Morgenthau notes that African deputies were marginalized within the National Assembly, colonial questions were rarely addressed there, and most legislators did not attend the sessions in which they were.

89　These included the Territorial Assemblies law of February 6, 1952, the new Code du Travail passed on December 15, 1952, and the second Lamine Guèye law, equalizing earnings for overseas civil service workers. Morgenthau, *Political Parties*, 54–61; Cooper, *Decolonization*, 182–201, 277–322; Cooper, *Africa since 1940*, 40–49; Chafer, *End of Empire*, 56–67. Forced labor was prohibited, trade unions legalized, and wages and benefits for African civil servants were made equivalent to their metropolitan counterparts. Development assistance began to be channeled through FIDES. The *indigénat* legal code was abolished, rights of assembly and association were granted, and African representation on local assemblies was increased.

90　Morgenthau, *Political Parties*, 54–61.

91　Senghor, "Les négro-africains," 205–8.

92　Senghor, "Les négro-africains," 208.

93　Senghor, "Les négro-africains," 208.

94 Morgenthau, *Political Parties*, 145–53. Morgenthau describes the troubling alliance in the National Assembly of the BDS with the MRP, the very party that had opposed the more progressive constitution. See also Vaillant, *Black, French, and African*, 235–41.

95 Echenberg, " 'Morts pour la France,' " 3775–80; Cooper, " 'Our Strike,' " 81–118; Dewitte, "La CGT," 3–32.

96 Senghor, "Rapport sur la méthode, 1949," 53.

97 Senghor, "Rapport sur la méthode, 1949," 52.

98 Senghor, "Rapport sur la méthode, 1949," 52–53.

99 Senghor, "Rapport sur la méthode, 1949," 53.

100 Senghor, Assemblée nationale, 30 juin 1950, *JORF, Débats parlementaires, Assemblée Nationale*, no. 79, July 1, 1950, 5309.

101 Senghor, Assemblée nationale, 30 juin 1950, 5310.

102 Senghor, Assemblée nationale, 30 juin 1950, 5310. Senghor reminded the assembly that "the French economy, whether by law or in fact, is not limited only to the metropole, or even to the Republic."

103 Senghor, Assemblée nationale, 30 juin 1950, 5310.

104 See Senghor, Assemblée consultative du Conseil de l'Europe, 25 septembre 1952, reprinted in *Liberté 2*: 95–100.

105 Senghor, Assemblée nationale, 20 octobre 1953, *JORF*, no. 71, 4399.

106 Senghor, Assemblée nationale, 27 novembre 1950, *JORF*, no. 122, November 28, 1950, 8181–83. Senghor also maintained that because France signed the UN charter and the Universal Declaration of Human Rights, international law compelled it to protect overseas workers' rights. For his thoughts on the Code du travail in French West Africa, see Senghor, Assemblée nationale, 7 avril 1951, *JORF*, no. 50, 2909. See also Cooper, *Decolonization*, 182–201, 277–322.

107 See Senghor Assemblée consultative, 95–100.

108 Senghor, Assemblée nationale, 20 octobre 1953, 4401.

109 Senghor, Assemblée nationale, 18 novembre 1953, 5250.

110 Senghor maintained that because the constitution defined the Republic as "indivisible" and "democratic" and because it identified the overseas territories as "members of the Republic," to exclude these territories from any future European accord would be illegal. Senghor, Assemblée nationale, 18 novembre 1953, 5249.

111 Senghor, Assemblée nationale, 18 novembre 1953, 5249.

112 Senghor, Assemblée nationale, 18 novembre 1953, 5250.

113 Senghor, Assemblée nationale, 18 novembre 1953, 5250.

114 Senghor, "Rapport sur la méthode, 1953," 104–5. He referred to the fact that since 1946 Chandernagor had been "ceded" to India and Tonkin to Vietnam. On Indochina's movement from colony to the autonomous status of an "associated state" in 1946, see Devillers, "Indochine, Indonésie"; Shipway, "British Perceptions"; and Marr, *Vietnam 1945*. Senghor also criticizes the contradictory character of the constitution in "Pour une solution fédéraliste," 161, 164.

115 Senghor, "L'Avenir," 419–20.

116 Senghor, "L'Avenir," 420–22.

117 Senghor, "L'Avenir," 422.

118 In 1955 Tunisia and Morocco became autonomous states within the French Union
and politically independent in 1956. See Catroux, "France, Tunisia and Morocco,"
282–94; Balafrej, "Morocco Plans," 483–89; Julien, "Morocco," 199–211; Mitchell,
"Development of Nationalism," 427–34; Moore, *Tunisia since Independence*, 71–131;
Perkins, *History of Modern Tunisia*, 105–56; Pennell, *Morocco since 1830*, 268–96.

119 Senghor, "L'Avenir," 423.

120 Senghor, "Union française et fédéralisme," 197.

121 Senghor, "Union française et fédéralisme," 204.

122 Senghor, "Rapport sur la méthode, 1953," 105; "Union française et fédéralisme,"
203–9. Senghor insisted that a new constitution have language defining the republic as federal rather than indivisible (Senghor, "Pour une solution fédéraliste," 159).

123 Senghor, "Pour une solution fédéraliste," 159.

124 Senghor, "L'Avenir," 424. He proposed creating one federation comprising Senegal,
Mauritania, Soudan, and Guinée, with its capital in Dakar, and another comprising
Côte d'Ivoire, Haute-Volta, Niger, and Dahomey, with its capital in Abidjan.

125 Senghor, "L'Avenir," 423.

126 Senghor, "Pour une solution fédéraliste," 159. Senghor's federation would have thus
differed from the British Commonwealth model, essentially an economic confederation of independent states.

127 Senghor, "Pour une solution fédéraliste," 167.

128 Senghor, "Union française et fédéralisme," 205.

129 Senghor, "Union française et fédéralisme," 206.

130 Senghor, "Union française et fédéralisme," 206–7. Senghor explains that according
to the terms of federation, the metropole would have to subsidize overseas social
benefits such as family allocations and public education.

131 Senghor, "L'Avenir," 425.

132 Senghor, "L'Avenir," 425.

133 Senghor, "L'Avenir," 425.

134 Senghor, "L'Avenir," 426.

135 Morgenthau, *Politics Parties*, 61–71. On the resistance of the colonial administration
to citizenship provisions for overseas people, see Coquery-Vidrovitch, "Nationalité
et citoyenneté," 296–304.

136 Benot, *Les parlementaires Africains*, 155–59.

137 Morgenthau, *Politics Parties*, 44–48; Tyre, "From Algérie Française," 276–96.
For metropolitan discussions of federalism that raised questions about the
French Union, see Labouret, *Colonisation, colonialisme, décolonisation*; Jacqmin,
États-Unis de France; Rossillion, *Le régime législatif*; Mus, *Le Destin de l'Union
française*; Grenier, *L'Union française*; Fabre, "L'Union française"; Lavergne,
Problèmes africaines; Borella, *L'Évolution politique*. See also the issue devoted to
federalism of *Union française et parlement*, 7, no. 64 (July 1955), and the articles
from this period in *La Nouvelle Revue française d'outre-mer*. For examples of the
broader academic discourse on federalism from the fifties, see Walton, "Fate of
Neo-Federalism," 366–90; Macmahon, *Federalism*; Neumann, "Federalism and
Freedom"; Berger et al., *Le fédéralisme*; Brugmans and Duclos, *Le fédéralisme
contemporaine*.

138 Morgenthau, *Political Parties*, 66–74. She adds that this gesture toward African self-rule was criticized as violating the legal order of the Fourth Republic by dividing state sovereignty.

139 Atlan, "Senghor député."

140 See Morgenthau, *Political Parties*, 88–119, 301–29.

141 Senghor, "Union française et fédéralisme," 199. Cf. Shepard, *Invention of Decolonization*, 82–100. Whereas Shepard questions how decolonization as such was made to appear inevitable, I question the naturalized association between decolonization and national liberation.

142 Senghor, "Pour une solution fédéraliste," 159–61.

143 Senghor, "Union française et fédéralisme," 208.

144 Senghor, "Union française et fédéralisme," 203.

145 Senghor, "Pour une solution fédéraliste," 161.

146 Senghor, "Pour une solution fédéraliste," 169.

147 Senghor, "Union française et fédéralisme," 199.

148 Senghor, "Union française et fédéralisme," 202.

149 Senghor, "L'Eurafrique, unité économique de l'avenir," *Liberté 2*, 93.

150 Senghor, "Pour une solution fédéraliste," 161.

151 Senghor, "Union française et fédéralisme," 202.

152 Senghor, "Pour une solution fédéraliste," 161. He compares France, along with Egypt, India, and ancient Greece, to "a grafted tree."

153 Senghor, "Union française et fédéralisme," 202–3.

154 Senghor, "Union française et fédéralisme," 203.

155 Senghor, "Union française et fédéralisme," 203.

156 Senghor, "Union française et fédéralisme," 202.

157 Senghor, "Union française et fédéralisme," 202.

158 Senghor, "Union française et fédéralisme," 203.

159 See Senghor, *Liberté 3*, and *Liberté 5*.

160 Senghor, "Union française et fédéralisme," 203.

161 See Schuman, "Declaration of 9 May 1950."

162 For an imperial version of Eurafrique as a realpolitik attempt to prevent African secession and preserve French international stature with respect to the US and the USSR, see Nord, *L'Eurafrique*. For a history of the concept, see Liniger-Goumaz, *L'Eurafrique*. Eurafrique as a program for cultural symbiosis and postnational federation persisted into the 1970s. See the first publication of the Fraternité Eurafricaine, *Vers une nouvelle nation de l'être*. For historical discussions of the early debates around Eurafrique and the European Economic Community, see Gosnell, "France, Empire, Europe," 203–12, and Sicking, "Colonial Echo," 207–28.

163 Although the position of Senghor and the IOM was not purely instrumental, they allied on Eurafrique with their "realist" colleagues in the MRP, RPF, and Radical parties. Senghor participated in debates about a European community not only as a deputy in the National Assembly but as a French delegate to the European Consultative Assembly. See the recollections by Senghor's colleague Émile-Derlin Zinsou, then a senator, vice president of the Assembly of the French Union, and secretary general of the IOM group. Zinsou, "Il aura honoré," 68–69.

164 Senghor, Assemblée nationale, 30 juin 1950, reprinted in *Liberté* 2: 79. Senghor thus anticipated more recent arguments that French decolonization was motivated by a deliberate economic turn toward the European market and away from Africa; see Marseille, *Empire colonial*, and Cooper, *Decolonization*.

165 Sutton, *France and the Construction of Europe*, 52–62.

166 Senghor, Assemblée nationale, 17 janvier 1952, *JORF*, no. 2, January 18, 1952, 260. Senghor also suggested that Eurafrique would counterbalance the "Eurasian" Soviet bloc.

167 Senghor, Assemblée nationale, 17 janvier 1952, 260.

168 Senghor, Assemblée nationale, 17 janvier 1952, 160.

169 Senghor, "L'Afrique et l'Europe," 148.

170 Senghor, "L'Afrique et l'Europe," 148.

171 Diagne rightly argues that for Senghor "art is knowledge" and treats "African art as a philosophy in search of its expression." Diagne, "Bergson in the Colony," 131, 130, and *Léopold Sédar Senghor*.

172 Senghor, "L'Afrique et l'Europe," 149.

173 Senghor, "L'Afrique et l'Europe," 150.

174 Senghor, "L'Afrique et l'Europe," 150–51.

175 Senghor, "L'Afrique et l'Europe," 154.

176 Senghor, "L'Afrique et l'Europe," 154. Emphasis added.

177 Senghor, "L'Afrique et l'Europe," 155.

178 Senghor elaborated this distinction at the First International Congress of Black Writers and Artists in Paris in 1956: "Traditionally the Nègre is not devoid of reason as I am often accused of saying. But his reason is not discursive; it is synthetic. It is not antagonistic; it is sympathetic. It is another modality of knowledge" that transcends the opposition between subject and object. Senghor, "L'esprit de la civilisation," 52, 64.

179 Senghor, "L'Afrique et l'Europe," 155.

180 Senghor, "L'Afrique et l'Europe," 157.

181 Senghor, "L'Afrique et l'Europe," 157.

182 He began his talk at the First International Congress by asserting that "world Civilization .. will be the work of all or it will be nothing . . . each people, each race, each continent cultivates, with a particular direction, certain human virtues, in which resides precisely its originality." Senghor, "L'esprit de la civilisation," 51, 65.

183 Senghor, "L'Afrique et l'Europe," 148.

184 Senghor, "La décolonisation," 217.

185 Senghor, "La décolonisation," 216.

186 Senghor, "La décolonisation," 217–18.

187 Senghor, "La décolonisation," 217.

188 Senghor, "La décolonisation," 217.

189 Senghor, "La décolonisation," 216.

190 Senghor, "La décolonisation," 218.

191 Senghor, "La décolonisation," 217.

192 Senghor, "La décolonisation," 218, 219.

193 Senghor, "La décolonisation," 221.

194 Senghor, Assemblée nationale, 13 mai 1958, *JORF*, no. 46, May 14, 1958, 2266.

195 Senghor, Assemblée nationale, 13 mai 1958, 2266.

196 Marx writes about how cooperative labor within large-scale industry and the increasing centralization of capital created the conditions for elevated forms of socialized labor and social property. Marx, *Capital*, 929. He develops this thinking in 443–54, 476–77, 480–82, 486–91, 508, 530–32, 617–19, 635–39. Elsewhere he writes, "It is generally the fate of completely new historical creations to be mistaken for the counterpart of older and even defunct forms of social life, to which they may bear a certain likeness." *The Civil War in France*, 59. Cf. Benjamin's similar insight about "the world to come" in which "everything will be the same as here—only a little bit different." Benjamin, "In the Sun," 664.

197 Bloch, *Philosophy of the Future*, 91–92, and Harvey, *Spaces of Hope*, 182–98. See also Bloch and Adorno, "Something's Missing."

198 Marx, "To Make the World Philosophical," 9.

199 Would all organs and agents of colonial administration be abolished? Would the metropole stand for the federation as a whole? Would local autonomy function to exclude Africans from French national politics and effectively restrict their citizenship rights to the overseas territories?

200 Senghor's thinking resembles Proudhon's insofar as both insist on free consent as a condition of any federation and that a federation by definition must be republican. Senghor, like Proudhon, was concerned with political decentralization and regional autonomy; he insisted on local self-government and *autogestion*; he challenged the Jacobin tradition of unitary republicanism; he sought to relate political federalism to economic associationism through agricultural cooperatives of autonomous peasant producers. See Proudhon, *Du principe fédératif*. Senghorian federalism also resonated with a tradition of French legal sociology that joined *solidarisme* and federalism, including Léon Duguit, Louis Le Fur, and Georges Scelle. See Koskenniemi, *Gentle Civilizer*, 327–37. See also Kant, "Perpetual Peace"; Rossiter, ed., *Federalist Papers*; Kymlicka, "Federalism, Nationalism, and Multiculturalism."

201 E.g., Senghor voted to fund the Algerian war despite his stated opposition to it. He followed the Socialist Party directive not to attend the crucial 1947 Bamako Congress, in which the RDA was formed. He failed to take a public stand during the 1947 Dakar railway strike.

202 Cf. Amin, *Re-Reading the Postwar Period*; Habermas, "Post-national Constellation"; Balibar, *We the People of Europe?*; Rosanvallon, *Democracy Past and Future*; Cheah, *Inhuman Conditions*. For left critiques of federalism, see Laski, "Obsolescence of Federalism"; Neumann, "Federalism and Freedom"; Strachey, *Federalism or Socialism?*.

203 Camus, "Algeria 1958," 143–53; LeSeuer, *Uncivil War*, 55–74; Connelly, *Diplomatic Revolution*, 215–48; Shepard, *Invention of Decolonization*, 50–51, 234–35; Tyre, "From Algérie Française," 276–96.

CHAPTER 7. *Antillean Autonomy and the Legacy of Louverture*

1 Rice-Maximin, *Accommodation and Resistance*; Wall, "French Communists," 521–43. On the PCF belief that the Algerian people did not constitute a proper nation, see Shepard, *Invention of Decolonization*, 79–81.

2 Maurice Thorez, Secretary General of the PCF, famously affirmed that colonial peoples' right to self-determination did not entail an obligation to divorce. Pervillé, "La révolution algérienne," 55–66; Wall, "French Communists," 521–43.

3 Césaire, "La mort des colonies," 1366. Also published as Césaire, "Les Temps du régime colonial." Other speakers included Jean Amrouche, Alioune Diop, Daniel Guérin, Michel Leiris, André Mandouze, Moulay Merbah, Jean Rous, and Jean-Paul Sartre. For a discussion of the committee and event, see LeSueur, *Uncivil War*, 36–54.

4 Césaire, "La mort des colonies," 1368, 1369.

5 Césaire, "La mort des colonies," 1369–70.

6 Established in 1947, Présence Africaine explored many of the ideas first formulated by the Negritude cohort in the 1930s. See Mudimbe, *Surreptitious Speech*, and Jules-Rosette, *Black Paris*, 34–78.

7 Other notable presenters included Jacques Rabemananjara, Paul Hazoumé, Amadou Hampaté Ba, Franz Fanon, Louis T. Achille, Jacques Stéphen Alexis, Jean Price-Mars, G. Lamming, Cheikh Anta Diop, and Richard Wright.

8 Diop, "Discours d'ouverture," 12–13. This talk echoed many of the concerns of the programmatic essay he published in the inaugural issue of *Présence Africaine* a decade earlier. Alioune Diop, "Niam n'goura."

9 Diop, "Discours d'ouverture," 14–15, 17.

10 Diop, "Discours d'ouverture," 15.

11 Diop, "Discours d'ouverture," 14.

12 Césaire, "Culture et colonisation," 195–96. This essay should be read alongside similar interventions that also anticipated by decades the postcolonial critique of imperial knowledge, including Leiris, "L'ethnographe," 357–74, Balandier, "La situation coloniale," 44–79, Fanon, "Racisme et culture." It should also be read in relation to contemporary discussions of race sponsored by UNESCO. "Statement on Race, Paris, July 1950" and "Statement on the Nature of Race and Race Differences, Paris, June 1951," collected in *Four Statements on the Race Question*; also, *Race Question; Race Concept; Race Question in Modern Science*, which includes reprints of pamphlets published in the UNESCO series of the same title, including Lévi-Strauss, "Race et histoire"; Leiris, "Race et culture"; and Klineberg, "Race and Society." See also Leiris, *Race et civilisation*, and *Contacts de civilisations*.

13 Césaire, "Culture et colonisation," 196–97.

14 Césaire, "Culture et colonisation," 198, 199.

15 Césaire, "Culture et colonisation," 200.

16 Césaire, "Culture et colonisation," 202.

17 Césaire, "Culture et colonisation," 202.

18 Césaire, "Culture et colonisation," 202, 203.

19 Césaire, "Culture et colonisation," 204.

20 Césaire, "Culture et colonisation," 205.

21 Césaire, "Culture et colonisation," 205.

22 This perspective may help us understand Césaire's insistence on the structural resemblance between the predicament of colonized peoples and that of black Americans. His point was not that blacks were as foreign to the United States as Africans were to France but that black citizens of imperial France were as thoroughly

French as their US black counterparts were clearly American. This issue generated heated exchanges following Césaire's presentation. Mercer Cook and John Davis, Americans, and Louis Achille, from Martinique, challenged Césaire's contention that black Americans inhabited a colonial situation. Senghor supported Césaire on this point but disagreed with his claim that colonialism made true cultural *métissage* impossible. Césaire, "Culture et colonisation," 215–16.

23 Nicolas, *Histoire de la Martinique*, 166.

24 Nicolas, *Histoire de la Martinique*, 167–69.

25 Quoted in Moutoussamy, *Aimé Césaire*, 63.

26 Quoted in Moutoussamy, *Aimé Césaire*, 62.

27 Quoted in Moutoussamy, *Aimé Césaire*, 62.

28 Nicolas, *Histoire de la Martinique*, 169–70. On the events surrounding Césaire's resignation, including his 1953 trip to Moscow for Stalin's funeral, see Hale and Véron, "Aimé Césaire's Break," 47–55.

29 On Césaire's dispute with fellow communist intellectuals Louis Aragon and René Depestre over CP orthodoxy concerning "revolutionary" poetic forms and properly national poetry, which played out in the pages of *Présence Africaine*, see Arnold, *Modernism and Negritude*, 180–84, Césaire, "Sur la poésie nationale," Depestre, "Réponse à Aimé Césaire," 39–41, 42–62, and Césaire, "Réponse à Depestre." The latter is a poem that was published in revised form as "Le verbe maronner. À René Depestre, poète haïtien." *La Poésie*, 481–83. It is a rich source for thinking with Césaire about the (non-necessary) relationship between a given poetic form and radical politics.

30 Césaire, *Lettre à Maurice Thorez*, 14. According to Nicolas, Césaire wrote his letter of resignation on October 24, 1956, and it was published the following day in the Parisian weekly *France-Observateur*. Thorez wrote a reply to Césaire (October 25) in which he wondered why Césaire never communicated with him about his disaffection with the PCF. His colleagues in the Communist Federation of Martinique adopted a resolution on October 29 that expressed regret for Césaire's resignation and disagreement with his arguments against the party. Nicolas, *Histoire de la Martinique*, 169–72; Fonkoua, *Aimé Césaire*, 236–44.

31 Césaire, *Lettre à Maurice Thorez*, 12.

32 Césaire, *Lettre à Maurice Thorez*, 13.

33 Césaire, *Lettre à Maurice Thorez*, 14.

34 Césaire, *Lettre à Maurice Thorez*, 16.

35 Césaire, *Lettre à Maurice Thorez*, 15.

36 Césaire, *Lettre à Maurice Thorez*, 15.

37 Césaire, *Lettre à Maurice Thorez*, 16.

38 Césaire, *Lettre à Maurice Thorez*, 9.

39 For rare and valuable attempts to grapple directly with Césaire's radical universalism, see Nesbitt, "Incandescent I," and Constant, "Aimé Césaire et la politique."

40 On 1956 as a pivotal year for Césaire's political thought, see Daniel, "Aimé Césaire," 27–28; Hale and Véron, "Aimé Césaire's Break"; and Edwards, "Introduction," 115–25.

41 Guérin was a libertarian communist who became a militant anticolonial anarchist. He served with Césaire on the Comité d'Action des Intellectuels contre la Guerre. His book, which attributed deplorable Antillean social conditions to the neocolonial

arrangements created by departmentalization, concluded by proposing a pan-Caribbean federation. For an overview of his politics, see Berry, "'Un Contradicteur permanent.'"

42 Césaire, Introduction, 9.
43 Césaire, Introduction, 10.
44 Césaire, Introduction, 10.
45 Césaire, Introduction, 10.
46 Césaire, Introduction, 10.
47 Césaire, Introduction, 10.
48 Césaire, Introduction, 11.
49 Césaire, Introduction, 11.
50 Césaire, Introduction, 12.
51 Césaire, Introduction, 13.
52 Césaire, Introduction, 14. By insisting on the specificity of a hybrid Antillean history, language, and culture, Césaire anticipated the positions later developed, supposedly in contrast to his African-oriented negritude, by Edouard Glissant as *antillanité* and then Patrick Chamoiseau and Raphaël Confiant as *créolité*.
53 On Césaire's public dispute with the PCF and his Martinican communist colleagues, including summaries of Césaire's anti-Stalinist speech of November 22, 1956, at the Maison du Sport, see Hale and Véron, "Aimé Césaire's Break," 47–55, and Fonkoua, *Aimé Césaire*, 263–84. In a public pamphlet (November 4) Césaire declared, "It is true that I left the French Communist Party, but I remain no less aligned with the Martinican people and communists" Quoted in Fonkoua, *Aimé Césaire*, 278.
54 Nicolas, *Histoire de la Martinique*, 169–75.
55 Nicolas, *Histoire de la Martinique*, 176; Darsières, *Des origines*, 187–96.
56 Césaire served not only as deputy to the National Assembly but mayor of Fort-de-France, president of the Conseil Régional de la Martinique, and conseiller général de Fort-de-France.
57 See Miles, "Mitterand in the Caribbean," 63–79; Miles, *Elections and Ethnicity*; Constant, *La retraite aux flambeaux*; Burton, *Assimilation or Independence*.
58 Césaire, "Pour la transformation," 478.
59 Césaire, "Pour la transformation," 478.
60 Césaire, "Pour la transformation," 478.
61 Césaire, "Pour la transformation," 479, 480.
62 Césaire, "Pour la transformation," 483–84.
63 Césaire, "Pour la transformation," 482.
64 Césaire, "Pour la transformation," 482.
65 Césaire, "Pour la transformation," 483.
66 Césaire, "Pour la transformation," 484.
67 Césaire, "Pour la transformation," 487.
68 Césaire, "Pour la transformation," 487.
69 Césaire, "Pour la transformation," 487. Césaire here refers to the USA and the USSR and quotes Charles Durand, who coedited a volume of essays on federalism in 1956 along with Gaston Berger, the phenomenologist who influenced Senghor's political thinking in the late 1950s (Berger et al., *Le fédéralisme*).

70 Césaire, "Pour la transformation," 487.

71 Césaire, "Pour la transformation," 491.

72 Césaire, "Pour la transformation," 491.

73 Césaire, "Pour la transformation," 491.

74 Césaire, "Pour la transformation," 492.

75 Césaire, "Pour la transformation," 491–92. Here he refers to Senghor, Félix Houphouët-Boigny, Pierre Mendès France, François Mitterand, and René Pleven.

76 Césaire, "Pour la transformation," 492.

77 On the escalation of the war in 1956/57, see Stora, *Algeria 1830–2000*, 43–68.

78 The evolution of the Algerian war into a civil conflict repeated uncannily the Franco-French divisions during the Vichy period. Similarly, this constitutional crisis reprised the consequences of the 1939 act through which the National Assembly of the Third Republic divested itself of its constituted sovereignty and delivered state power to Pétain.

79 On the unconstitutional and antirepublican character of de Gaulle's emergency rule, see Shepard, *Invention of Decolonization*, 248–68.

80 Durand, "État unitaire."

81 Sylvestre, "Vers une République fédérale"; Césaire, "L'heure du choix"; "Les opiomanes du mensonge"; "De la constitution"; and "Une occasion manqué."

82 Aliker, "C'est le moment."

83 Césaire, "L'heure du choix."

84 Césaire, "Relire Schoelcher," 1.

85 Césaire, "Les opiomanes du mensonge."

86 Césaire, "De la constitution."

87 Césaire, "Une occasion manqué."

88 Césaire, "Une occasion manqué."

89 Césaire, "Une occasion manqué." Césaire was equally concerned about article 72, which risked re-creating the gubernatorial rule of the colonial epoch.

90 Césaire, "Imaginer ou mourir," 1.

91 Darsières, *Des origines*, 197.

92 Darsières, *Des origines*, 198.

93 "Un meeting historique."

94 Nicolas, *Histoire de la Martinique*, 178–79, and Fonkoua, *Aimé Césaire*, 306–11.

95 Rimbaud, "Farewell," 242–43. "Sometimes in the sky I see endless sandy shores covered with white rejoicing nations . . . I was the creator of every feast, every triumph, every drama. I tried to invent new flowers, new planets, new flesh, new languages. I thought I had acquired supernatural powers. Ha! I have to bury my imagination and my memories! What an end to a splendid career as an artist and storyteller! / I! I called myself a magician . . . I am sent back to the soil to seek some obligation, to wrap gnarled reality in my arms! [. . .] True, the new era is nothing if not harsh. [. . .] Never mind hymns of thanksgiving: hold on to a step once taken. [. . .] And at dawn, armed with glowing patience, we will enter the cities of glory."

96 Césaire, "Tenir le pas gagné," 1.

97 Darsières, *Des origines*, 198–201.

98 Constitution, Oct. 4 1958.

99 Moutoussamy, *Aimé Césaire*, 68.

100 Campaign flyer, reprinted in Moutoussamy, *Aimé Césaire*, 69.

101 Moutoussamy, *Aimé Césaire*, 69–70.

102 Nicolas, *Histoire de la Martinique*, 179.

103 Nicolas, *Histoire de la Martinique*, 180–92, and Placide, *Les émeutes de décembre 1959*.

104 Césaire, "L'Homme de culture," 116.

105 Césaire, "L'Homme de culture," 117.

106 Césaire, "L'Homme de culture," 119.

107 Césaire, "L'Homme de culture," 119.

108 Césaire, "L'Homme de culture," 121.

109 Césaire, "L'Homme de culture," 121.

110 Césaire, "L'Homme de culture," 121.

111 Césaire, "L'Homme de culture," 121.

112 Césaire, "L'Homme de culture," 121.

113 Césaire, "L'Homme de culture," 121–22.

114 Césaire, "L'Homme de culture," 121–22.

115 Césaire, "L'Homme de culture," 122.

116 On Louis Delgrès and abolition in Guadeloupe, see Dubois, *Colony of Citizens*. On the memory of Delgrès, see Dubois, "Haunting Delgrès," and Nesbitt, *Voicing Memory*, 49–75. For a synoptic history of the Haitian Revolution, see Dubois, *Avengers of the New World*.

117 Césaire, "Memorial for Louis Delgrès," 330 (I have modified this translation in places).

118 Césaire, "Memorial for Louis Delgrès," 333.

119 Césaire, "Memorial for Louis Delgrès," 332.

120 "Parage," *Oxford English Dictionary Online*, www.oed.com.

121 Césaire, "Memorial for Louis Delgrès," 335.

122 Senghor frequently employed the trope of "grafting" in his criticism and poetry about politics and culture under imperial conditions.

123 Césaire, "Memorial for Louis Delgrès," 337.

124 Césaire, "Memorial for Louis Delgrès," 335.

125 Césaire, "Memorial for Louis Delgrès," 337.

126 Césaire, *Et les chiens*.

127 Césaire, "Relire Schoelcher," 1.

128 Césaire, "Relire Schoelcher," 1.

129 Césaire, "Relire Schoelcher," 1.

130 On "colonial democracy" in Martinique under the Third Republic, see Constant, *La retraite aux flambeaux*, 27–66.

131 See Schoelcher, *Colonies étrangères*.

132 Schoelcher, *Conférence sur Toussaint Louverture*. Following the talk, Ernest Legouvé, one of the organizers, presented a celebratory summary of Schoelcher's role in the 1848 abolition of slavery, concluding with the proposal that he now be called "Schoelcher Louverture" (51).

133 Schoelcher, *Vie de Toussaint Louverture*.

134 Schoelcher, *Vie de Toussaint Louverture*, 297.

135 Toumson and Henry-Valmore, *Aimé Césaire*, 95–97.

136 Césaire, *Nègre je suis*, 56.

137 Alex Gil has discovered an existing copy of this lost play which he analyzes in Gil, "La découverte de l'Ur-texte," 145–56

138 Quoted in Véron, "Césaire at the Crossroads," 437, 441.

139 Césaire, *Toussaint Louverture*.

140 James, *Black Jacobins*, 190–240; Dubois, *Avengers of the New World*, 194–242.

141 On Toussaint's modern state apparatus, see James, *Black Jacobins*, 241–63. On his strict labor regulations, see Dubois, *Avengers of the New World*, 239–40.

142 Titre Premier, Article 6, Constitution du 5 Fructidor an III (22 août 1795), www .assemblee-nationale.fr/histoire/constitutions/constitution-de-1795-an3.asp.

143 Article 91, Constitution du 22 Frimaire an VIII (13 décembre 1799), www.assem-blee-nationale.fr/histoire/constitutions/constitution-de-1-an-8.asp.

144 No ex-slaves were included in the assembly. See James, *Black Jacobians*, 262, and Dubois, *Avengers of the New World*, 242.

145 Dubois, *Avengers of the New World*, 240–42.

146 Quoted in Schoelcher, *Vie de Toussaint Louverture*, 299.

147 Quoted in Schoelcher, *Vie de Toussaint Louverture*, 300.

148 "Haitian Constitution of 1801," 46.

149 "Haitian Constitution of 1801," 46–47.

150 "Haitian Constitution of 1801," 49.

151 "Haitian Constitution of 1801," 51.

152 "Haitian Constitution of 1801," 47, 59.

153 "Haitian Constitution of 1801," 48.

154 "Haitian Constitution of 1801," 60.

155 Schoelcher, *Vie de Toussaint Louverture*, 293.

156 "Haitian Constitution of 1801," 46.

157 "Haitian Constitution of 1801," 46.

158 "Haitian Constitution of 1801," 60–61.

159 Schoelcher, *La vie de Toussaint Louverture*, 299.

160 Schoelcher, *Vie de Toussaint Louverture*, 300.

161 Césaire, *Toussaint Louverture*, 282.

162 Quoted in Schoelcher, *Vie de Toussaint Louverture*, 303–4.

163 Schoelcher, *Vie de Toussaint Louverture*, 317.

164 Schoelcher, *Vie de Toussaint Louverture*, 317–18.

165 Schoelcher, *Vie de Toussaint Louverture*, 317.

166 Schoelcher, *Vie de Toussaint Louverture*, 317.

167 Schoelcher, *Vie de Toussaint Louverture*, 301.

168 Quoted in James, *Black Jacobins*, 280–81.

169 On Toussaint as a "hero of correspondence," see Jenson, "Toussaint Louverture," 45–80.

170 Dubois, *Avengers of the New World*, 253–61.

171 Quoted in Césaire, *Toussaint Louverture*, 295.

172 Césaire, *Toussaint Louverture*, 325–31; James, *Black Jacobins*, 324–29.

173 James, *Black Jacobins*, 213.

174 James, *Black Jacobins*, 291. On James's view of Toussaint as a tragic figure, see Scott, *Conscripts of Modernity*, 132–78.

175 James, *Black Jacobins*, 291.

176 James, *Black Jacobins*, 282–92, 310.

177 James, *Black Jacobins*, 291, 290.

178 James, *Black Jacobins*, 321.

179 James, *Black Jacobins*, 325.

180 Césaire, *Toussaint Louverture*, 305.

181 James, *Black Jacobins*, 313.

182 James, *Black Jacobins*, 345.

183 James, *Black Jacobins*, 250.

184 This reading of Louverture's politics is based in part on his own writings, which are generously excerpted in Schoelcher, *Vie de Toussaint Louverture*; Césaire, *Toussaint Louverture*; and Tyson, *Toussaint L'Ouverture*. It is also indebted to James, *Black Jacobins*; Blackburn, *Overthrow of Colonial Slavery*; Fick, *Making of Haiti*; Geggus, *Haitian Revolutionary Studies*; and Dubois, *Avengers of the New World*.

185 Scholars have generally been more concerned with explaining Louverture's despotism than with examining the particular political vision expressed in his constitutional act. The latter has typically been understood as a de facto declaration of independence, an attempt to buy time until such a declaration could be made, or a missed opportunity to do so properly. For notable exceptions, see Moïse, *Le projet national*, Dubois, *Avengers of the New World*, and Dubois, "Louverture," which argues persuasively that Louverture chose not to declare independence. On Toussaint's insistence that the people of Saint-Domingue retain French nationality, see Gaffield, "Complexities of Imagining Haiti," 81–103. On Toussaint's commitment to postracial universalism, see Nesbitt, *Universal Emancipation*.

186 See Dubois, *Avengers of the New World*, 251–79.

187 Dubois, *Avengers of the New World*, 251–301.

188 Schoelcher, *Vie de Toussaint Louverture*; Dubois, *Avengers of the New World*.

189 Césaire, *Toussaint Louverture*, 279, 283.

190 This proliferation of discourse must be recalled as a counterpoint to Michel Rolph Trouillot's influential argument about the later unthinkability of the Haitian Revolution in *Silencing the Past*. See Forsdick, "Situating Haiti," 17–34.

191 Such anxious warnings of Antillean revolutions that would come unless slavery were abolished extend back to prerevolutionary Saint-Domingue in the writings of Louis Sebastien Mercier and the Abbé Raynal. See Dubois, *Avengers of the New World*, 57–59. Césaire was also evoking a tradition of successive uprisings, unrest, and strikes in Martinique extending from the 1820s to the 1960s. See Adélaide-Merlande, *Les origines*.

192 For other interpretations of how Césaire reflected on his own situation by writing about Toussaint, see Hurley, "Is he, am I, a hero?" 113–33, and Walsh, "Césaire reads Toussaint Louverture," 110–24.

193 Césaire made similar points about the lifelong struggles and repeated setbacks of Grégoire and Schoelcher. See Césaire, "Discours d'inauguration."

194 Moutoussamy, *Aimé Césaire*, 74.

195 Reprinted in Moutoussamy, *Aimé Césaire*, 74.

196 Moutoussamy, *Aimé Césaire*, 75.

197 Moutoussamy, *Aimé Césaire*, 75.

198 Moutoussamy, *Aimé Césaire*, 76.

199 Moutoussamy, *Aimé Césaire*, 76.

200 Moutoussamy, *Aimé Césaire*, 76.

201 Moutoussamy, *Aimé Césaire*, 77.

202 Moutoussamy, *Aimé Césaire*, 80.

203 Nicolas, *Histoire de la Martinique*, 192–99. On February 14, 1960, the PCM drafted a plan to re-create Martinique as an autonomous federated territory of the French republic.

204 Nicolas, *Histoire de la Martinique*, 198.

205 Nicolas, *Histoire de la Martinique*, 200–206.

206 Nicolas, *Histoire de la Martinique*, 199, 206–13.

207 Césaire, "Crise dans les départements d'Outre-Mer," 109.

208 Césaire, "Crise dans les départements d'Outre-Mer," 109.

209 Césaire, "Crise dans les départements d'Outre-Mer," 109.

210 Césaire, "Crise dans les départements d'Outre-Mer," 110, 111.

211 Césaire, "Crise dans les départements d'Outre-Mer," 111.

212 Césaire, "Crise dans les départements d'Outre-Mer," 111.

213 Reprinted in Moutoussamy, *Aimé Césaire*, 81.

214 Césaire, "Crise dans les départements d'Outre-Mer," 86.

215 Césaire, "Crise dans les départements d'Outre-Mer," 96.

216 Césaire, *Toussaint Louverture*, 32.

217 Césaire, Interview with Nicole Zand. Quoted in Ngal, *Aimé Césaire*, 248.

218 Césaire, *La tragédie du roi Christophe*.

219 Dubois, *Haiti*, 52–88.

220 Césaire, "Aimé Césaire crée un Faust africain," 25–26. Quoted in Toumson and Henry-Valmore, *Aimé Césaire*, 235.

221 G. De Préville, "Entretien avec Aimé Césaire," Club des Lecteurs d'expression française, Bulletin no. 3 (Nov.–Dec. 1964), quoted in Ngal, *Aimé Césaire*, 347.

222 On the production history, see Toumson and Henry-Valmore, *Aimé Césaire*, 234–36.

223 Césaire, *Une saison au Congo*.

224 See De Witte, *Assassination of Lumumba*.

225 Toumson and Henry-Valmore, *Aimé Césaire*, 234–36.

226 Césaire, Interview with Nicole Zand. Quoted in Ngal, *Aimé Césaire*, 250.

227 By enacting and meditating on the interpenetration of historical epochs, these plays resonate with Edouard Glissant's later call for a "prophetic vision of the past" in his 1961 play organized around "the simultaneity of the two time frames in which Toussaint lives" and marked by "the equivalence of past and present" (preface to the 1st ed. of Glissant, *Monsieur Toussaint*, 15, 16).

228 Rancière, "The Paradoxes of Political Art." This is why Dash, while right to insist on the nonreferentiality of Césaire's poetry and his resistance to creating message-based political work, is mistaken to question its status as political. Dash, "Aimé Césaire," 737–42.

CHAPTER 8. *African Socialism and the Fate of the World*

1 On Senghor's African socialism as a party or state ideology, see Andrain, "Guinea and Senegal"; LeMelle, "Return to Senghor's Theme," 330–43; Skurnik, "Léopold Sédar Senghor," 349–69; Hazard, "Negritude," 778–809; Markovitz, *Léopold Sédar Senghor*; Cox and Kessler, "Après Senghor," 327–42; Vaillant, *Black, French, and African*. On African socialism as a project for Africa to "realize itself without denying itself," which would be "Negritude's contribution to planetary humanism," see Thomas, *Le socialisme et l'Afrique*. For attempts to relate African socialism to socioeconomic conditions after independence, see Wallerstein, "Elites in French-Speaking West Africa," 1–33, and Arrighi and Saul, "Socialism and Economic Development," 141–69.

2 Cf. Diouf, "Assimilation coloniale," 565–87, and "Les Quatre Communes, 135–56; Coquery-Vidrovitch, "Nationalité et citoyenneté," 285–305.

3 Senghor, Lettre à Guy Mollet, 47, 49.

4 Senghor, Lettre à Guy Mollet, 50. On Senghor's resignation, see Morgenthau, *Political Parties*, 127–45, and Vaillant, *Black, French, and African*, 222–35.

5 Senghor, 'Lettre à Guy Mollet," 50.

6 On the formation of the BDS, see Dia, *Mémoires*, 9–62, and *Afrique*, 11–91. On Dia and N'Daw, see Vaillant, *Black, French, and African*, 187–88, 222–28.

7 Morgenthau, *Political Parties*, 145–53. On Dia and the BDS newspaper *Condition Humaine*, see Vaillant, *Black, French, and African*, 224–28.

8 Vaillant, *Black, French, and African*, 228, 301–2.

9 "Mamadou Dia."

10 See Dia, "Notre dette," 68–69. On cooperative development, see Perroux, *La Coexistence pacifique*; *Autarcie et expansion*; and *Communauté et société*. Perroux was a contradictory figure who supported the Vichy regime during the war and later supervised Samir Amin's economics thesis on capitalist polarization on a world scale (Amin, *Life Looking Forward*). Equally influential was the work of Louis Joseph Lebret, the Dominican priest and development economist. Lebret was commissioned by Senghor and Dia to design humanist development planning initiatives for Senegal after independence. Diouf, "Senegalese Development." On Lebret's formulations of "integrated" and harmonized" development through "human economy," see his talks republished in Becker, *Le père Lebret*, as well as Malley, *Le père Lebret*.

11 Dia outlined his program for rural cooperatives in *Condition Humaine*; e.g., Dia, "La Révolution Économique au Sénégal," 1–2; "La Révolution Économique," 1; "L'offensive," 1; and "Les Coopératives Vivront," 3–4. For overviews of his vision of African socialism, see Dia, *Réflexions*; *Contribution à l'étude*; and *L'Économie africaine*. For Dia's role in Senegalese nation building and economic development, see Diouf, "Léopold Sédar Senghor," 171–89. See also Diouf, "Senegalese Development," and Diop, *Le Sénégal à l'heure*, 20–49.

12 These ideas are summarized in Dia, *Nations africaines*.

13 Morgenthau, *Political Parties*, 145–53; Vaillant, *Black, French, and African*, 235–41; Boone, *Political Topographies*, 46–67. See O'Brien, *Mourides of Senegal*.

14 Senghor offered private but not public support to the 1947 railway strike in French West Africa yet instrumentalized and thereby domesticated it partly by incorpo-

rating the more radical syndicalist leader Ibrahima Sarr into the BDS party. See Cooper, " 'Our Strike.' "

15 Senghor, Rapport sur la méthode, VIe, 125.

16 Senghor, Rapport sur la méthode, VIe, 125.

17 Senghor describes his social, economic, and political legislative activities and plans between 1946 and 1956 in "Sénégal (1951)," and "Sénégal (1956)." On his efforts to pass the Code du Travail, see Cooper, *Decolonization*, 277–322. Senghor used *Condition Humaine* to update his constituency on his legislative efforts in Paris and his policy proposals for education and health reform, veterans' pensions, agricultural production, development funds, and electoral rules for colonial representation in the National Assembly. E.g., Senghor, "La Condition de Notre Évolution," 1–2; "Actions parlementaires," 2; "Questions écrites," 2; "Le Problème de l'Arachide," 1; "Le problème du F.I.D.E.S.," 1; "Le Reclassement," 1–2; "La S.F.I.O.," 1–2.

18 Senghor, Rapport sur la méthode, VIe, 140.

19 Senghor, Rapport sur la méthode, VIe, 140.

20 Senghor, Rapport sur la méthode, VIe, 140.

21 Senghor, Rapport sur la méthode, VIe, 136–37.

22 Senghor, Rapport sur la méthode, VIe, 138.

23 Senghor recounts that after being elected to the National Assembly, in the library of the Palais Bourbon, he began to read Marx's early works, followed by those of Lenin, Henri Lefebvre, the utopian socialists, Jean Jaurès, Léon Blum, Mao Tse-tung, and Gandhi. Senghor, *La poésie de l'action*, 11–12, 131, 132, 138, 210.

24 It appeared in the same journal that published extracts on alienated labor from Marx's newly discovered 1844 Manuscripts. Marx, "Le travail aliéné," 154–68. On the importance of Marx's early writings for postwar French Marxism, see Judt, *Marxism and the French Left*, 169–98. A piece by Senghor on African socialism was included in Fromm, *Socialist Humanism*. It should be compared with contemporaries in that volume, Goldmann, "Socialism and Humanism"; Marcuse, "Socialist Humanism?"; Schaff, "Marxism," 40–52, 107–17, 141–50. Cf. Lefebvre, *Critique of Everyday Life*, and Merleau-Ponty, *Humanisme et terreur*.

25 Senghor, "Marxisme et humanisme," 29–44.

26 Senghor, "Marxisme et humanisme," 37.

27 Senghor, "Marxisme et humanisme," 42.

28 Senghor, "Marxisme et humanisme," 43.

29 Senghor, Rapport sur la méthode, IIe, 67–68.

30 Senghor, "Le népotisme," 72.

31 Jacques Maritain, quoted in Senghor, "Marxisme et humanisme," 29–30. See Maritain, *Humanisme intégral*; *Principes d'une politique humaniste*; *La Personne et le bien commun*. Cf. Mounier, *Le Personnalisme*. After the war Maritain sought to link his vision of freedom to a "world political society" and "world government" (*L'homme et l'état*).

32 Senghor, "Marxisme et humanisme," 44.

33 As he later wrote, "The problem for socialism today is less to abolish class inequalities than the inequalities that exist between nations, between wealthy and proletarian peoples, 'developed' and 'developing' countries . . . that is where there is true exploitation of man by man." Senghor, *La poésie de l'action*, 219.

34 Senghor, Rapport sur la méthode, Ière, 57, and Rapport sur la méthode, v^e, 102–3. This debatable claim about the absence of classes was not simply a statement about traditional African social formations but about the structure of colonial social relations. For similar claims by other African socialists, including Sékou Touré and Kwame Nkrumah, see Friedland and Rosberg, *African Socialism*. Senghor felt more sympathetic to Nyerere's cooperativist vision of African socialism than to Sékou Touré's statist version. Senghor, *La poésie de l'action*, 209–12. See Touré, *L'Action du Parti Démocratique*, and *Expérience guinéene*; Nyerere, *Ujamaa*. Cf. Nkrumah, *Building a Socialist State*; *Consciencism*; and *Some Aspects of Socialism*; Mboya, "African Socialism," and *Freedom and After*, 164–78.

35 Senghor, "Naissance du Bloc," 56.

36 Senghor, "Naissance du Bloc," 137–38.

37 Senghor, "La conscience," 126–34. Senghor here describes the system of economic exploitation to which Senegal remained subject. On the *pacte coloniale* and the *économie de traite* in French Africa, see Suret-Canale, *L'Afrique noire*; Coquery-Vidrovitch, *Le Congo*; Amin, *Neo-Colonialism*, 3–33. See also Hodeir, "Grand patronat colonial français," 223–44.

38 Senghor, "La conscience," 135.

39 Senghor, "Marxisme et humanisme," 35.

40 Senghor, "Naissance du Bloc," 59.

41 Senghor, "Socialisme, fédération, religion," 106. See also Senghor, "L'esprit de la civilization," 65.

42 Senghor, "Marxisme et humanisme," 33, "Naissance du Bloc," 57–58, and "Socialisme, fédération, religion," 101.

43 Senghor, "Socialisme, fédération, religion," 102.

44 Senghor, "Socialisme, fédération, religion," 106.

45 Senghor, "Marxisme et humanisme," 35.

46 Senghor, "Le népotisme," 72.

47 Senghor, "Le népotisme," 72.

48 Senghor, "Socialisme, fédération, religion," 106–7. He maintained a distinction between *laïcité*, the secularism supported by Jules Ferry, which promoted neutrality and respect for all beliefs, and *laïcisme*, which Senghor defined as a doctrinaire hypersecularism that opposed all religion. Senghor, "Naissance du Bloc," 59.

49 Senghor, "Le népotisme," 72.

50 Senghor, "Le népotisme," 72.

51 Senghor, "Socialisme, fédération, religion," 107.

52 Senghor, "La conscience," 137.

53 Senghor, "Le népotisme," 68–70.

54 Senghor, "Socialisme, fédération, religion," 108.

55 See Adorno, *Negative Dialectics*.

56 Senghor's attempted to link religion and politics paralleled efforts by Benjamin, Bloch, and Adorno to reconcile Marxism and messianism but with less of a ruptural revolutionary charge. See Löwy, "Jewish Messianism," 105–15, and Rabinbach, "Between Apocalypse and Enlightenment." Senghor's African socialism might also be compared fruitfully with Cornel West's "prophetic pragmatism"; West, *American Evasion of Philos-*

ophy. These approaches to the dialectic of religion and politics differ markedly from the apolitical forms of political theology in interwar central Europe, which in many ways find their heirs in Levinas and Derrida. Gordon, "Concept of the Apolitical," 855–78.

57 Senghor, "La conscience," 141,
58 Senghor, "La conscience," 141, 137.
59 Senghor, "La conscience," 137–38.
60 Senghor, "La conscience," 140.
61 Proudhon, *Du principe fédératif.*
62 Senghor, "La conscience," 140.
63 Senghor, "Socialisme, fédération, religion," 109.
64 My emphasis. Senghor, "Socialisme, fédération, religion," 106.
65 Senghor, "Socialisme, fédération, religion," 106.
66 Cf. Marx, "On the Jewish Question." Whereas Bruno Bauer developed a critique of religious emancipation from the standpoint of political emancipation, Marx developed a critique of political emancipation from the standpoint of human emancipation.
67 Senghor, "La conscience," 135.
68 Senghor, "La conscience," 141.
69 Senghor, "Le népotisme," 71.
70 Senghor, "Le népotisme," 71–72.
71 Senghor, "Socialisme, fédération, religion," 107. He draws these terms from the Italian communist Remo Cantoni, who published an essay in *Esprit*, June 1948.
72 Senghor, Rapport sur la méthode, VIIIe, 189.
73 Senghor, "La conscience," 136.
74 Senghor, "Socialisme et culture," 184.
75 Senghor, "Socialisme et culture," 185.
76 Senghor, "Socialisme et culture," 190–91. He identifies "rhythmic images" as the means through which black art expresses social reality and collective spirit in a nonrealist fashion.
77 Senghor, "Socialisme et culture," 196. In 1956 he wrote, "We have seen that the spirit of Negro-African civilization *incarnates* itself in the most quotidian reality. But it always transcends it in order to express the meaning (*sens*) of the world." Senghor, "L'esprit de la civilization," 65.
78 Senghor, "L'Afrique et l'Europe," 154.
79 Senghor, "L'Afrique et l'Europe," 154.
80 Senghor, "La conscience," 141.
81 Tony Chafer describes how this system transformed territorial assemblies from representative organs through which Africans could make demands on the French state to targets of demands that they had neither the resources nor power to meet. This created a dilemma for African leaders, who could either maintain salaries and working conditions at metropolitan levels, which they could no longer afford to do and which would divert funds from rural development initiatives, or risk alienating their urban and trade-union supporters. Chafer, *The End of Empire*, 165–72. See also Morgenthau, *French Political Parties*, 65–73.
82 The French state grouped its west and central African colonies into separate administrative "federations."

83 On this conflict, see Morgenthau, *Political Parties*, 301–8, Chafer, *End of Empire*, 208–11. See Kipré, *Le Congrès de Bamako*.

84 Morgenthau, *Political Parties*, 153–61; Boone, *Political Topographies*, 60–67.

85 Morgenthau, *Political Parties*, 161–62.

86 Morgenthau, *Political Parties*, 162–64, Chafer, *End of Empire*, 174–79.

87 Article 77, Constitution du 4 octobre 1958.

88 Article 78, Constitution du 4 octobre 1958.

89 Article 77, Constitution du 4 octobre 1958.

90 Article 73, Constitution du 4 octobre 1958.

91 Article 74, Constitution du 4 octobre 1958.

92 Under the new community, overseas territories would no longer send deputies to the French National Assembly. Chafer, *End of Empire*, 174–80, 187.

93 Morgenthau, *Political Parties*, 311.

94 Senghor, "Le Référendum en Afrique Noire," 227.

95 Constitution du 4 octobre 1958.

96 Senghor, "Le Référendum en Afrique Noire," 228.

97 Senghor, "Le Référendum en Afrique Noire," 225.

98 Senghor, "Le Référendum en Afrique Noire," 225.

99 Senghor, "Le Référendum en Afrique Noire," 231.

100 Senghor, "Le Référendum en Afrique Noire," 226.

101 Senghor, "Le Référendum en Afrique Noire," 226.

102 Senghor, *Rapport sur la doctrine*, 8.

103 Senghor, "Balkanization ou fédération," 180–83. Morgenthau argues that Senegal had a material interest in federation (maintaining the port of Dakar, keeping the Dakar–Bamako railroad profitable) while Houphouët-Boigny's antifederalism was motivated partly by the fear that a relatively wealthy Côte d'Ivoire would have to subsidize poorer member states. Morgenthau, *Political Parties*, 164, 321.

104 See Snyder, "Political Thought of Modibo Keita," 79–106.

105 Chafer, *End of Empire*, 183–85, and Morgenthau, *Political Parties*, 313–14. On the Mali Federation, see Dia, *African Nations*, 106–32, Foltz, *From French West Africa*, and Cissoko, *Un combat pour l'unité*.

106 Senghor, *Rapport sur la doctrine*, 17.

107 Senghor, *Rapport sur la doctrine*, 17.

108 Senghor, *Rapport sur la doctrine*, 18–19.

109 Senghor, *Rapport sur la doctrine*, 72.

110 Senghor, *Rapport sur la doctrine*, 18.

111 Senghor, *Rapport sur la doctrine*, 72.

112 Senghor, *Rapport sur la doctrine*, 88.

113 Quoted in Senghor, *Rapport sur la doctrine*, 88–89.

114 Senghor, *Rapport sur la doctrine*, 74.

115 Senghor, *Rapport sur la doctrine*, 87.

116 Cf. Balandier, *Le Tiers-Monde*.

117 Senghor, *Rapport sur la doctrine*, 27.

118 Quoted in Senghor, *Rapport sur la doctrine*, 88.

119 Senghor, *Rapport sur la doctrine*, 26.

120 Senghor, *Rapport sur la doctrine*, 26.
121 Senghor, *Rapport sur la doctrine*, 27.
122 Senghor, *Rapport sur la doctrine*, 89, 28.
123 Senghor, *Rapport sur la doctrine*, 89.
124 Senghor, *Rapport sur la doctrine*, 89.
125 Senghor, *Rapport sur la doctrine*, 89–90.
126 Senghor, *Rapport sur la doctrine*, 29.
127 Senghor, *Rapport sur la doctrine*, 28.
128 Senghor, *Rapport sur la doctrine*, 36.
129 Senghor, *Rapport sur la doctrine*, 46.
130 Senghor, *Rapport sur la doctrine*, 33.
131 Senghor, *Rapport sur la doctrine*, 41.
132 Senghor, *Rapport sur la doctrine*, 50.
133 Senghor, *Rapport sur la doctrine*, 43–44.
134 Senghor, *Rapport sur la doctrine*, 49
135 Senghor, *Rapport sur la doctrine*, 47. In this report Senghor cites contemporary thinkers who had developed noneconomistic readings of Marx, including Henri Lefebvre, Lucien Goldmann, Pierre Bigo, André Vène, Karl Kautsky, Jean-Paul Sartre, and Georg Lukács.
136 Senghor, *Rapport sur la doctrine*, 36.
137 Senghor, *Rapport sur la doctrine*, 51.
138 Senghor, *Rapport sur la doctrine*, 37.
139 Senghor, *Rapport sur la doctrine*, 50.
140 Senghor, *Rapport sur la doctrine*, 43
141 Senghor, *Rapport sur la doctrine*, 56.
142 Senghor, *Rapport sur la doctrine*, 56–57.
143 Senghor, *Rapport sur la doctrine*, 61.
144 Senghor, *Rapport sur la doctrine*, 57.
145 Senghor, *Rapport sur la doctrine*, 58.
146 Senghor, *Rapport sur la doctrine*, 59.
147 Quoted in Senghor, *Rapport sur la doctrine*, 63. See Teilhard de Chardin, *Le Phénomène humain*, and *L'Avenir de l'homme*.
148 Senghor, *Rapport sur la doctrine*, 63.
149 Senghor, *Rapport sur la doctrine*, 59.
150 Senghor, *Rapport sur la doctrine*, 64.
151 Senghor, *Rapport sur la doctrine*, 64.
152 Senghor, *Rapport sur la doctrine*, 64.
153 Senghor, *Rapport sur la doctrine*, 65.
154 Senghor, *Rapport sur la doctrine*, 46.
155 Senghor, *Rapport sur la doctrine*, 66.
156 Senghor, *Rapport sur la doctrine*, 67.
157 Senghor, *Rapport sur la doctrine*, 69.
158 Senghor, "Éléments constructifs," 250.
159 Senghor, "Éléments constructifs," 275.
160 Senghor, "Éléments constructifs," 276.

161 Senghor, "Éléments constructifs," 276.
162 Senghor, "Éléments constructifs," 277.
163 Senghor, "Éléments constructifs," 279.
164 Senghor, *Théorie et pratique*, 34.
165 Senghor, "La voie africaine du socialism," 96–100.
166 Senghor, "La voie africaine du socialism," 108
167 Senghor, "La voie africaine du socialism," 108.
168 Senghor, "La voie africaine du socialism," 104, 112, 105.
169 Senghor, "La voie africaine du socialism," 122. Cf. Bachelard, *Le nouvel esprit philosophique*.
170 For Senghor's engagement with currents of European modernist, vitalist, and phenomenological thinking, see Senghor "Négritude et modernité," 215–42; "La révolution de 1889 et Leo Frobenius"; "Pierre Teilhard de Chardin"; and "Gaston Berger." See also Hymans, *Léopold Sédar Senghor*; Irele, *African Experience*, 67–88; Irele, *Negritude Moment*, 39–121, Steins, "Les antecedents"; Wilder, *French Imperial Nation-State*, 262–65; Diagne, "Bergson in the Colonies"; *Léopold Sédar Senghor*; and *Bergson Postcolonial*; Jones, *Racial Discourses*. Although Irele's thoughtful readings remain within the "cultural nationalism" debate, they challenge the superficial and polemical dismissals of Senghor's supposedly reactionary and metaphysical thinking that arose within debates about decolonization and African philosophy. Among the many merits of Diagne's careful engagements with the philosophical implications of Senghor's thought is his reading of Senghor's dialogical and *métis* understanding of alterity, which challenges one-sided understandings of Senghor as a separatist, nativist, or nationalist thinker. Jones, who claims to expose the supposed biologism, essentialism, and irrationalism of what she calls Senghor's conservative epistemology, reproduces precisely the kind of narrow reading (which has purported to unmask his culturalism, racialism, metaphysics, essentialism, or vitalism) that has overdetermined discussions of Senghor since the 1960s.
171 Senghor, *Théorie et pratique*, 7
172 Senghor, *Théorie et pratique*, 7.
173 Senghor, *Théorie et pratique*, 37.
174 Senghor, *Théorie et pratique*, 41.
175 Senghor, *Théorie et pratique*, 41.
176 Senghor, *Théorie et pratique*, 42.
177 Senghor, *Théorie et pratique*, 44.
178 Senghor, *Théorie et pratique*, 44.
179 Senghor, *Théorie et pratique*, 45.
180 Senghor, *Théorie et pratique*, 45.
181 Senghor, *Théorie et pratique*, 58.
182 Senghor, *Théorie et pratique*, 50.
183 Senghor, *Théorie et pratique*, 51.
184 Senghor, *Théorie et pratique*, 55.
185 Senghor, *Théorie et pratique*, 57, 58.
186 Senghor, *Théorie et pratique*, 58.

187 A student of the Catholic action philosopher Maurice Blondel, Gaston Berger was a Franco-Senegalese philosopher, born in Saint-Louis, who became best known for helping to introduce Husserl in France, for his writings on "characterology," and for his futurist phenomenology of "la prospective"; see Senghor, "Gaston Berger." The ideas upon which Senghor draws are developed in Berger, *Phénoménologie*; "L'Attitude prospective," 43–46; and *De la prospective*. See also Lacroze, "Gaston Berger," 317–26; Tournier, "Gaston Berger," 379–88; *Hommage à Gaston Berger*; Cournand and Lévy, *Shaping the Future*; Diagne, "La leçon de Gaston Berger," 15–18; "Sur la Théorique," 69–84; and "On Prospective: Development," 55–69.

188 Senghor, *Théorie et pratique*, 60, 61.

189 Gaston Berger quoted in Senghor, *Théorie et pratique*, 61.

190 Senghor, *Théorie et pratique*, 61.

191 Senghor, *Théorie et pratique*, 61.

192 Senghor, *Théorie et pratique*, 62.

193 Senghor, *Théorie et pratique*, 64.

194 Senghor, *Théorie et pratique*, 67.

195 Senghor, *Théorie et pratique*, 68.

196 Senghor, *Théorie et pratique*, 68. Here Senghor cites Mustapha al-Siba'i, "A Propos du 'Socialisme de l'Islam,'" *Orient*, no. 20 (1961).

197 Senghor, *Théorie et pratique*, 69.

198 Senghor, *Théorie et pratique*, 70.

199 Senghor refers to Jaeger's *Early Christianity and Greek Paideia* (1961) to make this point.

200 Senghor, *Théorie et pratique*, 70–71.

201 On Senghor's socialism, his support for African Unity, and the 1962 International Colloquium on African Socialism in Dakar, see Zolberg, "Dakar Colloquium." On African socialism as a state ideology that sought to ensure national unity and consolidate party power, see Friedland and Rosberg, *African Socialism*.

202 On how Senegalese cooperatives in the 1960s allowed the central state and conservative rural forces, including marabouts, to maintain peasants in a condition of endebted dependency, see Diop and Diouf, "L'administration Sénégalaise," 65–87, and Boone, *Political Topographies*, 70–72.

203 See Dia, *Mémoires*, 143–207; Vaillant, *Black, French, and African*, 304–16; Diop, *Le Sénégal*, 124–66, 203–82.

204 Vaillant, *Black, French, and African*, 282–84.

205 See Wylie, *Myth of Iron*.

206 Senghor, "Chaka," 118.

207 Senghor, "Chaka," 122.

208 Senghor, "Chaka," 122.

209 Senghor, "Chaka," 123.

210 Senghor, "Chaka," 120, 123, 124.

211 Senghor, "Chaka," 120.

212 Senghor, "Chaka," 124.

213 Senghor, "Chaka," 123, 124, 126.

214 Senghor, "Chaka," 123.

215 Senghor, "Chaka," 127.

216 Senghor, "Chaka," 127, 129.

217 Senghor, "Chaka," 129, 130, 131.

218 Senghor, "Chaka," 130.

219 Senghor, "Chaka," 132.

220 Senghor, "Chaka," 133.

221 Many parallels obviously link Senghor's Chaka and Césaire's Christophe and Lumumba. Senghor also explored the troubled relationship between politics and poetics, action and imagination, public life and interior experience in his next collection of poems, *Nocturnes* (1961).

222 For Senghor's continuing engagement with Marx and socialism in relation to state planning and development after Senegalese independence, see Senghor, *Rapport sur la doctrine*; *Théorie et pratique*; *Pour une relecture africaine*; and *Liberté 4*.

223 See Adorno's comments on reified objects being more than they actually are, precisely because of what they are; *Negative Dialectics*, 19, 28, 52, 163.

224 Gandhi, *Selected Political Writings*, 99. Gandhi then adds, "If India converts . . . Englishmen, it can become the predominant partner in a world commonwealth of which England can have the privilege of becoming a partner if she chooses." See Chatterjee, *Nationalist Thought*, 85–130. On Nehru's attempt to conjugate national independence with world government and a postcolonial federal union, see Bhagavan, "A New Hope," 1–37, and "Princely States," 427–56.

225 Habermas, "The Postnational Constellation."

CHAPTER 9. *Decolonization and Postnational Democracy*

1 Vaillant, *Black, French, and African*, 316–19. See also O'Brien, *Mourides of Senegal*, 274–84; Diouf, *Histoire du Sénégal*, 203–10; Boone, *Political Topographies*, 67–140.

2 Vaillant, *Black, French, and African*, 316–27, 332–37. See also O'Brien, "Political Opposition," 557–66; O'Brien, "Ruling Class," 209–27; O'Brien, "Clans, Clienteles," 149–52, 171–82; Boone, *Merchant Capital*, 78–103; Diop, *Le Sénégal*, 246–80.

3 Vaillant, *Black, French, and African*, 328–31, 337–38. See also Senghor, "Pour un humanisme," 542–52.

4 Verschave, *La Françafrique*, and Médard, "France-Africa."

5 Silverman, *Deconstructing the Nation*; Hargreaves, *Immigration*.

6 Silverman, *Deconstructing the Nation*; Hargraves, *Immigration*; Schnapper, *La France de l'integration*; Rosanvallon, *Le sacre du citoyen*; Balibar, "Racism and Crisis"; Weil, *La France et ses étrangers*, and *How to Be French*; DeClair, *Politics on the Fringe*.

7 Dubois, "Republic at Sea," 64–79; Fassin, "Biopolitics of Otherness," 3–7; Silverstein, "Immigrant Racialization," 363–84; Fassin, "Compassion and Repression," 362–87; Guéye, "Colony Strikes Back," 225–42; Mann, *Native Sons*, 183–216; Ticktin, *Casualties of Care*.

8 Silverstein and Tetreault, "Urban Violence in France"; Mbembe, "La France peut-elle?"; Balibar, "Uprisings," 47–71; and the essays collected at http://riotsfrance.ssrc.org.

9   Sarkozy, "Discours," and Diop, "Le Discours inacceptable."

10 Sarkozy, "Allocution"; Thioub, "À Monsieur Nicolas Sarkozy"; Mbembe, "L'Afrique de Nicolas Sarkozy"; Mbembe, "France-Afrique." See also Makhily et al., *L'Afrique répond à Sarkozy.*

11 Shepard, *Invention of Decolonization*; Mann, *Native Sons*; Crapanzano, *The Harkis.*

12 On Sarkozy's initiative to create a Mediterranean Union trading bloc, see Muselier and Guibal, "Comment construire?"; and Déclaration commune.

13 Crusol, "Quelques aspects économiques," 20–31; Miles, *Elections and Ethnicity*, 141–58; Constant, *La retraite aux flambeaux*, 67–86; Burton, "French West Indies," 1–19; Nosel, "Appréciation," 25–71; François-Lubin, "Les méandres"; Nicolas, *Histoire de la Martinique*, 243–86; Anselin, *L'émigration antillais*; Constant, "La politique migratoire," 97–132; Beriss, *Black Skin, French Voices*, 1–21, 61–72; Dobie, "Invisible Exodus," 149–83.

14 At the 1971 "Convention pour l'Autonomie des Quatres DOM" at Morne Rouge, representatives from across the anticolonialist left in all four departments denounced departmentalization and declared their support for self-determination through a new autonomy status. Nicolas, *Histoire de la Martinique*, 294–95.

15 On the independence movement and parties, see Miles, *Elections and Ethnicity*, 45–55, 207–16; Burton, "Idea of Difference," 150–52, and "French West Indies," 16–18. Alfred Marie-Jeanne of the Mouvement indépendantiste martiniquais party was elected deputy to the National Assembly in 1997 and president of the Conseil Régionale in 1998. But according to Justin Daniel, this is more a function of his association with effective management and good governance than of popular support for national independence (Daniel, "L'espace politique," 250–52). In 1999, along with the presidents of the regional councils of Guyane and Guadeloupe, Marie-Jeanne signed "La déclaration de Basse-Terre," demanding official autonomous status for the three departments.

16 On Gaullism in Martinique, see Miles, *Elections and Ethnicity*, 129–38; Daniel, "L'éspace politique," 240–47; and Nicolas, *Histoire de la Martinique*, 64–85, 178–242. A survey of Antillean leaders conducted by Arvin W. Murch in the late 1960s indicated great support for departmental status (Murch, "Political Integration," 544–62). Such concerns led the Martinican public to vote against François Mitterrand in May 1981 despite the close alliance between the PPM and the French Socialist Party; Miles, "Mitterrand in the Caribbean," 63–79. The same dynamic appears to have been at work in the December 7, 2003, referendum on whether to create a single territorial council, which was defeated by an electorate reluctant to make any adjustment to the department's legal status. See Daniel, "Les élus," and Zander, "La consultation," 113–51. On this dynamic in Réunion, see Vergès, *Monsters and Revolutionaries*, 123–84.

17 Césaire's speech was printed in "Aimé Césaire propose," 13–15. See also Constant, "Les usages politiques," 43–65; Reno, "Re-sourcing dependency," 9–22; Daniel, "Aimé Césaire," 29–31.

18 Miles, *Elections and Ethnicity*, 230–46; Constant, *La retraite aux flambeaux*, 141–221; Daniel, "L'espace politique," 233–37, 247–52; Bernabé, Capgras, and Murgier, "Les politiques culturelles," 133–52; Blatt, "Immigrant Politics," 40–58.

19 Blérald, *Négritude et politique*; Glissant, *Le discours antillais*; Bernabé, Chamoiseau, and Confiant, *Eloge de la créolité*; Confiant, *Aimé Césaire*; Condé, "Order, Disorder, Freedom," 121–35; Dash, *Edouard Glissant*; Chamoiseau et al., "Créolité Bites," 124–61; Burton, "Idea of Difference"; Giraud, "De la négritude"; Price and Price, "Shadowboxing," 3–36; Murray, "Cultural Citizen," 79–90; Beriss, *Black Skin, French Voices*, 67–104.

20 Such debates marked commemorations in 1998 of the 150th anniversary of the abolition of slavery. They informed the 2001 Loi Taubira, which classified slavery as a crime against humanity and mandated that the history of slavery be taught in French public schools. Following the recommendations of the Comité pour la Mémoire de l'Esclavage, whose president was Maryse Condé, President Jacques Chirac established May 10 as an official holiday commemorating the abolition of slavery. Memory politics surrounded protests against the law of February 23, 2005, which publicly recognized the "positive" aspects of overseas French colonialism and mandated that they be taught to French schoolchildren. A small but vocal campaign by Antilleans to demand that the state pay reparations to the descendants of French slaves emerged. Beriss, *Black Skin, French Voices*, 25–33, 51–54; Dubois, *Colony of Citizens*, 423–38; Comité pour la Mémoire de l'Esclavage, *Mémoires*; Vergès, *La mémoire enchaînée*. In *Esprit*, no. 332, "Antilles: La république ignorée," see Maximin, Pocrain, and Taubira, "Quelle mémoire?," 62–70; Landi and Larcher, "La mémoire coloniale," 84–97; Constant, "Pour une lecture sociale," 105–16; Weil, "Politique de la mémoire," 124–43; Miller, *The French Atlantic*.

21 Daniel, "L'espace politique," 247–52; Jos, "Identité culturelle," 335–71; Daniel, "Les élus," 123–37.

22 Civil servants in the DOM are paid the famous 40% premium over their colleagues in metropolitan agencies. Various forms of "positive discrimination" have extended opportunity preferences to Antillean populations regarding employment, training, and social security. The 1958 Constitution allowed the laws of the republic to be subject to "adaptations" in the DOMs. A decree on April 26, 1960, gave the Conseils Généraux in the Antilles a special right to advise the central government on legislation that would affect the DOM in particular ways. The decentralization law of March 2, 1982, led local governmental structures in Martinique to evolve in ways distinct from the metropolitan model. Miles, *Ethnicity and Elections*, 231–34; Constant, *La retraite aux flambeaux*, 141–221. Decentralization has continued to evolve through the laws of July 5, 1994, and December 13, 2000; the constitutional revisions of March 28, 2003; the debate over Martinique's legal status around the referendum of December 7, 2003; and the law of August 13, 2004. See François-Lubin, "Les méandres," 83–93; Daniel, *L'outre-mer à l'épreuve*; and the essays collected in part 2 of Michalon, *Entre assimilation et émancipation*, 200–362. On legal autonomy, see Le Pourhiet, "La perception du droit," 451–72, and Vimon, "Assimilation," 433–50.

23 Daniel, "L'espace politique." Other accounts of the specificity of the Martinican political system include Constant, *La retraite aux flambeaux*; Reno, "La créolisation," 405–32; "Politics and Society," 34–47; and "Re-sourcing Dependency."

24 Daniel argues that the "autonomization of political space" has also led to its "enlargement" such that Martinique identifies simultaneously with the Antilles, the

wider Caribbean, France, and the EU ("L'espace politique," 252). On the EU, see Jos, "Declaration," 86–97; and Daniel, "L'espace politique," 242–55. Departmentalization thus expanded the boundaries of "Europe" and created opportunities for Antilleans, as Europeans, to pursue their interests directly through the EU without the intermediation of the French state. Yet because they are formal departments of France, the DOMs are excluded from many of the economic subsidies, development funding, and security pacts designed to aid "ultraperipheral" regions of the EU. And their already diminished agricultural economy is further threatened by a common market without protections from low-priced competitors. Historically, Martinique has been only weakly integrated into the Caribbean region, where it has enjoyed better living conditions, social protections, and political stability than its independent counterparts. See Sutton, *Dual Legacies*; Burac, "French Antilles," 98–111; Constant and Daniel, *Politique et développement*, esp. Daniel, "Crise ou mutations," 99–153; and Daniel, "Développement et compétition politique," 185–223.

25 Giraud, "Le malheur," 49–61.

26 See Letchimy, *Discours sur l'Autonomie*; Lozès, *Noirs de France*; and Taubira, Site officiel.

27 See Daniel, "L'espace politique," and "Crise ou mutations"; Giraud, "De la négritude"; "Le malheur"; "Crispation identitaire," 129–51; "Dialectics of Descent," 75–85; "Sur l'assimilation," 89–102; and "L'arbre et la forêt," 81–83; Maximin, Pocrain, and Taubira, "Quelle mémoire?" Edouard Glissant, from Martinique, and Maryse Condé, from Guadeloupe, continued to extend Césaire's legacy.

28 Giraud and Weil, "À la pointe," 48; Maximin, Pocrain, and Taubira, "Quelle mémoire?," 68–69.

29 See Habermas, "Postnational Constellation," 58–112; "Kant's Idea," 113–53; and "Constitutionalization of International Law," 115–93.

30 Cf. Scott, *Conscripts of Modernity*, and my discussion of his argument in Wilder, "Untimely Vision," 101–40.

31 Bonilla, "Guadeloupe on Strike," 6–10. Here Puerto Rico serves as a crucial reference point in the non-Francophone Caribbean. See Grosfoguel, *Colonial Subjects*. On the resonances between Césaire's political legacy and the Guadeloupe general strike, see Bonilla, "Césairean Transcripts," and Wilder "Historical Constellations." Whether or not intentionally, Antilleans in 2009 joined Césaire's orientation to an open future through experimental forms of political association to popular direct action. In so doing, they created a political movement that Césaire, the syndicalists, and the communists could not in the 1950s.

32 Habermas, "Postnational Constellation," 61, 62.

33 Habermas, "Postnational Constellation," 61.

34 Habermas, "Postnational Constellation," 61.

35 Mbembe, "Necropolitics."

36 Balibar, "World Borders," 110.

37 Balibar, "World Borders," 110–11.

38 Balibar, "World Borders," 110.

39 Balibar, "World Borders," 113.

40 Balibar, "Outline," 131.

41 Balibar, "Outline," 131–32.

42 Drew, "East Timor Story," 651–84. See also Cristecu, *Right to Self-Determination*; Pomerance, *Self-Determination*; Berman, "Sovereignty in Abeyance," 51–105; Hannum, *Autonomy*; Gayim, *Principle of Self-Determination*; Tomuschat, *Modern Law*; Koskenniemi, "National Self-Determination Today"; Grovogui, *Sovereigns*; McCorquodale, *Self-Determination*; Knop, *Diversity and Self-Determination*; Hannum and Babbitt, *Negotiating Self-Determination*; Crawford, *Creation of States*.

43 Engle, "On Fragile Architecture," and *Elusive Promise*; Polanco, *Indigenous Peoples*. On the autonomous political practices and arrangements pioneered in Chiapas, see Mattiace, *To See with Two Eyes*, and Mora, "Zapatista Anticapitalist Politics," 64–77. On autonomous movements in Argentina, see Sitrin, *Horizontalism*.

44 Woodman, "Legal Pluralism," 152–67; Himonga and Bosch, "African Customary Law," 306–41; Lehnert, "Role of the Courts," 241–77; Cornell and Muvangua, *uBuntu and the Law*. On the challenges and contradictions of South Africa's attempt to constitutionalize legal pluralism, see Comaroff and Comaroff, "Liberalism, Policulturalism."

45 Said, "One-State Solution"; Abu-Odeh, "Case for Binationalism"; Said, *From Oslo to Iraq*; Judt, "Israel"; Tilley, "One State Solution"; Tilley, *One-State Solution*; Makdisi, "Secular Democratic State."

46 Soysal, *Limits of Citizenship*; Shaw, "Peoples, Territorialism and Boundaries," 478–507; Derrida, *On Cosmopolitanism*; Balibar, *We, the People*; Benhabib, *Another Cosmopolitanism*; Bosniak, "Citizenship Denationalized" "Multiple Nationality," and *Citizen and the Alien*. Sassen, "Need to Distinguish";

47 Beck and Grande, *Cosmopolitan Europe*; Fabbrini, *Democracy and Federalism*; Hoskyns and Newman, *Democratizing*; Ferrara, "Europe," 315–31.

48 Teubner, *Global Law*; Fassbender, "United Nations Charter," 529–620, and "'We the Peoples of the United Nations'"; Dunoff and Trachtman, *Ruling the World?*; Teubner, *Constitutional Fragments*.

49 Held, *Political Theory*; Archibugi, Held, and Kohler, *Re-Imagining Political Community*; Held, *Democracy and the Global Order*; Falk, *On Humane Global Governance*, and "Reforming the United Nations."

50 Kennedy, "Politics of the Invisible College"; *International Legal Structures*, 193–201; "Challenging Expert Rule"; and "Mystery of Global Governance"; Teubner, "Contracting Worlds"; Berman, "Intervention," 743–69. See also Koskenniemi, *From Apology to Utopia*, and "Fate of Public International Law," 1–30.

51 Habermas, *Postnational Constellation*, and *Divided West*; Balibar, *We, the People*; Rosanvallon, *Democracy Past and Future*; Benhabib, *Another Cosmopolitanism*; Sassen, *Losing Control?*

52 Badiou, *Communist Hypothesis*; Douzinas and Žižek, *Idea of Communism*; Holloway, *Change the World*, and *Crack Capitalism*; Hardt and Negri, *Commonwealth*.

53 On the legal pluralism of French family law as a legacy of empire and a real but unacknowledged aspect of the contemporary republican state, see Surkis, "Hymenal Politics," 531–56, and Saada, *Empire's Children*.

54 Ticktin, *Casualties of Care*; Silverstein, *Algeria in France*; Bowen, *French Don't Like Headscarves*; Scott, *Politics of the Veil*; Fernando, "Reconfiguring Freedom," 19–35,

Bonilla, "Past Is Made by Walking," 313–39, and "Guadeloupe Is Ours," 125–37, Beriss, *Black Skin, French Voices*; Dubois, *Soccer Empire*; Scott, *Parité!*; Fassin, "Same Sex, Different Politics."

55 Here we might think of David Scott's "aftermaths of sovereignty," Emanuel Eze's "post-racial humanity," Edward Said's "fields of coexistence," Paul Gilroy's "cosmopolitan conviviality," Achille Mbembe's "Afropolitanism" and "ethic of mutuality," and Samir Amin's "internationalism of peoples." Equally resonant are Jacques Rancière's "part of no part," Jean-Luc Nancy's "being singular plural," Jacques Derrida's "New International" and "cities of refuge," Étienne Balibar's "droit de cité" and "community of fate," William Connolly's "pluralization," Susan Buck-Morss's "universal history," Michael Hardt and Antonio Negri's "commonwealth," Wendy Brown's "waning sovereignty," and Judith Butler's "cohabitation." Scott, "Aftermaths of Sovereignty," 1–26; Eze, *Achieving Our Humanity*; Said, *Humanism and Democratic Criticism*; Mbembe, *Sortir de la grande nuit*; Amin, "Pour la cinquième international," 204–9. Rancière, *Disagreement*; Derrida, *Specters of Marx*, 84–94; Nancy, *Being Singular Plural*; Derrida, *On Cosmopolitanism*, 4–23; Balibar, *We, the People*, 31–50, 131–32; Connolly, *Ethos of Pluralization*; Buck-Morss, *Hegel, Haiti, and Universal History*, 87–152; Hardt and Negri, *Commonwealth*; Brown, *Walled States*; Butler, "Is Judaism Zionism?," 79–89.

56 Jameson, "Politics of Utopia," 54.

57 Benjamin, "Some Reflections on Kafka," 144.

58 Adorno, "Notes on Kafka," 251–52.

59 On the indispensable utopian dimension of recent Latin American politics, see Coronil, "Future in Question," 231–92.

60 Adorno, *Minima Moralia*, 247.

61 Césaire and Vergès, *Ne'gre je suis*, 63.

WORKS CITED

Abu-Odeh, Lama. "The Case for Binationalism: Why One State, Liberal and Constitu-tionalist, May Be the Key to Peace in the Middle East." *Boston Review* 26, no. 6 (Dec. 2001–Jan. 2002).

Adélaide-Merlande, Jacques. *Les origines du mouvement ouvrier en Martinique: 1870–1900*. Paris: Khartala, 2000.

Adorno, Theodor. "The Actuality of Philosophy," in *The Adorno Reader*, ed. Brian O'Connor. London: Blackwell, 2000, 23–39.

Adorno, Theodor. *Minima Moralia: Reflections on a Damaged Life*. New York: Verso: 2006.

Adorno, Theodor. *Negative Dialectics*. New York: Continuum, 1983.

Adorno, Theodor. "Notes on Kafka," in *Prisms*, trans. Samuel Weber and Shierry Weber. Cambridge, MA: MIT Press, 1983.

Theodor W. Adorno, "Progress," in *Critical Models: Interventions and Catchwords*. New York: Columbia University Press, 2005.

Alduy, Paul. *L'Union française: Mission de la France*. Paris: Fasquelle, 1948.

Alessandrini, Anthony C. "Humanism in Question: Fanon and Said," in *A Companion to Postcolonial Studies*, ed. Henry Schwartz and Sangeeta Ray. London: Blackwell, 2000, 431–50.

Aliker, Pierre. "C'est le moment." *Le Progressiste* 1, no. 12 (June 21, 1958).

Almeida, Lilian Pestre de. "Les versions successives du Cahier d'un retour au pays natal," in *Césaire 70*, ed. George Ngal and Martin Steins. Youandé: Éditions Silex, 2004, 35–90.

Amin, Samir. *A Life Looking Forward: Memoirs of an Independent Marxist*. London: Zed Books, 2006.

Amin, Samir. *Neo-Colonialism in West Africa*. New York: Monthly Review Press, 1973.

Amin, Samir. "Pour la cinquième international." *Nouvelles Fondations* 3, nos. 7–8 (2007): 204–9.

Amin, Samir. *Re-Reading the Postwar Period: An Intellectual Itinerary*. New York: Monthly Review Press, 1994.

Andrain, Charles F. "Guinea and Senegal: Contrasting Types of African Socialism," in *African Socialism*, ed. William H. Friedland and Carl G. Rosberg Jr. Stanford, CA: Hoover Institute/Stanford University Press, 1964.

Anghie, Antony. *Imperialism, Sovereignty, and the Making of International Law*. Cambridge: Cambridge University Press, 2004.

Anselin, Alain. *L'émigration antillais en France: La troisième île.* Paris: Karthala, 1990.

Arana, Marie. *Bolivar: American Liberator.* New York: Simon and Schuster, 2013.

Archibugi, Daniele, David Held, and Martin Kohler, eds. *Re-Imagining Political Community: Studies in Cosmopolitan Democracy.* Stanford, CA: Stanford University Press, 1998.

Arendt, Hannah. "Can the Jewish-Arab Question Be Solved?," in *The Jewish Writings.* New York: Schocken, 2007.

Arendt, Hannah. "A Christian Word about the Jewish Question," in *The Jewish Writings.* New York: Schocken, 2007.

Arendt, Hannah. "Confusion," in *The Jewish Writings.* New York: Schocken, 2007.

Arendt, Hannah. "Home to Roost," in *Responsibility and Judgment.* New York: Schocken, 1993.

Arendt, Hannah. *The Human Condition.* Chicago: University of Chicago Press, 1958.

Arendt, Hannah. *The Jewish Writings.* New York: Schocken, 2007.

Arendt, Hannah. *The Life of the Mind.* Vol. 1, *Thinking*; vol. 2, *Willing.* New York: Harcourt, 1978.

Arendt, Hannah. "The Minority Question (copied from a letter to Eric Cohn-Bendit, summer 1940)," in *The Jewish Writings.* New York: Schocken, 2007, 127.

Arendt, Hannah. *On Revolution.* New York: Viking, 1963.

Arendt, Hannah. *The Origins of Totalitarianism.* New York: Harcourt Brace Jovanovich, 1951.

Arendt, Hannah. "Peace or Armistice in the Near East," in *The Jewish Writings.* New York: Schocken, 2007.

Arendt, Hannah. "Preface: The Gap between Past and Future," in *Between Past and Future: Six Essays.* New York: Penguin, 1968.

Arendt, Hannah. "The Return of Russian Jewry," in *The Jewish Writings.* New York: Schocken, 2007.

Arendt, Hannah. "A Way toward the Reconciliation of Peoples," in *The Jewish Writings.* New York: Schocken, 2007.

Arendt, Hannah. "What Is Freedom?," in *Between Past and Future: Six Essays.* New York: Penguin, 1968.

Aristotle. "Physics, Book IV." *Basic Works of Aristotle.* New York: Modern Library, 2001.

Arnold, A. James. *Modernism and Negritude: The Poetry and Poetics of Aimé Césaire.* Cambridge, MA: Harvard University Press, 1981.

Aron, Raymond. *L'Âge des empires et l'avenir de la France.* Paris: Défense de la France, 1945.

Aron, Raymond. *Memoirs: Fifty Years of Political Reflection.* New York: Holmes and Meier, 1990.

Aron, Raymond. "Révolution et rénovation," in *Chroniques de Guerre.* Paris: Gallimard, 1946.

Arrighi, Giovanni. *The Long Twentieth Century: Money, Power, and the Origins of Our Times.* Rev. ed. New York: Verso, 2010.

Arrighi, Giovanni, and John S. Saul, "Socialism and Economic Development in Tropical Africa." *Journal of Modern African Studies* 6, no. 2 (Aug. 1968): 141–69.

Assemblée nationale constituante. *Journal Officiel de la République Française* (JORF). Débats de l'assemblée nationale constituante, no. 29 (Mar. 22, 1946).

Atlan, Catherine. "Senghor député: L'apprentisage de la politique," in *Léopold Sédar Senghor: La pensée et l'action politique: Actes du Colloque*. Paris: Assemblée Nationale/Assemblée Parlementaire de la Francophonie, Section Française, 2006. Accessed September 29, 2008, assemblee-nationale.fr/international/colloque_senghor.pdf.

Badiou, Alain. *The Communist Hypothesis*. New York: Verso, 2010.

Bahloul, Joelle. *The Architecture of Memory: A Jewish-Muslim Household in Colonial Algeria, 1937–1962*. Cambridge: Cambridge University Press, 2006.

Balafrej, Ahmed. "Morocco Plans for Independence." *Foreign Affairs* 34, no. 3 (Apr. 1956): 483–89.

Balandier, Georges. "La situation coloniale: Approche théorique." *Cahiers internationaux de sociologie* 11 (1951): 44–79.

Balandier, Georges, ed. *Le Tiers-Monde, sous-développement et développement*. Paris: PUF, 1956.

Balibar, Étienne. "Outline of a Topography of Cruelty: Citizenship and Civility in the Era of Global Violence," in *We, the People of Europe?* Princeton, NJ: Princeton University Press, 2003.

Balibar, Étienne. "Racism and Crisis," in Étienne Balibar and Immanuel Wallerstein, *Race, Nation, Class: Ambiguous Identities*. New York: Verso, 1992.

Balibar, Étienne. "Uprisings in the Banlieue." *Constellations* 14, no. 1 (2007): 47–71.

Balibar, Etienne. *We, the People of Europe? Reflections on Transnational Citizenship*. Trans. James Swenson. Princeton, NJ: Princeton University Press, 2003.

Balibar, Étienne. "World Borders, Political Borders," in *We, the People of Europe?* Princeton, NJ: Princeton University Press, 2003.

Bangou, Henri. *La Guadeloupe*, vol. 3: *1939 à nos jours, ou la nécessaire decolonization*. Paris: L'Harmattan, 1987.

Baptiste, F.-A. "Le régime de Vichy à la martinique (juin 1940–juin 1943)." *Revue d'histoire de la Deuxième Guerre mondiale* 28, no. 111 (July 1978): 1–24.

Barma, Kothj. "L'Étudiant de la France d'Outre mer," *Chronique des foyers* 1 (July 1, 1943).

Beauvoir, Simone de. *Force of Circumstance*, vol. 1: *After the War, 1944–1952*. Trans. Richard Howard. New York: Paragon House, 1992.

Beck, Ulrich, and Edgar Grande. *Cosmopolitan Europe*. Cambridge: Polity Press, 2007.

Becker, Charles, ed. *Le père Lebret, un dominicain économiste au Sénégal (1957–1963)*. Paris: Khartala, 2007.

Benhabib, Seyla. *Another Cosmopolitanism: Hospitality, Sovereignty, and Democratic Iterations*. New York: Oxford University Press, 2006.

Benjamin, Walter. "The Author as Producer," in *Reflections: Essays, Aphorisms, Autobiographical Writings*. New York: Harcourt Brace Jovanovich, 1978.

Benjamin, Walter. "In the Sun," in *Selected Writings*, vol. 2: *1927–1934*. Cambridge, MA: Belknap Press/Harvard University Press, 199.

Benjamin, Walter. "On the Concept of History," in *Selected Writings*, vol. 4, *1938–1940*. Cambridge, MA: Belknap Press/Harvard University Press, 2003.

Benjamin, Walter. *The Origin of German Tragic Drama*. London: Verso, 2003.

Benjamin, Walter. "Paralipomena to 'On the Concept of History,'" in *Selected Writings*, vol. 4. Cambridge, MA: Belknap Press/Harvard University Press, 2003.

Benjamin, Walter. "Some Reflections on Kafka," in *Illuminations*, ed. Hannah Arendt, trans. Harry Zohn. New York: Schocken, 1969.

Benjamin, Walter. "Surrealism: Last Snapshot of the European Intelligentsia," in *Reflections: Essays, Aphorisms, and Autobiographical Writings*. New York: Schocken, 1978.

Benot, Yves. *Massacres coloniaux*. Paris: La Découverte 1994.

Benot, Yves. *Les parlementaires Africans à Paris (1914–1958)*. Paris: Éditions Chaka, 1989.

Berger, Gaston. "L'attitude prospective." *Management International* 4, no. 3 (1964): 43–46.

Berger, Gaston. *De la prospective: Textes fondamentaux de la prospective française, 1955–1966*. Paris: L'Harmattan, 2007.

Berger, Gaston. *Phénoménologie du temps et prospective*. Paris: Presses Universitaires de France, 1964.

Berger, Gaston, J. J. Chevallier, et al. *Le fédéralisme*. Paris: PUF, 1956.

Bergson, Henri. *The Creative Mind: An Introduction to Metaphysics*. New York: Dover, 2007.

Bergson, Henri. *Matter and Memory*. London: Allen and Unwin, 1911.

Bergson, Henri. *Time and Free Will: An Essay on the Immediate Data of Consciousness*. London: George Allen, 1913.

Beriss, David. *Black Skin, French Voices: Caribbean Ethnicity and Activism in Urban France*. Boulder, CO: Westview Press, 2004.

Berman, Nathaniel. "'But the Alternative Is Despair': European Nationalism and the Modernist Renewal of International Law." *Harvard Law Review* 106 (June 1993): 1792–1903.

Berman, Nathaniel. "Intervention in a 'Divided World': Axes of Legitimacy." *European Journal of International Law* 17, no. 4 (2006): 743–69.

Berman, Nathaniel. "Sovereignty in Abeyance: Self-Determination and International Law." *Wisconsin International Law Journal* 7 (1988): 51–105.

Bernabé, Jean, Patrick Chamoiseau, and Raphaël Confiant. *Éloge de la créolité*. Paris: Gallimard/Presses Universitaires Créoles, 1989.

Bernabé, Yves, Viviane Capgras, and Pascal Murgier. "Les politiques culturelles à la Martinique depuis la decentralization," in *1946–1996: Cinquante ans de départementalisation outre-mer*, ed. Fred Constant and Justin Daniel. Paris: L'Harmattan, 1997, 133–52.

Bernstein, Richard J. *The Pragmatic Turn*. Cambridge: Polity Press, 2010.

Berry, David. "'Un Contradicteur permanent': The Ideological and Political Itinerary of Daniel Guérin," in *After the Deluge: New Perspectives on the Intellectual and Cultural History of Postwar France*, ed. Julian Bourg. Lanham, MD: Lexington Books, 2004.

Bey, Salma Mardam. *Syria's Quest for Independence, 1939–1945*. Ithaca, NY: Garnet and Ithaca Press, 1994.

Bhagavan, Manu. "A New Hope: India, the United Nations and the Making of the Universal Declaration of Human Rights." *Modern Asian Studies* (2009): 1–37.

Bhagavan, Manu. "Princely States and the Making of Modern India: Internationalism, Constitutionalism, and the Postcolonial Moment." *Indian Economic and Social History Review* 46, no. 3 (2009): 427–56.

Blackburn, Robin. *The Overthrow of Colonial Slavery, 1776–1848*. London: Verso, 1989.

Blatt, David. "Immigrant Politics in a Republican Nation," in *Postcolonial Cultures in France*, ed. Alec G. Hargreaves and Mark McKinney. New York: Routledge, 1997, 40–58.

Blérald, Alain. *Négritude et politique aux Antilles*. Paris: Éditions Caribéennes, 1981.

Bloch, Ernst. "Nonsynchronism and the Obligation to Its Dialectics." *New German Critique* 11 (Spring 1977): 22–38.

Bloch, Ernst. *The Principle of Hope*, vol. 1. Cambridge, MA: MIT Press, 1986.

Bloch, Ernst. *Spirit of Utopia*. Stanford, CA: Stanford University Press, 2000.

Bloch, Ernst, and Theodor Adorno, "Something's Missing: A Discussion between Ernst Bloch and Theodor Adorno on the Contradictions of Utopian Longing (1964)," in Ernst Bloch, *The Utopian Function of Art and Literature: Selected Essays*. Cambridge, MA: MIT Press, 1989.

Bloch, Marc. *Strange Defeat: A Statement of Evidence*. New York: Norton, 1999.

Boittin, Jennifer Anne. *Colonial Metropolis: The Urban Grounds of Anti-Imperialism and Feminism in Interwar Paris*. Lincoln: University of Nebraska Press, 2010.

Bonilla, Yarimar. "Césairean Transcripts." *The Work of Man Has Just Begin: Legacies of Césaire*. http://cesairelegacies.cdrs.columbia.edu/.

Bonilla, Yarimar. "Guadeloupe Is Ours: The Prefigurative Politics of the Mass Strike in the French Antilles." *Interventions: International Journal of Postcolonial Studies* 12, no. 1 (2010): 125–37.

Bonilla, Yarimar. "Guadeloupe on Strike: A New Chapter in the French Antilles." *NACLA Report on the Americas* 42 (3): 6–10.

Bonilla, Yarimar. "The Past Is Made by Walking: Labor Activism and Historical Production in Postcolonial Guadeloupe." *Cultural Anthropology* 26, no. 3 (2011): 313–39.

Boone, Catherine. *Merchant Capital and the Roots of State Power in Senegal: 1930–1985*. Cambridge: Cambridge University Press, 2006.

Boone, Catherine. *Political Topographies of the African State: Territorial Authority and Institutional Choice*. Cambridge: Cambridge University Press, 2003.

Borella, François. *L'Évolution politique et juridique de l'Union française depuis 1946*. Paris: R. Pichon et R. Durand-Auzias, 1958.

Borgwardt, Elizabeth. *A New Deal for the World: America's Vision for Human Rights*. Cambridge, MA: Harvard University Press, 2005.

Bosniak, Linda. *The Citizen and the Alien: Dilemmas of Contemporary Membership*. Princeton, NJ: Princeton University Press, 2006.

Bosniak, Linda. "Citizenship Denationalized." *Indiana Journal of Global Legal Studies* 447 (Spring 2000).

Bosniak, Linda. "Multiple Nationality and the Postnational Transformation of Citizenship." *Virginia Journal of International Law* 42 (2002): 979–1004.

Bowen, John B. *Why the French Don't Like Headscarves: Islam, the State, and Public Space*. Princeton, NJ: Princeton University Press, 2006.

Brecht, Bertolt. "The Modern Theater Is the Epic Theater," in *Brecht on Theater: The Development of an Aesthetic*, ed. John Willett. New York: Hill and Wang, 1964.

Breton, André. "Martinique charmeuse de serpents. Un grand poète noir." *Tropiques*, no. 11 (May 1944).

Brocheux, Pierre, and Daniel Hémery. *Indochina: An Ambiguous Colonization, 1858–1954.* Berkeley: University of California Press, 2011.

Brown, Wendy. "Untimeliness and Punctuality: Critical Theory in Dark Times," in *Edgework: Critical Essays on Knowledge and Politics.* Princeton, NJ: Princeton University Press, 2005.

Brown, Wendy. *Walled States, Waning Sovereignty.* New York: Zone Books, 2010.

Brugmans, Henri, and Pierre Duclos, *Le fédéralisme contemporaine: Critères, institutions, perspectives.* Leyden: Styhoff, 1962.

Buber, Martin. "The Bi-National Approach to Zionism," in *Towards Union in Palestine: Essays on Zionism and Jewish-Arab Cooperation,* ed. M. Buber, J. L. Manges, and A. E. Simon. Palestine: Ihud Assn., 1947.

Buck-Morss, Susan. *Dreamworld and Catastrophe: The Passing of Mass Utopia in East and West.* Cambridge, MA: MIT Press, 2002.

Buck-Morss, Susan. "The Gift of the Past." *Small Axe* 33 (Nov. 2010): 173–85.

Buck-Morss, Susan. "Universal History," in *Hegel, Haiti, and Universal History.* Pittsburgh: University of Pittsburgh Press, 2009.

Buck-Morss, Susan. *The Origin of Negative Dialectics.* New York: Free Press, 1977.

Burac, Maurice. "The French Antilles, and the Wider Caribbean," in *French and West Indian: Martinique, Guadeloupe, and French Guiana Today,* ed. Richard D. E. Burton and Fred Reno. Charlottesville: University Press of Virginia, 1994, 98–111.

Burton, Richard D. E. *Assimilation or Independence: Prospects for Martinique.* Toronto: Center for Developing-Area Studies, McGill University, 1978.

Burton, Richard D. E., and Fred Reno, eds. *French and West Indian: Martinique, Guadeloupe, and French Guiana Today.* Charlottesville: University Press of Virginia, 1994.

Burton, Richard D. E. "The French West Indies à l'heure de l'Europe: An Overview," in *French and West Indian: Martinique, Guadeloupe, and French Guiana Today,* ed. Richard D. E. Burton and Fred Reno. Charlottesville: University Press of Virginia, 1994, 1–19.

Burton, Richard D. E. "The Idea of Difference in Contemporary French West Indian Thought: Négritude, Antillanité, Créolité," in *French and West Indian: Martinique, Guadeloupe, and French Guiana Today,* ed. Richard D. E. Burton and Fred Reno. Charlottesville: University Press of Virginia, 1994.

Burton, Richard D. E. "Ke Moun Nou Ye? The Idea of Difference in Contemporary French West Indian Thought." *New West Indian Guide* 67, nos. 1–2 (1993).

Butler, Judith. "Is Judaism Zionism?," in *The Power of Religion in the Public Sphere,* ed. Judith Butler, Eduardo Mendieta, and Jonathan VanAntwerpen. New York: Columbia University Press, 2011, 79–89.

Callard, Keith. "The Republic of Bourguiba." *International Journal* 16, no. 1 (Winter 1960/1961): 17–36.

Camus, Albert. "Algeria 1958," in *Resistance, Rebellion, and Death: Essays.* New York: Vintage, 1995.

Camus, Albert. *Camus at Combat: Writing, 1944–1947,* ed. Jacqueline Lévi-Valensi. Princeton, NJ: Princeton University Press, 2006.

Camus, Albert. *The Plague.* New York: Penguin, 1966.

Casimir, Jean. *La culture opprimé*. Delmas, Haiti: Lakay, 2001.

Catroux, Georges. "France, Tunisia and Morocco." *International Journal* 9, no. 4 (Autumn, 1954): 282–94.

Caygill, Howard. *Levinas and the Political*. New York: Routledge, 2002.

Césaire, Aimé. *Aimé Césaire: The Collected Poetry*. Trans. Clayton Eshelman and Annette Smith. Berkeley: University of California Press, 1983.

Césaire, Aimé. "Aimé Césaire crée un Faust africain. La tragédie du roi Christophe." Entretien avec Dominique Désanti. *Jeune Afrique*, no. 161 (Dec. 9–15, 1963): 25–26.

Césaire, Aimé. "Aimé Césaire propose à la Martinique un moratoire." *Le Naif* 329 (June 3–9, 1981): 13–15.

Césaire, Aimé. *Les armes miraculeuses*. Paris: Gallimard, 1946.

Césaire, Aimé. "Cahier d'un retour au pays natal," in *Aimé Césaire: La Poésie*. Paris: Seuil, 1994.

Césaire, Aimé. "Crise dans les départements d'Outre-Mer ou crise de la departmentalization." *Présence Africaine* 36 (1961).

Césaire, Aimé. "Culture et colonization," in Le 1er congrès international des écrivains et artistes noirs. Paris, Sorbonne, Sept. 19–22, 1956. *Présence Africaine*, special issues 8–10 (June–Nov. 1956).

Césaire, Aimé. "De la constitution." *Le Progressiste*, August 2, 1958, 1.

Césaire, Aimé. "Discours d'inauguration de la place de l'abbé Grégoire, Fort-de-France, 28 décembre 1950," in *Aimé Césaire: Oeuvres completes, vol. 3: Oeuvre historique et politique: Discours et communications*. Fort-de-France: Désormeaux, 1976.

Césaire, Aimé. "Discours prononcé en l'honneur de la visite de L. S. Senghor (Feb. 13, 1976)," in *Aimé Césaire: Oeuvres complètes*, vol. 3: *Oeuvre historique et politique: Discours et communications*. Paris: Éditions Désormais, 1976.

Césaire, Aimé. "Discours prononcé par M. Aimé Césaire," in Gaston Monnerville, Léopold Sédar Senghor, and Aimé Césaire, *Commémoration du centenaire de l'abolition de l'esclavage: Discours prononcés à la Sorbonne le 27 avril 1948*. Paris: Presses Universitaires de France, 1948.

Césaire, Aimé. "Discours sur le colonialisme," in *Aimé Césaire: Oeuvres complètes*, vol. 3: *Oeuvres historique et politique: Discours et communications*. Paris: Éditions Désormaux, 1976.

Césaire, Aimé. *Et les chiens se taisent*. Paris: Présence Africaine, 1956.

Césaire, Aimé. *Ferrements*. Paris: Seuil, 1960.

Césaire, Aimé. "Fragments d'un Poème," *Tropiques*, nos. 1, 9 (April 1941).

Césaire, Aimé. "L'heure du choix." *Le Progressiste* 1, no. 15 (July 5, 1958).

Césaire, Aimé. "Hommage à Victor Schoelcher." *Tropiques*, nos. 13–14 (1945).

Césaire, Aimé. "L'Homme de culture et ses responsabilités." *Présence Africaine*, special issue: "Deuxième congrès international des écrivains et artistes noirs (Rome Mar. 26–Apr. 1, 1959)": tome 1: "L'unité des cultures négro-africaines," nos. 24–25 (Feb.–May 1959).

Césaire, Aimé. "Imaginer ou mourir." *Le Progressiste* 1, no. 22 (Aug. 30, 1958): 1.

Césaire, Aimé. Introduction to Daniel Guérin, *Les Antilles décolonisées*. Paris: Présence Africaine, 1956.

Césaire, Aimé. *Lettre à Maurice Thorez*. Paris: Présence Africaine, 1956.

Césaire, Aimé. "Memorial for Louis Delgrès," in *The Collected Poetry*, trans. Clayton Eshelman and Annette Smith. Berkeley: University of California Press, 1984.

Césaire, Aimé. "La mort des colonies." *Les temps modernes* 11, no. 123 (Mar.–Apr. 1956).

Césaire, Aimé. *Nègre je suis, nègre je resterai: Entretiens avec Françoise Vergès*. Paris: Michel, 2005.

Césaire, Aimé. "Une occasion manqué." *Le Progressiste* 1, no. 19 (Aug. 9, 1958).

Césaire, Aimé. "Les opiomanes du mensonge." *Le Progressiste* 1, no. 17 (July 26, 1958).

Césaire, Aimé. "Panorama." *Tropiques*, no. 10 (Feb. 1944).

Césaire, Aimé. "La poésie," in *La Poésie*, ed. Daniel Maximin and Gilles Carpentier. Paris: Seuil, 2006.

Césaire, Aimé. "Poésie et connaissance." *Tropiques* no. 12 (Jan. 1945).

Césaire, Aimé. "Poetry and Knowledge," trans. A. James Arnold, in Arnold, *Aimé Césaire: Lyric and Dramatic Poetry, 1946–82*. Charlottesville: University Press of Virginia, 1990.

Césaire, Aimé. "Pour la transformation de la Martinique en region dans le cadre d'une union française fédérée," in *Aimé Césaire, Oeuvres complètes*, vol. 3: *Oeuvre historique et politique: Discours et communications*. Paris: Éditions Désormeaux, 1976.

Césaire, Aimé. "Relire Schoelcher." *Le Progressiste* 1, no. 16 (July 19, 1958): 1.

Césaire, Aimé. "Réponse à Depestre, poète haïtien. Éléments d'un art poétique." *Présence Africaine*, nos. 1–2 (Apr.–July 1955): 113–15.

Césaire, Aimé. *Une saison au Congo*. Paris: Seuil, 1966.

Césaire, Aimé. "Sur la poésie nationale," and René Depestre, "Réponse à Aimé Césaire (Introduction à un art poétique haïtien)." *Présence Africaine*, no. 4 (Oct.–Nov. 1955): 39–41, 42–62.

Césaire, Aimé. "Les Temps du régime colonial est passé," in *Guerre d'Algérie et colonialisme: Textes des interventions et messages prononcés au cours du meeting du 27 janvier 1956*. Paris: Comité d'Action des Intellectuels contra la Poursuite de la Guerre en Afrique du Nord, 1956.

Césaire, Aimé. "Tenir le pas gagné." *Le Progressiste* 1 (Sept. 27, 1958): 1.

Césaire, Aimé. *Toussaint Louverture: La Révolution française et le problème colonial*. Paris: Présence Africaine, 1962.

Césaire, Aimé. *La tragédie du roi Christophe*. Paris: Présence Africaine, 1970.

Césaire, Aimé. "Le verbe maronner. À René Depestre, poète haïtien." *La Poésie*, 481–83.

Césaire, Aimé. "Victor Schoelcher et l'abolition de l'esclavage," in Victor Schoelcher, *Esclavage et colonization*, ed. Aimé Césaire. Paris: Presses Universitaires de France, 1948.

Césaire, Aimé, and Françoise Vergès. *Ne'gre je suis, ne'gre je resterai*. Paris: Albin Michel, 2005.

Césaire, Suzanne. "1943: Le Surréalisme et nous," *Tropiques* 8–9 (October 1943).

Césaire, Suzanne. "André Breton," *Tropiques* 3 (October 1941).

Césaire, Suzanne. *Le grand camouflage: Ecrits de dissidence (1941–1945)*. Paris: Seuil, 2009.

Césaire, Suzanne. "Léo Frobénius," *Tropiques* 1 (April 1941).

Césaire, Suzanne. "Malaise d'une civilization," *Tropiques* 5 (April 1942).

Chafer, Tony. *The End of Empire in French West Africa: France's Successful Decolonization?* London: Berg, 2002.

Chakrabarty, Dipesh. *Provincializing Europe: Postcolonial Thought and Historical Difference.* Rev. ed. Princeton, NJ: Princeton University Press, 2007.

Chamoiseau, Patrick, Raphaël Confiant, Jean Bernabé, and Lucien Taylor. "Creolité Bites." *Transition*, no. 74 (1997): 124–61.

Charter of the United Nations and Statute of the International Court of Justice. San Francisco 1945. Accessed July 14, 2011. www.un.org/en/documents/charter.

Chatterjee, Partha. *Nationalist Thought and the Colonial World: A Derivative Discourse.* Minneapolis: University of Minnesota Press, 1986.

Cheah, Pheng. *Inhuman Conditions: On Cosmopolitanism and Human Rights.* Cambridge, MA: Harvard University Press, 2006.

Cissoko, Sékéné Mody. *Un combat pour l'unité de l'Afrique de l'Ouest, la Fédération du Mali (1959–1960).* Dakar: Nouvelles Éditions Africaines du Sénégal, 2005.

Cleary, A. S. "The Myth of Mau Mau in Its International Context." *African Affairs* 89, no. 355 (Apr. 1990): 227–45.

Cole, Jennifer. *Forget Colonialism? Sacrifice and the Art of Memory in Madagascar.* Berkeley: University of California Press, 2001.

Collier, Simon. "Nationality, Nationalism, and Supranationalism in the Writings of Simón Bolívar." *Hispanic American Historical Review* 63, no. 1 (Feb. 1983): 37–64.

Comaroff, Jean, and John L. Comaroff. "Liberalism, Policulturalism, and ID-ology: Thoughts on Citizenship and Difference," in *Theory from the South; or, How Euro-America Is Evolving toward Africa.* Boulder, CO: Paradigm, 2011.

Comité pour la Mémoire de l'Esclavage. Mémoires de la traite négrière, de l'esclavage et de leurs abolitions, Apr. 12, 2005. Accessed June 30, 2008. www.ladocumentationfrancaise.fr/rapports -publics/054000247/index.shtml.

Condé, Maryse. "Order, Disorder, Freedom, and the West Indian Writer." *Yale French Studies*, no. 83 (1993): 121–35.

La conférence africaine française. Brazzaville, 30 janvier 1944–8 février 1944. Algiers: Commissariat aux Colonies, 1944.

Confiant, Raphaël. *Aimé Césaire: Une traversée paradoxale du siècle.* Paris: Stock, 1993.

Connelly, Matthew. *A Diplomatic Revolution: Algeria's Fight for Independence and the Origins of the Post-Cold War Era.* New York: Oxford University Press, 2003.

Connolly, William E. *The Ethos of Pluralization.* Minneapolis: University of Minnesota Press, 2005.

Connolly, William E. *Pluralism.* Durham, NC: Duke University Press, 2005.

Constant, Fred. "Aimé Césaire et la politique: Sept leçons de leadership." *French Politics, Culture, and Society* 27, no. 3 (Winter 2009): 34–42.

Constant, Fred. "La politique migratoire: Essai d'un evaluation," in *1946–1996: Cinquante ans de départementalisation outre-mer,* ed. Fred Constant and Justin Daniel. Paris: L'Harmattan, 1997, 97–132.

Constant, Fred. "Pour une lecture sociale des revendications mémorielles 'victimaires,'" *Esprit* no. 332, special issue, "Antilles: La république ignorée" (2007): 105–16.

Constant, Fred. *La retraite aux flambeaux: Société et politique en Martinique.* Paris: Éditions Caribéennes, 1988.

Constant, Fred. "Les usages politiques de la décentralisation dans les DOM: Le cas de la Martinique." *Cahiers de l'administration outre-mer* 2 (May 1989): 43–65.

Constant, Fred, and Justin Daniel, eds. *1946–1996: Cinquante ans de départementalisation outre-mer*. Paris: L'Harmattan, 1997.

Constant, Fred, and Justin Daniel, eds. *Politique et développement dans les Caraïbes*. Paris: L'Harmattan, 1999.

Constitution du 27 octobre 1946. Accessed May 1, 2007. http://www.conseil-constitu tionnel.fr/conseil-constitutionnel/francais/la-constitution/les-constitutions-de-la -france/constitution-de-1946-ive-republique.5109.html.

Constitution du 4 octobre 1958. Accessed May 1, 2007. http://www.conseil-constitu tionnel.fr/conseil-constitutionnel/francais/la-constitution/la-constitution-du-4 -octobre-1958/texte-integral-de-la-constitution-du-4-octobre-1958-en-vigueur.5074 .html.

Cooper, Frederick. *Africa since 1940: The Past of the Present*. New York: Cambridge University Press, 2002.

Cooper, Frederick. "Alternatives to Empire: France and Africa after World War II," in *The State of Sovereignty: Territories, Laws, Populations*, ed. Douglas Howland and Luise White. Bloomington: Indiana University Press, 2009.

Cooper, Frederick. *Citizenship between Empire and Nation: Remaking France and French Africa, 1945–1960*. Princeton, NJ: Princeton University Press, 2014.

Cooper, Frederick. *Decolonization and African Society: The Labor Question in French and British Africa*. Cambridge: Cambridge University Press, 1996.

Cooper, Frederick. " 'Our Strike': Equality, Anticolonial Politics, and the 1947–1948 Railway Strike in French West Africa." *Journal of African History* 37, no. 1 (1996): 81–118.

Cooper, Frederick. "Provincializing France," in *Imperial Formations*, ed. Ann Laura Stoler, Carole McGranahan, and Peter Purdue. Santa Fe: School for Advanced Research Press, 2007.

Coquery-Vidrovitch, Catherine. "Le Congo au temps des grandes compagnies concessionaires 1898–1930." Paris: Mouton, 1972.

Coquery-Vidrovitch, Catherine. "Nationalité et citoyenneté en Afrique occidentale français: Originaires et citoyens dans le Sénégal colonial." *Journal of African History* 42 (2001): 296–304.

Cornell, Drucilla, and Nyoko Muvangua. *uBuntu and the Law: African Ideals and Postapartheid Jurisprudence*. New York: Fordham University Press, 2011.

Coronil, Fernando. "The Future in Question: History and Utopia in Latin America (1989–2010)," in *Business as Usual: The Roots of the Global Financial Breakdown*, ed. Craig Calhoun and Georgi Derluguian. New York: New York University Press and Social Science Research Council, 2011, 231–92.

Cottias, Myriam. " 'L'oubli du passé' contre la 'citoyenneté': Troc et ressentiment à la Martinique (1848–1946)," in *1946–1996: Cinquante ans de départementalisation outre-mer*, ed. Fred Constant and Justin Daniel. Paris: L'Harmattan, 1997, 293–313.

Cournand, André, and Maurice Lévy, eds. *Shaping the Future: Gaston Berger and the Concept of Prospective*. London and New York: Gordon and Breach, 1973.

Courtois, Patrick. "Le noisetier, le coudrier." *L'arbre mémoire de l'homme*. Accessed September 28, 2012. http://patrick.moostik.net/.

Covenant of the League of Nations. Boston: World Peace Foundation, 1920.

Cox, Pamela, and Richard Kessler, "Après Senghor—a Socialist Senegal?" *African Affairs* 79, no. 316 (Jul. 1980): 327–42.

Crapanzano, Vincent. *The Harkis: The Wound That Never Heals*. Chicago: University of Chicago Press, 2011.

Crawford, James R. *The Creation of States in International Law*. 2nd ed. New York: Oxford University Press, 2007.

Cristecu, Aureliu. *The Right to Self-Determination: Historical and Current Development on the Basis of United Nations Instruments*. New York: United Nations, 1981.

Crowder, Michael. "Independence as a Goal in French Speaking West African Politics 1944–60," in *Colonial West Africa: Collected Essays*. New York: Routledge, 1978.

Crusol, Jean. "Quelques aspects économiques de la departmentalization aux Antilles françaises." *Caribbean Studies* 15, no. 1 (Apr. 1975): 20–31.

Daniel, Justin. "Aimé Césaire et les Antilles françaises: Une histoire inachevée?" *French Politics, Culture and Society* 27, no. 3. (Winter 2009): 24–33.

Daniel, Justin. "Crise ou mutations des institutions: La quête de nouveaux modèles," in *Politique et développement dans les Caraïbes*, ed. Fred Constant and Justin Daniel. Paris: L'Harmattan, 1999, 99–153.

Daniel, Justin. "Développement et compétition politique: Vers une mutation du modèle portoricain?," in *Les îles caraïbes: Modèles politiques et stratégies de développement*. Paris: Karthala, 1996, 185–223.

Daniel, Justin. "Les élus face à la réforme institutionnelle et à l'acte II de la décentralisation: La difficile conciliation d'aspirations contradictoires," in *Entre assimilation et émancipation*, ed. Thierry Michalon. Paris: Les Perséides, 2006.

Daniel, Justin. "L'espace politique martiniquais à l'épreuve de la départmentalisation," in *1946–1996: Cinquante ans de départementalisation outre-mer*, ed. Fred Constant and Justin Daniel. Paris: L'Harmattan, 1997.

Daniel, Justin, ed. *L'outre-mer à l'épreuve de la décentralisation: Nouveaux cadres institutionnels et difficultés d'adaptation*. Paris: L'Harmattan, 2007.

D'Arboussier, Gabriel. *Une dangereuse mystification: La théorie de la négritude*. Paris: La nouvelle critique, 1949.

Darsières, Camille. *Des origines de la nation martiniquaise*. Pointe-à-Pitre: Desormeaux, 1974.

Dash, J. Michael. "Aimé Césaire: The Bearable Lightness of Becoming." PMLA 125, no. 3 (2010): 737–42.

Dash, J. Michael. *Édouard Glissant*. Cambridge: Cambridge University Press, 1995.

Dash, J. Michael. *The Other America: Caribbean Literature in a New World Context*. Charlottesville: University Press of Virginia, 1998.

Davis, Gregson. *Aimé Césaire*. Cambridge: Cambridge University Press, 1997.

DeClair, Edward G. *Politics on the Fringe: The People, Policies and Organization of the French National Front*. Durham, NC: Duke University Press, 1999.

Déclaration commune du sommet de Paris pour la Méditerranée, Paris, 13 juillet 2008, Conseil de l'Union Européene, Bruxelles, le 15 juillet 2008 11887/08 (Presse 213).

Décret d'abolition de l'esclavage dans les colonies françaises April 27, 1848. Reprinted in Nelly Schmidt, *Victor Schoelcher et l'abolition de l'esclavage*. Paris: Fayard, 1994, 381–82.

de Francesco, Antonio. "Popular Sovereignty and Executive Power in the Federalist Revolt of 1793." *French History* 5, no. 1 (1991): 74–101.

de Gaulle, Charles. "Discours de Bayeux, 16 juin 1946," in *Discours et messages, 1: Pendant la guerre, juin 1940–janvier 1946*. Paris: Plon, 1971.

de Gaulle, Charles. "Discours de Brazzaville, 30 janvier 1944." La conférence africaine française. Brazzaville, 30 janvier 1944–8 février 1944. Algiers: Commissariat aux Colonies, 1944.

De Gaulle, Charles. "Discours de l'Hôtel de Ville de Paris, 25 août 1944." Accessed June 15, 2012. http://www.charles-de-gaulle.org/pages/1-homme/accueil/discours/pendant-la-guerre-1940–1946/discours-de-1-hotel-de-ville-de-paris-25-aout-1944.php.

de Gaulle, Charles. *Discours et messages: Dans l'attente, février 1946–avril 1958*. Paris: Plon, 1970.

de Gaulle, Charles. *Discours et messages, 1: Pendant la guerre, juin 1940–janvier 1946*. Paris: Plon, 1947.

DeGrazia, Victoria. *Irresistible Empire: America's Advance through Twentieth-Century Europe*. Cambridge, MA: Harvard University Press, 2006.

Delavignette, Robert. "L'Union française: À l'échelle du Monde, à la mésure de l'Homme." *Esprit* 112 (July 1, 1945): 214–36.

Derrida, Jacques. *Archive Fever: A Freudian Impression*. Chicago: University of Chicago Press, 1996.

Derrida, Jacques. "Force of Law," in *Deconstruction and the Possibility of Justice*, ed. Drucilla Cornell, Michel Rosenfeld, and David Gray Carlson. New York: Routledge, 1992.

Derrida, Jacques. "Hostipitality," in *Acts of Religion*. New York: Routledge, 2002.

Derrida, Jacques. *Of Hospitality*. Stanford, CA: Stanford University Press, 2000.

Derrida, Jacques. *On Cosmopolitanism and Forgiveness*. New York: Routledge, 2001.

Derrida, Jacques. *The Other Heading: Reflections on Today's Europe*. Bloomington: Indiana University Press, 1992.

Derrida, Jacques. *Politics of Friendship*. Verso: 1997.

Derrida, Jacques. *Rogues: Two Essays on Reason*. Stanford, CA: Stanford University Press, 2005.

Derrida, Jacques. *Specters of Marx: The State of the Debt, the Work of Mourning and the New International*. New York: Routledge, 1994.

Deschamps, Hubert. *L'Union française: Évolution politique et juridique*. Paris: Institut d'études politiques, 1949.

Devèze, Michel. *La France d'Outre-Mer: De l'empire colonial a l'Union française*. Paris: Hachette, 1948.

Devillers, Philippe. "Indochine, Indonésie: Deux décolonisations manquées," in *L'ère des décolonisations, Actes du colloque international*, ed. Charles-Robert Ageron and Marc Michel. Paris: Khartala, 1995.

Dewey, John. *The Essential Dewey*, vol. 1: *Pragmatism, Education, Democracy*. Bloomington: Indiana University Press, 1998.

Dewey, John. *The Public and Its Problems*. New York: Holt, 1927.

De Witte, Ludo. *The Assassination of Lumumba*. New York: Verso, 2001.

Dewitte, Philippe. "La CGT et les syndicats d'Afrique occidentale française (1945–1957)." *Le mouvement social*, no. 117 (Oct.–Dec. 1981): 3–32.

Dewitte, Philippe. *Les mouvements nègres en France, 1919–1939*. Paris: L'Harmattan, 1985.

Dia, Mamadou. *The African Nations and World Solidarity*. New York: Praeger, 1961.

Dia, Mamadou. *Afrique: Le prix de la liberté*. Paris: L'Harmattan, 2001, 11–91.

Dia, Mamadou. *Contribution à l'étude du mouvement cooperatif en Afrique noire*. Paris: Présence Africaine, 1957.

Dia, Mamadou. "Les Coopératives vivront en Afrique comme sous les Ciel Toulpusain" (letter). *Condition Humaine*, no. 14 (Oct. 5, 1948): 3–4.

Dia, Mamadou. *L'Économie africaine: Études et problèmes nouveaux*. Paris: PUF, 1957.

Dia, Mamadou. *Mémoires d'un militant du tiers-monde*. Paris: Éditions Publisud, 1985.

Dia, Mamadou. "Notre dette envers François Perroux," in François Denoël, *François Perroux*. Lausanne: Éditions L'Âge d'Homme, 1990, 68–9.

Dia, Mamadou. "L'offensive contre les Coopératives". *Condition Humaine*, no. 12 (Sept. 1, 1948): 1.

Dia, Mamadou. *Réflexions sur l'économie de l'Afrique noire*. Paris: Éditions Africaines, 1952.

Dia, Mamadou. "La Revolution Economique: Les Coopératives Indigènes." *Condition Humaine*, no. 4 (Apr. 7, 1948).

Dia, Mamadou. "La Révolution Économique au Sénégal." *Condition Humaine*, no. 3 (Mar. 10, 1948): 1–2.

Diagne, Souleymane Bachir. "Bergson in the Colonies: Intuition and Duration in the Thought of Senghor and Iqbal." *Qui Parle* 17, no. 1 (Fall/Winter 2008): 125–45.

Diagne, Souleymane Bachir. *Bergson Postcolonial: L'élan vital dans la pensée de Léopold Sédar Senghor et de Mohamed Iqbal*. Paris: CNRS Éditions, 2011.

Diagne, Souleymane Bachir. "La leçon de Gaston Berger," in *Gaston Berger, introduction à une philosophie de l'avenir*, ed. Souleymane Bachir Diagne. Dakar: Nouvelles Éditions Africaines du Sénéga1, 1997, 15–18.

Diagne, Souleymane Bachir. *Léopold Sédar Senghor: L'art africain comme philosophie*. Paris: Reveneuve, 2007.

Diagne, Souleymane Bachir. "On Prospective: Development and a Political Culture of Time." *Africa Development* 29, no. 1 (2004): 55–69.

Diagne, Souleymane Bachir. "Sur la théorique de Gaston Berger," in *Gaston Berger, introduction à une philosophie de l'avenir*, ed. Souleymane Bachir Diagne. Dakar: Nouvelles Éditions Africaines du Sénéga1, 1997, 69–84.

Diop, Adama Baytir. *Le Sénégal à l'heure de l'indépendance: Le projet politique de Mamadou Dia (1957–1962)*. Paris: L'Harmattan, 2008, 20–49.

Diop, Alioune. "Discours d'ouverture," in Le 1er congrès international des écrivains et artistes noirs. Paris, Sorbonne, Sept. 19–22, 1956. *Présence Africaine*, special issues 8–10 (June–Nov. 1956).

Diop, Alioune. "Niam n'goura ou les raisons d'être de Présence Africaine." *Présence Africaine* 1 (November–December 1947): 7–14.

Diop, Boubacar Boris "Le Discours inacceptable de Nicolas Sarkozy" (Aug. 13, 2007). Accessed March 14, 2008. http://www.rewmi.com/le-discours-inacceptable-de-nicolas-sarkozy-par-boubacar-boris-diop_a3409.html.

Diop, Momar Coumba, and Mamadou Diouf. "L'administration Sénégalaise, les confréries religieuses, et les paysanneries." *Africa Development* 17, no. 2: 65–87.

Diouf, Mamadou. "Assimilation coloniale et identités religieuses de la civilité des originaires des Quatre Communes (Sénégal)." *Canadian Journal of African Studies/ Revue Canadienne des Études Africaines* 34, no. 3, special issue, "On Slavery and Islam in African History: A Tribute to Martin Klein" (2000): 565–87.

Diouf, Mamadou. *Histoire du Sénégal: Le modèle islamo-wolof et ses périphéries.* Paris: Maisonneuve and Larose, 2001.

Diouf, Mamadou. "Léopold Sédar Senghor et la construction de la nation sénégalaise," in *Léopold Sédar Senghor: La pensée et l'action politique: Actes du Colloque.* Paris: Assemblée Nationale/Assemblée Parlementaire de la Francophonie, Section Française, 2006. Accessed September 29, 2008. www.assemblee-nationale.fr/international /colloque_senghor.pdf.

Diouf, Mamadou. "Les Quatre Communes, histoire d'une assimilation particulière," in *Histoire du Sénégal: Le modèle islamo-wolof et ses périphéries.* Paris: Larose, 2001, 135–56.

Diouf, Mamadou. "Senegalese Development: From Mass Mobilization to Technocratic Elitism," in *International Development and the Social Sciences: Essays on the History and Politics of Knowledge,* ed. Frederick Cooper and Randall Packard. Berkeley: University of California Press, 1997.

Dobie, Madeleine. "Invisible Exodus: The Cultural Effacement of Antillean Migration." *Diaspora* 13 (2004): 149–83.

Douzinas, Costas, and Slavoj Žižek, eds. *The Idea of Communism.* New York: Verso, 2010.

Drew, Catriona. "The East Timor Story: International Law on Trial." *European Journal of International Law* 12, no. 4 (Sept. 1, 2001): 651–84.

Dubois, Laurent. *Avengers of the New World: The Story of the Haitian Revolution.* Cambridge, MA: Harvard University Press 2004.

Dubois, Laurent. *A Colony of Citizens: Revolution and Slave Emancipation in the French Caribbean, 1787–1804.* Chapel Hill: University of North Carolina Press, 2004.

Dubois, Laurent. *Haiti: The Aftershocks of History.* New York: Metropolitan Books, 2012.

Dubois, Laurent. "Haunting Delgrès," in Daniel Walkowitz and Lisa Maya Knauer, eds., *Contested Histories in Public Space: Memory, Race, and Nation.* Durham, NC: Duke University Press, 2009.

Dubois, Laurent. "Louverture, Dessalines, and the Quest for Sovereignty." Unpublished.

Dubois, Laurent. "Republic at Sea." *Transition,* no. 79 (1999): 64–79.

Dubois, Laurent. *Soccer Empire: The World Cup and the Future of France.* Berkeley: University of California Press, 2010.

DuBois, W. E. B. *Black Reconstruction in America, 1860–1880.* New York: Free Press, 1992.

Duiker, William J. *Ho Chi Minh: A Life.* New York: Hyperion, 2000.

Dumont, Jacques. "La quête de l'égalité aux Antilles. La départmentalisation et les manifestations des années 1950." *Le Movement Social* no. 230 (January–March 2010): 79–98.

Dunoff, Jeffrey L., and Joel P. Trachtman, eds. *Ruling the World?: Constitutionalism, International Law, and Global Governance.* Cambridge: Cambridge University Press, 2009.

Durand, Charles. "État unitaire, état unitaire decentralize, et état fédéral." *Le Progressiste* 1, no. 8 (May 21, 1958).

Durand, J., André de la Far, A. Gauthier-Waltern, and R. Mangin, eds. *L'Union française sera fédérale ou ne sera pas*. Paris: La Fédération, Centre d'Études Institutionnelles pour l'Organisation de la Société Française, 1947.

Duroselle, J. B. "The Turning-Point in French Politics: 1947." *Review of Politics* 13, no. 3 (July 1951): 302–28.

Echenberg, Myron. "'Morts pour la France': The African Soldier in France during the Second World War." *Journal of African History* 26, no. 4, World War II and Africa (1985): 3775–80.

Edwards, Brent Hayes. "Aimé Césaire and the Syntax of Influence." *Research in African Literatures* 36, no. 2 (Summer 2005): 1–18.

Edwards, Brent Hayes. "Introduction: Césaire in 1956." *Social Text*, no. 103 (Summer 2010): 115–25.

Edwards, Brent Hayes. *The Practice of Diaspora: Literature, Translation, and the Rise of Black Internationalism*. Cambridge, MA: Harvard University Press, 2003.

Eley, Geoff. "Europe after 1945." *History Workshop Journal* 65 (Spring 2008): 195–212.

Engle, Karen. *The Elusive Promise of Indigenous Development: Rights, Culture, Strategy*. Durham, NC: Duke University Press, 2010.

Engle, Karen. "On Fragile Architecture: The UN Declaration on the Rights of Indigenous Peoples in the Context of Human Rights." *European Journal of International Law* 22, no. 1 141 (2011): 141–63.

Eze, Emmanuel Chukwudi. *Achieving Our Humanity: The Idea of the Postracial Future*. New York: Routledge, 2001.

Fabbrini, Sergio, ed. *Democracy and Federalism in the European Union and the United States: Exploring Post-national Governance*. New York: Routledge, 2004.

Fabre, Michel-Henry. "L'Union française," in *Le fédéralisme*, ed. Gaston Berger, J. J. Chevallier, et al. Paris: PUF, 1956.

Fabre, Michel. *From Harlem to Paris: Black American Writers in France, 1840–1980*. Champaign-Urbana: University of Illinois Press, 1991.

Falk, Richard. *On Humane Global Governance: Toward a New Global Politics*. Cambridge: Polity Press, 1995.

Falk, Richard. "Reforming the United Nations: Global Civil Society Perspectives and Initiatives." *Global Civil Society Yearbook 2005–2006*. Accessed September 28, 2012. www.gcsknowledgebase.org/.

Fall, Bernard B. *Street without Joy: The French Debacle in Indochina*. Mechanicsburg, PA: Stackpole Books, 1994.

Fanon, Frantz. *Black Skin, White Masks*. New York: Grove, 1967.

Fanon, Frantz. "Racisme et culture." Paper presented at 1er congrès international des écrivains et artistes noirs, Paris, Sept. 19–22, 1956. *Présence Africaine*, special issue, 8–10, June–Nov. 1956.

Fanon, Frantz. "West Indians and Africans," in *Toward the African Revolution*. New York: Grove Press, 1967, 21–22.

Fanon, Frantz. *The Wretched of the Earth*. New York: Grove Press, 2004.

Fassbender, Bardo. "The United Nations Charter as the Constitution of the International Community." *Columbia Journal of Transnational Law* 36 (1998): 529–620.

Fassbender, Bardo. "'We the Peoples of the United Nations': Constituent Power and Constitutional Form in International Law," in *The Paradox of Constitutionalism: Constituent Power and Constitutional Form,* ed. Martin Loughlin and Neil Walker. New York: Oxford University Press, 2008.

Fassin, Didier. "The Biopolitics of Otherness: Undocumented Foreigners and Racial Discrimination in French Public Debate." *Anthropology Today* 17, no. 1 (Feb. 2001): 3–7.

Fassin, Didier. "Compassion and Repression: The Moral Economy of Immigration Policies in France." *Cultural Anthropology* 20, no. 3, Ethnographies of the Biopolitical (Aug. 2005): 362–87.

Fassin, Éric. "Same Sex, Different Politics: 'Gay Marriage' Debates in France and the United States." *Public Culture* 13, no. 2 (Spring 2001).

Fernando, Mayanthi. "Reconfiguring Freedom: Muslim Piety and the Limits of Secular Law and Public Discourse in France." *American Ethnologist* 37, no. 1 (2010): 19–35.

Ferrara, Alessandro. "Europe as a 'Special Area for Human Hope.'" *Constellations* 14, no. 3 (2007): 315–31.

Fick, Carolyn E. "The French Revolution in Saint Domingue: A Triumph or a Failure?," in *A Turbulent Time: The French Revolution and the Greater Caribbean,* ed. David Barry Gaspar and David Patrick Geggus. Bloomington: Indiana University Press, 1997.

Fick, Carolyn E. *The Making of Haiti: The Saint Domingue Revolution from Below.* Knoxville: University of Tennessee Press, 1991.

Fitzgerald, Gerald E. "Introduction," in *The Political Thought of Bolívar: Selected Writings,* ed. Gerald E. Fitzgerald. The Hague: Martinus Nijhoff, 1972.

Foltz, William. *From French West Africa to the Mali Federation.* New Haven, CT: Yale University Press, 1965.

Fonkoua, Romuald. *Aimé Césaire (1913–2008).* Paris: Perrin, 2010.

Fontana, Biancamaria. "The Napoleonic Empire and the Europe of Nations," in *The Idea of Europe: From Antiquity to the European Union,* ed. Anthony Pagden. Cambridge: Cambridge University Press/Woodrow Wilson Institute, 2002, 116–28.

Forsdick, Charles. "Situating Haiti: On Some Early Nineteenth-Century Representations of Toussaint Louverture." *International Journal of Francophone Studies* 10, no. 1 (2007): 17–34.

Four Statements on the Race Question. Paris: UNESCO, 1969.

Franck, Robert. "France and the Idea of Europe," in *The Columbia History of Twentieth-Century French Thought,* ed. Laurence D. Kritzman, Brian J. Reilly, and M. B. DeBevoise. New York: Columbia University Press, 2007.

François-Lubin, Bertrand. "Les méandres de la politique sociale outre-mer," in *1946–1996: Cinquante ans de départementalisation outre-mer,* ed. Fred Constant and Justin Daniel. Paris: L'Harmattan, 1997.

Fraternité Eurafricaine. *Vers une nouvelle nation de l'être.* Paris: Michel Touroude, 1974.

Freud, Sigmund. *Beyond the Pleasure Principle.* New York: Norton, 1990.

Freud. Sigmund. *The Interpretation of Dreams.* Trans. James Strachey. New York: Avon/Harper Collins, 1965.

Freud, Sigmund. "The Uncanny," in *The Standard Edition of the Complete Psychological Works of Sigmund Freud,* vol. 17 (1917–1919): *An Infantile Neurosis and Other Works.* London: Hogarth Press, 1955 (1919).

Friedland, William H., and Carl G. Rosberg Jr., eds. *African Socialism*. Stanford, CA: Stanford University Press, 1964.

Friedlander, Saul, ed. *Memory, History, and the Extermination of the Jews of Europe*. Bloomington: Indiana University Press, 1993.

Friedlander, Saul. *Probing the Limits of Representation: Nazism and the "Final Solution."* Cambridge, MA: Harvard University Press, 1992.

Fromm, Erich, ed. *Socialist Humanism: An International Symposium*. New York: Anchor, 1965.

Gaffield, Julia. "Complexities of Imagining Haiti: A Study of National Constitutions, 1801–1807." *Journal of Social History* 41 (2007): 81–103.

Gallagher, John, and Ronald Robinson. "The Imperialism of Free Trade." *Economic History Review* 6, no. 1, NS (1953): 1–15.

Gandhi, Mahatma. *Selected Political Writings*. Indianapolis: Hackett, 1996.

Gauvin, Gilles. "Le parti communiste de la Réunion (1946–2000)." *Vingtième Siècle: Revue d'historie*, no. 68 (Oct.–Dec. 2000): 73–94.

Gavronsky, Serge. "Aimé Césaire and the Language of Politics." *French Review* 56, no. 2 (Dec. 1982): 272–80.

Gayim, Essau. *The Principle of Self-Determination: A Study of Its Historical and Contemporary Legal Evolution*. Norwegian Institute of Human Rights, Oslo, Publication no. 5, 1990.

Geggus, David Patrick. *Haitian Revolutionary Studies*. Bloomington: Indiana University Press, 2002.

Genova, James Eskridge. *Colonial Ambivalence, Cultural Authenticity, and the Limitations of Mimicry in French-Ruled West Africa, 1914–1956*. New York: Peter Lang, 2004.

Gil, Alex. "La découverte de l'Ur-texte de *Et les chiens se taisent*," in *Aimé Césaire à l'œuvre: Actes du colloque international*, ed. Marc Cheymol and Philippe Ollé-Laprune. Paris: Éditions des archives contemporaines, 2010, 145–56.

Gilroy, Paul. *Postcolonial Melancholia*. New York: Columbia University Press, 2006.

Ginio, Ruth. *French Colonialism Unmasked: The Vichy Years in French West Africa*. Lincoln: University of Nebraska Press, 2006.

Giraud, Michel. "L'arbre et la forêt: À propos de quelques polémiques récentes." *Esprit*, no. 332 (2007): 81–83.

Giraud, Michel. "Crispation identitaire et antisémitisme: Le cas d'Antilla." *Traces*, no. 11 (1985): 129–51.

Giraud, Michel. "De la négritude a' la créolité: Une évolution paradoxale a' l'e're départmentale," in *1946–1996: Cinquante ans de départementalisation outre-mer*, ed. Fred Constant and Justin Daniel. Paris: L'Harmattan, 1997, 373–401.

Giraud, Michel. "Dialectics of Descent and Phenotypes in Racial Classification in Martinique," in *French and West Indian: Martinique, Guadeloupe, and French Guiana Today*, ed. Richard D. E. Burton and Fred Reno. Charlottesville: University Press of Virginia, 1994, 75–85.

Giraud, Michel. "Le malheur d'être parties." *Esprit*, no. 332 (2007): 49–61.

Giraud, Michel. "Sur l'assimilation: Les paradoxes d'un objet brouillé," in *Entre assimilation et émancipation*, ed. Thierry Michalon. Paris: Les Perséides, 2006, 89–102.

Giraud, Michel, and Patrick Weil, "À la pointe avancée de la République." *Esprit*, no. 332 (2007): 48.

Girollet, Anne. *Victor Schoelcher, abolitionniste et républicain: Approche juridique et politique de l'oeuvre d'un fondateur de la République*. Paris: Karthala, 2000.

Glissant, Édouard. *Le discours antillais*. Paris: Seuil, 1981.

Glissant, Édouard. *Monsieur Toussaint: A Play*, trans. J. Michael Dash and Édouard Glissant. Boulder, CO: Rienner, 2005.

Godineau, Henri. *L'Union française et les principles du droit public*. Bordeaux: Imprimerie Bière, 1949.

Gordon, Peter Eli. "The Concept of the Apolitical: German, Jewish Thought, and Weimar Political Theology." *Social Research* 74, no. 3 (Fall 2007): 855–78.

Gosnell, Jonathan K. "France, Empire, Europe: Out of Africa?," *Comparative Studies of South Asia, Africa and the Middle East* 26, no. 2 (2006): 203–12.

Grenier, René. *L'Union française sera fédérale ou ne sera pas!* Paris: Éditions du Scorpion, 1956.

Grosfoguel, Ramón. *Colonial Subjects: Puerto Ricans in a Global Perspective*. Berkeley: University of California Press, 2003.

Grosz, Elizabeth. *The Nick of Time: Politics, Evolution, and the Untimely*. Durham, NC: Duke University Press, 2004.

Grovogui, Siba N'Zatioula. *Sovereigns, Quasi Sovereigns, and Africans*. Minneapolis: University of Minnesota Press, 1996.

Guérin, Daniel. *Les Antilles décolonisées*. Paris: Présence Africaine, 1956.

Gueye, Abdoulaye. "The Colony Strikes Back: African Protest Movements in Postcolonial France." *Comparative Studies of South Asia, Africa, and the Middle East* 26, no. 2 (2006): 225–42.

Guèye, Lamine. *Étapes et perspectives de l'Union française*. Paris: Éditions de l'Union Française, 1955.

Guillemin, Philippe. "Les Élus d'Afrique Noire à l'Assemblée Nationale sous la Quatrième République." *Revue française de science politique* 8, no. 4 (1958): 861–77.

Habermas, Jürgen. "Does the Constitutionalization of International Law Still Have a Chance?," in *The Divided West*, ed. and trans. Ciaran Cronin. Cambridge: Polity Press, 2006, 115–93.

Habermas, Jürgen. "Kant's Idea of Perpetual Peace, with the Benefit of Two Hundred Years' Hindsight," in *Perpetual Peace: Essays on Kant's Cosmopolitan Ideal*, ed. James Bohman and Mattias Lutz-Bachmann. Cambridge, MA: MIT Press, 1997, 113–53.

Habermas, Jürgen. "The Postnational Constellation and the Future of Democracy," in *The Postnational Constellation: Political Essays*. Cambridge, MA: MIT Press, 2001.

"Haitian Constitution of 1801," in *Toussaint Louverture: The Haitian Revolution*, ed. Nick Nesbitt. New York: Verso, 2008.

Halbwachs, Maurice. *On Collective Memory*. Chicago: University of Chicago Press, 1992.

Hale, Thomas. "Littérature orale: Le discours comme arme de combat chez Aimé Césaire," in *Soleil éclaté*, ed. Jacqueline Leiner. Tübingen: Gunter Narr, 1984.

Hale, Thomas. "Two Decades, Four Versions: The Evolution of Aimé Césaire's 'Cahier d'un retour au pays natal,'" in *When the Drumbeat Changes*, ed. Carolyn Parker. Washington, DC: Three Continents, 1981.

Hale, Thomas A., and Kora Véron. "Aimé Césaire's Break from the Parti Communiste Français: Nouveaux élans, nouveaux defis." *French Politics, Culture, and Society* 27, no. 3 (Winter 2009): 47–62.

Hale, Thomas A., and Kora Véron. "Is There Unity in the Writings of Aimé Césaire?," *Research in African Literatures* 41, no. 1 (Spring 2010): 46–70.

Hannum, Hurst. *Autonomy, Sovereignty, and Self-Determination: The Accommodation of Conflicting Rights.* Philadelphia: University of Pennsylvania Press, 1990.

Hannum, Hurst, and Eileen Babbitt, eds. *Negotiating Self-Determination.* Lanham, MD: Lexington Books, 2006.

Hanson, Paul R. "The Federalist Revolt: An Affirmation or Denial of Popular Sovereignty." *French History* 6, no. 3 (1992): 335–55.

Hardt, Michael, and Antonio Negri. *Commonwealth.* Cambridge, MA: Belknap Press/ Harvard University Press, 2011.

Hargreaves, Alec. *Immigration, "Race" and Ethnicity in Contemporary France.* New York: Routledge, 1995.

Hargreaves, Alec, ed. *Memory, Empire, and Postcolonialism: Legacies of French Colonialism.* Lanham, MD: Lexington Books, 2005.

Harvey, David. *Spaces of Hope.* Berkeley: University of California Press, 2000.

Hazard, John N. "Negritude, Socialism, and the Law." *Columbia Law Review* 65, no. 5 (May 1965): 778–809.

Hegel, G. W. F. *Introduction to the Philosophy of History.* Indianapolis: Hackett, 1987.

Held, David. *Democracy and the Global Order: From the Modern State to Cosmopolitan Governance.* Stanford, CA: Stanford University Press, 1995.

Held, David. *Political Theory and the Modern State: Essays on State, Power, and Democracy.* Stanford, CA: Stanford University Press, 1989.

Hick, Frederick Charles. *The New World Order: International Organization, International Law, International Cooperation.* New York: Doubleday, 1920.

Hiddleston, Jane. "Aimé Césaire and Postcolonial Humanism." *Modern Language Review* 105, no. 1 (Jan. 2010): 87–102.

Hilderbrand, Robert C. *Dumbarton Oaks: The Origins of the United Nations and the Search for Postwar Security.* Chapel Hill: University of North Carolina Press, 1990.

Himonga, Chuma, and Craig Bosch. "The Application of African Customary Law under the Constitution of South Africa: Problems Solved or Just the Beginning?," *South African Law Journal* 117, no. 2 (2000): 306–41.

Hodeir, Catherine. "Grand patronat colonial français et domination blanche au tournant des indépendances." *French Colonial History* 8 (2007): 223–44.

Hoffmann, Stanley. "Paradoxes of the French Political Community," in *In Search of France,* ed. Stanley Hoffmann. Cambridge, MA: Harvard University Press, 1963, 90–98.

Holloway, John. *Change the World without Taking Power: The Meaning of Revolution Today,* 3rd ed. New York: Pluto Press, 2010.

Holloway, John. *Crack Capitalism.* New York: Pluto Press, 2010.

Holt, Thomas. *The Problem of Freedom: Race, Labor, and Politics in Jamaica and Britain, 1832–1938.* Baltimore: Johns Hopkins University Press, 1991.

Hommage à Gaston Berger: Colloque du 17 février 1962. Aix-en-Provence: Éditions Oph-rys, 1964.

Hook, Sidney. *Pragmatism and the Tragic Sense of Life*. New York: Basic Books, 1975.

Hopkins, Anthony G. "Rethinking Decolonization." *Past and Present*, no. 200 (2008): 211–47.

Hoskyns, Catherine, and Michael Newman, eds. *Democratizing the European Union: Issues for the Twenty-First Century*. Manchester: Manchester University Press, 2000.

Hurley, E. Anthony. "'Is He, Am I, a Hero?': Self-Referentiality and the Colonial Legacy in Aimé Césaire's Toussaint Louverture," in *Tree of Liberty: Cultural Legacies of the Haitian Revolution in the Atlantic World*, ed. Doris Garraway. Charlottesville: University of Virginia Press, 2008.

Hymans, Jacques Louis. *Léopold Sédar Senghor: An Intellectual Biography*. Edinburgh: University Press, Edinburgh, 1971.

Inden, Ronald B. *Imagining India*. London: Blackwell: 1990.

Irele, Abiola. *The African Experience in Literature and Ideology*. Bloomington: Indiana University Press, 1990.

Irele, Abiola. *The Négritude Moment: Explorations in Francophone African and Caribbean Literature and Thought*. Trenton, NJ: Africa World Press, 2011.

Jacqmin, René. *États-Unis de France: Ce que doit être l'Union française*. Paris: Larose, 1953.

James, C. L. R. *The Black Jacobins: Toussaint Louverture and the San Domingo Revolution*. New York: Random House, 1963.

James, William. *Pragmatism and Other Writings*. Harmondsworth, UK: Penguin Classics, 2000.

Jameson, Frederic. "The Politics of Utopia." *New Left Review* 25 (Jan.–Feb. 2004): 35–54.

Jennings, Eric. *Vichy in the Tropics: Pétain's National Revolution in Madagascar, Guadeloupe, and Indochina, 1940–1944*. Stanford, CA: Stanford University Press, 2001.

Jenson, Deborah. "Toussaint Louverture, 'Spin Doctor'? Launching the Haitian Revolution in the Media Sphere," in *Beyond the Slave Narrative: Politics, Sex, and Manuscripts in the Haitian Revolution*. Liverpool: Liverpool University Press, 2011, 45–80.

Joint Statement by President Roosevelt and Prime Minister Churchill, Aug. 14, 1941, *Avalon Project*, Yale Law School. http://avalon.law.yale.edu/wwii/at10.asp.

Jones, Donna V. *The Racial Discourses of Life Philosophy: Négritude, Vitalism, and Modernity*. New York: Columbia University Press, 2010.

Jos, Emmanuel. "Identité culturelle et identité politique: Le cas Martiniquais," in *1946–1996: Cinquante ans de départementalisation outre-mer*, ed. Fred Constant and Justin Daniel. Paris: L'Harmattan, 1997, 335–71.

Journal Officiel de la République française (JORF). Débats parlementaires de la 4ème république et constituantes. Assemblée Nationale. http://4e.republique.jo-an.fr/.

Journal Officiel de la République française (JORF). Débats de l'Assemblée nationale constituante. Paris: Journaux officiels, 1946.

Journal Officiel de la République française (JORF). Documents de l'Assemblée nationale constituante. Paris: Journaux officiels, 1946.

Judt, Tony. "Israel: The Alternative." *New York Review of Books* 50, no. 16 (Oct. 2003).

Judt, Tony. *Marxism and the French Left: Studies in Labour and Politics in France, 1830–1981*. Oxford: Oxford University Press, 1986.

Judt, Tony. *Postwar: A History of Europe since 1945*. New York: Penguin, 2005.

Jules-Rosette, Benetta. *Black Paris: The African Writers' Landscape*. Champaign-Urbana: University of Illinois Press, 1998.

Julien, Charles-André. "Morocco: The End of an Era." *Foreign Affairs* 34, no. 2 (Jan. 1956): 199–211.

Kant, Immanuel. "The Contest of the Faculties," in *Immanuel Kant: Political Writings*. Cambridge: Cambridge University Press, 1991.

Kant, Immanuel. *Critique of Pure Reason*. New York: Penguin, 2007.

Kant, Immanuel. "Perpetual Peace: A Philosophical Sketch," in *Immanuel Kant: Political Writings*. Cambridge: Cambridge University Press, 1991.

Kant, Immanuel. *The Philosophy of Law*. Gloucester: Dodo Press, 2009.

Kant, Immanuel. "Universal History with a Cosmopolitan Intent," in *Immanuel Kant: Political Writings*. Cambridge: Cambridge University Press, 1991.

Kebede, Messay. "Negritude and Bergsonism." *Journal on African Philosophy* (2003). Accessed November 26, 2013. http://www.africaknowledgeproject.org/index.php /jap/article/view/18.

Kelley, Robin D. G. *Freedom Dreams: The Black Radical Imagination*. Boston: Beacon Press, 2002.

Kelly, John D., and Martha Kaplan. *Represented Communities: Fiji and World Decolonization*. Chicago: University of Chicago Press, 2001.

Kennedy, David. "Challenging Expert Rule: The Politics of Global Governance." *Sydney Law Review*, 27 (2005): 1–24.

Kennedy, David. *International Legal Structures*. Baden-Baden: Nomos, 1987.

Kennedy, David. "The Mystery of Global Governance," in *Ruling the World?: Constitutionalism, International Law, and Global Governance*, ed. Jeffrey L. Dunoff and Joel P. Trachtman. Cambridge: Cambridge University Press, 2009.

Kennedy, David. "The Politics of the Invisible College: International Governance and the Politics of Expertise." *European Human Rights Law Review* 5 (2001): 463–598.

Kent, Raymond K. *From Madagascar to the Malagasy Republic. Madagascar 1947: La tragédie oubliee*. Colloque AFASPA des 9–11 octobre 1997, Université Paris VIII–Saint Denis: Actes. Paris: Temps des cerises, 1999.

Kipré, Pierre. *Le Congrès de Bamako; ou, La naissance du RDA en 1946*. Paris: Chakra, 1989.

Knop, Karen. *Diversity and Self-Determination in International Law*. Cambridge: Cambridge University Press, 2004.

Kosellek, Reinhart. *Futures Past: On the Semantics of Historical Time*. New York: Columbia University Press, 2004.

Kosellek, Reinhart. "Historia Magistra Vitae: The Dissolution of the Topos into the Perspective of a Modernized Historical Process," in *Futures Past*. New York: Columbia University Press, 2004.

Kosellek, Reinhart. "History, Histories, and Formal Time Structures," in *Futures Past*. New York: Columbia University Press, 2004.

Kosellek, Reinhart. "Neuzeit: Remarks on the Semantics of Modern Concepts of Movement," in *Futures Past*. New York: Columbia University Press, 2004.

Kosellek, Reinhart. "Perspective and Temporality: A Contribution to the Historiographical Exposure of the Historical World," in *Futures Past*. New York: Columbia University Press, 2004.

Kosellek, Reinhart. " 'Space of Experience' and 'Horizon of Expectation,' Two Historical Categories," in *Futures Past*. New York: Columbia University Press, 2004.

Koskenniemi, Martti. "The Fate of Public International Law: Between Technique and Politics." *Modern Law Review* 70, no. 1 (Jan. 2007): 1–30.

Koskenniemi, Martti. *From Apology to Utopia: The Structure of International Legal Argument*. Cambridge: Cambridge University Press, 2006.

Koskenniemi, Martti. *The Gentle Civilizer of Nations: The Rise and Fall of International Law 1870–1960*. Cambridge: Cambridge University Press, 2004.

Koskenniemi, Martti. "National Self-Determination Today: Problems of Legal Theory and Practice." *International and Comparative Law Quarterly*, Apr. 1994.

Krog, Antjie. *Country of My Skull: Guilt, Sorrow, and the Limits of Forgiveness in the New South Africa*. New York: Crown, 1998.

Kuisel, Richard. *Seducing the French: The Dilemma of Americanization*. Berkeley: University of California Press, 1993.

Kunz, Josef L. "The Idea of 'Collective Security' in Pan-American Developments." *Western Political Quarterly* 6, no. 4 (Dec. 1953): 658–79.

Kymlicka, Will. "Federalism, Nationalism, and Multiculturalism," in *Multicultural Citizenship: A Liberal Theory of Minority Rights*. Oxford: Oxford University Press, 1996.

Labouret, Henri. *Colonisation, colonialisme, decolonization*. Paris: Larose, 1952.

LaCapra, Dominick. *History and Criticism*. Ithaca, NY: Cornell University Press, 1985.

LaCapra, Dominick. *History and Memory after Auschwitz*. Ithaca, NY: Cornell University Press, 1998.

LaCapra, Dominick. *History in Transit: Experience, Identity*. Ithaca, NY: Cornell University Press, 2004.

LaCapra, Dominic. *Representing the Holocaust: History, Theory, Trauma*. Ithaca, NY: Cornell University Press, 1996.

LaCapra, Dominick. *Writing History, Writing Trauma*. Baltimore: Johns Hopkins University Press, 2000.

Lacroze, René. "Gaston Berger devant le mystère du temps." *Les Études philosophiques* 16, no. 4, NS (Oct.–Dec. 1961): 317–26.

Lampué, Pierre. *La citoyenneté de l'Union française*. Paris: Librairie générale de droit et de jurisprudence, 1950.

Lampué, Pierre. *L'Union française d'après la constitution*. Paris: Librairie générale de droit et de jurisprudence, 1947.

Landi, Élisabeth, and Silyane Larcher. "La mémoire coloniale vue de Fort-de-France." *Esprit*, no. 332 (2007), special issue, "Antilles: La république ignorée": 84–97.

Laplanche, J., and J.-B. Pontalis. "Deferred Action," in J. Laplanche and J.-B Pontalis, *The Language of Psycho-Analysis*. New York: Norton, 111–14.

Laplanche, Jean. "On Afterwardness," in *Essays on Otherness*. London: Routledge, 1999.

Laplanche, Jean. "Time and the Other," in *Essays on Otherness*. London: Routledge, 1999.

Laski, Harold. "The Obsolescence of Federalism," in *Theories of Federalism: Why Federations Fail*, ed. Thomas M. Franck. New York: New York University Press, 1968.

Lavergne, Bernard. *Problèmes africaines: Afrique noire, Algérie, Affaire de Suez*. Paris: Éditions Larose, 1957.

Lawrence, Mark Atwood. "Forging the 'Great Combination': Britain and the Indochina Problem, 1945–1950," in *The First Vietnam War: Colonial Crisis and Cold War Conflict*, ed. Mark Atwood Lawrence and Fredrik Logevall. Cambridge, MA: Harvard University Press, 2007, 105–29.

Lawrence, Mark Atwood, and Fredrik Logevall, eds. *The First Vietnam War: Colonial Conflict and Cold War Crisis*. Cambridge, MA: Harvard University Press, 2007.

Lefebvre, Henri. *The Critique of Everyday Life*, vol. 1. New York: Verso 1990.

Lefebvre, Henri. *Introduction to Modernity: Twelve Preludes*. New York: Verso, 1995.

Lefebvre, Henri. "The Worldwide Experience," in *Lefebvre, State, Space, World: Selected Essays*, ed. Neil Brenner and Stuart Elden. Minneapolis: University of Minnesota Press, 2009, 274–89.

Lehnert, Wieland. "The Role of the Courts in the Conflict between African Customary Law and Human Rights." *South African Journal on Human Rights* 2, no. 2 (2005): 241–77.

Leiner, Jacqueline. "Entretien avec Aimé Césaire," in *Tropiques, 1941–1945: Collection Complète*. Paris: Jean Michel Place, 1978.

Leiris, Michel. *Contacts de civilisations en Martinique et en Guadeloupe*. Paris: UNESCO-Gallimard, 1955.

Leiris, Michel. "L'ethnographe devant le colonialisme." *Les Temps modernes* 6, no. 58 (Aug. 1950): 357–74.

Leiris, Michel. *Race et civilisation*. Paris: UNESCO, 1951.

LeMelle, Wilbert T. "A Return to Senghor's Theme on African Socialism." *Phylon* 26, no. 4 (1965): 330–43.

Lenin, V. I. "Continuation of the Notes (December 31, 1922)," in *The Lenin Anthology*, ed. Robert Tucker. New York: Norton, 1975.

Lenin, V. I. "The Right of Nations to Self-Determination," in *The Lenin Anthology*, ed. Robert Tucker. New York: Norton, 1975.

Le Pourhiet, Anne-Marie. "La perception du droit à la Martinique," in *1946–1996: Cinquante ans de départementalisation outre-mer*, ed. Fred Constant and Justin Daniel. Paris: L'Harmattan, 1997, 451–72.

LeSueur, James D. *Uncivil War: Intellectuals and Identity Politics during the Decolonization of Algeria*, 2nd ed. Lincoln: University of Nebraska Press, 2005.

Letchimy, Serge. *Discours sur l'autonomie*. Martinique: Ibis Rouge, 2002.

Levinas, Emmanuel. *Otherwise Than Being; or, Beyond Essence*. Pittsburgh: Duquesne University Press, 1981.

Levinas, Emmanuel. "Peace and Proximity," in *Basic Philosophical Writings*. Bloomington: Indiana University Press, 1996.

Levinas, Emmanuel. *Totality and Infinity: An Essay on Exteriority*. Pittsburgh: Duquesne University Press, 1969.

Lévi-Strauss, Claude. *Tristes Tropiques*. New York: Atheneum, 1984.

Lewin, André. *Ahmed Sékou Touré (1922–1984), tome 4 (1960–1962): Président de la Guinée*. Paris: L'Harmattan, 2009.

Lewis, James I. "The MRP and the Genesis of the French Union, 1944–1948." *French History* 12, no. 3 (1998): 276–314.

Liniger-Goumaz, Max. *L'Eurafrique, utopie ou réalité? Les métamorphoses d'une idée*. Yaoundé: Éditions Clé, 1972.

Louis, William Roger. *Imperialism at Bay: The United States and the Decolonization of the British Empire, 1941–1945*. Oxford: Oxford University Press, 1987.

Louis, William Roger, and Ronald Robinson. "Empire Preserv'd: How the Americans Put Anti-Communism before Anti-Imperialism," in *Decolonization: Perspectives from Then and Now*, ed. Prasenjit Duara. London and New York: Routledge, 2004.

Louis, William Roger, and Ronald Robinson. "The Imperialism of Decolonization." *Journal of Imperial and Commonwealth History*, 22, no. 3 (1994): 462–511.

Löwy, Michael. "Jewish Messianism and Libertarian Utopia in Central Europe (1900–1933)." *New German Critique*, no. 20 (Spring–Summer 1980): 105–15.

Löwy, Michael. "Marxism and Revolutionary Romanticism." *Telos*, Sept. 21, 1981, 83–95.

Lozès, Patrick. *Nous, les Noirs de France*. Paris: Danger Public, 2007.

Luard, Evan. *A History of the United Nations*, vol. 1: *The Years of Western Domination, 1945–1955*. New York: Saint Martin's Press, 1982.

Luard, Evan. *A History of the United Nations*, vol. 2: *The Age of Decolonization, 1955–1965*. New York: Saint Martin's Press, 1989.

Lukács, Georg. "The Old Culture and the New Culture." *Telos*, no. 5 (1970): 21–30.

Mabille, Pierre. *Le Merveilleux*. Paris: Les Éditions des Quatre Vents, 1946.

Macey, David. *Frantz Fanon: A Biography*. New York: Picador, 2000.

Macmahon, Arthur, ed. *Federalism: Mature and Emergent*. New York: Doubleday, 1955.

MacMillan, Margaret. *Paris 1919: Six Months That Changed the World*. New York: Random House, 2003.

Magnes, Judah. "A Solution through Force," in *Towards Union in Palestine: Essays on Zionism and Jewish-Arab Cooperation*, ed. M. Buber, J. L. Manges, and A. E. Simon. Palestine: Ihud Assn., 1947.

Magnes, Judah. "Toward Peace in Palestine" and "Report on Palestine," in *Dissenter in Zion: From the Writings of Judah L. Magnes*. Cambridge, MA: Harvard University Press, 1982.

Maier, Charles, and Stanley Hoffmann, eds. *The Marshall Plan: A Retrospective*. Boulder, CO: Westview Press, 1984.

Makdisi, Saree. "For a Secular Democratic State." *The Nation*, June 18, 2007.

Makhily, Gassama, et al., eds. *L'Afrique répond à Sarkozy: Contre le discours de Dakar*. Paris: Philippe Rey, 2008.

Malley, François. *Le Père Lebret: L'économie au service des homes*. Paris, Cerf, 1968.

"Mamadou Dia (1910–2009)." Assemblée Nationale. Extrait du *Dictionnaire des parlementaires français: Notices biographiques sur les parlementaires français de 1940 à 1958*. Paris: Documentation française, 2005. http://.assemblee-nationale.fr/sycomore/fiche.asp?num_dept=2495.

Mamdani, Mahmood. *When Victims Become Killers: Colonialism, Nativism, and the Genocide in Rwanda*. Princeton, NJ: Princeton University Press, 2001.

Manela, Erez. *The Wilsonian Moment: Self-Determination and the International Origins of Anticolonial Nationalism*. New York: Oxford University Press, 2007.

Mann, Gregory. *Native Sons: West African Veterans and France in the Twentieth Century*. Durham, NC: Duke University Press, 2006.

Maritain, Jacques. *L'homme et l'état*. Paris: PUF, 1953.

Maritain, Jacques. *Humanisme integral*. Paris: Le Cerf, 1936.

Maritain, Jacques. *La Personne et le bien commun*. Paris: Desclée de Brower, 1947.

Maritain, Jacques. *Principes d'une politique humaniste*. New York: Éditions de la Maison Française, 1944.

Markovitz, Irving Leonard. *Léopold Sédar Senghor and the Politics of Negritude*. New York: Atheneum, 1969.

Marr, David G. *Vietnam 1945: The Quest for Power*. Berkeley: University of California Press, 1997.

Marseille, Jacques. *Empire colonial et capitalisme français: Histoire d'un divorce*. Paris: Albin Michel, 1989.

Marshall, D. Bruce. *The French Colonial Myth and Constitution Making in the Fourth Republic*. New Haven, CT: Yale University Press, 1973.

Marx, Karl. *Capital*, vol. 1. New York: Vintage, 1976.

Marx, Karl. "Concerning Feuerbach," in *Early Writings*. London: Penguin, 1992, 421–23.

Marx, Karl. "For a Ruthless Criticism of Everything," in *The Marx-Engels Reader*, 2nd ed., ed. Robert Tucker. New York: Norton, 1989.

Marx, Karl. "On the Jewish Question," in *Early Writings*. London: Penguin, 1992, 211–41.

Marx, Karl. "To Make the World Philosophical," in *The Marx-Engels Reader*, 2nd ed., ed. Robert Tucker. New York: Norton, 1989.

Marx, Karl. "Le travail aliéné." *La Revue socialiste*, no. 2 (1947): 154–68.

Mattiace, Shannan L. *To See with Two Eyes: Peasant Activism and Indian Autonomy in Chiapas, Mexico*. Albuquerque: University of New Mexico Press, 2003.

Mauss, Marcel. *The Gift: The Form and Reason for Exchange in Archaic Societies*. London and New York: Routledge, 1990.

Maximin, Daniel, Stéphane Pocrain, and Christiane Taubira. "Quelle mémoire de l'esclavage? Table ronde." *Esprit*, no. 332 (2007), special issue, "Antilles: La république ignorée": 62–70.

Mazower, Mark. *No Enchanted Palace: The End of Empire and the Ideological Origins of the United Nations*. Princeton, NJ: Princeton University Press, 2009.

Mazzini, Giuseppe. *A Cosmopolitanism of Nations: Giuseppe Mazzini's Writings on Democracy, Nation Building, and International Relations,"* ed. Stefano Recchia and Nadia Urbinati. Princeton, NJ: Princeton University Press, 2009.

Mbembe, Achille. "L'Afrique de Nicolas Sarkozy." *Le Messager*, Aug. 1, 2007.

Mbembe, Achille. "France-Afrique: Ces sottises qui divisent." *Le Messager*, Aug. 10, 2007.

Mbembe, Achille. "La France peut-elle réinventer son identité?," *Le Messager*, Dec. 2005. Accessed Septeber, 3, 2007. http://www.ldh-toulon.net/spip.php?article2221.

Mbembe, Achille. *Sortir de la grande nuit: Essai sur l'Afrique decolonize*. Paris: La Découverte, 2010.

Mboya, Tom. "African Socialism and Its Application to Planning in Kenya," in *The Challenge of Nationhood: A Collection of Speeches and Writings*. London: Heinemann, 1980.

Mboya, Tom. *Freedom and After*. London: André Deutsch, 1963.

McCorquodale, Robert, ed. *Self-Determination in International Law*. Farnham, Surrey: Ashgate, 2000.

Médard, Jean-François. "France-Africa: Within the Family," in *Democracy and Corruption in Europe*, ed. Donatella Della Porta and Yves Mény. London: Pinter, 1997.

Menand, Louis. *The Metaphysical Club: A Story of Ideas in America.* New York: Farrar, Straus and Giroux, 2002.

Menand, Louis, ed. *Pragmatism: A Reader.* New York: Vintage, 1997.

Ménil, René. "Introduction au Merveilleux," *Tropiques,* no. 3 (October 1941).

Ménil, René. "Naissance de notre art," *Tropiques,* no. 1 (April 1941).

Ménil, René. "Situation de la poésie," *Tropiques,* no. 11 (May 1944).

Ménil, René. *Tracées: Identité, négritude, esthétique aux Antilles.* Paris: Éditions Robert Laffont, 1992.

Merleau-Ponty, Maurice. *Humanisme et terreur.* Paris: Gallimard, 1947.

Merleau-Ponty, Maurice. "The War Has Taken Place," in *Sense and Non-Sense.* Evanston, IL: Northwestern University Press, 1964.

Michalon, Thierry, ed. *Entre assimilation et émancipation: L'outre-mer français dans l'impasse?* Paris: Les Perséides, 2006.

Miles, William F. S. *Elections and Ethnicity in French Martinique: A Paradox in Paradise.* New York: Praeger, 1985.

Miles, William F. S. "Mitterand in the Caribbean: Socialism(?) Comes to Martinique." *Journal of Interamerican Studies and World Affairs* 27, no. 3 (Autumn 1985): 63–79.

Miller, Christopher L. *The French Atlantic Triangle: Literature and Culture of the Slave Trade.* Durham, NC: Duke University Press, 2008.

Mitchell, Harriett. "The Development of Nationalism in French Morocco." *Phylon* (1940–56) 16, no. 4 (4th qtr. 1955): 427–34.

Moïse, Claude. *Le projet national de Toussaint Louverture.* Port-au-Prince: Mémoire, 2001.

Moore, Clement Henry. *Tunisia since Independence: The Dynamics of One-Party Government.* Berkeley: University of California Press, 1965.

Mora, Mariana. "Zapatista Anticapitalist Politics and the 'Other Campaign': Learning from the Struggle for Indigenous Rights and Autonomy." *Latin American Perspectives* 34, no. 2 (Mar. 2007): 64–77.

Morgenthau, Ruth Schachter. *Political Parties in French-Speaking West Africa.* Oxford: Oxford University Press, 1964.

Mounier, Emmanuel. *Le Personnalisme.* Paris: PUF, 1949.

Moutoussamy, Ernest. *Aimé Césaire: Député à l'Assemblée nationale, 1945–1993.* Paris: L'Harmattan, 1993.

Moyn, Samuel. *Origins of the Other: Emmanuel Levinas between Revelation and Ethics.* Ithaca, NY: Cornell University Press, 2007.

Mudimbe, Valentin. *The Surreptitious Speech: Présence Africaine and the Politics of Otherness, 1947–1987.* Chicago: University of Chicago Press, 1992.

Murch, Arvin W. "Political Integration as an Alternative to Independence in the French Antilles." *American Sociological Review* 33 (1968): 544–62.

Murray, David A. B. "The Cultural Citizen: Negations of Race and Language in the Making of Martiniquais." *Anthropological Quarterly* 70 (1997): 79–90.

Mus, Paul. *Le Destin de l'Union française: De l'Indochine à l'Afrique.* Paris: Seuil, 1954.

Muselier, Renaud, and Jean-Claude Guibal. "Comment construire l'Union méditerranéenne?" Assemblée nationale, Commission des affaires étrangères, Documents d'information de l'Assemblée nationale no. 449, Assemblée nationale, Dec. 5, 2007.

Nancy, Jean-Luc. *Being Singular Plural*. Trans. Robert Richardson and Anne O'Byrne. 1st ed. Stanford, CA: Stanford University Press, 2000.

Nancy, Jean-Luc. "Urbi and Orbi," in *The Creation of the World or Globalization*. Albany: State University of New York Press, 2007, 31–55.

Nesbitt, Nick. "Departmentalization and the Logic of Decolonization." *L'esprit créateur* 47 (2007): 32–43.

Nesbitt, Nick. "The Idea of 1804." *Yale French Studies*, 107. The Haiti Issue: 1804 and Nineteenth-Century French Studies (2005): 6–38.

Nesbitt, Nick. "The Incandescent I, Destroyer of Worlds." *Research in African Literatures* 41, no. 1 (Spring 2010): 121–41.

Nesbitt, Nick. "Troping Toussaint, Reading Revolution." *Research in African Literatures* 35, no. 2, (Summer 2004): 18–33.

Nesbitt, Nick. *Universal Emancipation: The Haitian Revolution and the Radical Enlightenment*. Charlottesville: University of Virginia Press, 2008.

Neumann, Franz L. "Federalism and Freedom: A Critique," in *Theories of Federalism: Why Federations Fail*, ed. Thomas M. Franck. New York: New York University Press, 1968.

Newton, Isaac. *Principia*, vol. 1: *The Motion of Bodies*. Berkeley: University of California Press, 1962.

Ngal, Georges. *Aimé Césaire: Un homme à la recherché d'une patrie*. Paris: Présence Africaine, 1994.

Nicolas, Armand. *Histoire de la Martinique*, tome 3: *De 1939 à 1971*. Paris: L'Harmattan, 1998.

Nietzsche, Friedrich. *Beyond Good and Evil (Prelude to a Philosophy of the Future)*. New York: Vintage, 1966.

Nietzsche, Friedrich. *The Gay Science: With a Prelude in Rhymes and an Appendix of Songs*. Trans. Walter Kaufmann. 1st ed. New York: Vintage, 1974.

Nietzsche, Friedrich. *Untimely Mediations*. Cambridge: Cambridge University Press, 1997.

Nkrumah, Kwame. *Building a Socialist State*. Accra: Government Printer, 1961.

Nkrumah, Kwame. *Consciencism: Philosophy and Ideology for De-colonization*. London: Heinemann, 1964.

Nkrumah, Kwame. *Some Aspects of Socialism in Africa*. Accra: Publicity Secretariat, 1963.

Nora, Pierre. "General Introduction: Between Memory and History," in *Realms of Memory: The Construction of the French Past*, vol. 1: *Conflicts and Divisions*. New York: Columbia University Press, 1986.

Nord, Philip. *France's New Deal: From the Thirties to the Postwar Moment*. Princeton, NJ: Princeton University Press, 2012.

Nord, Pierre. *L'Eurafrique, notre dernière chance*. Paris: Librairie Arthème Fayard, 1955.

Nosel, José. "Appréciation de l'impact économique de la départmentalisation à la Martinique," in *1946–1996: Cinquante ans de départementalisation outre-mer*, ed. Fred Constant and Justin Daniel. Paris: L'Harmattan, 1997, 25–71.

Nussbaum, Arthur. *A Concise History of the Law of Nations*. 2nd printing. New York: Macmillan, 1950.

Nyerere, Julius K. *Ujamaa: The Basis of African Socialism*. Dar es Salaam: Tanu, 1962.

O'Brien, Donal B. "Ruling Class and Peasantry in Senegal: 1960–1976," in *The Political Economy of Underdevelopment: Dependence in Senegal*, ed. Rita Cruise O-Brien. London: Sage 1976.

O'Brien, Donal B. Cruise. "Clans, Clienteles, and Communities: A Structure of Political Loyalties," in *Saints and Politicians: Essays in the Organization of a Senegalese Peasant Society*. Cambridge: Cambridge University Press, 1975, 149–52, 171–82.

O'Brien, Donal B. Cruise. *The Mourides of Senegal: Political and Economic Organization of an Islamic Brotherhood*. Oxford: Oxford University Press, 1971.

O'Brien, Donal B. Cruise. "Political Opposition in Senegal: 1960–1967." *Government and Opposition* 2, no. 4 (July–Oct. 1978): 557–66.

"One-State Declaration Statement," Nov. 29, 2007. http://onestate.net/articles.htm.

Pagden, Anthony. "Fellow Citizens and Imperial Subjects: Conquest and Sovereignty in Europe's Overseas Empires." *History and Theory* 44, no. 4: 28–46. Theme of issue 44: Theorizing Empire (Dec. 2005).

"Parage." *Oxford English Dictionary Online*. Accessed September 28, 2012. http://www.oed.com.ezproxy.gc.cuny.edu/view/Entry/137401?redirectedFrom=parage&.

"Paris Liberation Made 'Whites Only.'" BBC News (Apr. 6, 2009, 10:48:15 GMT). Accessed October 4, 2012. http://news.bbc.co.uk/go/pr/fr/-/2/hi/europe/7984436.stm.

Parker, Janet, Alice Mills, and Julie Stanton, eds. *Mythology: Myths, Legends and Fantasies*. Capte Town: Struik, 2007.

Pennell, C. R. *Morocco since 1830: A History*. New York: New York University Press, 2001.

Perina, Mickaëlla. *Citoyenneté et sujetion aux Antilles francophones*. Paris: L'Harmattan, 1997.

Perkins, Kenneth. *A History of Modern Tunisia*. Cambridge: Cambridge University Press, 2004.

Perroux, François. *Autarcie et expansion: Empire ou empires?* Paris: Librairie de Médicis, 1940.

Perroux, François. *Communauté et société*. Paris: PUF, 1941.

Perroux, François. *La coexistence pacifique*. Paris: PUF, 1958.

Pervillé, Guy. "La révolution algérienne et la 'guerre froide' (1954–1962)." *Études internationales* 16, no. 1 (1985): 55–66.

Pickles, Dorothy Maud. *France: The Fourth Republic*. London: Metheun, 1955.

Placide, Louis-Georges. *Les émeutes de décembre 1959 en Martinique: Un repère historique*. Paris: L'Harmattan, 2009.

Polanco, Hector Diaz. *Indigenous Peoples in Latin America: The Quest for Self-Determination*. Boulder, CO: Westview Press, 1997.

Pomerance, Michla. *Self-Determination in Law and Practice: The New Doctrine in the United Nations*. Leiden: Martinus Nijhoff, 1982.

Postone, Moishe. *Time, Labor, and Social Domination: A Reinterpretation of Marx's Critical Theory*. Cambridge: Cambridge University Press, 1993.

Postone, Moishe, and Eric Santner, eds. *Traumatic Realism: The Demands of Holocaust Representation, Catastrophe and Meaning: The Holocaust and the Twentieth Century*. Chicago: University of Chicago Press, 2003.

Price, Richard. *The Convict and the Colonel: A Story of Colonialism and Resistance in the Caribbean*. Durham, NC: Duke University Press, 2006.

Price, Richard, and Sally Price, "Shadowboxing in the Mangrove." *Cultural Anthropology* 12 (1997): 3–36.

Programme du Conseil National de la Résistance, March 15, 1944. http://fr.wikisource.org.

Proudhon, Pierre-Joseph. *Du principe fédératif et de la nécessité de reconstituer le parti de la revolution*. Paris: Éditions Bossard, 1921.

Proudhon, Pierre-Joseph. *General Idea of the Revolution in the Nineteenth Century*. New York: Cosimo, 2007.

Proudhon, Pierre-Joseph. *What Is Property? An Inquiry into the Principle of Right and Government*, trans. Benjamin R. Tucker. Princeton, MA, 1876.

Quatrième République, Projet de constitution du 19 avril 1946. http://mjp.univ-perp.fr /france/co1946p.htm#8.

Rabinbach, Anson. "Between Apocalypse and Enlightenment: Benjamin, Bloch, and Modern German-Jewish Messianism," in *In the Shadow of Catastrophe: German Intellectuals between Apocalypse and Enlightenment*. Berkeley: University of California Press, 2001.

The Race Question. Paris: UNESCO, 1950.

The Race Concept: Results of an Inquiry. Paris: UNESCO, 1952.

The Race Question in Modern Science. Paris: UNESCO, 1956.

Racine, Daniel. *Léon-Gontran Damas: L'homme et l'œuvre*. Paris: Présence Africaine, 1983.

Ranciére, Jacques. *Disagreement: Politics and Philosophy*. Minneapolis: University of Minnesota Press, 1995.

Rancière, Jacques. "The Paradoxes of Political Art," in *Dissensus: On Politics and Aesthetics*. London: Continuum International, 2010.

Reinhardt, Catherine A. *Claims to Memory: Beyond Slavery and Emancipation in the French Caribbean*. Oxford, New York: Berghahn, 2008.

Reno, Fred. "Aimé Césaire ou l'ambivalence fecund." *French Politics, Culture, and Society* 27, no. 3 (Winter 2009): 19–23.

Reno, Fred. "La créolisation de l'espace publique à la Martinique," in *1946–1996: Cinquante ans de départementalisation outre-mer*, ed. Fred Constant and Justin Daniel. Paris: L'Harmattan, 1997, 405–32.

Reno, Fred. "Politics and Society in Martinique," in *French and West Indian: Martinique, Guadeloupe, and French Guiana Today*, ed. Richard D. E. Burton and Fred Reno. Charlottesville: University Press of Virginia, 1994, 34–47.

Reno, Fred. "Re-sourcing Dependency Decolonisation and Post-colonialism in French Overseas Departments." *European Journal of Overseas History* 25 (2001): 9–22.

Rice-Maximin, Edward Francis. *Accommodation and Resistance: The French Left, Indochina, and the Cold War, 1944–1954*. Westport, CT: Greenwood, 1986.

Richter, Gerhard. *Thought-Images: Frankfurt School Writers' Reflections from Damaged Life*. Stanford, CA: Stanford University Press, 2007.

Rimbaud, Arthur. "Farewell," in *Complete Works*, trans. Paul Schmidt. New York: Harper Perennial, 2008, 242–43.

Rioux, Jean-Pierre. *The Fourth Republic, 1944–1958*. Cambridge: Cambridge University Press, 1987.

Rodríguez O., Jaime E. "The Emancipation of America." *American Historical Review* 105, no. 1 (Feb. 2000): 131–52.

Rolland, Patrice. *L'unité politique de l'Europe: Histoire d'une idée: Les grands texts*. Brussels: Bruylant, 2006.

Rorty, Richard. *Consequences of Pragmatism: Essays 1972–1980*. Minneapolis: University of Minnesota Press, 1982.

Rosanvallon, Pierre. *Democracy Past and Future*. New York: Columbia University Press, 2006.

Rosanvallon, Pierre. *Le sacre du citoyen: Histoire du suffrage universel en France*. Paris: Gallimard, 1992.

Rosello, Mireille. "The 'Césaire Effect,' or How to Cultivate One's Nation." *Research in African Literatures* 32, no. 4 (Winter 2001): 77–91.

Ross, Kristin. *May '68 and Its Afterlives*. Chicago: University of Chicago Press, 2002.

Rossillion, Claude. *Le régime législatif de la France d'outre-mer*. Paris: Éditions de l'Union Française, 1953.

Rossiter, Clinton, ed. *The Federalist Papers*. New York: Penguin Putnam, 1961.

Rothberg, Michael. *Multidirectional Memory: Remembering the Holocaust in the Age of Decolonization*. Stanford, CA: Stanford University Press, 2009.

Rousso, Henry. *The Vichy Syndrome: History and Memory in France since 1944*. Cambridge, MA: Harvard University Press, 1991.

Saada, Emmanuelle. *Empire's Children: Race, Filiation, and Citizenship in the French Colonies*. Trans. Arthur Goldhammer. Chicago: University of Chicago Press, 2012.

Sablé, Victor. *Les Antilles sans complexes: Une expérience de decolonization*. Paris: Larose, 1972.

Sablé, Victor. *La transformation des Isles d'Amérique en départements français*, Paris: Larose, 1955.

Said, Edward. *From Oslo to Iraq and the Road Map: Essays*. New York: Pantheon, 2004.

Said, Edward. *Humanism and Democratic Criticism*. New York: Columbia University Press, 2004.

Said, Edward. "The One-State Solution." *New York Times Magazine*, Jan. 10, 1999.

Sankalé, Marc. "L'ainé du Quartier Latin, ou déjà la passion de la culture," in *Hommage à Lèopold Sédar Senghor, homme de culture*. Paris: Présence Africaine, 1976.

Sarkozy, Nicolas. "Allocution de M. Nicolas Sarkozy, Président de la République, prononcé à l'Université de Dakar." Accessed September 3, 2007. http://www.elysee.fr/elysee/root/bank/print/79184.htm.

Sarkozy, Nicolas. "Discours. Réunion publique Agen, 22 juin 2006." Accessed March 9, 2012. www.u-m-p.org.

Sartre, Jean-Paul. "The Liberation of Paris: An Apocalyptic Week," in *Selected Prose: The Writings of Jean-Paul Sartre*, ed. Michel Contat and Michel Rybalka. Evanston, IL: Northwestern University Press, 1974.

Sassen, Saskia. *Losing Control? Sovereignty in an Age of Globalization*. New York: Columbia University Press, 1996.

Sassen, Saskia. "The Need to Distinguish Denationalized and Postnational." *Indiana Journal of Global Legal Studies* 7, no. 2 (2000): 575–84.

Sayre, Robert, and Michael Löwy. "Figures of Romantic Anti-Capitalism." *New German Critique* 32 (Spring–Summer 1984): 42–92.

Schmidt, Nelly. *Abolitionnistes de l'esclavage et réformateurs des colonies: 1820–1851: Analyse et documents*. Paris: Karthala, 2000.

Schmidt, Nelly. *Victor Schoelcher et l'abolition de l'esclavage*. Paris: Fayard, 1994.

Schmitt, Carl. *The Nomos of the Earth in the International Law of the Jus Publicum Europaeum*. New York: Telos Press, 2006.

Schnapper, Dominique. *La France de l'integration: Sociologie de la nation en 1990*. Paris: Gallimard, 1991.

Schoelcher, Victor. *Abolition de l'esclavage: Examen critique du prejugé contre la couleur des Africains et des sang mêlé*. Paris: Pagnerre, 1840.

Schoelcher, Victor. "Aux électeurs de la Guadeloupe et de la Martinique" (Sept. 29, 1848). Reprinted in Nelly Schmidt, *Victor Schoelcher et l'abolition de l'esclavage*. Paris: Fayard, 1994, 385–86.

Schoelcher, Victor. *Colonies étrangeres et Haiti: Résultats de l'émancipation anglaise*. Paris: Pagnerre, 1842–43.

Schoelcher, Victor. *Conférence sur Toussaint Louverture, général en chef de l'armée de Saint- Domingue*. Port-au-Prince: Panorama, 1966.

Schoelcher, Victor. *De la pétition des ouvriers pour l'abolition immediate de l'esclavage*. Paris: Pagnerre, 1844.

Schoelcher, Victor. *Des colonies françaises: Abolition immédiate de l'esclavage*. Paris: Pagnerre, 1842.

Schoelcher, Victor. "Deuxième rapport au Ministre de la Marine sure les derniers travaux de la Commission" (July 21, 1848). Reprinted in Nelly Schmidt, *Victor Schoelcher et l'abolition de l'esclavage*. Paris: Fayard, 1994, 380.

Schoelcher, Victor. *L'esclavage des Noirs et de la legislation colonial*. Paulin: Paris, 1833.

Schoelcher, Victor. *Histoire de l'esclavage pendant les deux dernières années*. Paris: Pagnerre, 1847.

Schoelcher, Victor. *Histoire des crimes de 2 décembre*. London: J. Chapman, 1852.

Schoelcher, Victor. "Petition pour l'abolition complète et immediate de l'esclavage addressee à MM. les members de la Chambre des Pairs de la Chambre des Députés, par les soins de la Société Française pour l'Abolition de l'esclavage, 30 August 1847." Reprinted in Nelly Schmidt, *Abolitionnistes de l'esclavage et réformateurs des colonies: 1820–1851: Analyse et documents*. Paris: Karthala, 2000.

Schoelcher, Victor. *Polémique coloniale*, vol. 1. Paris: Dentu, 1882. Vol. 2. Paris: Dentu, 1886.

Schoelcher, Victor. "Premier rapport fait au Ministre de la Marine et des Colonies par la Commission d'Émancipation." *Le Moniteur*, May 2, 1848. Reprinted in Nelly Schmidt, *Victor Schoelcher et l'abolition de l'esclavage*. Paris: Fayard, 1994.

Schoelcher, Victor. *Le Procés de Marie-Galante*. Paris: Éditions de Soye, 1851.

Schoelcher, Victor. "Profession de foi de Victor Schoelcher, candidat aux élections legislatives à Paris, avril 1848." Reprinted in Nelly Schmidt, *Victor Schoelcher et l'abolition de l'esclavage*. Paris: Fayard, 1994, 383–84.

Schoelcher, Victor. "Proposition d'une ligue de la paix." *Le Temps*, Apr. 26, 1871. Reprinted in Nelly Schmidt, *Victor Schoelcher et l'abolition de l'esclavage*. Paris: Fayard, 1994, 395–97.

Schoelcher, Victor. *Protestations des citoyens français nègres et mulâtres contre des accusations calonmieuses*. Paris: Éditions de Soye, 1851.

Schoelcher, Victor. *La Verité aux ouvriers et cultivateurs de la Martinique*. Paris: Pagnerre, 1849.

Schoelcher, Victor. *Vie de Toussaint Louverture*. Paris: Karthala, 1982.

Schuman, Robert. "Declaration of 9 May 1950: The Schuman Plan for European Integration," in *Theories of Federalism: A Reader*, ed. Dimitrios Karmis and Wayne Norman. London: Palgrave Macmillan, 2005.

Scott, David. "The Aftermaths of Sovereignty: Postcolonial Criticism and the Claims of Political Modernity." *Social Text* 48 (Autumn 1996): 1–26.

Scott, David. *Conscripts of Modernity: The Tragedy of Colonial Enlightenment*. Durham, NC: Duke University Press, 2004.

Scott, David. *Refashioning Futures: Criticism after Postcoloniality*. Princeton, NJ: Princeton University Press, 1999.

Scott, Joan Wallach. *Parité!: Sexual Equality and the Crisis of French Universalism*. Chicago: University of Chicago Press, 2005.

Scott, Joan Wallach. *The Politics of the Veil*. Princeton, NJ: Princeton University Press, 2007.

Sengor, Léopold Sédar. "Actions parlementaires: Pour les anciens combattants africains." *Condition Humaine*, no. 1 (Feb. 11, 1948): 2.

Senghor, Léopold Sédar. "L'Afrique et l'Europe: Deux mondes complémentaires." *Marchés coloniaux* (May 14, 1955). Reprinted in *Liberté 2*.

Senghor, Léopold Sédar. "L'apport de la poésie nègre au demi-siècle," in *Liberté 1*.

Senghor, Léopold Sédar. "L'Avenir de la France dans l'Outre-Mer." *Politique étrangère* 19, no. 4 (1954): 419–26.

Senghor, Léopold Sédar. "Balkanization ou fédération." *Afrique nouvelle*, December 1956. Reprinted in *Liberté 2*.

Senghor, Léopold Sédar. "Ce que l'homme noir apporte," in *L'homme de couleur*. Paris: Plon, 1939.

Senghor, Léopold Sédar. "Comme les lamantins vont boire à la source" (1954). Postface to *Ethiopiques*, in *Poèmes*. Paris: Seuil, 1984.

Senghor, Léopold Sédar. "La Condition de notre évolution: Réforme de l'enseignement." *Condition Humaine*, no. 1 (Feb. 11, 1948): 1–2.

Senghor, Léopold Sédar. "La décolonisation, condition de la communauté Franco-Africaine." *Le Monde*, Sept. 4, 1957. Reprinted in *Liberté 2*.

Senghor, Léopold Sédar. "Défense de l'Afrique noire." *Esprit*, 112 (July 1945): 237–48.

Senghor, Léopold Sédar. "Éléments constructifs d'une civilisation d'inspiration négro-africaine." Deuxiéme congrès international des écrivains et artistes noirs (Rome, Mar. 26–Apr. 1, 1959). Tome 1: L'unité des cultures négro-africaines. *Présence Africaine*, nos. 24–25 (Feb.–May 1959).

Senghor, Léopold Sédar. "L'esprit de la civilisation, ou les lois de la culture négro-africaine." Le 1er congrès international des écrivains et artistes noirs. Paris, Sorbonne, Sept. 19–22, 1956. *Présence Africaine*, special issues 8–10 (June–Nov. 1956).

Senghor, Léopold Sédar. "L'Eurafrique, unité économique de l'avenir," in *Liberté 2*.

Senghor, Léopold Sédar. "Gaston Berger, le philosophe de l'action," in *Hommage à Gaston Berger*. Dakar: Université de Dakar, 1962.

Senghor, Léopold Sédar. Interview with *Gavroche*, August 8, 1946. Reprinted in Léopold, *Liberté, 2*.

Senghor, Léopold Sédar. Lettre à Guy Mollet, Sécrétaire Général du Parti Socialiste, SFIO, Dakar 27 September 1948." Reprinted as "Vers un socialisme africain," in *Liberté 2*.

Senghor, Léopold Sédar. *Liberté 1: Negritude et humanisme*. Paris: Seuil, 1964.

Senghor, Léopold Sédar. *Liberté 2: Nation et voie africaine du socialisme*. Paris: Seuil, 1971.

Senghor, Léopold Sédar. *Liberté 3: Négritude et civilisation de l'universel*. Paris: Seuil, 1977.

Senghor, Léopold Sédar. *Liberté 4: Socialisme et planification*. Paris: Seuil, 1983.

Senghor, Léopold Sédar. *Liberté 5: Le dialogue des cultures*. Paris: Seuil, 1993.

Senghor, Léopold Sédar. "Marxisme et humanisme." *La Revue socialiste* 19 (Mar. 1948): 201–16.

Senghor, Léopold Sédar. "Le message de Goethe aux nègres-nouveaux" in *Liberté 1*.

Senghor, Léopold Sédar. "La Négritude comme culture des peoples noirs, ne saurait être dépassé," in *Liberté 5*.

Senghor, Léopold Sédar. "Négritude et modernité, ou la négritude est un humanisme du xxe siècle," in *Liberté 3*: 215–42.

Senghor, Léopold Sédar. "Les négro-africains et l'union française." *Revue politique et parliamentaire* (June 1947): 205–8.

Senghor, Léopold Sédar. "Pierre Teilhard de Chardin et la politique africaine," in *Cahiers Pierre Teilhard de Chardin 3*. Paris: Seuil, 1962.

Senghor, Léopold Sédar. *Poèmes*. Paris: Seuil, 1984.

Senghor, Léopold Sédar. *La poésie de l'action: Conversations avec Mohamed Aziza*. Paris: Stock, 1980.

Senghor, Léopold Sédar. "Pour une solution fédéraliste." *La Nef*, special issue, "Où va l'Union française" (June 1955): 151–55.

Senghor, Léopold Sédar. "Pour un humanisme de la francophonie," in *Liberté 3*.

Senghor, Léopold Sédar. *Pour une relecture africaine de Marx et d'Engels*. Dakar: Nouvelles Éditions Africaines du Sénégal, 1976.

Senghor, Léopold Sédar. "Le problème culturel en AOF," in *Liberté 1*.

Senghor, Léopold Sédar. "Le problème de l'Arachide." *Condition Humaine*, no. 7 (May 26, 1948): 1.

Senghor, Léopold Sédar. "Le problème du FIDES." *Condition Humaine*, no. 10 (Jul. 25, 1948): 1.

Senghor, Léopold Sédar. "Rapport supplémentaire fait au nom de la commission de la constitution." Assemblée Nationale Constituante, séance du 5 avril 1946, no. 885, Annexe 1.

Senghor, Léopold Sédar. *Rapport sur la doctrine el la politique générale; ou, Socialisme, unité africaine, construction nationale*. Union Progressiste Sénégalaise: Dakar: 1962.

Senghor, Léopold Sédar. "Questions écrites: Cadre unique et médecins africains." *Condition Humaine*, no. 6 (May 10, 1948).

Senghor, Léopold Sédar. "Questions écrites: Pension des A. C. Africains." *Condition Humaine*, no. 6 (May 10, 1948): 2.

Senghor, Léopold Sédar. "Rapport sur la doctrine et le programme du parti." Congrès Constitutif du Parti de la Fédération Africaine (Dakar, 1–3 juillet 1959). Paris: Présence Africaine, 1959.

Senghor, Léopold Sédar. "Rapport sur la méthode au Ier congrès du BDS, 15, 16, 17 avril 1949 à Thiès," in *Liberté 2*.

Senghor, Léopold Sédar. "Rapport sur la méthode du Parti, 11e congrès du BDS, 22–24 avril 1950." Reprinted as "Le népotisme contre la révolution sociale," in *Liberté 2*.

Senghor, Léopold Sédar. "Rapport sur la méthode, v^e congrès du BDS, 3, 4, 5 juillet 1953." Reprinted as "Socialisme, fédération, religion," in *Liberté 2*.

Senghor, Léopold Sédar. Rapport sur la méthode, VIe congrès du BDS, 21 avril 1954." Reprinted as "La conscience: Vertu majeure du socialisme," in *Liberté 2*, 125.

Senghor, Léopold Sédar. "Rapport sur la méthode, VIIIe congrès du BDS, 19–21 mai 1956." Reprinted as Senghor, "Socialisme et culture," in *Liberté 2*.

Senghor, Léopold Sédar. "Le Reclassement de la fonction publique outre-mer." *Condition Humaine*, no. 11 (Aug. 11, 1948): 1–2.

Senghor, Léopold Sédar. "Le Référendum en Afrique noire." *Les cahiers de la république* (1958), in *Liberté 2*.

Senghor, Léopold Sédar. "La révolution de 1889 et Léo Frobenius." *Ethiopiques: Revue socialiste de culture négro-africaine*, no. 30, 1982.

Senghor, Léopold Sédar. "Sénégal," in *Programmes et engagements électoraus des députés proclamés élus à la suite des elections génerales du 17 juin 1951*. Paris: Imprimerie de l'Assemblée Nationale, 1952.

Senghor, Léopold Sédar. "Sénégal," in *Programmes et engagements électoraus des députés proclamés élus à la suite des elections génerales du 2 janvier 1956*, tome 2. Paris: Imprimerie de l'Assemblée Nationale, 1956.

Senghor, Léopold Sédar. "La SFIO a vote contre le college unique, La SFIO a vote contre l'égalité des pensions des Anciens Combattants, La SFIO a vote contre la représentation proportionnelle, La SFIO est contre la démocratie en Afrique." *Condition Humaine*, no. 14 (Oct. 5, 1948): 1–2.

Senghor, Léopold Sédar. *Théorie et pratique du socialisme sénégalais: Seminaire des cadres politique, Union progressiste sénégalais, novembre–décembre 1962*. Dakar: Ministère de l'information, des télécommunications et du tourisme, 1964.

Senghor, Léopold Sédar. "Union française et fédéralisme." *Université des Annales*, Nov. 21, 1956, in *Liberté 2*.

Senghor, Léopold Sédar. "La voie africaine du socialisme: Essai de definition (Séminaire des Jeunes du PFA, 16–19 mai 1960)," in *Nation et voie africaine du socialisme*. Paris: Présence Africaine, 1961, 96–100.

Senghor, Léopold Sédar. "Vues sur l'Afrique noire ou assimiler, non être assimilés," in Robert Lemaignen, Léopold Sédar Senghor, and Prince Sisowath Youtévong, *La Communauté imperiale française*. Paris: Éditions Alsatia, 1945.

Sharpley-Whiting, T. Denean. *Negritude Women*. Minneapolis: University of Minnesota Press, 2002.

Shaw, Malcolm. "Peoples, Territorialism and Boundaries." *European Journal of International Law* 3 (1997): 478–507.

Shepard, Todd. *The Invention of Decolonization: The Algerian War and the Remaking of France*. Ithaca, NY: Cornell University Press, 2006.

Shipway, Martin. "British Perceptions of French Policy in Indochina from the March 1946 Accords to the Inception of the Bao Dai Regime 1946–1949: A Meeting of 'Official Minds'?," in *L'ère des décolonisations*, ed. Charles Robert Ageron and Marc Michel. Paris: Karthala, 1995.

Shipway, Martin. "Madagascar on the Eve of Insurrection, 1944–47: The Impasse of a Liberal Colonial Policy." *Journal of Imperial and Commonwealth History* 24, no. 1 (1996): 72–100.

Sicking, Louis. "A Colonial Echo: France and the Colonial Dimension of the European Economic Community." *French Colonial History* 5 (2004): 207–28.

Silverman, Maxime. *Deconstructing the Nation: Immigration, Racism, and Citizenship in Modern France*. New York: Psychology Press, 1992.

Silverstein, Paul. *Algeria in France: Transpolitics, Race, and Nation*. Bloomington: University of Indiana Press, 2004.

Silverstein, Paul A. "Immigrant Racialization and the New Savage Slot: Race, Migration, and Immigration in the New Europe." *Annual Review of Anthropology* 34 (2005): 363–84.

Silverstein, Paul, and Chantal Tetreault, "Urban Violence in France." *Middle East Report Online* (Nov. 2005). Accessed September 3, 2007. www.merip.org/mero/interventions /silverstein_tetreault_interv.htm.

Simon, Yves R. *The Community of the Free*, trans. Williard R. Trask. New York: University Press of America, 1984.

Singer Barnett, and John Langdon. *Cultured Force: Makers and Defenders of the French Empire*. Madison: University of Wisconsin Press, 2004.

Sinha, Mrinalini. *Colonial Masculinity: The "Manly Englishman" and the "Effeminate Bengali" in the Late Nineteenth Century*. Manchester: Manchester University Press, 1995.

Sissoko, Fily-Dabo. *Coups de sagaie: Controverses sur l'Union française*. Paris: Éditions de Latour du Guet, 1957.

Sitrin, Marina. *Horizontalism: Voices of Popular Power in Argentina*. Oakland, CA: AK Press, 2006.

Skurnik, Walter A. E. "Léopold Sédar Senghor and African Socialism." *Journal of Modern African Studies* 3, no. 3 (Oct. 1965): 349–69.

Smith, Andrea L. *Colonial Memory and Postcolonial Europe: Maltese Settlers in Algeria and France*. Bloomington: Indiana University Press, 2006.

Smith, Neil. *American Empire: Roosevelt's Geographer and the Prelude to Globalization*. Berkeley: University of California Press, 2004.

Snyder, Francis G. "The Political Thought of Modibo Keita." *Journal of Modern African Studies* 5, no. 1 (May 1967): 79–106.

Soysal, Yasemin Nuhoglu. *Limits of Citizenship: Migrants and Postnational Membership in Europe*. Chicago: University of Chicago Press, 1995.

Steins, Martin. "Les antecedents et la genèse de la négritude senghorienne." Ph.D. diss., Université de Paris III, 1981.

Stoler, Ann Laura, Carole McGranahan, and Peter C. Perdue, eds. *Imperial Formations*. Santa Fe: SAR Press, 2007.

Stora, Benjamin. *Algeria 1830–2000: A Short History*. Ithaca, NY: Cornell University Press, 2001.

Stovall, Tyler. *Paris Noir: African Americans in the City of Light*. New York: Houghton Mifflin, 1996.

Strachey, John. *Federalism or Socialism?* London: Victor Gollancz, 1940.

Suret-Canale, Jean. *L'Afrique noire: L'ère coloniale 1900–1945*. Éditions Sociales: Paris: 1961.

Surkis, Judith. "Hymenal Politics: Marriage, Secularism, and French Sovereignty." *Public Culture* 22, no. 3 (2010): 531–56.

Sutton, Paul, ed. *Dual Legacies in the Contemporary Caribbean: Continuing Aspects of British and French Dominion*. London: Cass, 1986.

Sylvestre, Constantin. "Vers une république fédérale." *Le Progressiste* 1, no. 12 (June 21, 1958).

Taubira, Christiane, Députée de Guyane. Site officiel. Accessed Nov. 10, 2008. www .christiane-taubira.org.

Teilhard de Chardin, Pierre. *L'Avenir de l'homme*. Paris: Seuil, 1959.

Teilhard de Chardin, Pierre. *Le Phénomène humain*. Paris: Seuil, 1955.

Teubner, Gunther. *Constitutional Fragments: Societal Constitutionalism and Globalization*. New York: Oxford University Press, 2012.

Teubner, Gunther. "Contracting Worlds: The Many Autonomies of Private Law." *Social and Legal Studies* 399 (2000): 399–417.

Teubner, Gunther. *Global Law without a State*. Farnham, Surrey: Ashgate: 1996.

Thiam, Cheikh. "Beyond Bergson's Lebensphilosophie: Senghor, Negritude, and African Vitalism." *West Africa Review* 19 (2011). Accessed October 9, 2013. http://www .africaknowledgeproject.org/index.php/war/article/view/1440.

Thioub, Ibrahima. "À Monsieur Nicolas Sarkozy, Président de la République française," Aug. 9, 2007. Accessed November 19, 2007. http://www.africultures.com/index.asp ?menu=affiche_article&no=6818.

Thomas, L. V. *Le socialisme et l'Afrique*, tome 1: *Essai sur le socialisme africain*, and tome 2: *Idéologie socialiste et les voies africaines de developpement*. Paris: Le Livre Africain, 1966.

Thomas, Martin. "Colonial Violence in Algeria and the Distorted Logic of State Retribution: The Sétif Uprising of 1945." *Journal of Military History* 75, no. 1 (2011): 45–91.

Thomas, Martin. "French Imperial Reconstruction and the Development of the Indochina War, 1945–1950," in *The First Vietnam War: Colonial Conflict and Cold War Crisis*, ed. Mark Atwood Lawrence and Fredrik Logevall. Cambridge, MA: Harvard University Press, 2007.

Ticktin, Miriam I. *Casualties of Care: Immigration and the Politics of Humanitarianism in France*. Berkeley: University of California Press, 2011.

Tilley, Virginia. "The One-State Solution." *London Review of Books* 25, no. 21 (Nov. 6, 2003).

Tilley, Virginia. *The One-State Solution: A Breakthrough for Peace in the Israeli-Palestinian Deadlock*. Ann Arbor: University of Michigan Press, 2005.

Tomuschat, Christian. *Modern Law of Self-Determination*. The Hague: Martinus Nijhoff, 1993.

Tonnesson, Stein. "Franklin Roosevelt, Trusteeship, and Indochina: A Reassessment," in *The First Vietnam War: Colonial Conflict and Cold War Crisis*, ed. Mark Atwood Lawrence and Fredrik Logevall. Cambridge, MA: Harvard University Press, 2007.

Toumson, Roger, and Simonne Henry-Valmore. *Aimé Césaire: Le nègre inconsolé*. La Roque d'Anthéron: Vents d'ailleurs, 2002.

Touré, Sékou. *L'Action du Parti Démocratique de Guinée et la lutte pour l'émancipation africaine*. Paris: Présence Africaine, 1959.

Touré, Sékou. *Expérience guinéene et unité africaine*. Paris: Présence africaine, 1961.

Tournier, Gilbert. "Gaston Berger et la prospective." *Les études philosophiques*, NS, 16, no. 4 (Oct.–Dec. 1961): 379–88.

Towa, Marcien. *Léopold Sédar Senghor: Négritude ou servitude?* Yaoundé: Éditions Cle, 1971.

Travaux de la Congrès international de philosophie consacré aux problèmes de la connaissance. Organisé par la Société Haïtienne d'Études Scientifiques et tenu à Port-au-Prince du 24 au 30 septembre 1944. Republished in *Moun: Revue de philosophie*, special issue, 4, no. 8 (May 2008).

Tronchon, Jacques. *L'insurrection malgache de 1947: Essai d'interprétation historique*. Paris: François Maspero, 1974.

Tropiques, 1941–1945: Collection complète. Paris: Jean-Michel Place, 1978.

Trouillot, Michel Rolph. *Silencing the Past: Power and the Production of History*. Boston: Beacon Press, 1997.

Tyre, Stephen. "From Algérie Française to France Musulmane: Jacques Soustelle and the Myths and Realities of 'Integration,' 1955–1962." *French History* 20, no. 3 (2006): 276–96.

Tyson, George F., Jr., ed. *Toussaint L'Ouverture*. Englewood Cliffs, NJ: Prentice Hall, 1973.

UN Resolution 1513 (xv). Declaration on the granting of independence to colonial countries and peoples, December 14, 1960. General Assembly–15th Session, 67. Accessed November 15, 2007. http://www.un.org/documents/ga/res/15/ares15.htm.

UN Resolution 1541 (xv). Principles which should guide members in determining whether or not an obligation exists to transmit the information called for under Article 73 of the Charter, December 15, 1960. Accessed November 15, 2007. http://www.un.org/documents/ga/res/15/ares15.htm.

UN Resolution 1542 (xv). Transmission of information under Article 73e of the Charter, December 15, 1960. Accessed November 15, 2007. http://www.un.org/documents/ga/res/15/ares15.htm.

UN Resolution 1654 (xvi). The situation with regard to the implementation of the Declaration on the granting of independence to colonial countries and peoples, November 27, 1961. Accessed November 15, 2007. http://www.un.org/documents/ga/res/16/ares16.htm.

Vaillant, Janet. *Black, French, and African: A Life of Léopold Sédar Senghor*. Cambridge, MA: Harvard University Press, 1990.

Vergès, Françoise. *La mémoire enchaînée: Questions sur l'esclavage*. Paris: Albin Michel, 2006.

Vergès, Françoise. *Monsters and Revolutionaries: Colonial Family Romance and Métissage*. Durham, NC: Duke University Press, 1999.

Véron, Kora. "Césaire at the Crossroads in Haiti: Correspondence with Henri Seyrig." *Comparative Literature Studies* 50, no. 3 (2013): 434.

Verschave, François-Xavier. *La Françafrique: Le plus long scandale de la République*. Paris: Stock, 1998.

"Victor Schoelcher (1804–1893). Une vie, un siècle: L'esclavage d'hier à aujourd'hui." Accessed July 11, 2011. www.senat.fr/evenement/victor_schoelcher/engagements .html.

Vimon, Jack. "Assimilation et dédoublement des ordres normatifs: Le cas des Amérindiens de Guyane française," in *1946–1996: Cinquante ans de départementalisation outremer*, ed. Fred Constant and Justin Daniel. Paris: L'Harmattan, 1997, 433–50.

Wall, Irwin M. "The French Communists and the Algerian War." *Journal of Contemporary History* 12 (1977): 521–43.

Wallerstein, Immanuel. "Elites in French-Speaking West Africa: The Social Basis of Ideas." *Journal of Modern African Studies* 3, no. 1 (May 1965): 1–33.

Wallerstein, Immanuel. *Unthinking the Social Sciences: The Limits of Nineteenth-Century Paradigms*. Cambridge: Polity Press, 1991.

Walsh, John Patrick. "Césaire Reads Toussaint Louverture: The Haitian Revolution and the Problem of Departmentalization." *Small Axe* 15, no. 1 (Mar. 2011): 110–24.

Walsh, John Patrick. *Free and French in the Caribbean: Toussaint Louverture, Aimé Césaire, and Narratives of Loyal Opposition*. Bloomington: Indiana University Press, 2013.

Walton, Clarence C. "The Fate of Neo-Federalism in Western Europe." *Western Political Quarterly* 5, no. 3 (Sept. 1952): 366–90.

Weil, Patrick. *La France et ses étrangers: L'aventure d'une politique de l'immigration de 1938 à nos jours*. Paris: Gallimard, 1995.

Weil, Patrick. *How to Be French: Nationality in the Making since 1789*. Trans. Catherine Porter. Durham, NC: Duke University Press, 2008.

Weil, Patrick. "Politique de la mémoire: L'interdit et la commemoration." *Esprit* (February 2007): 124–43.

Weil, Simone. "The Colonial Question and the Destiny of the French People," in *Simone Weil on Colonialism: An Ethic of the Other*, ed. and trans. J. P. Little. Lanham, MD: Rowman and Littlefield, 2003.

Weinstein, Brian. *Éboué*. New York: Oxford University Press, 1972.

Wells, H. G. *The Shape of Things to Come*. New York: Macmillan, 1933.

West, Cornel. *The American Evasion of Philosophy: A Genealogy of Pragmatism*. Madison: University of Wisconsin Press, 1989.

White, Hayden. *Metahistory: The Historical Imagination in Nineteenth-Century Europe*. Baltimore: Johns Hopkins University Press, 1975.

Wilder, Gary. "Aimé Césaire: Contra Commemoration." *African and Black Diaspora: An International Journal* 2, no. 1 (2009): 121–23.

Wilder, Gary. "*Eurafrique* as the Future Past of Black France: Recognizing Léopold Sédar Senghor's Postwar Vision," in *France Noire—Black France*, ed. Trica Danielle Keaton and Tyler Stovall. Durham, NC: Duke University Press, 2012.

Wilder, Gary. *The French Imperial Nation-State: Negritude and Colonial Humanism between the Two World Wars*. Chicago: University of Chicago Press, 2005.

Wilder, Gary. "From Optic to Topic: The Foreclosure Effect of Historiographic Turns." *American Historical Review* 117, no. 3 (2012): 723–45.

Wilder, Gary. "Historical Constellations and Political Futures (Past)." *The Work of Man Has Just Begin: Legacies of Césaire.* http://cesairelegacies.cdrs.columbia.edu/.

Wilder, Gary. "Race, Reason, Impasse: Césaire, Fanon, and the Legacy of Emancipation." *Radical History Review* 90 (Fall 2004): 31–61.

Wilder, Gary. "Response Essay," online forum on *The French Imperial Nation-State. H-France Forum*, no. 3 (Summer 2006). Accessed September 10, 2006. http://h-france.net/forum/h-franceforumv011.html.

Wilder, Gary. "Telling Histories: A Conversation with Laurent Dubois and Greg Grandin." *Radical History Review* 115 (2013): 11–25.

Wilder, Gary. "Unthinking French History: Colonial Studies beyond National Identity," in *After the Imperial Turn: Critical Approaches to 'National' Histories and Literatures,* ed. Antoinette Burton. Durham, NC: Duke University Press, 2003, 125–43.

Wilder, Gary. "Untimely Vision: Aimé Césaire, Decolonization, Utopia." *Public Culture* 21, no. 1 (Winter 2009): 101–40.

Wilks, Jennifer M. *Race, Gender, and Comparative Black Modernism: Suzanne Lacascade, Marita Bonner, Suzanne Césaire, Dorothy West.* Baton Rouge: Louisiana State University Press, 2008.

William, Jean-Claude. "Aimé Césaire: Les contrariétés de la conscience nationale," in *1946–1996: Cinquante ans de départementalisation outre-mer,* ed. Fred Constant and Justin Daniel. Paris: L'Harmattan, 1997.

Wilson, Peter. *The International Theory of Leonard Woolf: A Study in Twentieth Century Idealism.* London: Palgrave Macmillan, 2003.

Wilson, Woodrow. *Essential Writings and Speeches of the Scholar-President,* ed. Mario DiNunzio. New York: New York University Press, 2006.

Wolin, Richard. *Heidegger's Children: Hannah Arendt, Karl Löwith, Hans Jonas, and Herbert Marcuse.* Princeton, NJ: Princeton University Press, 2001.

Wolin, Richard. *Walter Benjamin: An Aesthetic of Redemption.* Berkeley: University of California Press, 1994.

Woodcock, George. *Pierre-Joseph Proudhon: A Biography.* Montreal: Black Rose Books, 1996.

Woodman, Gordon R. "Legal Pluralism and the Search for Justice." *Journal of African Law* 40, no. 2, (1996): 152–67.

Woolf, Leonard. *The Framework of a Lasting Peace.* Ithaca, NY: Cornell University Library, 2009.

Woolf, Leonard. *International Government.* London: George Allen, 1916.

Wylie, David. *Myth of Iron: Shaka in History.* Athens: Ohio University Press, 2008.

Yerushalmi, Yosef Hayim. *Zakhor: Jewish History and Jewish Memory.* New York: Schocken, 1989.

Young-Bruehl, Elisabeth. *Hannah Arendt: For Love of the World.* 2nd ed. New Haven, CT: Yale University Press, 2004.

Zander, Ulrike. "La consultation du 7 décembre 2003 et les manifestations d'inquiétude de l'opinion martiniquaise," in *Entre assimilation et émancipation,* ed. Thierry Michalon. Paris: Les Perséides, 2006.

Zinsou, Émile-Derlin. "Il aura honoré l'Homme . . . ," in *Léopold Sédar Senghor: La pensée et l'action politique.* Accessed September 29, 2008. www.assemblee-nationale.fr /international/colloque_senghor.pdf.

Zisser, Eyal. *Lebanon: The Challenge of Independence.* London: Tauris, 2000.

Zolberg, Aristide R. "The Dakar Colloquium: The Search for a Doctrine," in *African Socialism,* ed. William Friedland and Carl Rosberg. Stanford, CA: Stanford University Press, 1964.

INDEX

194–205; Kant on free forms of, 98–101, 105, 293n185; Mazzini on concrete cosmopolitanism and, 102–4, 118; Proudhon on cooperative association and, 104–5, 118, 294n208; Senghor on the *afro-français* community and, 60–64, 135, 137–47, 153–66, 286n86, 307n124, 307nn162–64, 309nn199–201. *See also* decolonization without state sovereignty

Federation of French Indochina, 84–86

Ferrements (Césaire), 182–85

Ferry, Jules, 320n48

Fifth Republic, 2–3; anticolonization movements and, 196–205; Césaire's demands of, 195–99; constitutional referendum of, 177–81, 195, 219–20, 313n89; de Gaulle's presidency of, 176–77, 219, 247, 271, 313n79; DOMS under, 246–51, 327nn15–16, 328n24; French Community of, 177–81, 219–20, 271, 322n92; positive discrimination under, 328n22

First International Congress of Black Artists and Writers, 168, 270, 309–10nn6–8, 310n12

Fonds d'investissements pour le developpement economique et social (FIDES), 141, 150, 304n89

Forces françaises de l'intérieur (FFI), 74–75, 86

forgiveness, 69–73

"For the Transformation of Martinique into a Region within the Framework of a Federated French Union" (Césaire), 173–76

Foucault, Michel, 254

Fougeyrollas, Pierre, 228

Fourier, Charles, 115, 228

Fourth Republic, 2–3, 86–87; Césaire's vision of, 33, 63; citizenship rights of, 148–49, 154, 304n87; collapse of, 162, 176–77, 271, 313n78; Constituent Assembly of, 64–65, 86, 109–12, 137–47; constitution of, 146–50, 152–53, 163, 211, 267; Indépendants d'outre-mer (IOM) coalition of, 150, 154–55; Loi-Cadre of 1956 of, 155, 218, 220, 270, 321nn81–82; overseas departments (DOMS) of, 109–12, 124–27, 147–52. *See also* French Union

"Fragments of a Poem" (Césaire), 24–26, 279n43

la françafrique system, 244–46, 327n14

France, 1–3; abolition of slavery by, 17–20, 112–20, 122, 262, 328n20; African military recruits of, 53, 55–59, 74, 82, 137, 246, 288n1; anticolonial wars against, 84–86, 127–28, 141, 151, 154,

162, 165, 167, 170, 293n151; anti-immigrant nationalism and racism in, 245–46, 250, 273; *banlieue* uprising of 2005 in, 245–46, 249, 273; Camp Thiaroye massacre in, 57–58; Commission for the Abolition of Slavery of, 115–17; de Gaulle's postwar vision for, 82–87, 137–38, 141, 281n84, 290n82; 1848 revolution in, 104–5, 115–17, 119–20; global relationships of, 14–15; labor migration to, 197, 244–46, 257–58; *la françafrique* system of, 244–46, 327n14; Mitterrand's socialist government of, 247–48; plural imperial polity of, 5–7, 37, 60–64; postwar politics of time of, 39–48; revolutionary republican tradition of, 33–35, 46–47, 101, 144; social security system of, 122–23; U.S. Marshall Plan in, 86. *See also* Fifth Republic; Fourth Republic; World War II

La France Libre journal, 78

Franc Jeu bulletin, 108

freedom: Arendt on federal citizenship and, 95–98, 253, 255, 293n164; Arendt on revolutionary rupture of, 76–77; of de Gaulle on empire and, 82–87, 137–38, 141, 290n82, 291n85; historical precedents for, 98–105, 118, 293–94nn185–187, 294n190, 294n208; liberation as political performance and, 74–76, 288n1; narratives of the postwar era on, 95–105; postnational political formations and, 251–55; public freedom and happiness in, 46–47; socialist ideals of, 77–81, 98, 141, 149, 151, 289n26, 289nn33–34, 295n19; UN's nationalist logic of, 84, 87–95, 291n109. *See also* decolonization; United Nations

Free French Forces, 74–75, 77–78; de Gaulle's narrative of, 82; West African participants in, 53, 55–59, 74, 82, 137, 162, 288n1

French Antilles: abolition of slavery in, 17–20, 112–18, 122, 262, 298n100, 328n20; anticipation of self-determination in, 20–21; Césaire on form of revolution in, 32–35; decolonization in, 196–205; departmentalization of, 20–21, 106–12, 122–32, 167–81; historic legacy of, 182–95; labor repression in, 17–20, 32, 117–18, 120–21, 186–90; language use in, 34; Napoleon's reinstatement of slavery in, 19, 188–93; postnational political arrangements in, 246–51, 328n24, 329n31; postwar unrest in, 85, 196–99; Schoelcherism in, 112–13, 118–22, 126–27, 176–77, 185–87; Senghor's

Louis, William Roger, 94–95

Louis-Napoléon (Napoleon III), 121, 262, 298n111

Louverture, François-Dominique Toussaint, 14, 132, 185–95, 258, 261; Césaire's engagement with, 185–95, 199–201, 251, 314n137, 316nn191–93; imprisonment and death of, 191–92; on partnership with France, 189–91, 193–94; repressive governance by, 18–19, 189–90, 193–94, 316n185; revolution of, 18, 33, 101–2, 186–89, 192–93, 201, 316n190; writings of, 316n184

"Louverture" (Dubois), 316n185

Lozès, Patrick, 249

Lukács, 323n135

Lumumba, Patrice, 201–4, 271–72, 326n221

Lyannaj Kont Pwofitasyon (LKP), 251

Lyautey, Hubert, 62–63

Mabille, Pierre, 29, 280n72

MacMillan, Margaret, 90

Madagascar, 86, 127, 154

Magnes, Judah, 293n164

Mali, 245–46

Mali Federation, 221–24, 271

Malinowski, Bronisław, 168

Malraux, André, 178

mandate system, 91–92, 94

Manela, Erez, 90, 292n141

Manville, Marcel, 22

Marie-Jeanne, Alfred, 327n15

Maritain, Jacques, 29–30, 210, 264, 319n31

Marr, David, 290n82

Marshall, C. Bruce, 141, 302n52, 303n80

Martinique: 1943 return to republican government in, 107–12; anticipation of self-determination in, 20–21; Césaire on form of revolution in, 32–35; Césaire's teaching in, 22–23; Communist party in, 107–12, 127, 130, 169–71, 173, 180, 197, 247, 270, 311nn29–30, 312n53; decolonization in, 196–205; departmentalization in, 20–21, 106–12, 122–32, 296n35; Fifth Republic and, 195–99, 247–49, 327nn15–16, 328n22, 328n24; opposition to departmentalization in, 169–81, 247–49, 327nn15–16; positive discrimination under, 328n22; postwar social unrest in, 85, 122–24, 180–81, 197; Robert's Vichy regime in, 23–24, 107, 279n33; Senghor's visit to, 49–51; slave revolts in, 113, 298n100, 316n191; slavery and

labor repression in, 19–20, 32, 298n100. *See also* Césaire, Aimé; French Antilles

Marx, Karl/Marxism, 13–14, 118, 258; on capitalism and personal liberty, 17–18; on cultural creativity, 51; on dream images, 42; 1844 manuscripts of, 267, 319n24; Senghor on humanist vision of, 209–18, 225–26, 319nn23–24, 320n48, 321n66, 323n135; Senghor's critique of, 225–34; on socialized labor and property, 308n196; on untimely processes, 43–44, 283n137, 283n139

"Marxism and Humanism" (Senghor), 209–10

Massu, Jacques, 291n85

Maugée, Aristide, 271

Mau Mau rebellion, 84, 95

Mauretania, 245–46

Mauss, Marcel, 71, 263

Maximin, Daniel, 249

Mazzini, Giuseppe, 102–5, 118, 130, 172, 182

Mbembe, Achille, 275n7, 331n55

McKay, Claude, 263

Mediterranean Union, 246

"Memorial for Louis Delgrès" (Césaire), 182–85

memory. *See* time

Ménil, René, 23, 279n34; on the Antillean future, 27–29, 33, 279nn34–35; governance role of, 107–8; vision of concrete universality of, 36–37

Mercier, Louis Sebastien, 316n191

Merleau-Ponty, Maurice, 77–78, 231, 267–68, 289nn33–34

Merlet, Jean-François, 303n63

methodological nationalism, 3–5, 8

métissage: early religion and, 234–36; Senghor's vision of, 52–59, 72–73, 156–61, 164, 224–25, 244, 308n178, 308n182

Mitterrand, François, 247–48, 327n16

Moch, Jules, 124

modernity, 10–11, 128–30

Mollet, Guy, 207

Monnerot, Jules, 107

Monnerville, Gaston, 109, 111, 118–19, 268, 303n71

Monnerville Commission, 64, 137

Morgenthau, Ruth Shachter, 154–55, 208, 302n58, 307n138, 322n103

Morin, Edgar, 228

Morocco, 86, 153–54, 305n118

Mounier, Emanuel, 263

Moutoussamy, Ernst, 179

Pompidou, Georges, 178
Ponton, Georges Louis, 107–8
Portugal, 291n109
postcolonial theory, 3, 8–12, 257–59
postnational democracy, 241–59; citizenship in,
251–55, 257–58; in the DOMs, 246–51, 328n24,
329n31
Postwar (Judt), 275n2
pragmatism: of Césaire, 21–22, 127, 195, 204–5;
of Senghor, 154, 243–46
"Prayer for Peace" (Senghor), 58–59
"Prayer for the Senegalese Soldier"
(Senghor), 56
Présence Africaine, 168, 182–85, 237, 267, 309n6
Le Progressiste newspaper, 176–77, 185
Proudhon, Pierre-Joseph, 13–14, 102–5, 228,
309n200; on federalism, 104–5, 118, 223,
294n208; on mutualism, 214; on political
assimilation, 174
Provincializing Europe (Chakrabarty), 10–11
psychoanalysis and dreams, 42–43
Puerto Rico, 329n31

radical literalism, 7
Rancière, Jacques, 71, 204–5, 288n134, 331n55
Rassemblement démocratique africain (RDA),
86, 155, 221, 267, 268, 309n201
Rassemblement du Peuple Français (RPF), 78,
87, 268, 307n163
Ravoahangy, Raset, 303n71
Raynal, Abbé, 316n191
Reno, Fred, 248
"Réponse à Depestre" (Césaire), 311n29
"Reports on Method" (Senghor), 150–52,
210–14
republicanism: Césaire's vision of, 173–81,
194–205; France's tradition of, 33–35, 46–47,
101, 144; Kant's free federalism and, 98–101,
105, 293n185, z; in Martinique, 107–12;
Mazzini on concrete cosmopolitanism and,
102–4, 118; Proudhon on Jacobin form of,
101–5, 118, 223, 294n208; racism in postcolonial France and, 245–46, 250, 273; Senghor's
vision of, 60–64, 135, 137–47, 153–66,
286n86, 307n124, 307nn162–64, 309n200,
309nn199–201
Réunion, 109–12, 123, 296n35
Richepanse, General, 183
Rigaud, André, 187
Rimbaud, Arthur, 25, 31–32, 50, 178–79, 313n96

Robert, Georges, 23–24, 107, 279n33
Robinson, Ronald, 94–95
romantic anticapitalism, 277n21
Roosevelt, Franklin D., 85
Rousso, Henry, 283n133
Ruge, Arnold, 118, 211

Said, Edward, 275n7, 331n55
Sand, Nicole, 200
Saravane, Lambert, 303n71
Sarkozy, Nicholas, 245–46, 273
Sarr, Ibrahima, 318n14
Sartre, Jean-Paul, 74–75, 77, 182, 262,
265–68, 323n135
Schlegel, Friedrich, 45
Schmidt, Nelly, 115, 118, 298n100
Schmitt, Carl, 254, 294n186
Schoelcher, Victor, 14, 111, 125, 258, 261–62,
298n93; abolition of slavery and, 19, 112–18,
122, 186, 296n46, 314n132; impact on Cés-
aire of, 112–13, 118–22, 126–27, 176–77, 185–87,
298n117; on Toussaint Louverture, 185–87,
316n184; utopian vision of, 114–15, 120,
296n35, 297nn83–84, 298n106, 298nn111–12
Schuman Declaration, 269
Scott, David, 15–16, 282n113, 331n55
A Season in the Congo (Césaire), 200, 201–3
Second International Congress of Black Writers and Artists, 181–82, 271
Second Republic, 117, 262
self-determination, 1–5; Césaire's anticipation
of, 20–48; Lenin's views on, 90–91; nation-
states as normative goals of, 87–95, 101;
in postwar federation proposals, 95–105,
153–57, 153–61; radical literalist approaches
to, 5–7; UN's nationalist logic of, 87–95,
140; Wilson's views on, 89–90. *See also*
decolonization
Seminar for Political Cadres of the Senegalese
Progressive Union, 231
Senegal: BDS reform project for, 149–52, 206–16,
304n94; Dakar railway strike in, 309n201,
318n14; French Socialist Party (SFIO) of, 137,
149, 207–8; labor migration from, 245–46;
Lamin Guèye faction in, 207; in the Mali Federation, 221–23, 271; Muslim Brotherhood of,
243; postwar social unrest in, 150; Senghor's
research in, 53, 65; UPS coalition of, 218–19.
See also French West Africa; Senghor,
Léopold Sédar